THE CIVILIZATION OF THE AMERICAN INDIAN SERIES

INDIAN CLOTHING BEFORE CORTÉS

Indian Clothing

University of Oklahoma Press:

Norman and London

Before Cortés

MESOAMERICAN COSTUMES FROM THE CODICES

BY Patricia Rieff Anawalt

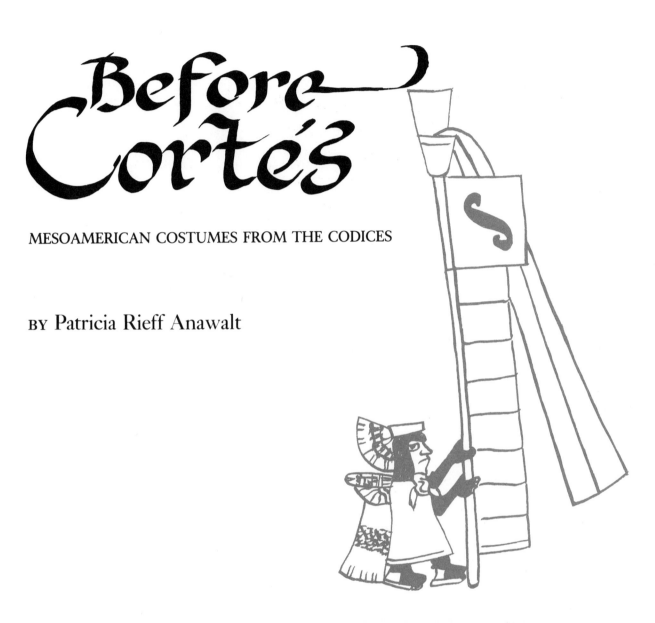

FOREWORD BY H. B. Nicholson

CHARTS PREPARED BY Jean Cuker Sells

To my husband, Richard, and children,
Dave, Doyle, Kate, Chuck, and Fred,
and grandchildren,
Rieff, Ryland, and Natalie,
who continue to
supply—and demand—a
sensible balance.

Anawalt, Patricia Rieff, 1924–
    Mesoamerican costumes from the codices.

    (The civilization of the American Indian series; no. 156)
    Bibliography: p. 219
    Includes index.
        1. Indians of Mexico—Costume and adornment.
2. Indians of Mexico—Art. 3. Indians of Central
America—Costume and adornment. 4. Indians of Central
America—Art. I. Title. II. Series: Civilization of the American
Indian series; no. 156.

F1219.3.C75A5   391'.00972   80–5942
                                                   AACR2

ISBN: 0–8061–2288–9

FIGURE 1, on the title page, depicts an Aztec priest carrying a banner
bearing the ilhuitl ("feast day") symbol. *Codex Borbonicus*, p. 29.

CONTENTS

ILLUSTRATIONS

MAP

TABLE

FOREWORD

By H. B. Nicholson

Impressive progress in our knowledge of the Mesoamerican Area Co-Tradition—that portion of North America where advanced cultures fully comparable to the earliest Old World civilizations (Mesopotamia, Egypt, northwest India, China) flourished in pre-European times—has been achieved in the past few decades. This progress is the result of the dedicated efforts of many students, of various nationalities, working with data in two major categories, archaeological and ethnohistorical.

What can be considered modern scientific archaeology gradually emerged in Middle America at the end of the nineteenth and the beginning of the present century. Major well-funded archaeological projects, both domestic and foreign, increased in tempo during the 1920s and 1930s, and especially during the years following World War II. The excavations have yielded a tremendous body of new data concerning the surviving artifactual and architectural remains of the indigenous Mesoamerican civilizations, as well as providing a much-improved understanding of their developmental histories.

Ethnohistorical research, which focuses on the documentary and pictorial sources relating to the late pre-Hispanic and early colonial Mesoamerican cultures, has made commensurate strides during the same period. By now most of the ethnohistorical sources containing significant amounts of information on pre-Hispanic Mesoamerica have been published, and important analyses and syntheses based on these materials are appearing in steadily increasing numbers. The organization of the complex bibliography of Mesoamerican ethnohistory has also recently been substantially improved, above all, in the four volume *Guide to Ethnohistorical Sources*, volumes 12 to 15 of the Handbook of Middle American Indians series (1972–75).

Pre-Hispanic ethnohistory necessarily concentrates on the mature, final expression of Mesoamerican civilization during the Postclassic period and as it was functioning when it was overrun and profoundly altered by the Spanish conquistadors in the sixteenth century. As a point of departure for both the recovery and the interpretation of earlier, pre-Postclassic cultures and, moving forward in time, the understanding of transculturative processes during the post-Conquest epoch, as full a reconstruction as possible of the various Mesoamerican cultures at the moment of initial contact with the European invaders is vitally important. Unfortunately, the available ethnohistorical documentation crucial to this indispensable task

is shot full of gaps and uneven in quality and degree of reliability. The area for which there is by far the most information is central Mexico, which at the time of the Conquest was the political power heart and the most densely populated zone of Mesoamerica. It is, therefore, particularly important to compile as complete a record as is feasible of the richly documented culture of contact-period Central Mexico—traditionally called "Aztec"—since it will always serve as the basic touchstone for the reconstruction and interpretation of all other Mesoamerican cultures.

Although great progress has also been made in this endeavor, especially in recent years, one very significant aspect of Aztec culture that has not been satisfactorily researched until now is the full costume repertory and the role costume played in the over-all culture pattern. Clearly, this role was of considerable significance. As Patricia Anawalt states in her opening chapter:

> . . . dress was identity; even a god had to don his proper attire. To the Aztecs and their neighbors, the wearing of appropriate ethnic and class apparel was strictly controlled by both custom and law. As a result, an individual's clothing immediately designated not only cultural affiliation but rank and status as well. Since each Indian group dressed in a distinctive and characteristic manner, a great deal of ethnographic and historical information is contained in depictions of their clothing.

The importance of this book is that it constitutes much the most comprehensive description and analysis of costume in late pre-Hispanic and contact Mesoamerica yet published, focusing on six major groups for which a substantial body of pictorial data is available. As would be expected, significantly more information is extant concerning central Mexican, or Aztec, culture, and the costume patterns of this area provide the author with her fundamental point of departure. Following her extensive treatment of Aztec, she moves on to reconstruct and analyze the costume inventories of the Tlaxcaltecans; the Tarascans of Michoacán; the Mixtecs of Oaxaca; the groups of uncertain location who produced the ritual divinatory screenfolds of the Codex Borgia Group; and the lowland Mayas of Yucatán.

Before undertaking this broad cultural survey, in her first chapter, she provides a valuable and necessary discussion of the relevant primary sources and the methodology she has employed in her descriptions and analyses of the costume repertory of each group. To begin with, she points out that the environment of the area encompassed within Mesoamerica is not, in general, very conducive to the long-term preservation of textiles and other perishable costume items. Therefore, only a very few actual specimens of materials from pre-Hispanic costumes have survived. Fortunately, the rich representational art, which constituted one of the most typical and impressive Mesoamerican cultural achievements, significantly makes up — in part — for this irreparable loss. Somewhat ironically, a class of artifact that was, like the textiles, also manufactured from perishable materials (bark paper, tanned animal skin, cloth), has provided most of the information concerning Mesoamerican costume in the final pre-Hispanic period: the native tradition pictorials, usually designated "codices." The tiny handful of indubitably pre-Hispanic examples survived largely because most of them were sent or taken early to Europe as souvenirs of the exotic newly discovered land, while most of the colonial specimens owe their preservation to the fact that they were considered of sufficient importance to retain for various "practical" reasons (rarely, "ethnographic" in the modern sense). These pictorials, of many types (ritual-divinatory, historical-genealogical, cartographic, administrative-economic, litigative, and so on), were the commonest media for the expression of the native embryonic writing system, essentially picto-ideo-logographic but with some limited phoneticism in place and personal name signs. Particularly the members of the first two categories, ritual-divinatory and historical-genealogical, feature a vast number of representations of deities and persons, and it is on this remarkable corpus — without neglecting some pertinent archaeological data — that Patricia Anawalt has primarily based her study. With adequate reproductions of most of the major pre-Hispanic and sixteenth-century native-tradition pictorials now available, no one has examined them for their information on costume patterns more carefully or more thoroughly than the author of this book.

In this preliminary chapter she also develops an effective costume typology, which she proceeds, in the subsequent chapters, systematically to apply to each of the six groups. This typology is an adaptation of the scheme, involving five fundamental "archetypes" of costume construction techniques, enumerated in a 1966 publication by the leading French costume historian Françoise Boucher: draped, slip-on, open-sewn, closed-sewn, and limb-encasing garments. She clearly defines each category, and the usefulness and general applicability of this typology is demonstrated in her first pictorial chart. She also includes in this chapter a useful summary of the technological and socioeconomic aspects of the production of the textiles that provided the bulk of Mesoamerican costume, focusing on the basic weaving apparatus, the backstrap loom.

In her discussion of the costume inventory of each of the six groups selected, Anawalt's presentation is considerably enhanced by the wealth of illustrations taken from the relevant primary pictorial sources, typically summarized in charts schematized according to her general, cross-cultural categories of costume construction. This pictorial chart method of presenting her basic data particularly facilitates comparisons between the groups, a subject to which she devotes explicit attention in chapter 8. The book, consequently, among its many other obvious merits, constitutes a valuable repository of illustrations of great utility for any student of the costume aspect of Mesoamerican civilization.

Her detailed comparisons in chapter 8 of the costume repertories of the six groups reveal some interesting differences between them — within the fundamental, widely shared costume patterns that pervaded pre-Hispanic Mesoamerica. Although casual comparisons of this type have previously been made, Anawalt presents here a much more comprehensive, structured discussion than has been undertaken heretofore. What is revealed here as much as anything else is the typical Mesoamerican cultural richness and variety, featuring considerable ethnic and regional differentiation. Clearly, costume was no exception.

In the same chapter, comparing and contrasting the costume repertories of the Mixteca and that of the painters of the core members of the Borgia Group, Anawalt makes a significant contribution to the still controversial question of the precise proveniences of the highly important pre-Hispanic ritual-divinatory screenfolds of the latter group. Her detailed comparisons, usefully summarized in the table in chapter 8, clearly reveal some very significant differences in costume patterns between the Borgia Group and those from Mixteca, which appear to indicate, in the author's words, that "the ritual books of the Borgia Group...probably...did not come from the Mixtec heartland, for they do not reflect Mixtec ritual clothing patterns." She goes on further to suggest that the frequency of topless females in the Borgia Group might point to a provenience in "a lowland area bordering the Mixteca," more precisely, the Gulf Coast. Although the question is still obviously somewhat open, Anawalt's costume analysis adds a significant new dimension to the discussion of the long-standing, challenging problem of the provenience of these uniquely valuable sources for late pre-Hispanic western Mesoamerican religious iconography.

In her final chapter, the author provides a convenient pan-Mesoamerican summary of the costume patterns she has described and analyzed separately for each group. She also enters into an interesting discussion of the possible reasons for certain significant discrepancies between descriptions of costume in the colonial textual sources, particularly the 1579–85 series of *Relaciones geográficas*, and in the pictorial sources from which she drew many of her data. She proposes various hypotheses to account for these seeming contradictions, all of which appear cogent, though the desirability of further analysis and discussion of this problem is clearly implied. In her concluding discussion, regarding the role of native military attire in the events of the Conquest, she reasonably relates the theatrical, highly symbolic military costumes worn by the leading Indian warriors to the strongly ritualized Mesoamerican concept of warfare. This approach contrasted sharply with the devastating, tactically more effective European concept, and—entirely aside from European superiority in military technology—unquestionably put the natives at a considerable disadvantage in their desperate, ultimately unsuccessful attempts to defend themselves against these unexpected invaders from overseas.

Throughout the book the author displays a very "functional," genuinely anthropological approach, consistently attempting to interrelate costume patterns with other aspects of the culture, especially in the religious-ritual and sociopolitical spheres. She recognizes that the study of costume should never be treated in isolation but always in relation to the cultural whole of which it is only one facet—and that costume patterns strongly reflect, often in a very subtle and significant fashion, basic cultural values and themes. Her book, therefore, not only constitutes a valuable study of Mesoamerican costume but also, *inter alia*, conveys much additional information on overall cultural patterns of late pre-Hispanic and Conquest-period Mesoamerican civilization. It is a major new contribution to the field and will, I feel certain, be warmly welcomed by all serious students of Mesoamerica's past.

PREFACE

In retrospect, I realize that this book really began in July, 1956, on the morning of my first day in Mexico, when I unexpectedly discovered the unique visibility of the Mexican historical sequence.

On the night of my arrival in Mexico City I had little background or knowledge of what to expect, which made the following morning even more dramatic, when I was taken by my hosts on a picnic to Malinalco, an Aztec archaeological site in a remote valley several hours' drive southwest of the capital. On the ride out of the city and over the mountains toward Toluca, I was much impressed by the sharp contrast between the colorful and imaginative modern architecture of central Mexico City and the old colonial buildings and the simple adobe houses of the outlying areas. When we turned off the main highway, I was even more intrigued.

The road to Malinalco begins in the small town of Tenancingo, where we stopped at the Sunday outdoor market. I had never seen an Indian marketplace before, and the sounds, smells, and sights fascinated me. Everything was of interest: the physical layout; the manner of displaying goods at ground level; the predominance of the area's specialized product, the *rebozo* (a woman's shawl); and the stylized behavior of the quiet and orderly participants. My overwhelming impression was one of abiding antiquity; I had come upon an anachronism and was captivated.

This sense of the past revisited increased as we left the marketplace and began the tortuous drive over the mountains and then down abruptly into the beautiful valley in which Malinalco rests. That jarring, breathtaking ride was unforgettable. In 1956 the Tenancingo–Malinalco road was truly appalling, with the result that it served as a barrier, preserving the sixteenth-century atmosphere of the area. The way to the archaeological site led along the narrow cobblestone streets of the village and past a towering early-sixteenth-century convent. Leaving the town, we walked through verdant gardens and old orchards and climbed the path up the hillside to the cliff overlooking the valley where the ruins stand.

The Aztec temple at Malinalco is an architectural tour de force. The small, well-proportioned structure is a single unit—sculpture and all—hewn out of the rock. The temple, complete with a roof of fresh thatch, looks much as it must have in the fifteenth century, when it was carved. To me it seemed the inevitable destination for the time-machine journey I had unknowingly embarked upon that morning.

Standing beside the ruins, I was dumbfounded by all that I had seen. In a few short hours we had traveled backward in time from modern Mexico City to a peasant market, back through the sixteenth-century colonial period, and then, finally, even farther back, into the pre-Hispanic era. The experience was overwhelming. That Sunday morning my involvement with Mexican historical research began.

On my return to Los Angeles, I was fortunate to be able to study at the Univerity of California with Ralph Beals, the renowned ethnographer who had worked in Mexico for many years. I learned from him that the phenomenon to which I was committed was called acculturation: the ongoing process that occurs when two disparate cultures meet, meld, and produce a new entity. I also discovered that in no other area of the world is the acculturative process more fruitfully studied than in Mexico and Central America. There in 1519 the two totally divergent civilizations of the Old and New Worlds fatefully met, when Hernán Cortés and his conquistadors landed in Veracruz. For three hundred years following the Conquest, the Spanish crown jealously guarded her valuable colonies, allowing almost no foreigners to enter. Most of the Spanish colonial administrators were methodical record keepers. The result is that Middle America is the most homogenous and best-documented acculturative laboratory in the world.

Thanks to Malinalco and to Ralph Beals, I acquired the theoretical orientation that has continued to structure my research. However, acculturation cannot be studied in a vacuum. To calibrate the acculturative process, some specific social system or item of material culture has to be monitored. Acculturation can be observed only by noting the changes that take place within some social or cultural entity. I found my own subject as the result of a chance remark by Beals. One day he mentioned that to see what Mexico was like fifty years before one should visit the conservative Indian villages in Highland Guatemala. Shortly after finishing my undergraduate work, I went there.

The marketplaces of Guatemala were even more exciting than that of Tenancingo. Most of the highland villages had their own unique costumes, which the Indians still regularly wore. When the villagers gathered en masse in their magnificently colored handwoven clothing, a pageantlike scene was created. With each successive market—I could not seem to see enough—I became increasingly fascinated by these garments. While their color, design motifs, and intricate workmanship were all of interest, what really intrigued me was the antiquity of their basic shapes. Although many of the costumes resembled those worn in the pre-Hispanic pictorial codices, other clothing incorporated what were clearly Spanish colonial elements. Just how, when, and why had these latter traits been introduced?

This Guatemalan experience provided the topic for my doctoral dissertation, which was the basis for this book. My plan was to monitor the acculturative process through the study of changes in Middle American Indian costume from the sixteenth to the twentieth centuries. In the initial stages of my research the work of Hilda Delgado Pang was particularly appreciated. In her study of modern highland Guatemalan Indian costume, she briefly discussed the Spanish side of the Indian costume equation, and this material, together with her encouragement, was most helpful.

Once I had defined my research project, it was necessary to determine at what time period the acculturation study should begin. The obvious baseline was European contact. Since no one had ever demonstrated what the Indians were wearing when the Spaniards arrived, I would have to do it. Such a reconstruction demanded the use multiple examples of each garment type to adjust for idiosyncrasies of the native artists or aberrant costume depictions.

Sufficient clothing data were not available on extant pre-Hispanic sculpture or wall paintings, but did exist in the indigenous pictorial books of Middle America. Since these codices are discussed in detail in Chapter 1, I will comment here only that for their utilization I came into Mesoamerican ethnohistory at precisely the right time. Facsimile reproductions of the pictorial manuscripts had begun appearing in the late 1960s, and by the early 1970s most of the major ones were accessible to scholars in excellent editions. Keeping pace with codices publication was the increasing availability of guides to the colonial ethnohistorical sources. Before that time, simply determining how to find these invaluable documents was extremely difficult, confusing, and frustrating. Thanks to the patient and careful work of a small group of dedicated Mesoamerican ethnohistorians, the tangled snarl of bibliographic references was slowly unraveled and set aright. Between 1972 and 1975 four volumes containing guides to the sources were added to the Handbook of Middle American Indians series. As a result of this contribution, it was possible for me to make use of previously hard-to-find textual material to aid in interpreting the pictorial codices.

The more I became involved with the problems of four hundred years of Indian costume change the more it became apparent that the topic was much too broad for a dissertation (indeed, the subject is large enough to last a

reasonable scholar a lifetime). I soon decided that the establishment of the contact-period Mesoamerican costume repertory would more than suffice.

In developing the work, I had the initial problem of devising a method for organizing the clothing data of the codices. Several colleagues contributed to this work. Ann Rowe made valuable suggestions on my initial typology, as did Alice McCloskey, who also provided some appropriate examples for chart 1. At a later stage Irmgard Johnson clarified several puzzling pre-Hispanic costume enigmas and also generously shared the products of her own research.

To organize the clothing depictions, it was first necessary to photograph each individual garment example and then arrange these 299 figures on a series of charts. I have had excellent technical assistance with this undertaking. Susan Einstein did all of the photography, outstanding work with often difficult subjects. Jean Cuker Sells, whose experience, patience, and good humor could always be counted on, supervised the physical construction of the charts and also painstakingly traced each figure so that the chart illustrations are exact copies of photographs of facsimiles from the codices. Carrie Rodionoff contributed to the other art work in the book, and her sure hand and cheerful nature were always a pleasure.

Several of the more complicated costume problems were first presented as papers at scholarly meetings. In this way I met many Mesoamerican ethnohistorians, several of whom were particularly helpful. Nancy Troike and Emily Rabin were consulted on matters Mixtec, and Doris Heyden generously shared her research on the *quechquemitl*. Wayne Ruwet assisted with difficult bibliographic problems, as well as generous loans of rare books from his outstanding Mesoamerican library.

After the dissertation was accepted in 1975, I continued with my research on pre-Hispanic clothing. I became a traveling lecturer for the Archaeological Institute of America, and on my tours I was gratified to find there was sustained interest in the work. Repeated requests for articles and copies of the dissertation convinced me that I should rewrite it for publication, incorporating subsequent research. To encourage me in this undertaking, Anne-Louise Schaffer carefully read the dissertation and made many excellent suggestions which have been incorporated here.

This book, then, is the first volume in my magnum opus, a study of four hundred years of Indian costumes. The involvement is already almost twenty-five years long, and for such a prolonged project moral support has been of paramount importance. From the beginning of my scholarly endeavors, my long-term friend Mary Anne Thompson has read my papers, offered helpful suggestions, and encouraged me in every way. I will always be in her debt for that. I have also benefited from the kind support and gentle guidance of my erudite friend Hasso von Winning. This knowledgeable man has long been familiar with the Mesoamerican archaeological scene, and I have learned much from him that no one else could have taught me.

In addition to the aid of those listed above, I have had the fortunate opportunity of graduate work with three truly outstanding scholars, each of whom has contributed in an important way to this book. Studying with Frances Frei Berdan, I have been able to observe sophisticated methodology and dedicated scholarship operating at the highest level. Consistently she has been my demanding but diplomatic mentor, valued colleague, and devoted friend. In each of these capacities she has enriched my life.

It was with the distinguished Andeanist Christopher Donnan that I initially became involved in the technological side of material culture and also learned the value of working in painstaking detail with multiple examples. Drawing on experience gained in assembling his Moche archive data bank, he has helped me with perceptive suggestions that have been crucial in the development of both

typology and charts. His wise counsel, tough-minded editing, and supportive friendship have been invaluable.

I have been privileged to have H. B. Nicholson as my graduate adviser, colleague, and friend. He is justly renowned for his encyclopedic knowledge of Mesoamerican archaeology and ethnohistory and for the soundness of his research. I would like further to attest to the infectiousness of his enthusiasm for all matters Middle American and unrelenting goad contained in his repeated contention concerning scholarly matters: "Nothing is right but right!"

My final acknowledgment is for my cherished family, to whom this book is dedicated. To them, and to all those listed above, I owe a deep debt of gratitude, for each has helped to make this undertaking possible.

PATRICIA RIEFF ANAWALT
Fowler Museum of Cultural History
University of California, Los Angeles

ACKNOWLEDGMENT

I wish to acknowledge here the great contribution made to Mesoamerican research by Akademische Druck- u. Verlangsanstalt (Graz, Austria) with the publication of their Codices Selecti, Series C Manuscripts from Central America. This unique series makes available faithful facsimile reproductions of documents previously often unavailable to scholars.

Because of the highly specialized nature of this book, only twelve codices (*Borbonicus*, *Cospi*, Dresden, *Fejérváry-Mayer*, *Ixtililxochitl*, *Laud*, Madrid, *Magliabechiano*, Paris, *Vaticanus B*, *Vindobonensis*, and Seler 1960) of the Codice Selecti Series C publications were used. This outstanding series, however, contains a total of sixty-six works, all of invaluable aid to Americanist scholars.

Akademische Druck- u. Verlangsanstalt has been most generous in allowing the material to be reproduced in this book. Their prompt attention and courteous co-operation are in keeping with the superb quality of their publications.

PATRICIA RIEFF ANAWALT

INDIAN CLOTHING BEFORE CORTÉS

FIGURE 2. An Aztec mother teaching her fourteen-year-old daughter to weave on the backstrap loom. *Codex Mendoza*, vol. 3, fol. 6or.

CHAPTER ONE

The Data, the Method, the Clothing

MOCTEZUMA WAS A TROUBLED MAN.[1]

By the early summer of 1519 the Aztec emperor was already unnerved by the increasing frequency of a series of ill omens. Then came further disquieting news that the group of extraordinary floating towers that had been reported proceeding up the Gulf Coast had come to rest offshore (near present-day Veracruz).[2] These strangers came from out of the east in an anniversary year connected with the prophesied return of the tenth-century Toltec ruler Quetzalcóatl. Moctezuma surmised that they might well represent the return of that deity with his entourage. Accordingly an appropriate offering was assembled to be carried down to the new arrivals.

The first official contact between the Aztec Empire and the future conqueror of Mexico, Hernán Cortés, was the presentation of this gift, whose content the Spaniards carefully recorded. The itemized inventory, which also listed gifts received on the journey along the coast, included elaborate textiles, animal skins, feather plumes, ornamental featherwork incorporating jewels and gold, finely wrought gold and silver jewelry, two native books,[3] gold dust and gold nuggets, and two enormous wheels, one of gold, measuring some twelve feet in circumference,

and another, somewhat smaller, of silver.[4]

A generation later this first memorable meeting was also described by the Aztecs.[5] The contrast is revealing. In the Indian account no reference is made to gifts of gold or jewels or even textiles per se. Instead, for this most important of meetings Indian legend records only that the emperor sent clothing; the traditional attire of three major deities is described in careful detail.

In the lands to which Cortés had come, dress was identity; even a god had to don his proper attire. To the Aztecs and their neighbors the wearing of appropriate ethnic and class apparel was strictly controlled by both custom and law. An individual's clothing immediately signaled not only cultural affiliation but rank and status as well. Since each Indian group dressed in a distinctive and characteristic manner, a great deal of ethnographic and historical information is contained in depictions of their clothing.

Climatic conditions have a great effect on the preservation or deterioration of articles of clothing over long periods of time. In Egypt or coastal Peru, for example, the combination of burial practices and dry climate has preserved ancient textiles down to the present day. The dampness and humidity of Middle America have destroyed all but occasional textile fragments and all com-

---

[1] In classical Nahuatl, the language of the Aztec Empire, the emperor's name was Motecuhzoma Xocoyotzin, the Angry Lord, the Younger (to distinguish him from his great-grandfather Huehue Motecuhzoma Ilhuicamina, The Elder Angry Lord, Archer of the Skies). For the past century, in English-language literature the name Motecuhzoma has commonly appeared as Montezuma, a version not used in the Spanish-speaking world. Moctezuma is a grammatically legitimate contraction of the original form, but increasingly the term Moctezuma is used in both English and Spanish, and this more familiar form is used in this book.

[2] A stylized Indian version of the Spanish conquest is presented in the *Floren-*

tine Codex (Sahagún 1950–69), bk. 12, *The Conquest of Mexico*.

[3] The two native books were probably not part of Moctezuma's official gift but were received on the journey up the Gulf Coast.

[4] See Pagden (1971, pp. 40–46) for Cortés's inventory of the objects he was preparing to send back to Spain from Veracruz. They included not only the gifts from Moctezuma but also the articles obtained from other Indian leaders encountered earlier on the voyage along the Yucatán-Campeche coast. Wagner (1969, pp. 85, 120–29) has presented a very interesting discussion of the inventory and its subsequent fate.

[5] Sahagún 1950–69, bk. 12, pp. 9–20.

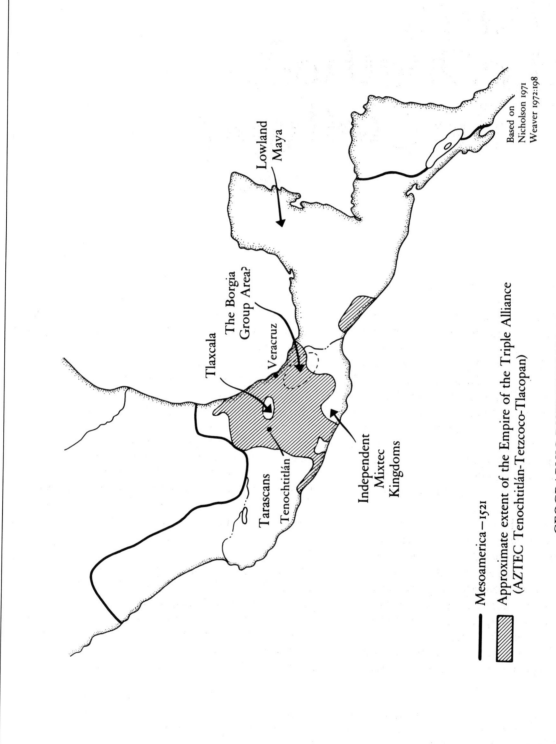

Tarascans

Tenochtitlán

Tlaxcala

The Borgia
Group Area?

Veracruz

Lowland
Maya

Independent
Mixtec
Kingdoms

Based on
Nicholson 1971
Weaver 1972:198

—— Mesoamerica – 1521

Approximate extent of the Empire of the Triple Alliance
(AZTEC Tenochtitlán-Tetzcoco-Tlacopan)

GEOGRAPHIC DISTRIBUTION OF INDIAN GROUPS
AT THE TIME OF SPANISH CONTACT

plete costumes. That does not mean, however, that there is no knowledge of pre-Conquest garments. As Cortés early discovered, the New World civilization had manuscripts in which matters of importance were recorded in a pictographic system. Thanks to the realism of this picture writing, hundreds of depictions of pre-Hispanic garments are extant.

Within Mesoamerica[6]—that portion of present-day Mexico and Central America where the great Indian high cultures flourished—there existed a number of distinctive ethnic groups.[7] From the surviving native pictorial documents and Spanish colonial records the costume repertory of six of these groups can be reconstructed: that of the Aztecs,[8] the Tlaxcalans, the Tarascans, the Mixtecs, the creators of the Borgia Group Codices, and the lowland Mayas.

THE DATA: CLOTHING DEPICTED IN THE MESOAMERICAN CODICES

It is possible to compile and interpret the pre-Cortesian clothing of these six groups because of the survival of indigenous Middle American codices. The term *codex*, the Latin word for a type of book, has come to imply an ancient manuscript. Since the late nineteenth century the term, as used in Mesoamerican studies, has designated any document compiled in a native tradition. These indigenous records contain hundreds of pictures of Mesoamerican individuals and deities, each dressed in appropriate pre-Hispanic attire. The depictions are examples of the recognizable graphic images employed in Mesoamerican writing, a system whose level of structural complexity differs from that of the writing of ancient Egypt and Mesopotamia.

One usually associates a writing system with an alphabet, but the Mesoamerican system did not evolve to that point. In 1952, I. J. Gleb, an Oriental-language specialist and author of the most influential recent general study of

writing systems, considered the "so-called Maya and Aztec writings" as "limited systems" and regarded them not as writings proper but as forerunners of writings.[9] He contended that, "although the beginning of phonetization can be observed among both the Aztecs and the Maya, neither even approximately reached the phonetic state of writing which we find so well developed already in the oldest Sumerian inscriptions."[10]

The research of the last twenty-five years has somewhat revised the picture Gelb presented in 1952. It is becoming increasingly apparent that the Maya writing system of the Classic Period, from A.D. 300 to 900, should be accorded far more credit than is reflected in Gelb's appraisal. It must also be acknowledged, however, that the Maya system did not continue its dynamic development; by the time of sixteenth-century Spanish contact it had atrophied.

The Mesoamerican system appears to be overall an unusually sophisticated "picture writing" that reveals several degrees of complexity. In its simplest form it is pictographic, representing events by means of images. At this level a picture of a man hunting means only that, a hunter. The next stage of abstraction is the ideographic, where an image conveys an idea. In the pre-Cortesian and early colonial histories and genealogies from the Mixtec area, an ideogram of an intertwined *A* and *O* represents a year sign:

In the Mixtec and Highland Mexican pictorials an ideogram of a footprint denotes a path, and hence a journey:

[6] The term Mesoamerica defines a specific culture area, a location on the earth's surface inhabited by people who share a similar way of life. The concept grew out of the diffusionist thinking of the Boasian school. In the early part of the twentieth century American anthropologists, led by Franz Boas, became increasingly disillusioned with their nineteenth-century predecessors, the Evolutionists. As the Boasians went out into the field and collected data, they soon found that the grandiose schemes of the Evolutionists, based on the accounts of others, ran afoul of the facts. A part of the Boasian reaction was the belief that human beings were not too inventive; innovations were assumed to have entered cultural inventories through diffusion from an original hearth of invention. Their procedure was to analyze cultures into traits and then trace the movement of these traits through time and space. The area of highest trait concentration was regarded as the most likely center of its invention. In America this orientation culminated in the elaboration of culture areas, relatively small geographic units based on the contiguous distribution of cultural elements. Although the emphasis of American anthropological theory is no longer so strongly on diffusion, the cultural-area concept continues to be a useful device for summing up the diagnostic cultural features of a specific location.

In 1943, Paul Kirchhoff (1952, p. 23) defined Mesoamerica as a culture area determined by the distribution of certain cultural traits throughout the region. Geographically the area involved is indigenous Mexico and Central America extending from Sinaloa and the Pánuco River on the Pacific coastal side down to northwestern Costa Rica. On the east, on the Gulf Coast side, the boundary extends roughly from present-day Tampico south into Honduras (see map).

[7] H. B. Nicholson (1967a, pp. 64–65) has summarized thirteen (a good Mesoamerican sacred number) of the outstanding diagnostic cultural features of fully developed Mesoamerica as it was flourishing at the time of Spanish conquest: (1) An intensive agricultural system featuring maize, beans, and squash; (2) a dense population; (3) the importance of the institution of the market and the powerful influence of well-organized merchant groups; (4) the importance in the commercial structure of the cacao bean, used both for the status beverage chocolate and for currency; (5) the fundamental importance of the large town and its dependent satellites as the basic sociopolitical unit; (6) the sharply aristocratic bias of the society correlated with a high degree of social stratification; (7) the pervasive influence of the complex religious-ritual system; (8) the many typical cosmological and cosmogonical concepts in the religious ideology; (9) the great elaboration of art and architecture in the service of religious ideology; (10) the complex calendrical systems serving both divinatory-religious and more practical, secular ends; (11) the development of hieroglyphic writing systems; (12) the possession of bark paper and skin screenfold books; (13) the importance of jade or jadelike stones as the ultimate in preciousness and value (the diamonds and sables of Mesoamerica were jade and quetzal feathers).

[8] The term Aztecs is used here as a generic name, intended to encompass all the Nahuatl-speaking peoples of the Basin of Mexico, not just the inhabitants of the city of Tenochtitlán.

[9] Gelb 1974, p. v.

[10] Ibid., p. 51.

A further principle in Mesoamerican writing is the logographic principle. Numbers are examples of logograms, where a certain symbol stands for a specific word: 3 = three. This is evident in some of the Maya glyphs, where each sign or grapheme stands for a particular term; for example:

 stands for the number 13; and

 stands for *Ahau*, one of the twenty day signs.

The logographic principle also occurs in certain Nahuatl place-names, for example, in the toponym for the community of Coatepec. Written logographically, this toponym combines the logogram for snake: *coatl*

with that of hill: *tepetl*

The result is Coatepec:

This logographic system was also employed in Chinese writing, which has been in existence for thirty-five hundred years and now employs over thirty thousand characters plus some phoneticism.

The most abstract level of development in a pictorial system such as that of Mesoamerica is the phonetic. The characters portrayed represent sounds rather than images or ideas. In rebus writing, an example of the phonetic principle, a symbol is utilized only for the sound value it represents. The sentence, "I can see Aunt Peg," is written:

The pictures have lost all relation to or mental association with the objects they portray; their value is only in the phonetic transfer.

In western Mesoamerica the pictographic writing system apparently reached only the phonetic level in depictions of proper names: places, persons, and titles. For example, in the Aztec codices certain pictorial elements, or graphemes, were employed to convey—entirely independent of their semantic connotations—all or part of the sound values of the Nahuatl names for what they represent to form all or parts of words containing similar sounds.[11] This can be demonstrated with the place-name Tochpan. This toponym is formed by combining *tochtli* ("rabbit"):

with a suffix to denote a place. The sound-alike suffix is taken from *pantli* ("banner"):

In Nahuatl the term *pan* means "on, on top of, over." The result of combining elements of *tochtli* and *pantli* is the rebus form:

on the rabbit: Tochpan (Place of the Rabbit). It was only in the depiction of such proper names that genuine phoneticism was a feature of the pre-Hispanic writing system.

All the types of Middle American writing in use at the time of the Spanish conquest were no doubt genetically related, because they shared certain basic patterns reflecting what was probably the prime function of the pre-Hispanic writing and counting system—divination. It was the Mesoamerican belief that an individual's entire life was strongly determined by his date of birth, although a

---

[11] Nicholson 1973*a*, p. 3.

whole battery of other influences was also considered applicable. Since each day was perceived as fortunate, unfortunate, or neutral, it was mandatory to mark the passage of time; only by knowing the burden of good or ill carried by each day could men and women prepare themselves to deal with the gods.

In such a belief system the maintenance of a consistent calendric count was essential, and fundamental to all Middle American cultures was the sacred almanac of 260 days. The almanac was formed by combining a sequence of the numbers 1 to 13 with the twenty day names. The general uniformity in the names and glyphs assigned those days throughout Mesoamerica suggests that all such almanacs, despite differences which arose over the course of a millennium, probably had a common ancestry.[12]

Where and when hieroglyphs representing the twenty day names first appeared is uncertain, but they are found in Period I—approximately 500 B.C.—at the Zapotec site Monte Albán, Oaxaca. This incipient writing was apparently the mother script of all Middle America, which each culture then fashioned to meet its needs. One system developed in the Mixtec region of western Oaxaca, southern Puebla, and eastern Guerrero and represents a widespread Postclassic iconographic tradition generally known as the Mixteca-Puebla style. This writing incorporates images of human figures, geographic features, and objects to convey both real and symbolic meanings. Within the Mixtec codices, which are principally historical-genealogical manuscripts, there are certain toponyms and proper names that Caso contends have phonetic value.[13]

Some scholars, such as H. B. Nicholson, believe that a higher degree of phoneticism was reflected in the native-style documents produced by the Nahuatl-speaking peoples of the Valley of Mexico.[14] The Aztec pictorials ranged in content from the historical-genealogical to divinatory. In addition the Aztec imperial emphasis also produced economic documents. As the empire expanded, regions and towns in non-Nahuatl areas were given Nahuatl names that were then recorded hieroglyphically and hence could be understood across language and cultural barriers. At the same time historical codices were recording imperial conquests, listing the names of specific rulers. The increase in pictorials containing personal and place names focused attention on the recording of the single word and hence was moving the pictographic system toward phoneticism.[15] In comparison to the Lowland Mayas of the Classic Period, however, the Postclassic Mixtecs and Aztecs never really carried phonetic writing beyond a rudimentary stage.

Although the Classic Mayas left detailed glyphic passages on temples, stelae, and various portable objects, it is somewhat difficult to contrast their writing system with that of the Late Postclassic Mixtec and Aztec texts because no comparable historical or genealogical codices have survived. There are, however, comparable religious documents. In contrast to the Maya passages, the ritualistic codices from the Mixteca and central Mexico almost completely lack accompanying explanatory glyphic texts; one must depend on the pictorial matter alone to recognize the subject of the divinations. Of all the Mesoamerican peoples the Mayas alone supplemented their pictorial representations with glyphic symbols to convey meaning more fully. Fray Cuidad Real, who traveled extensively in Middle America in the 1580s, aptly noted that only the Mayas of Yucatán "had characters and letters in which they wrote [of ceremonial matters] in their books."[16]

The Maya scholar Sir J. Eric S. Thompson noted that the Maya hieroglyphic system comprised approximately 350 main-sign characters, 370 affixes, and about 100 portrait glyphs, principally of deities.[17] Omitting the portrait glyphs and deducting for variants and overlappings between main signs and affixes would lower the total Maya glyphs to about 650, but those glyphic elements were combined to form many more compounds. In compensating for their limited range of glyphs, the Mayas ingeniously utilized ideograms, pictograms, synonyms, but above all rebus writing to express themselves.[18] As a result the Maya language was the most phonetic of the Mesoamerican pictographic writing systems.

A great many of the Maya glyphs are still undeciphered. Also, one of the big problems in decipherment is deciding which Maya language was used.[19] Gelb, believing that the language the glyphs expressed is known and spoken to this day in the Lowland Maya region, contends that this is conclusive proof that the Mayas did not have a phonetic script.[20] According to him the most important principle in the theory of decipherment is that a phonetic writing can and ultimately must be deciphered if the underlying language is known. Thompson, however, offered as a partial explanation for the decipherment problem the fact that most Maya ritual terms and religious imagery, unrecorded in Maya-Spanish dictionaries, were lost with the disappearance of the Maya hierarchy.[21] Fortunately great strides have been taken in the past few years by such scholars as David Kelley,[22] Floyd Lounsbury[23] and Linda Schele,[24] who are making increasingly enlightening breakthroughs in Maya glyphic decipherment.

[12] Thompson 1972a, p. 21.
[13] Caso 1965, p. 951.
[14] Nicholson 1973a.
[15] Dibble 1971, p. 330.
[16] Thompson 1965, p. 652.
[17] Thompson 1972a, p. 9.
[18] Ibid., p. 68.

[19] Robertson and Jeffers 1979.
[20] Gelb 1974, p. 56.
[21] Thompson 1972a, pp. 9–10.
[22] Kelley 1976.
[23] Lounsbury 1974, 1976.
[24] Schele 1974, 1976, 1979.

Discussing the limitations of the pictographic writing system, Thompson noted that the Maya hieroglyphic texts "were the bones on which a priest moulded the flesh of oratory."[25] The same observation applies to every Mesoamerican codex regardless of its degree of complexity. Since all the Middle American writing systems were pictographic, they could not record subtle detail or, beyond a limited scope, handle abstraction. Because of this the codices present only a skeletonized version of the information; they served as memory prompters.

Many of the Mesoamerican pictorials, be they religious or historical in content, are in screenfold form (that is, a single long strip was folded, in the manner of a modern folding screen, into pages of equal size into whose dimensions the entire document condensed). The material used was either scraped deerskin or *amatl* paper, made of the pounded inner bark of the fig tree. Over the skin or bark paper a thin coat of lime gesso was applied, creating a smooth, even surface upon which to work. The extant codices vary in size, often even those from the same region. Their general dimensions may reflect either the idiosyncratic decisions of their artisan or priestly creators or the prevailing style at the time of their execution.

Only a few of the thousands of screenfold books that must have existed at the time of the Conquest have survived. Many of the pictorials, particularly the calendric-divinatory codices, were burned by the Spanish missionaries. They assumed, correctly, that the pictorials reflected native beliefs that stood in the way of the conversion of the Indians to the true faith. Most of the extant religious documents owe their survival to Europeans who sent them home as exotic relics of the New World (like the two books listed in the itemized inventory that included Moctezuma's gift). To date no one is certain which if any of the surviving codices are indeed these two famous pictorials. As will be seen below, there is no dearth of contenders for the title.

If all the facts were known, an adventurous saga could be written tracing the turbulent and circuitous history of the few surviving codices. It is an indication of the esoteric appeal and tremendous value of these fascinating documents that today almost all of them are guarded carefully within European museums and libraries and designated by European names. Because the colorful pictorials have appealed to collectors for centuries, many still carry the names of the individuals who formerly possessed them. *Codex Zouche-Nuttall* bears the names both of a one-time owner and of a subsequent discoverer-interpreter; *Codex Selden* and *Codex Bodley* carry the names of the men who collected them. *Codex Mendoza* is named for the first viceroy of Mexico, for whom it was reputedly made, whereas its cognate (sections of the two manuscripts apparently were copied from the same earlier source), the

Matrícula de tributos, bears a descriptive title, for it is an administrative tribute tally. Other pictorials, including the *Codex Dresden* and the *Florentine Codex*, are named for the cities where they are now held.

It is difficult to state precisely how many Mesoamerican codices are in existence today because the number depends upon how one defines the term. The Mesoamerican ethnohistorian John B. Glass, in his census of native Middle American pictorial manuscripts, lists 434.[26] He includes, however, any remnant, no matter how scant or damaged the fragment, that could be construed a "pictorial." Of these only sixteen are considered to have been made before European contact; all but one of these pre-Cortesian documents is represented in this book.

Not all the surviving codices contain depictions of a variety of clothing, and in some the garments are not clear enough to be useful as costume data. Only twenty-eight of the extant pictorials are represented in this book, but they include the most detailed, comprehensive, and refined of the Mesoamerican codices. They constitute the best examples from the six different groups for which there are costume data: the Aztecs, the Tlaxcalans, the Tarascans, the Mixtecs, the Borgia Group, and the Lowland Mayas.

The codices of the six Indian groups reflect considerable diversity at several levels. Geographically, their origins range from central Mexico to the lowlands of Yucatán. Internally, some of the pictorials are religious-divinatory manuals, whereas others contain secular, historical, or administrative information. Chronologically, some of the manuscripts were executed in the Late Postclassic period, while others were produced after the Conquest, in the latter part of the sixteenth century.

Given the diverse nature of the extant codices, it is difficult to organize their clothing data in such a way as to compare the costume repertory of one group with that of another. Of course, to be able to do this is mandatory if we are to understand pre-Hispanic Mesoamerican clothing. Problems abound, however. In addition to the difficulty of rendering the pictorial data into comparable units of analysis, there is also the problem of deciding at what level costume is to be viewed. Are such accessory elements as headdresses, jewelry, and other badges of office to be analyzed? Are such special-purpose garments as religious and warrior costumes to be treated separately? How is a study of pre-Cortesian clothing to deal with the status implications of costume? Obviously some system of organization is needed that will accommodate the variable data and at the same time cut through adornment detail, hold in abeyance the social implications of costume, and establish the mandatory comparable units of analysis. The explanation of such a method, developed for this book, follows.

---

[25] Thompson 1972a, p. 68.

[26] Glass 1975.

THE METHOD: CLOTHING ORGANIZED ACCORDING TO CONSTRUCTION PRINCIPLE

The system used throughout this book to categorize the pre-Hispanic clothing of the six different Mesoamerican groups is based on a concept originally developed by the anthropologist Homer G. Barnett.[27] Barnett contended that all material objects have three properties: principle, form, and function. His concept can be demonstrated with a garment example from the Mesoamerican costume repertory: the loincloth, *maxtlatl*, worn by Aztec men. This was the single piece of material wrapped around the lower torso. The principle—the scheme or theme around which an object is organized—is the draping of the garment. Its form—that aspect that can be observed and hence copied—is its visible shape. Its function—the contribution it makes to the needs of Aztec society—is the covering of the male lower torso.

To apply Barnett's model to a study of clothing, it is necessary to abstract the basic forms of costume into essential principles. To this end the work of the costume historian François Boucher[28] is most helpful. He has developed a scheme based on the premise that the manifold creations of costume, stripped of all accessory elements, can be reduced to five archetypes. To set up clothing categories that would accommodate the great diversity of illustrations from the codices, I have borrowed Boucher's scheme, changed and tightened his definitions somewhat, added further illustrative examples, and used his concepts thus augmented.

Chart 1, "The Five Basic Principles of Garment Construction," gives examples of the five principles that serve as the organizing categories for the clothing inventories of the six Mesoamerican groups. The five principles are illustrated in the left-hand section with examples from various points in time and space, demonstrating the universal applicability of the method. The right-hand side of the chart further illustrates the principles through the use of examples from a specific costume repertory, that of the Aztecs at the time of Spanish contact.

The first principle of garment construction is the draped garment, obtained by wrapping a piece of material around the body. Garments of this class can be worn directly from the loom with no cutting, sewing, or fitting required. Examples shown in chart 1 are (*a*) the Egyptian *shenti*, which drapes around the lower torso;[29] (*b*) the Grecian *himation*, draped over the shoulders;[30] (*c*) the Indonesian *sarong*, draped around the body to cover the upper and lower torso;[31] (*d*) the Aztec *maxtlatl* already discussed;[32] (*e*) the hip-cloth, which drapes over the hips (its Nahuatl name is unknown);[33] (*f*) the cloak, *tilmatli*, which drapes over the shoulder;[34] and (*g*) the male kilt, which wraps around the hips; and (*h*) the woman's skirt, *cueitl*, which wraps around the hips.[35]

The second of the five principles is the slip-on garment. This class of apparel slips over the head and is worn hanging from the shoulders. Cutting is necessary to produce the slit in the middle of the garment. Since (*j*) the Roman *paenula*[36] and (*k*) the Grecian *chlaina*[37] appear to have been wide, single webs, they probably needed no further work to make them wearable. But (*l*), the Aztec *quechquemitl*,[38] like (*i*) the Peruvian *poncho*,[39] was made of two loomed, joined webs. In this book, to accommodate the construction of the Mesoamerican *quechquemitl*, I define a slip-on garment as a garment pierced with a hole for the head, worn hanging from the shoulders, with no underarm seam.

The third principle is that of the open-sewn garment. It is made of several widths of material joined lengthwise by a continuous sewn seam and worn open in the front. This concept is illustrated by (*m*) the long Turkish mantle,[40] (*n*) the short English mantle,[41] and (*o*) the Indonesian warrior costume.[42] Although (*p*) the Aztec open *ichcahuipilli*,[43] and (*q*) the *xicolli*,[44] have ties to secure the two front panels, they are worn as open garments and therefore exemplify the same principle.

Closed-sewn garments constitute the fourth principle. Several webs of material are joined lengthwise by continuous sewn seams, but the garments are not worn open. They are either pulled on over the head or secured all the way up the front or back by some type of fasteners. Examples are (*r*) the Grecian *chiton*[45] and (*s*) the Anglo-Saxon tunic,[46] which appear to have been pulled over the head. Garments exemplified by (*t*) the French smock[47] could be either pulled on or buttoned up the back. Apparently (*u*) the closed *ichcahuipilli*[48] was a pull-on garment, as were (*v*) the *ehuatl*[49] and (*w*) the Aztec woman's *huipilli*.[50]

The final principle, that of limb-encasing garments, is the only category that involves the cutting and sewing of a garment to follow the lines of the body or to encase the

---

[27] Barnett 1942.
[28] Boucher 1966, p. 12.
[29] Bruhn and Tilke 1955, p. 1.
[30] Ibid., p. 12.
[31] Schreider 1962, p. 275.
[32] *Codex Mendoza*, vol. 3, fol. 60r.
[33] Ibid., fol. 68r.
[34] Ibid., fol. 64r.
[35] For (*g*), *Codex Magliabechiano*, fol. 34r; (*h*), *Codex Borbonicus*, p. 29.
[36] Bruhn and Tilke 1955, p. 17.
[37] Ibid., p. 12.
[38] *Codex Magliabechiano*, fol. 58r.
[39] Donnan 1973, p. 90.

[40] Bruhn and Tilke 1955, p. 91.
[41] Eworth 1938, plate 13.
[42] Schreider 1961, p. 618.
[43] *Codex Telleriano-Remensis*, fol. 29r.
[44] *Codex Mendoza*, vol. 3, fol. 63r.
[45] Bruhn and Tilke 1955, p. 12.
[46] Ibid., p. 34.
[47] Ibid., p. 141.
[48] *Codex Mendoza*, vol. 3, fol. 66r.
[49] This costume, which appears in Sahagún, *Codex Primeros memoriales*, 1:1, was photographed from Seler 1960, 2:576.
[50] *Codex Mendoza*, vol. 3, fol. 68r.

CHART 1

THE FIVE BASIC PRINCIPLES OF GARMENT CONSTRUCTION

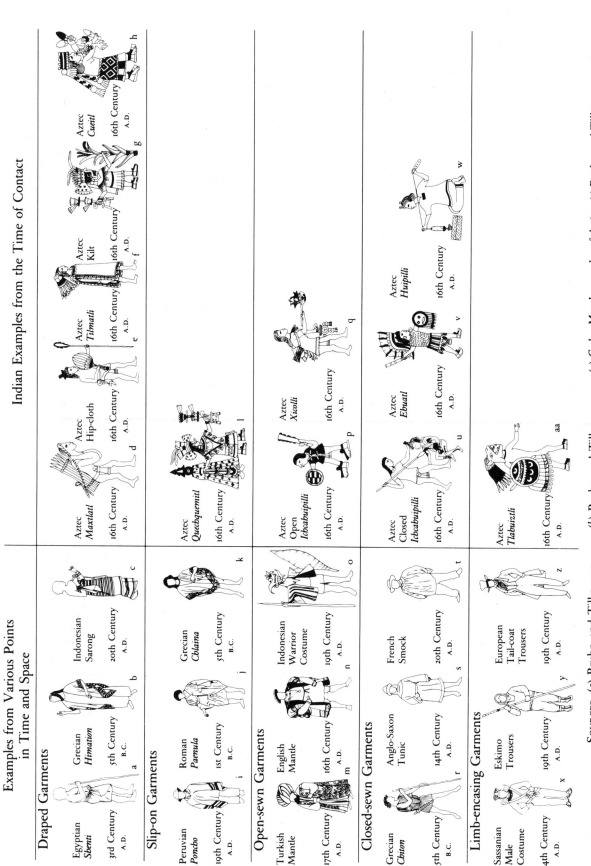

Examples from Various Points
in Time and Space

Indian Examples from the Time of Contact

Draped Garments

Egyptian *Sbenti* 3rd Century A.D.

Grecian *Himation* 5th Century B.C. — a

Indonesian Sarong 20th Century A.D. — b

Peruvian *Poncho* 19th Century A.D. — c

Aztec *Maxtlatl* 16th Century A.D.

Aztec Hip-cloth 16th Century A.D. — d

Aztec *Tilmatli* 16th Century A.D. — e

Aztec Kilt 16th Century A.D. — f

Aztec *Cueitl* 16th Century A.D. — g,h

Slip-on Garments

Roman *Paenula* 1st Century B.C. — i

Grecian *Chlama* 5th Century B.C. — j

Aztec *Quechquemitl* 16th Century A.D. — k,l

Open-sewn Garments

Turkish Mantle 17th Century A.D. — m

English Mantle 16th Century A.D. — n

Indonesian Warrior Costume 19th Century A.D. — o

Aztec *Xicolli* 16th Century A.D. — p,q

Closed-sewn Garments

Grecian *Chiton* 5th Century B.C. — r

Anglo-Saxon Tunic 14th Century A.D. — s

French Smock 20th Century A.D. — t

Aztec Closed *Ichcahuipilli* 16th Century A.D. — u

Aztec *Ehuatl* 16th Century A.D. — v

Aztec *Huipilli* 16th Century A.D. — w

Limb-encasing Garments

Sassanian Male Costume 4th Century A.D. — x

Eskimo Trousers 19th Century A.D. — y

European Tail-coat Trousers 19th Century A.D. — z

Aztec *Tlahuiztli* 16th Century A.D. — aa

SOURCES: (*a*) Bruhn and Tilke 1955, p. 1; (*b*) Bruhn and Tilke 1955, p. 12; (*c*) Schreider 1962, p. 275; (*d*) Codex Mendoza, vol. 3, fol. 60r; (*e*) Codex Mendoza, vol. 3, fol. 68r; (*f*) Codex Mendoza, vol. 3, fol. 64r; (*g*) Codex Magliabechiano, fol 34r; (*h*) Codex Borbonicus, p. 29; (*i*) Donnan 1973, p. 90; (*j*) Bruhn and Tilke 1955, p. 17; (*k*) Bruhn and Tilke 1955, p. 12; (*l*) Codex Magliabechiano, fol. 58r; (*m*) Brunn and Tilke 1955, p. 91; (*n*) Eworth 1938, plate 13; (*o*) Schreider 1961, p. 618; (*p*) Codex Telleriano-Remensis, fol. 29r; (*q*) Codex Mendoza, vol. 3, fol. 65r; (*r*) Bruhn and Tilke 1955, p. 12; (*s*) Bruhn and Tilke 1955, p. 34; (*t*) Bruhn and Tilke 1955, p. 141; (*u*) Codex Mendoza, vol. 3, fol. 66r; (*v*) Seler 1960, 2:576; (*w*) Codex Mendoza, vol. 3, fol. 68r; (*x*) Bruhn and Tilke 1955, p. 23; (*y*) Bruhn and Tilke 1955, p. 200; (*z*) Bruhn and Tilke 1955, p. 119; (*aa*) Codex Mendoza, vol. 3, fol. 65r.

limbs. The latter concept is reflected in (x) the Sassanian man's costume[51] and in (y) the Eskimo trousers,[52] whereas (z) the nineteenth-century European topcoat and trousers[53] are tailored apparel. The only limb-encasing garment in the Aztec costume repertory was (aa) the warrior costume, *tlahuiztli*,[54] an untailored garment in that it did not follow the lines of the torso.

These then are the five principles that have been used to organize the clothing inventories of the six Mesoamerican groups.[55] By consistently using these categories, I found it possible not only to contrast the six inventories but also to compare individual garments across categories. This book will demonstrate, through the systematic presentation of data, that a similarity of clothing existed throughout Mesoamerica and will show the features these garments had in common. Before an examination of the individual costumes from the codices, it will be helpful to consider the characteristics the garments shared.

THE CLOTHING: PRODUCTION TECHNOLOGY, SOCIAL ATTITUDES, AND CONSTRUCTION COMMONALITIES

The socioeconomic importance of the textile production that provided the clothing of Mesoamerica cannot be exaggerated. From sixteenth-century sources for the Aztec world—the group for whom there is fullest Conquest-period documentation—it is evident that the weaving process and resulting fabrics were an indispensable part of the social framework. Weaving was the domain of women, and each household appears to have been responsible for its own needs plus whatever textiles were required for tribute payment. Aside from the palace and the temples, which had resident groups of weavers who produced the specialized fabrics needed by those institutions, no

evidence had been found that indicates the existence of organized weaving workshops. It was the wives and daughters of each family who wove the beautiful textiles that so dazzled the conquistadors at the time of Spanish contact.

The same type of weaving equipment was used throughout Mesoamerica. This assemblage of simple parts is generally known as a backstrap loom; it is also sometimes referred to as a girdle-back, hip, waist, belt, or occasionally stick loom. All these terms are descriptive, the last particularly so, because when the loom is not set up with the warp threads, it is literally just a bundle of sticks of various lengths and thicknesses. To judge by modern weavers' equipment—exactly the same type of loom is still used in Indian communities throughout present-day Middle America—the pre-Hispanic sticks were made of many kinds of wood, some hard, some soft, and some of bamboo.[56]

An illustration from the *Florentine Codex*[57] (fig. 3), the famous sixteenth-century encyclopedic compilation of Aztec life, depicts weaving and spinning equipment. These implements can be interpreted by utilizing modern analogues.[58] In the lower-right-hand corner of fig. 3 is the straw mat upon which the weaver sits or kneels as she works. On the mat rests a small bowl. A spindle filled with thread is illustrated at the left of the row above. To produce thread, the spindle—its end resting in the bowl—is rapidly whirled as clean and fluffed cotton or processed bast fiber, *ixtli*, is carefully played out and spun into thread. Spun skeins of undyed and dyed threads are shown in the middle section of fig. 3.

Above the straw mat is a warping frame whose purpose is to establish the length of the textile and the number of threads that will form its width. The thread is wound on

---

[51]Bruhn and Tilke 1955, p. 23.

[52] Ibid., p. 200.

[53] Ibid., p. 119.

[54] *Codex Mendoza*, vol. 3, fol. 65r.

[55] This approach is an innovation in the study of pre-Hispanic Mesoamerican dress. Although a number of scholars have dealt with modern Middle American Indian clothing, the pre-Cortesian antecedents of these costumes have received surprisingly little attention. Two excellent bibliographies for modern Mexican and Guatemalan Indian clothing are now available in the 1976 *Proceedings of the Irene Emery Roundtable on Museum Textiles: Ethnographic Textiles of the Western Hemisphere* (1977). The following brief review of the literature will mention only studies that deal with some aspect of pre-Hispanic dress.

Three books focus on describing Indian costumes of the period 1920–50; they include brief discussions of pre-Hispanic antecedents. Lilly de Jongh Osborne, in her 1935 description of the Highland Guatemalan Indian costumes, speculated on the possible survival of pre-Hispanic lineage-group affiliation symbols in modern design motifs. Flavio N. Rodas, in his 1938 study of symbolism in the costumes of Chichicastenango, Guatemala, discussed the possiblity of ancient religious significance in modern clothing. In 1968, Donald and Dorothy Cordry, in their well-illustrated descriptive study of modern Mexican Indian costumes, devoted their first chapter to connections between pre-Cortesian and contemporary costumes.

Irmgard Johnson has discussed the analysis of archaeological woven fragments and pre-Hispanic weaving techniques and textile production in several articles (1958, 1959, 1960, 1966). Miguel Othon de Mendizabal wrote on these subjects, as well as the role of cloth and clothing in Mexican colonial life (1943–47). Throughout the works of the great German scholar Eduard Seler (1900–1901, 1901–1902, 1902–1903, 1904, 1960, 1963, 1967) pre-Conquest costumes are repeatedly discussed and analyzed, particularly in religious

contexts.

The literature on Mesoamerican clothing also contains works concentrating on the dress of specific Indian groups. Barbro Dahlgren, in her 1954 study of the pre-contact Mixtecs, devoted a chapter to their clothing. Cottie Burland (1955) also described the Mixtec costumes of the codices, as did Smiley Karst (1972), who concentrated on female garments. The clothing of the ancient peoples of central Mexico has received attention in the descriptive studies of Josefina Barrera Fernández (1965), Eulalia Guzmán (1951), and Laurette Séjourné (1966), the latter concentrating on the Classic period site Teotihuacán. Thelma Sullivan (1972) translated a section of Sahagún dealing with the arms and insignia of the Aztecs, and H. B. Nicholson (1967b) did a detailed analysis of the royal headband of Tlaxcala and its social and political implications. For the Maya area Tatiana Proskouriakoff (1964) concentrated on female costumes as a means of understanding the sociopolitical role of the aristocratic women who appear in Classic Maya sculpture. Joy Mahler (1965) also studied the clothing of the Mayas, describing Lowland dress from Preclassic to Postclassic times.

Of all the aforementioned scholars only Joy Mahler mentioned costume commonalities extending beyond the confines of a single ethnic unit. She encompassed a broader geographic area than does my study when she stated (1965, p. 583) that all the basic types of Mesoamerican garments were in existence by the Classic period and were similar from Mexico to Peru. A consideration of clothing outside Middle America is beyond the bounds of this book. Even for Mesoamerica, however, no prior studies have attempted to demonstrate, through the systematic presentation of data, that a similarity of clothing existed throughout the area, nor have they shown what common features these garments displayed.

[56] Cordry and Cordry 1968, p. 32.

[57] Sahagún 1926, bk. 8, plate 75.

[58] Cordry and Cordry 1968, pp. 25–41.

the frame in a figure eight (thread wound in this manner is shown resting on a reed basket at the bottom left of fig. 3). The figure eight creates a cross, or lease. This gives each thread its proper position and will form, when placed on the loom, the shed through which the wooden bobbin or shuttle carrying the weft thread will pass. Before the warp threads are taken off the warping frame, the cross is tied to make it secure (this may be what is depicted in the drawing of the tied thread at the left of the three weaving sticks). After removal from the frame, the warp threads are usually washed in maize water to strengthen and stiffen them so that they can be handled more easily. A piece of hemp string is then slipped through the looped warp threads. It is this string, not the warps themselves, that is fastened to the loom by a series of spiral loops that bind it across the width of the warp beam.

The backstrap loom takes its name from the backstrap illustrated in the upper right-hand corner of fig. 3; this particular one appears to be woven of maguey or palm fiber. The strap goes about the hips of the weaver, who either sits or kneels; in the latter position she can better exert the considerable force needed to open the sheds and beat down the weft. This is done with a batten or sword, the largest of the three sticks illustrated.

The backstrap has cords at either end that attach to the cloth beam, the notched middle stick of the three illustrated. The cloth beam lies across the width of the textile and, together with the identically shaped warp beam at the opposite end of the loom, holds the warp threads in place. As the weaving proceeds, the cloth beam is used to roll up the finished textile and also to bring the unwoven warp threads closer to the weaver. The other end of the backstrap loom, the warp beam, is tied with a divided cord—illustrated at the upper left—to a tree, a post, a house corner, or a stake driven into the ground for that purpose (see fig. 2).

The smallest of the three sticks illustrated in fig. 3 is probably intended to depict the bobbin or shuttle that carries the weft threads back and forth through the warps. When all the weft threads have been woven into the warps, the finished textile is removed from the loom by cutting the spiral string that originally bound the warps to the warp beam. The resulting web of material now has four completely finished sides, or selvages, which makes it possible to utilize the textile immediately just as it comes from the loom; if it is a draped garment, no further processing is necessary.

In pre-Hispanic times, as today, most weaving was probably done outdoors because interiors were dark and space was limited. Since the backstrap loom was easily transportable, it could quickly be rolled up and subsequently stretched out again in a convenient area. Weaving may have had a certain seasonality to it. Modern weavers sometimes put their looms away during the rainy season, because handspun thread is believed to break more easily because of the dampness.

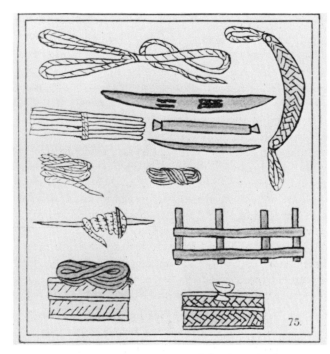

FIGURE 3. Aztec weaving apparatus. Sahagún 1926, *lámina* 49, *libro* 8, plate 75.

The fibers used in pre-Cortesian time were cotton for the upper classes and coarse bast fibers of maguey, yucca, pita, palm, and so on, for the commoners. All these latter vegetal fibers had to be laboriously processed—toasted, dressed, scraped, washed, and treated with maize water—before they could be spun and woven.

Many different kinds of dyes were used in Mesoamerica. Some colors came from flowers; the sixteenth-century friar Toribio de Benavente Motolinía said that when the Indians wanted to change colors they simply licked the brush clean, "for the paints were made from the juice of flowers."[59] Some vegetable dyes were also made of roots, wood bark, and fruit. Other sources included the famous shellfish dyes and the dried bodies of the female cochineal, the tiny insect that lives on the nopal (pricklypear) cactus. Mineral and earth dyes were also utilized, and feathers were used both to ornament cloth and to add warmth.

Although Mesoamerican garments were simply made, they were highly decorated. Many intricate designs were woven into the textiles. Weaving incorporated a number of demanding techniques, including brocade, figure gauze, tapestry, and warp-and-weft-face stripes. Designs were also applied by stamping, resist dying, and embroidering. For the embroidery of the finer garments a special thread composed of finely spun fur from the underbelly of the rabbit and strands of the indigenous wild silk were used. When dyed, this composite thread took on brilliant colors that were reputed to be fade-resistant. Fine embroidery work was so highly esteemed that a slave woman ac-

[59] Motolinía 1950, p. 220.

FIGURE 4. The equipment of Aztec women, presented to a baby girl at the time of her bathing ceremony. Sahagún 1926, *lámina* 40, *libro* 6, plate 30.

complished in this art, although destined for sacrifice, would be replaced by another so that she could continue working at her craft.[60]

The life of a woman from birth to death centered around the production of beautiful, well-made textiles. A newborn baby girl, at her bathing ceremony, was presented all the equipment of women: "the spinning whorl, the batten, the reed basket, the spinning bowl, the skeins, the shuttle, her little skirt, her little blouse" (see fig. 4).[61] When a woman died, her weaving equipment was burned with her in the funeral pyre to make it available to her for her journey after death. One of a mother's principal obligations was to teach her daughter to weave and spin, and this social emphasis appears repeatedly in the sixteenth-century Spanish chronicles. The *Florentine Codex* relates how the young girls were trained to weave:

> [Theirs was] the device with which [the loom] was held; the divided cord; the skein; the shuttle; the cane stalks; the wide batten, which swished [as it was used]; the thin batten, one made of bone; the small batten with which they worked designs; the heddle; the flail; the spindle whorl; the spinning bowl; chalk; the shallow whorl; when they spun with feathers; the basket for unspun cotton, one for rabbit hair, one for cotton thread, the basket for feathers, and the earthen bowl for feathers; the rack for yarn; the colored wood with which they dyed cotton when they wove; the bowl for colors in which they dissolved pigments; the paper patterns from

which they took the shape of whatsoever they made; maguey spines, with which they picked the cotton thread.[62]

One of the most famous of the Aztec pictorials, *Codex Mendoza*, shows the punishments administered by a mother if her daughter did not work well.[63] The girl's hand might be thrashed with a small stick, or her face might be held over a fire of burning chilis so that the acrid smoke would enter her nostrils.

It is apparent from the sixteenth-century sources that a woman who was a bad weaver was held in the lowest regard. Such a woman was described as lazy, indolent, nonchalant, sullen, and a deceiver.[64] A textile with a crooked hem was said to denote a selfish weaver.[65] A woman born under the sign One House was considered to be very lazy, much given to sleep and doing nothing useful: "...she could not twirl the spindle; she could not move nor raise the batten. She was incapable, witless, negligent, stupid, jeering and impudent."[66] The text goes on to imply that such a woman was good for nothing but sacrifice. Obviously in ancient Mesoamerica there was strong pressure to be a competent weaver.

The social importance of weaving is also reflected in iconographic and ritual symbolism. A weaving apparatus was part of certain deity costumes. The fertility goddess Tlazolteotl is often shown with spindles filled with thread stuck in an unspun fillet of cotton encircling her head, and

[60] Sahagún 1950–69, bk. 1, p. 44.
[61] Ibid., bk. 6, p. 201.
[62] Ibid., bk. 8, p. 49.
[63] *Codex Mendoza*, vol. 3, fols. 59r, 60r.

[64] Sahagún 1950–69, bk. 10, p. 36.
[65] Ibid., bk. 5, p. 192.
[66] Ibid., bk. 4, p. 95.

the goddess Xochiquetzal, patroness of weaving, is sometimes found in depictions associated with looms, spindles, and weaving. At one of the great Aztec public ceremonies, the Feast of Atemoztli, "Descent of the Water," edible images of the mountain fertility gods were made of amaranth-seed dough. These were subsequently "sacrificed" with weaving swords and then eaten. These are Aztec examples; the iconographic use of weaving apparatus also appears in pictorials of the other Mesoamerican ethnic groups (see fig. 50).

Since all the garments worn in pre-Cortesian Middle America were made of cloth produced on the same type of loom, it is understandable that the costumes of the diverse Mesoamerican Indian groups shared certain features and reflect an area-wide commonality of dress. Clothing requires broad, flat, flexible substances for its construction, and the size and shape of the materials available to a group have an influence on the apparel it

produces. In Mesoamerica the size of the woven textiles could not exceed the capacity of the backstrap loom. Cutting and sewing of cloth is a way of getting around the limitations of relatively narrow rectangular pieces; however this concept of cut and tailor, which involves quite a bit of waste, was not manifested in Mesoamerica. Instead, pieces of cloth were draped on the body just as they came from the loom, or slightly more complex garments were created by sewing together the selvages of two or more webs of material.

Throughout the codices this uncomplicated type of clothing is repeatedly illustrated. The pictorial world in which these simple garments are worn is a vital and colorful one where appropriately attired individuals and deities are engaged in a myriad of important activities. By focusing on their clothing and the context in which it is worn, we gain a particularly intimate and revealing glimpse of Mesoamerican culture before Cortés.

FIGURE 5. Four Aztec priest-warriors in their feather warrior suits complete with prestigious back devices and shields. *Codex Mendoza*, vol. 3, fol. 67r.

the Aztecs of Central Mexico

FOR OVER A MILLENNIUM before Spanish contact the northern heartland of Mesoamerica was the central plateau of Mexico, a high, dramatic region whose landscape is dotted with towering, snow-capped volcanoes interspersed with fertile mountain valleys. Since early times this *mesa central* had supported large populations and, during three separate periods, complex political systems. For some five hundred years, from about A.D. 100 to 650, the great empire of Teotihuacan flourished in the Valley of Mexico, only to fade and leave behind the massive ruins that have impressed subsequent peoples to the present day.

The next try at empire on the central plateau was that of the Toltecs, whose capital, Tula, was at its height around the beginning of the eleventh century. By mid-twelfth century this power too had fallen, and new waves of hunters and gatherers, drawn by the lure of an easier life, were breaking through the northern frontier to penetrate south into central Mexico.

Around the middle of the twelfth century there arrived in the fertile and desirable Valley of Mexico a small group of wandering Indians who in less than two hundred years were to forge the third highland empire and become the mighty Aztecs of Tenochtitlán. These newly arrived hunters and gatherers were one of seven tribes who had come out of the wild Chichimec ("barbarian") areas northwest of central Mexico; their legends tell of a semi-mythical homeland known as Aztlán, from which the name Aztec has subsequently evolved. They referred to themselves as the Mexicas.

Despite the rich resources of the central valley life was not easy for this small group of newcomers. They arrived, the last of the seven Chichimec groups, to find the desirable and fertile areas of the valley already settled. Competition for good land was keen, and the weak and despised Mexicas were forced to live in the most barren and inhospitable small islands and become the tributaries of more influential and settled masters. The new arrivals never questioned their destiny; they had been led thus far by their demanding and ferocious god Huitzilopochtli, who always promised that their reward awaited them. Following the dictates of their patron deity, the Mexicas searched and found a barren island in Lake Texcoco, where the prophesied eagle sat on a cactus, and there in 1325 they founded their city, Tenochtitlán.

For over one hundred years the Mexicas were forced to live modestly and at peace with their more powerful neighbors, but they always remembered their promised destiny. Finally in 1427 they had enough foothold to take advantage of a dispute that arose over water rights with the powerful lakeside city-state Azcapotzalco. The Mexicas, with the help of nearby Texcoco and the great powers of the Puebla basin, Tlaxcala and Huexotzinco, won this decisive battle. With their spoils, Tenochtitlán became an important city-state in its own right; the Aztec empire was under way.

Following the victory over Azcapotzalco, the Mexicas not only enlarged and glorified their city but also aggressively expanded their realm of influence. By the end of the fifteenth century the constantly shifting balance of power in the Valley of Mexico was coming to rest under control of ever-more-powerful Tenochtitlán. By 1430 the lakeside cities Tlacopán and Texcoco had joined the Mexicas to form the Triple Alliance, which eventually controlled an extensive empire of thirty-eight tribute-paying provinces. When Cortés arrived in 1519, the Aztec world was at its height.

It has been estimated that at the time of European contact the population of the Basin of Mexico was between 1 and 1.2 million. According to Spanish records there were about fifty small city-states in the valley, with populations of between 14,000 and 16,000 each, as well as a few larger cities. Tenochtitlán itself had between 122,000 and 200,000 inhabitants.[1] The feeding of this dense population was, of course, a vital matter in a land all too familiar with famines brought on not only by the ravages of recurrent warfare but also by natural disasters: plagues of locusts, drought, storms, and floods.

Richest of all the plateau zones, the Valley of Mexico has an elevation of over 7,200 feet and covers some 3,024 square miles.[2] Technically this area is not a valley at all but rather a closed basin whose most prominent feature in pre-Hispanic times was Lake Texcoco, a landlocked lake with no drainage outlet. This large body of water covered about 15 percent of the valley floor and had a profound influence not only on the environment but also on the social life of the basin.

All sections of the valley were utilized for agriculture, including the lake itself, where *chinampa* horticulture, one of the most productive gardening systems in the world, was extensively practiced.[3] Large areas of the shallow lake contained small fields built up out of layers of water plants and lake mud. Both Tenochtitlán and its twin island-city and subsidiary, Tlatelolco, were largely provisioned through the *chinampas* connected to the cities through a system of canals. Because the Mexicas lived on an island, many of their large-scale labor projects were in response to this particular and demanding environment; in addition to canals, dikes, and aqueducts, four major causeways joined the city to the surrounding mainland.

The ever-growing demands of a large population living in tight quarters in the island-city of Tenochtitlán necessitated constant provisioning that could be supplied only in part from the valley itself. Great quantities of food and other goods were brought into the city and distributed through marketplaces that contained an amazing variety of wares from the many diverse regions and climates of Mesoamerica. The greatest market in all of Middle America was that of Tenochtitlán's twin island-city, Tlatelolco; the conquistador Bernal Díaz del Castillo despaired of ever being able to enumerate all its varied wares.[4]

Tlatelolco's huge marketplace was part of its urban center, a great ceremonial precinct. Although Tenochtitlán's markets were not similarly situated adjacent to its temple complex, its massive central court was perhaps even more impressive. Around this huge plaza were grouped the major temples, administrative structures, palaces, and other pieces of monumental architecture. Sahagún listed about twenty-five pyramid-temples, nine attached priests' quarters, seven skull racks, two ball courts, arsenals, shops, and many other features in the

center of Tenochtitlán.[5]

Also living in the capital were the artisans—including metallurgists, featherworkers, jewelers, and dyers—who had the specialized skills to convert the exotic raw materials from the lowlands into highly coveted prestige goods. To highland Tenochtitlán came not only multicolored tropical feathers, jaguar pelts, gold dust, and turquoise and jade stones but also cotton. Since this plant will not grow at the high elevations of the *mesa central*, the Mexicas were dependent on trade and tribute for their supply of the important fiber; cotton was the Aztec status fabric par excellence, restricted solely to aristocratic wear. Tenochtitlán was the center for the luxury goods necessary to the maintenance of the Aztecs' highly complex, sharply stratified social structure.

The complexity and sophistication of development of Mesoamerican civilization is most clearly reflected in the elite class. Aztec society can be divided into roughly five categories. At the top were the aristocratic lineages, made up of the rulers of the city-states and their relatives. They were the *pipiltin* ("nobles"), who were supported by their own private lands and whose sons were educated in special schools, the *calmecac*. Directly below the ruling class were the highly specialized artisans, those who produced luxury goods, and the professional long-distance merchants. Both of these groups enjoyed special privileges not available to the class below them.

Most of the citizens were free commoners, *macehualtin*, organized into corporate landholding groups called *calpulli* ("big houses"). Membership in the *calpulli* was by birth, and the related families lived near one another, making up rural communities in the country and wards in the city.

All the land that members worked and lived on was held by the *calpulli* and allotted on a usufruct basis: plots were enlarged or withdrawn according to the needs and industriousness of each family. One of the most important functions of the head of each *calpulli*, who was traditionally drawn from one specific lineage, was to keep the land maps showing the distribution of plots.

The *calpulli* was the principal social, political, and religious unit of Aztec society. Through the *calpulli* craft specialization was carried out, children educated, taxes paid, labor drafts drawn, military units formed, and local temples maintained. This does not mean that all *calpulli* were equal, for even among the *macehualtin* there apparently was some degree of stratification. There appears to have been some affiliation between the noble classes and certain *calpulli*, but this connection is unclear. Certainly the members of the aristocracy, with their own private lands, were not dependent on the land-distribution control of the *calpulli* as were the *macehualtin*.

Below the *macehualli* class were the *mayeque* class, made

[1] Adams 1977, p. 26.
[2] Ibid.
[3] Calnek 1971.

[4] Díaz del Castillo 1967, 2:72.
[5] Sahagún 1950–69, bk. 2, pp. 165–80.

up of landless workers who were attached to and worked the estates of the nobles. Since this group had no *calpulli* affiliation with its attendant usufruct rights, its members were tied to the estates that provided their subsistence.

The lowest class of Aztec society was the slaves, who had no access to land and almost no individual rights. A person became a slave through adversity, which sometimes forced people to sell themselves or their children. Slave status was reversible, and one could buy out of bondage; the child of a slave was born free. Two factors that often drove people into slavery were famine and gambling. Many of the *tameme*—the porters, who were the only carriers of burdens in Mesoamerica—were slaves. War captives were occasionally enslaved, but most became sacrificial victims.

Despite the sharply defined social distances among the five segments of Aztec society, opportunities for upward mobility appear to have been available to the *macehualtin* through service to the state. Artisans, merchants, and warriors formed special subclasses ranking above the main class of farmer-laborers. Administrators played a key role in Aztec life; they were the civil servants through whom the aristocratic leaders controlled all affairs of importance.

At the time of Spanish contact the control exercised by the Triple Alliance, Tenochtitlán, Texcoco, and Tlacopán, had expanded to include five to six million people. This empire was administered by a well-developed system of graded bureaucrats, who carefully collected, transported, and tallied the valuable tribute that came in from the thirty-eight provinces. As long as these conquered groups adhered to imperial tribute demands, day-to-day life changed very little after they became part of the empire. Nothing was done to assimilate a conquered people beyond perhaps sending an Aztec governor and garrison to their territory and positioning an additional garrison at key points on the trade routes. As long as the assigned tribute was dutifully paid at agreed-upon, regular intervals, life in the conquered city-state continued much as before. Constant payment of the heavy tribute often chafed, and various provinces of the empire were frequently restive or in revolt. Aztec troops had to be sent to bring unruly groups back into line.

The artisan class produced status goods for the Aztec society from the exotic lowland products, much of which came into Tenochtitlán as tribute. Merchants also obtained goods through trade. The institution of the traveling merchant apparently had great time depth in central Mexico, perhaps because of the compressed ecological diversity within a small area that produced specialized crops easily transported short distances. By the time of Spanish contact the merchant class, the *pochteca*, held an important place in Aztec society. They had their own *calpulli* quarters in the towns as well as special schools, temples, and even a limited role in the ritual life otherwise dominated by the elite. In addition to trading, merchants acted as spies for their city-states, a role for which their long-distance trading ventures uniquely qualified them.

The gratitude of the state often allowed successful merchants to attain positions in the society that their social origins would not have predicted.

The most frequent route to social advancement, however, was the battlefield. The aggressive expansionist policies of the Aztec empire, coupled with the belief that continued functioning of the entire universe depended on constantly providing the gods with their necessary nourishment—human hearts and blood—had made warfare endemic by the time of Spanish contact. All young men were trained as warriors, and each was expected to take at least one captive in battle. As will be seen in the following discussion of Aztec clothing, the society richly rewarded those who continued on to greater martial feats. No greater service to the state could be offered than to provide captives for sacrifice. The need for such victims was unending, for the Aztecs' universe was envisioned as hostile, controlled by capricious gods who had to be ceaselessly propitiated. In the final analysis their adherence to their fatalistic religion strongly contributed to the destruction of their world.

Aztec religion was esoteric, all-pervasive, and complex, and its elitist composition mirrored the civilization as a whole. The complexities of the extensive pantheon, always prone to the incorporation of foreign deities, and the endless efforts to placate the myriad of gods necessitated detailed ritual knowledge. This body of information existed only at the upper levels of the priesthood and with certain higher nobles. Following the Conquest, when this relatively small group was eliminated, much of the ritual information was lost.

The pantheon was a crowded one, and the yearly round of ceremonies and ceaseless religious observances called for a large, active priesthood. Sons of the nobility, and apparently some outstanding boys from the *macehualli* class as well, were trained by priests in the *calmecac* schools. Those students who were chosen for religious life continued their studies into young adulthood, took vows of celibacy, and lived lives of austerity and service that included taking part in the ceaseless warfare. The Indian priests appear to have been loved and revered by the people, and even the Spanish friars admired the compassion, devotion, and dedication of their native counterparts.

In the Indian priesthood, as in administration, trade, or warfare, outstanding talent and service were recognized by the state and rewarded with special privileges. Among these was the wearing of garments that reflected achieved high status. In the tightly controlled and highly stratified Aztec society, each class and occupation had its own prescribed garments and badges of office that played a vital role not only as visual status markers but also as incentives to encourage further sustained and dedicated service to the state. Thus Aztec clothing reflected the structure and emphasis of Aztec society. Fortunately, illustrations of this revealing attire are available to us in the Aztec codices.

Nine pictorial documents from the Valley of Mexico

have been utilized to compile the Aztec costume reper- tory.[6] The *Codex Borbonicus* is the only Aztec ritual- calendrical screenfold still extant.[7] At one time this mag- nificent pictorial (see plate 3) was thought to have originated in Tenochtitlán-Tlateloco, but a recent study suggests that it may have come from the southern part of the basin — the *chinampa* region of Itztapalapa-Colhuacán.[8] The date of this beautiful and important pictorial is con- troversial; but if it is not pre-Hispanic, it certainly was ex- ecuted in the earliest part of the colonial period.

No one knows how or when the *Borbonicus* initially came to Europe, but it was first described in 1778, when it was in the Escorial in Spain. Sometime around 1826 the pictorial was either sold or given to the Library of the French Chamber of Deputies in Paris, where it still resides.

The manuscript includes not only a detailed 260-day divinatory almanac but also depictions of the eighteen monthly festivals as well as the last (1507) "New Fire" ceremony, which took place during the annual festival of Panquetzaliztli. Because of the religious nature of the *Codex Borbonicus*, all the figures are dressed in ritual attire. These resplendent and complex costumes are fascinating, but their very elaboration makes the garments themselves difficult to discern. In one instance, however, the ritual emphasis proves most helpful. The only fully visible wraparound skirt is found in the *Codex Borbonicus* (chart 2, example *p*), where it is worn topless. It is startling to realize that the figure is a male priest who is wearing the woman's garment over a female sacrificial victim's skin.

The *Codex Telleriano-Remensis* is considered to have been compiled in the Valley of Mexico in 1562–63.[9] It is named for the Frenchman Le Tellier, who in addition to being the royal librarian was also archbishop of Rheims. He apparently acquired the pictorial in the course of his travels in Europe in the late seventeenth century. Pres- ently in the collection of the Bibliothèque Nationale, in Paris, the codex contains three separate sections in several native styles dealing with ritual, calendrical, and historical subject matter. Fortunately the early Spanish priests wrote annotations on most of the pages, and these glosses are an important aid in understanding the pictorial's esoteric subject matter. Since the historical section deals with the many battles of the Mexicas between 1198 and 1562, it shows a considerable range of military attire.

Military attire also appears in the *Codex Vaticanus A*,[10] compiled between 1566 and 1589. This manuscript, presently in the Biblioteca Apostolica Vaticana, in Rome, is believed to have been copied by a non-Indian artist in Italy; its long Italian texts are thought to be based on a

commentary by Fray Pedro de los Ríos (this pictorial is also sometimes called *Codex Ríos*). Both *Vaticanus A* and *Telleriano-Remensis* are considered to be copies of a now- lost original manuscript, and, while there are duplications in the allied documents, each has fortuitous additions: leaves that are missing from the *Telleriano-Remensis* are preserved in its cognate, *Vaticanus A*.

Another colonial pictorial done in the native style before 1566 is the *Codex Magliabechiano*.[11] This manu- script came to light in early-seventeenth-century Europe in the collection of a royal librarian, Antonio Maglia- bechi, who served the Medicis. The codex was eventually added to their library, which in turn became a part of the Biblioteca Nazionale Centrale in Florence, where the pic- torial now resides. The *Magliabechiano*, which contains ritual-calendrical and ethnographic data, has been unusually valuable for this study of Aztec costume, pro- viding clothing examples in an informative series of ritual contexts. Some of these descriptions are enigmatic, however. For example, in scenes of ritual drinking the participants are shown wearing garments with crudely sewn seams,[12] but it is unclear why such clothing occurs only on these pages. All the male cloaks in the *Codex Magliabechiano* are short, whereas a number of early Spanish conquerors described carefully prescribed lengths available to the various social classes. It has been difficult to determine how much meaning to attach to such aber- rant examples; they could reflect the peculiarities of a specific community or artist.

Drawings from the early work of the famous sixteenth- century missionary and Aztec ethnographer Fray Bernar- dino de Sahagún have been most helpful in investigating military garments. Sahagún's earliest work with Indian in- formants and artists took place in the Valley of Mexico town Tepepulco, and this material is found in his *Primeros memoriales*.[13] The final pictorial sections of this helpful manuscript contain not only detailed drawings but also accompanying Nahuatl text. Using this combination, I was able to define the diagnostic features of a special military tunic, the *ehuatl*, and subsequently recognize that garment in the less-specific depictions of other codices.

Illustrations in two historical manuscripts from the Valley of Mexico have also been used to assemble the Aztec clothing inventory. The *Códice Azcatítlan*[14] deals with the Mexicas from their departure from Aztlán (Azca- títlan) through the migration and dynastic history of Tenochtitlán to the Spanish conquest. This document is helpful in further understanding military garments, par- ticularly variants of the basic martial attire, cotton armor.

The *Códice Xolotl*[15] comes from the Texcoco region of

[6] A more detailed description and history of all the Mesoamerican codices used in this book can be found in John B. Glass and Donald Robertson, "A Census of Native Middle American Pictorial Manuscripts" (1975). The census number for each of the codices used in this study is listed in the notes of the relevant chapter.

[7] Glass and Robertson 1975, *Codex Borbonicus*, census no. 32.

[8] Nicholson 1974a.

[9] Glass and Robertson 1975, *Codex Telleriano-Remensis*, census no. 308.

[10] Glass and Robertson 1975, *Codex Vaticanus A*, census no. 270.

[11] Glass and Robertson 1975, *Codex Magliabechiano*, census no. 188.

[12] *Codex Magliabechiano*, fols. 41r, 85r.

[13] Glass and Robertson 1975, *Codex Primeros memoriales*, census no. 271.

[14] Glass and Robertson 1975, *Códice Azcatítlan*, census no. 20.

[15] Glass and Robertson 1975, *Códice Xolotl*, census no. 412.

the Valley of Mexico and depicts the history of these people from their arrival in the valley (1224?) to 1427. The pictorial information is presented in map form. The tiny figures who people the landscape are often engaged in battle, as are those of the *Códice Azcatítlan.* Together the documents furnish valuable comparative clothing examples.

Both *Códices Azcatítlan* and *Xolotl* were part of the famous Boturini collection, compiled in Mexico between 1736 and 1743. Lorenzo Boturini Benaduci, a gentleman of high birth and good education, went to Mexico in 1736. He became interested in the story surrounding the Virgin of Guadalupe and resolved to collect available native documents to confirm her miracle. During his travels throughout Mexico he also acquired manuscripts that were vital to the history of New Spain but did not directly concern his objective. In the course of his quest he ran afoul of the all-powerful Spanish Council of the Indies and was deported to Spain. Boturini was never reunited with his collection, which was gradually dispersed. Part of it was acquired by the French collector Aubin, much of whose holdings eventually reached the Bibliothèque Nationale, where both *Azcatítlan* and *Xolotl* are now housed.

Probably the most valuable pictorial document of all for this study of Aztec clothing is the beautiful and informative *Codex Mendoza.*[16] This manuscript apparently was commissioned by the first Mexican viceroy, Antonio de Mendoza, in 1541–42 for presentation to Charles V. It is said to have been seized by French pirates on its way to Spain and is known to have been in the hands of the French royal cosmographer André Thevet by 1553. It is presently in the Bodleian Library at Oxford University, in England.

The *Codex Mendoza* is comprised of three parts, each containing a unified set of drawings and accompanying Spanish glosses. The first presents a history of the Mexica from the founding of Tenochtitlán through 1521. Since all these folios are stylized and contain no unique clothing depictions, that section was not helpful in the clothing study. The second part, however, is instructive. It is a pictorial record of the tribute sent from the thirty-eight provinces of the Aztec Empire.[17] Since much of the tribute was paid in textiles, pictograms of these clothes are shown repeatedly, often with the textiles' unique designs added. Even more detailed are the explicit drawings of the magnificent, brightly colored feathered warrior suits with attendant headgear and shields.

For this study of clothing the most valuable section of the *Codex Mendoza* is part three, a graphic portrayal of Aztec life. It was probably compiled especially for the codex and is done in a more Europeanized drawing style. One group of folios deals with a year-to-year history of Aztec men and women from birth through subsequent life stages. Other pages depict warriors, priests, and administrators, the palace of Moctezuma, and the laws and punishments of the emperor's reign.

The combination of secular individuals drawn in an easily recognizable Europeanized style and the accompanying Spanish glosses is extremely helpful because the diagnostic features of the clothing can thus be determined. It is then far easier to recognize variant forms in subsequent pictorials, many of whose styles differ markedly because of regional variation or artistic idiosyncrasies.

The problem of distinct differences among manuscripts in the portrayal of the same garments is perplexing. For example, were there really that many styles of capes and cotton armor? Does the diversity reflect the distinctive dress of a specific community or the unique artistic canon of a particular region? And what of the native artists themselves? Did all of them set about their tasks with approximately the same degree of training and supervision, or is the modern scholar at the mercy of their idiosyncratic quirks and priestly overseers with varying standards? From the standpoint of establishing the six clothing inventories, the best that can be done, more than four hundred years after the fact, is to strive constantly to determine the truth about a garment by using multi-example comparisons and exercising common sense in weighing the exceptional and aberrant cases.

The understanding of ancient Mesoamerican costumes shown in the pictorials is frequently aided by additional information on Middle American clothing available in the written sixteenth-century Spanish sources.

The conquistadors provided eyewitness accounts of contact-period life. Some of the reports of the European invaders have been viewed with skepticism. The Spaniards have been accused of exaggerating the size of Indian armies, and were it not for corroborative evidence in the pictorials, it might be supposed that the Spaniards' descriptions of Aztec martial apparel were also self-serving aggrandizement. Even a cursory examination of the *Codex Mendoza* indicates, however, that the reported grandeur of Aztec battle attire was accurate. And if the conquistadors described military costumes accurately, there was little to gain from biased reporting of secular or religious dress.

Four of the conquistadors' reports are of value. The first is the account of the conqueror himself, Hernán Cortés, who in the course of the Conquest sent six narrative letters to Charles V.[18] The first and last have been lost, but the remaining four contain progress reports, observations, and requests for aid. Since the letters were written to make a favorable impression on the Spanish crown, they must be judged accordingly. Unfortunately, Cortés said little about Indian clothing, but the few references to it are useful.

---

[16] Glass and Robertson 1975, *Codex Mendoza,* census no. 196.

[17] The same information exists in a cognate document, the *Matrícula de tributos,* census no. 368. Both manuscripts were apparently copied from a common original.

[18] Cortés 1971.

Both Bernal Díaz del Castillo[19] and Francisco (Alonso) de Aguilar[20] went to Mexico with Cortés in 1519 and took part in the whole course of the Conquest. Díaz's famous account is much fuller (and far more self-serving) than Aguilar's, but the latter contains some information not found elsewhere. That is also true of the account of the Anonymous Conqueror, whose true identity is still in question.[21]

In addition to the reports of the initial invaders, another rich source of information is the administrative reports. They were primarily political instruments, written either to report to higher officials on the general condition of the Indians or to gather specific information about native culture for some immediate practical use. The famous *Relaciones geográficas* fall into both categories.[22]

The *Relaciones geográficas* were compiled by order of Philip II. They constitute replies by Spanish officials in Middle and South America to a standard questionnaire prepared by imperial bureaucrats in Madrid. The purpose was to elicit basic information about the diverse European, Indian, and maritime communities and regions of the overseas realm. The form, composed of fifty questions, was accompanied by printed instructions on how it was to be answered. For the Mesoamerican area 166 *Relaciones geográficas* of the first series, 1579 to 1585, are extant. From this corpus the answers to a section of one particular query (question 15) regarding indigenous customs are especially important for this book: "Describe how they were governed; with whom they fought wars, and their manner of fighting; their former and present manner of dressing."[23]

In addition to the information drawn from the *Relaciones geográphicas* a further administrative source is Alonso de Zorita, who spent almost twenty years in New Spain traveling to various localities in his capacity as a judge.[24] He gave the Crown information regarding the government and tribute system of the Indians, and he was known for his protection of the natives against the Spanish *encomenderos*, settlers who controlled the labor of whole Indian villages.

The most detailed information on Indian life comes from the writings of the early-sixteenth-century missionaries, whose proselytizing fervor does not appear to have caused them to write biased descriptions of the "heathen" apparel of their idolatrous charges. Certainly there is, by mid-twentieth-century standards, undue concern with lack of modesty, proper covering of "shameful parts," and devil's work afoot in certain garments and design motifs. On the whole, however, costume descriptions of the clergy hold up well when compared with extant pictorial data. In their reports of the depravity of indigenous rites and the natives' delight in Christianity, the ecclesiastics must be read with caution; but, when discussing such everyday aspects of native life as clothing, they proved to be good informants. Just how much detail was withheld because it was deemed inappropriate can never be known. For example, the 1571 Nahuatl-Spanish dictionary of the Franciscan friar Francisco Molina does not include *xicolli*, the word for the Aztec ritual jacket often connected with human sacrifice.[25] The omission may have been an oversight, but such a deletion is in keeping with the friar's disapproval of all pagan religious matters.

Of all the missionaries who arrived in the early years following the Conquest, none is so important to the study of the indigenous culture as the Franciscan Bernardino de Sahagún.[26] Shortly after his arrival in New Spain in 1529, Sahagún mastered Nahuatl and gained a deep appreciation of the native culture. He did "fieldwork" with the Indians, utilizing what are now modern ethnographic techniques: he compiled questionnaires covering almost every aspect of the spiritual and material culture of the natives, selected with care knowledgeable older informants, and cross-checked the resulting data with another set of informants in another locale. He also had native artists illustrate certain customs, rites, and objects.

The result of Sahagún's more than forty years of labor are the twelve books collectively titled *Historia general de las cosas de Nueva España*, better known as the *Florentine Codex* after the city where it now resides. This outstanding work, which contains Nahuatl and paraphrased Spanish translations, is an encyclopedic compendium of the religion, customs, and natural history of the Aztecs. Not surprisingly, Sahagún provided the greatest wealth of information on Aztec apparel as well as on most other facets of their life.

In his description of Mesoamerican garments Sahagún used a diverse and specific Nahuatl terminology, providing an invaluable data corpus with which to investigate clothing from less-well-documented areas. While certain aspects of even Sahagún's work must be handled critically (for example, his contentions on the pernicious effects of pre-Hispanic religious beliefs[27]), his references to such mundane items as clothing, elicited as they were from native informants, have the ring of truth.

The Franciscan friar Toribio de Benavente—known as Motolinía because he took the Nahuatl word for "beggar" as his name—arrived in the New World in 1524.[28] He was one of the first twelve priests to arrive in New Spain after the Conquest. He traveled widely in Mexico and Guatemala, saw much of the still-unchanged native culture, and

[19] Díaz del Castillo 1967.
[20] Francisco (Alonso) de Aguilar 1954.
[21] Anonymous Conqueror 1858.
[22] Two articles dealing with the *Relaciones geográficas* have been utilized for this costume investigation: Howard F. Cline, "The Relaciones Geográficas of the Spanish Indies, 1577-1648" (1972); and H. R. Harvey, "The *Relaciones geográficas* 1579-1586: Native Languages" (1972).

[23] Cline 1972, p. 235.
[24] Zorita 1963.
[25] Molina 1970.
[26] Sahagún 1950-69.
[27] Ibid., bk. 1, pp. 55-76.
[28] Motolinía 1971.

became personally involved in indigenous life. Compared with Sahagún's, Motolinía's writings lack descriptive detail, and for this study he serves primarily as a corroborating, supplementary source.

Of more help is the work of the Dominican missionary Fray Diego Durán.[29] Although he wrote at a later date (between 1576 and 1581), Durán lived in Mexico City from the time he was a very young boy and drew much information from older natives who had known the indigenous patterns of the Aztec world at the time of its demise and also from older priests.

Like Sahagún's, Durán's stated purpose in writing was to help the missionaries combat the religious beliefs of the Indians who, forty years after the Conquest, were still holding to their pagan ways. Durán is not as informative or detailed as Sahagún, but he does provide additional information, particularly on the role of dress in the culture overall.

By combining the information on Aztec clothing found in eyewitness accounts of the conquistadors, administrators, and missionaries with the depictions from the codices, we can reconstruct the inventory of garments that made up the Aztec costume repertory. Of particular help in understanding the implications of this clothing is the work of a prodigious scholar whose pioneering research still forms the bulwark upon which future investigations of Mesoamerican iconography can rest. Eduard Seler (1849–1922) worked on Americanist material for thirty-five years, applying a disciplined, analytical methodology that continues to serve as a model for modern scholars.[30] He exemplified the thoroughness and critical positivism that were particular hallmarks of high-level German scholarship of his time.[31] Seler's work is valuable for understanding not only the Aztec clothing but also the apparel of the five other Mesoamerican groups.

AZTEC COSTUME REPERTORY

To examine and understand the Aztec clothing repertory, I organized representative garments according to the principle of construction that each exemplifies, as explained in chapter 1. These costume examples are arranged and presented in the five categories that represent the basic principles of clothing construction: draped, slip-on, open-sewn, closed-sewn, and limb-encasing garments.

Draped Garments

All of the clothing in this category is worn by wrapping or draping a piece of material on the body. The garments are complete as they come from the loom with no cutting, sewing, or fitting necessary. In this category appear the male *maxtlatl*, or loincloth; the hip-cloth; the *tilmatli*, or cloak; and the female *cueitl*, or skirt.

MAXTLATL. The first garment to be considered is the loincloth, which the Aztecs wore in two styles. In both, a long, narrow length of cotton or maguey fabric was wrapped around the lower torso, passed between the legs, and tied at the waist. In one style the two ends—often fringed and embroidered—were separated, with one falling in front and the other behind. In the other style the two ends remained in the front and were tied over the crotch in a distinctive knot, whose ends reached no lower than the knees. Since gods and their impersonators wore the first style, it may be the older, more archaic one.

The loincloth was the basic, indispensable item of clothing worn by Aztec males of all classes. Although many of these garments appear to have been plain, the loincloth could reflect the class of its wearer through the complexity and richness of its design motifs.

The Nahuatl word *maxtlatl* can be translated as either "loincloth" or "breechclout"; the former is used almost exclusively in the English texts. In etymologizing the Nahuatl word, Seler contended that the root *max* designates the place where the legs separate,[32] and the term is also applied to forks in the road and other forking objects. No reference is given for this statement, and it is difficult to assess its validity, for neither of the principal Nahuatl dictionaries lists the form *max*; the word *maxtlatl*, however, appears in both. Molina defined it as "short trousers or something similar."[33] The nineteenth-century Nahuatl dictionary of the Frenchman Rémi Siméon reads: "Belt, loincloth or a broad strip of cloth descending almost to the thighs."[34] A 1580 *Relación geográfica*[35] from the Aztec area (Otomi-speaking[36] Atitlalquía, east of Tollán, in the modern state of Hidalgo) provides a fuller description:

> . . . the men covered their privy parts with some woven bands of cotton like mufflers, which they wrapped around their loins a little above the hips and tie at the crotch and thus these bands formed (a) kind of open breeches or drawers with which the men cover their private parts. These bands they call *maxtles*.[37]

The Anonymous Conqueror also described the Aztec loincloth:

> [The men] cover their private parts, in front as well as in back, with very showy clothes like the large kerchiefs they put on their heads on journeys; they are in various

---

[29] Durán 1967.
[30] Seler 1900–1901, 1901–1902, 1902–1903, 1904, 1960, 1963, 1967.
[31] Nicholson 1973c, p. 362.
[32] Seler 1960, 2:466.
[33] Molina, p. 54v.
[34] Siméon 1965, p. 237.

[35] The *Relaciones geográficas* will be designated by their number in Cline's census (1972, pp. 185–88).
[36] Where possible the language spoken in these communities will also be listed; all linguistic affiliations are from Harvey's language index to the *Relaciones geográficas* (1972, pp. 283–94).
[37] Cline 1972, census no. 12; Paso y Troncoso 1905, 6:206.

CHART 2
AZTEC COSTUME REPERTORY
Examples of Draped Garments

Male
Maxtlatl

a

b

c

Hip-cloth

d

e

f

g

h

Tilmatli

i

j

k

l

m

n

Kilt

o

Female
Cueitl

p

q

r

s

t

Sources: (a) *Codex Mendoza*, vol. 3, fol. 60r; (b) *Codex Mendoza*, vol. 3, fol. 43r; (c) *Codex Telleriano-Remensis*, fol. 18r; (d) *Codex Mendoza*, vol. 3, fol. 68r; (e) *Codex Magliabechiano*, fol. 82r; (f) *Codex Telleriano-Remensis*, fol. 41v; (g) *Codex Borbonicus*, p. 26; (h) *Codex Magliabechiano*, fol. 63r; (i) *Codex Mendoza*, vol. 3, fol. 64r; (j) *Codex Mendoza*, vol. 3, fol. 68r; (k) *Códice Azcatítlan*, planche 22; (l) *Codex Magliabechiano*, fol. 35r; (m) *Codex Magliabechiano*, fol. 70r; (n) *Codex Magliabechiano*, fol. 85r; (o) *Codex Magliabechiano*, fol. 34r; (p) *Codex Borbonicus*, p. 29; (q) *Codex Magliabechiano*, fol. 67r; (r) *Codex Mendoza*, vol. 3, fol. 31r; (s) *Codex Mendoza*, vol. 3, fol. 60r; (t) *Codex Magliabechiano*, fol. 41r.

colors, with trimming of diverse colors also, and tassels that hang front and back.[38]

The *maxtlatl* was worn by men of all classes: slaves,[39] warriors,[40] and the ruler himself.[41] Sahagún's book *Kings and Lords* describes some of the designs found on the *maxtlatl* worn by the nobility: ivy design, embroidered at the ends; marketplace design; butterfly design at the ends; striped with many colors; breechclout made of twenty pieces of wind-jewel design at the ends; tawny-colored breechclout with embroidered ends; carmine-colored with ocelot head; ocelot breechclout with a step design; coyote-fur breechclout with the eagle head; breechclout with feathered disks at the end; and breechclout with radiating embroidery at the ends.[42]

In describing the investiture of the office of an Aztec lord, Motolinía wrote of the noble in one part of the ceremony as being naked "except for his *maxtlatl*."[43] Since the loincloth was the essential item of apparel for every male Aztec, its absence from the costume repertory of a neighboring people was cause for critical comment, noted in the attitutde of Sahagún's informants toward a group living in the lowlands on the northeast: "The defects of the Huastec: the men did not provide themselves with breech clouts."[44] Regarding another neighboring people, however, Sahagún reports: "These Otomi had a civilized way of life. The men wore capes, clothed themselves, wore breech clouts."[45]

The *maxtlatl* (example 2a) from *Codex Mendoza*, part three, is typical of all the loincloths in the *Codex Mendoza*, tying over the crotch and forming a distinctive knot. This folio deals with the training of boys and girls age eleven to fourteen. Aztec boys donned the *maxtlatl* only after reaching age thirteen, at which time they were considered men. Before that time they wore only a small cloak tied on the shoulder.

The figure portrayed, whose loincloth has a simple horizontal design at the end, is a young man of thirteen engaged in his chore of transporting reeds. (The accompanying Spanish annotation states that the standard fare for a young person of this age was two tortillas a meal, a sparse ration in keeping with what we know of the Aztecs as a frugal group little given to overindulgence. For most of the people the first food of the day was not served at dawn, the hour of arising, but in the middle of the morning. The main meal came at the beginning of the afternoon, during the hottest hours. Aside from perhaps a few sips of a corn or amaranth gruel before sleep, that made up the Mexicas' diet.)

The second *maxtlatl* depiction (example 2b) is from the tribute section of *Codex Mendoza*. Decorated loincloths

[38] Anonymous Conqueror 1858, pp. 576–77.
[39] Sahagún 1950–69, bk. 9, pp. 51, 59.
[40] Ibid., bk. 8, p. 88.
[41] Ibid., p. 56.
[42] Ibid., p. 25.
[43] Motolinía 1971, p. 381.
[44] Sahagún 1950–69, bk. 10, p. 186.
[45] Ibid., p. 176.

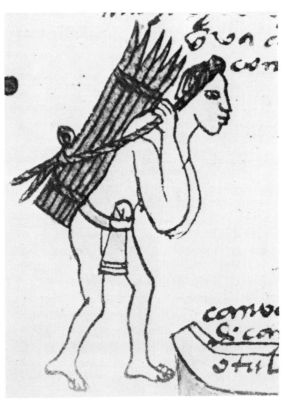

EXAMPLE *2a*. Aztec *maxtlatl*. *Codex Mendoza* vol. 3, fol. 60r. Note: The numeral and letter comprising the example number refer to the preceding numbered chart in which the sample appears.

EXAMPLE *2b*. Aztec *maxtlatl*. *Codex Mendoza*, vol. 3, fol. 43r.

were regularly given in tribute by some of the more than 350 towns of the thirty-eight provinces subject to the Aztec Triple Alliance. A pictographic record of this tribute was designated by drawing the distinctive knot of the *maxtlatl* on the standard representation of a *manta*, the large web of material often worn as a cloak. Nine such notations occur in part two of the *Codex Mendoza*, each representing 400 loincloths, for a total of 3,600 given every eighty days, with an annual total of 16,200.[46]

The third *maxtlatl* (example 2c) is worn by a male from the ritual calendar, the *tonalamatl*, a portion of the *Codex Telleriano-Remensis*. The garment is seen on the body of a hapless victim of a plumed serpent, patron of the fourteenth of the twenty periods that make up the sacred round of 260 days.

The *Codex Telleriano-Remensis* contains both ritual and historical sections. Twelve of the gods in the *tonalamatl* portion—those on whom it is possible to observe the full *maxtlatl*—are wearing the loincloth style with the ends hanging in front and back.[47] The nondeity figures in the same ritual calendar (such as the victim discussed above, who is a priest[48]) wear the distinctive knot-type *maxtlatl*. In the historical section the warriors generally wear the former type of loincloth; the distinctive knot style occurs only occasionally.[49]

In the *Codex Magliabechiano* the distinction between ritual and secular loincloths is marked. All the male deity impersonators wear the loincloths with ends hanging in front and back.[50] On two folios skeletonlike deities wear a snake for a loincloth, with the serpent's head hanging down in back.[51] Almost all the attendants and helpers in this pictorial wear the distinctive-knot loincloths.[52]

The same dichotomy also exists in the one extant Aztec pictorial devoted entirely to ritual matters, the *Codex Borbonicus*. Where it is possible to see the full *maxtlatl*, all the deities and their impersonators in this pictorial wear the style of loincloth with the ends hanging in front and back of the body. All subsidiary figures, however, wear the distinctive-knot type of *maxtlatl*.[53] Considering the conservative, slow-changing nature of religious accouterments, the manner in which the Aztec deities wear their loincloths probably reflects not only the style of an earlier period but also that of another area from which it diffused.

HIP-CLOTH. The second row of chart 2 contains examples of the hip-cloth. These garments appear repeatedly both in Aztec pictorials and in codices from other Mesoamerican groups, but very little is known about them. Although Seler mentioned hip-cloths (*Hüftentüchern*) and wrote of them as "girding loins,"[54] no further descriptive

EXAMPLE 2c. Aztec *maxtlatl. Codex Telleriano-Remensis*, fol. 18r.

information has been found, and the Nahuatl term for this garment is unknown.

The Aztec "triangular" hip-cloth was probably a square of material folded on the diagonal so as to form a triangle. It was worn around the waist and was usually tied on the right side. Since the hip-cloth is found in association with a warrior, a musician, a *cargador*, and a deity impersonator, it can be assumed that it was worn by all classes of Aztec males. Although the hip-cloth is not as ubiquitous as the *maxtlatl* over which it was always worn, it does appear to have been an all-purpose garment that could indicate the class of the wearer, depending on the type of fabric and the degree of decoration.

As the five examples of the hip-cloth in chart 2 demonstrate, the garment is associated with a number of activities. The first figure wearing a hip-cloth (example 2d) is from the section of *Codex Mendoza* that treats the secular life of the Aztecs. This individual's hair is arranged in a style called *temillotl* ("column of stone")[55] that signifies his high warrior rank. According to the text, he has reached the rank tequihua, "one who has captured at least four enemy warriors." He is shown with a lance and a fan, symbols of ambassadorial mission. Apparently he has

[46] Berdan 1975, p. 367.
[47] *Codex Telleriano-Remensis*, fols. 4v, 5r, 6v, 10r, 13r, 13v, 15r, 15v, 16v, 19v, 22r, 23v.
[48] Ibid., fol. 18r.
[49] E.g., ibid., fols. 29r, 41v.
[50] *Codex Magliabechiano*, fols. 49r–57r, 59r, 61r, 62r, 63r, 64r, 65r, 85r.

[51] Ibid., fols. 76r, 79r.
[52] Ibid., fols. 38r, 41r, 67r, 79r, 82r, 88r.
[53] E.g., *Codex Borbonicus*, pp. 10, 12, 15, 25, 27–30, 33.
[54] Seler 1960, 2:515.
[55] Clark 1938, 1:59.

EXAMPLE 2d. Aztec hip-cloth. *Codex Mendoza*, vol. 3, fol. 68r.

EXAMPLE 2e. Aztec hip-cloth. *Codex Magliabechiano*, fol. 82r.

been appointed to this honorable post by the ruler.

The next example of a male wearing a hip-cloth (example 2e) is from the *Codex Magliabechiano*. The individual is a drummer, one of a number of men from a ritual scene (fig. 6). The ceremony involves seven dancers, two of whom wear the hip-cloth. A second drummer is shown, but he is not wearing the garment. All the celebrants appear to wear the distinctive-knot type of *maxtlatl*.

Another male wearing a hip-cloth (example 2f) is from a section of the *Codex Telleriano-Remensis* dealing with the pre-Conquest history of the Aztecs. In the year 1505 there was a great famine in the Valley of Mexico, and many families emigrated to Pánuco, a lush and productive lowland region northeast of Tenochtitlán, from which they brought "bread," or corn. This area was part of the fabled "hot lands," a region of bounty that had long fascinated the inhabitants of the more austere *mesa central*. At the time of the Great Famine of 1450 to 1554, whole families had to sell themselves into lowland slavery to keep from starving. A subsequent famine is recorded in example 2f, the depiction of a man leaning on a walking staff and carrying corn with a tumpline (a carrying strap) supporting the heavily laden bag on his back. As on figures *d* and *e*, the *maxtlatl* is visible beneath the hip-cloth. This is the other style of Aztec *maxtlatl*: the two ends of the garment are not tied in front; one falls in front and one behind the body.

Another hip-cloth (example 2g) is shown on a deity impersonator from a section of *Codex Borbonicus* dealing with Toxcatl, the fifth of the eighteen annual festivals. This ceremony involved the sacrifice of impersonators of two deities: the patron god of the Mexica, Huitzilopochtli, and the omnipotent and capricious god Tezcatlipoca. It is the latter deity that this richly clad individual impersonates. His hip-cloth has a red border called *tenixyo* ("having eyes on the edge"),[56] often associated with Tezcatlipoca.

The final figure in the hip-cloth section (example 2h) is from the *Codex Magliabechiano*. It is Ixtlilton (Little Black Face), one of the fertility gods associated with sensuality, solar warmth, flowers, feasting, and pleasure.

Four of the five hip-cloth examples appear to tie on the right side, but an extant stone statue from the Tehuacán area (fig. 7) shows that the garment could also be tied in the front.[57] That is how the garment is worn today by the Tarahumara Indians of Sonora, Mexico (see fig. 8a and 8b).

Extrapolation from ethnographic evidence can throw further light on the hip-cloth. The collection of the Museum of Cultural History in the University of California, Los Angeles, contains two of these Tarahumara garments, which measure 38" × 31½" and 34" × 32". These nearly square pieces of material are worn folded diagonally to form an approximately triangular garment

FIGURE 6. Dancing before the Aztec god Mictlantecuhtli, ruler of the underworld. *Codex Magliabechiano*, fol. 82r.

EXAMPLE 2f. Aztec hip-cloth. *Codex Telleriano-Remensis*, fol. 41v.

EXAMPLE 2g. Aztec hip-cloth. *Codex Borbonicus*, p. 26.

(fig. 8*a* and 8*b*). A comparison with the hip-cloths depicted in the codices shows that the pre-Hispanic cloths were of similar dimensions. Since it was the custom in Mesoamerica to wear draped garments directly from the loom,[58] the pre-Hispanic triangular hip-cloth was undoubtedly also a square of material folded to form a triangle.

TILMATLI. The most important status item of male wearing apparel was the *tilmatli*, a word translated by the Spanish as "*manta*," and in the English literature as "cloak," "cape," or "mantle." As discussed earlier, Aztec society was sharply stratified, and the appropriate apparel for the different levels of the social hierarchy was precisely controlled by explicit sumptuary laws. Durán discussed the dress code at some length.[59] The common people wore maguey-, yucca-, or palm-fiber garments. Only the upper classes were allowed cotton clothing, and the decoration, colors, and amount of featherwork on these costumes were clearly specified. The twelve great lords wore certain cloaks, the minor lords others. The common soldier could wear only the simplest style of mantle, without any special design or fine embroidery that might set him off from the rest. Even the length of the capes was prescribed: the common man's mantle was not to be worn below the knee; if it reached the ankle, the penalty was death. The only exception was the warrior with leg wounds, who was permitted to wear a longer cloak only until his limbs healed. The jewelry and ornaments worn with the *tilmatli* were also rigidly controlled.

The nobleman's ascribed status, which permitted him to wear the magnificent cotton garments of his class, did not make him impervious to the anger of the ruler. Durán related the plight of some recalcitrant nobles of Tlatelolco whose punishment for failure to make a tribute payment was loss of the right to wear their splendid mantles, having instead to use cloaks of maguey fiber like those of people of lower rank.[60]

Ascribed status was not the only social condition reflected by Aztec clothing. A valiant warrior—noble or commoner—could earn the right to wear luxury garments. Durán vividly described the reward system established by the rulers to induce young men to put forth their greatest efforts on the field of battle:

I, Tlacaelel, wish to give more courage to the strong,
And embolden those who are weak. I wish to make a
    comparison to you:
When you go to the market place and see a precious ear-
    plug or nose pendant
Or when you see splendid and beautiful feathers
Or a rich gilded shield, or weapons done in feather work,

EXAMPLE 2*b*. Aztec hip-cloth. *Codex Magliabechiano*, fol. 63r.

FIGURE 7. The Aztec hip-cloth depicted on a stone statue from the Tehuacán area. Seler 1960, 2:789, fig. 4.

---

[58] A complete single breadth of handloomed material, referred to as a *web*, comes off the backstrap loom with four finished selvage edges. No cutting is involved to attain the desired size because the web is woven to a specific width and length.

[59] Durán 1967, 2:211–13.

[60] Ibid., pp. 264–65.

FIGURE 8. Present-day Tarahumara Indians wearing the hip-cloth. Photographs from "La Barrance del Cobre, Inigualable Paisaje Mexicano," *Excelsior* (Mexico City), November 24, 1974.

Do you not covet them, do you not pay the price that is asked?
Know now that the king, who is present, has willed that lip-plugs
Golden garlands, many-colored feathers, ear-plugs, arm-bands,
Shields, weapons, insignia, mantles, and loin cloths
Are not to be bought in the market any longer by brave men.
From now on the sovereign will deliver them as payment.
For memorable deeds. Each one of you, when he goes to war to fight,
Must think that he has journeyed to a market place
Where he will find precious stones. He who does not dare go to war
Even though he be the king's son, from now on will be deprived
Of all these things. He will have to wear the clothing

Of the common man. And in this way his cowardice, his weak heart
Will be known by all. He will not wear cotton garments,
He will not wear feathers, he will not receive flowers,
Like the great lords.[61]

Motolinía described the elaborate paraphernalia awarded for the taking of prisoners.[62] Sahagún told of the ceremony that was held after a young warrior took his first captive in battle: "...and at that time Moctezuma granted him favors; he gave him an orange cape with a striped border and a scorpion design to bind on and a carmine colored breech clout of many colors and then he began to wear capes with designs."[63] These special

[61] Ibid., p. 236, English translation from Heyden and Horcasitas 1964, p. 142.
[62] Motolinía 1971, p. 351.
[63] Sahagún 1950–69, bk. 8, pp. 76–77.

mantles granted for valor are detailed in part 3 of the *Codex Mendoza*[64] (fig. 9). A warrior who captured two prisoners was awarded an orange-bordered mantle; one who took three prisoners, a *manta* of the "jewel of *ehecatl*" design; and one who took four prisoners, a *nacazminqui* cloak.

Just as the nobles could lose the right to wear their high-status clothing, so too could the ruler revoke this privilege from the honored warrior who behaved badly on the field of battle: ". . .all with which they had bedight him—the precious capes and costly breech clouts—no longer could he assume. He might put on only a poor maguey fiber cape or a wretched yucca fiber cape, as he deserved."[65]

The tribute roles reflect the great variety of *mantas*. *Manta* designs recorded in the *Matrícula de tributos* include red-bordered; white-bordered; white; diagonally divided; quilted, twisted obsidian-serpent; jaguar; red stepped-fret; *ocuilteca* ("hummingbird"); elaborately painted; *ocuilteca* and shell; horizontally black-striped; vertically red-striped; and dark purple with shell border.[66] The total number of *mantas* given in tribute every eighty days was 51,600.

Of the aforementioned *mantas*, 5,200 are specified as maguey fiber, and 2,400 as palm fiber. Some of the maguey *mantas* are listed as white, white-bordered *ocuilteca* design, and elaborately painted. Naturally, far more maguey-fiber *tilmatli* were utilized in Aztec society than is indicated by this tribute count. The listed items may have been special insignia apparel, serving as visual status markers. In discussing the seller of coarse maguey capes, Sahagún mentioned ten different designs: the whirlpool design, as if with eyes painted; the turkey with the mat-designed interior; the small face; the twisted weave; broken cords, with husks outlined in black—in wide black lines, with the interior diagonal design; the jaguar design; the shiny maguey-fiber cape; the white-flowered design; the wavy design; and nettles.[67] Perhaps the *tilmatli* of the lower classes were more colorful and varied than the references to "poor" and "wretched" lower-class apparel would indicate. It must also be remembered that not all the *macehualtin* were "equal"; the variation in lower-class apparel may reflect that.

Sahagún also wrote of the maguey mantles as being sized with corn dough, which, when dried, was burnished to produce a high, pleasing luster.[68] Garments so treated apparently became stiff; hence they gave off a pottery-rattle when thumped. The chroniclers would have us believe that the dress of the masses was strictly regulated. It is questionable how true that is.[69] Certainly the sources show that the lower classes were not uninventive.

The cotton mantles varied in size. Some are listed as narrow, others as large. The latter are called *quachtli*,

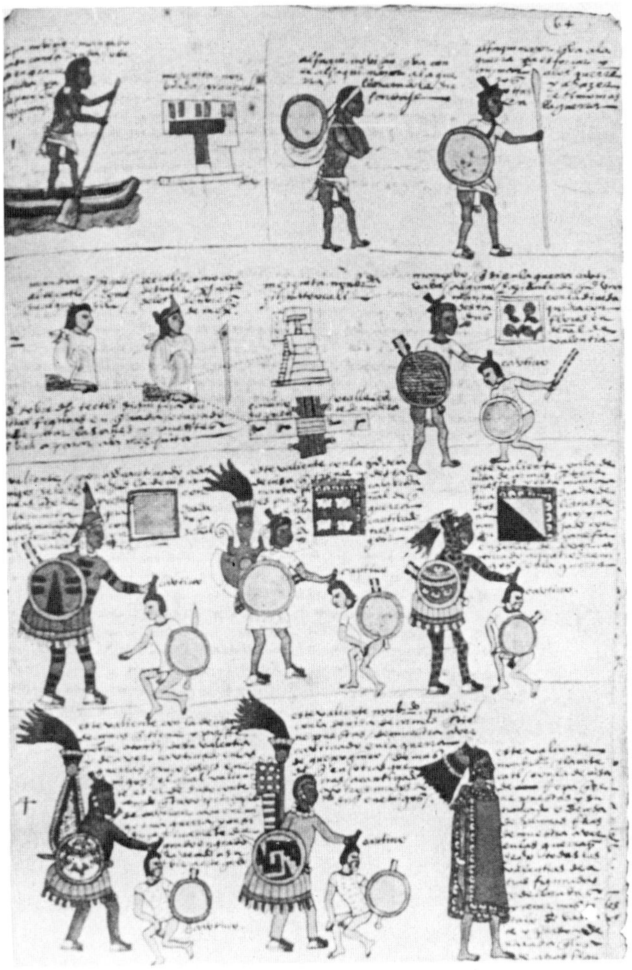

FIGURE 9. The grades of Aztec warriors as reflected in their feather warrior suits and accompanying cloaks. *Codex Mendoza*, vol. 3, fol. 64r.

which Molina translated as "*manta grande de algodón.*"[70] Some of the *mantas* are referred to as two, four, or eight *brazas* long. There is some confusion as to this unit of measurement, but approximately sixty-six inches is the increment generally used.[71] Since such cloths were too large to be worn, they must have been ritual or tribute cloths or both. They may have consisted of several lengths of hand-loomed fabric sewn together, because sixteen yards —two yards times eight *brazas*—is too large to be woven on a backstrap loom.

Large *mantas* were also utilized as items of exchange. Sahagún mentioned that thirty large cotton *quachtli* were paid for an ordinary slave, and forty for one who could both sing and dance.[72] Motolinía also mentioned the use of *mantas* as a form of economic exchange.[73]

Durán expressed surprise at the quantity and quality of the textiles given in tribute.

[64] *Codex Mendoza*, vol. 3, fol. 64r.
[65] Sahagún 1950–69, bk. 8, p. 88.
[66] Berdan 1975, pp. 318–64.
[67] Sahagún 1950–69, bk. 10, p. 73.
[68] Ibid.

[69] Anawalt 1980.
[70] Molina 1970, fol. 84r.
[71] Berdan 1975, p. 359.
[72] Sahagún 1950–69, bk. 9, p. 46.
[73] Motolinía 1971, p. 374.

A bewildering amount of cloth: strips twenty, ten, five, four and two yards long, according to the wealth of each province. Exceedingly rich mantles for the lords, differently woven and worked, some of them had rich fringes done in colors and feather work; others had insignia on them, others serpent heads, others jaguar heads, others the image of the sun, and yet others had skulls, or blowguns, figures of the gods—all of them embroidered in many colored threads and enriched with the down of ducks, all beautifully and curiously worked. Even though silk was unknown in this country, the natives were extremely skillful in embroidering and painting cotton cloth.[74]

The first twelve folios of the *Codex Magliabechiano* contain illustrations of forty-five ritual *mantas* and give an indication of the range of decoration and degree of elaboration of these magnificent textiles.

The Anonymous Conqueror likened the *tilmatli* to sheets:

> Their dress consists of cotton mantles like sheets, though not so large, finely worked in a variety of ways, and with decorated bands and borders. Each person has two or three, and they are knotted over the chest. In winter time they cover themselves with cloaks woven of tiny feathers. They are similar to red silk or woolen cloth, and like our fur hats. They have them in red, black, white, purple and yellow.[75]

Some presents sent from Mexico back to Spain in February, 1521, were described by a Spaniard named Zuazo who mentioned, among other items,

> many double-faced *mantas* made with turkey feathers so smooth that in drawing the hand across the grain they seemed nothing but a well-tanned sable marten skin. I had one of these weighed and it weighed no more than six ounces. They said that in the winter one was sufficient to cover the shirt and no other covering was necessary on the beds.[76]

Every aspect of the *tilmatli* conveyed meaning to members of Aztec society. Not only was control exercised over the material, design, and length of these mantles but also the manner of wearing them was prescribed. The usual style was to tie the knot of the mantle over the right shoulder. Certain nobles and priests, however, apparently were allowed to tie the cloak in the front (see plate 1).

The *tilmatli*, then, was a rectangular cloak of cotton, maguey, yucca, or palm fiber made in varying lengths and degrees of decoration. It was an all-purpose garment worn by all classes of Aztec men. The *tilmatli* was the principal visual status marker in Aztec society, and its material, decoration, length, and manner of wearing instantly revealed the class and rank of the wearer.

The initial example (*2i*) in the *Tilmatli* section of chart 2, from part 3 of *Codex Mendoza*, is worn by a warrior of

EXAMPLE *2i*. Aztec *tilmatli*. *Codex Mendoza*, vol. 3, fol. 64r.

EXAMPLE *2j*. Aztec *tilmatli*. *Codex Mendoza*, vol. 3, fol. 68r.

---

[74] Durán 1967, 2:206; translation from Heyden and Horcasitas 1964, p. 128.
[75] Anonymous Conqueror 1858, p. 576.
[76] Wagner 1969, p. 327.

EXAMPLE 2*k*. Aztec *tilmatli*. *Códice Azcatítlan, planche* 22.

EXAMPLE 2*l*. Aztec *tilmatli*. *Codex Magliabechiano*, fol. 35r.

the highest grade. His long cloak is red, with the *tenixyo* border, discussed in the hip-cloth section. The cape is tied on the right shoulder. In addition to the prestigious *tilmatli*, this seasoned captain also wears the important hair ornament, the *quetzallalpiloni*. This mark of military prowess was made of two great pompons of *quetzal* feathers, one at either end of a ribbon that could be tied to hold the hair in place.

The second *tilmatli* (example 2*j*) is worn by an assistant to or substitute for one of the important Aztec judges. The individual is of the noble class because he wears the *xiuhuitzolli*, the turquoise diadem; his *tilmatli* is shown tied on the right shoulder. The cloak is wrapped completely around the seated figure. Knowing the class of the individual, one can speculate that his mantle was long and full.

The third *tilmatli* (example 2*k*) is worn by the emperor Moctezuma, who is seated on a Spanish-type throne (before the Conquest a mat and backrest were used, so this colonial depiction is in error). He wears a nose jewel, and on his head is his symbol of rank, the *xiuhuitzolli*. Appropriately, Moctezuma's cloak is tied in the front rather than on the right shoulder. His elegant *tilmatli* has the *tenixyo* border.

The fourth *tilmatli* example (2*l*) is worn by a litter bearer for the human impersonator of the fertility god Xochipilli.[77] The deity representative is about to be sacrificed as part of the great festival Tecuilhuitontli (Small Feast Day of the Lords), when the nobles were hosts to the commoners at a banquet (at the great ceremonies, where human sacrifice was performed as a public display, the custom was to sacrifice an image of the god to the god). The bearer of the deity impersonator's litter wears a short, netted *tilmatli* with a *tenixyo* border; his *maxtlatl* hangs below. Perhaps this attire, which seems rather elegant for a bearer, reflects the glory of the god being honored.

The fifth *tilmatli* (example 2*m*) is worn by an onlooker standing at the bottom of a temple stairway as a human sacrifice is being performed (fig. 10). His cloak is white with a blue and red border and comes just to his knees, suggesting that he is of a lower class (it could also be a convention of the artist, for none of the *tilmatli* of the *Codex Magliabechiano* are full length). The mantle has a stiff, bell-like appearance; perhaps it is one of those made of maguey sized with corn dough.

The final figure (example 2*n*) in the *tilmatli* section, also from *Codex Magliabechiano*, is shown taking part in a feast of the pulque gods.[78] His cape is the shortest yet shown, coming only to the waist, and it appears to have a fringed border. It also has a visible seam, as does another cape on the same folio (fig. 11). These two cloaks are the only seamed *tilmatli* in the codices. The same folio shows four women in the traditional *huipilli*, or blouse (today re-

[77] Boone 1974, pp. 4–5.
[78] Ibid., p. 5.

31

FIGURE 10. Aztec sacrificial rite involving extraction of the heart. *Codex Magliabechiano*, fol. 70r.

EXAMPLE 2m. Aztec *tilmatli. Codex Magliabechiano*, fol. 70r.

EXAMPLE 2n. Aztec *tilmatli. Codex Magliabechiano*, fol. 85r.

FIGURE 11. Aztec ritual drinking during a pulque feast. *Codex Magliabechiano*, fol. 85r.

ferred to as a huipil) one of which is seamed (see chart 4, example *n*). Whether this seaming has significance is unknown. To complicate the analysis further, all three mantles of this folio are tied in front. At the present time I can offer no explanation for these unusual depictions.

KILT. In all of the extant Aztec pictorials there is only one male garment that can be likened to a kilt. It is usually depicted as pleated or with closely jointed panels attached to a belt. This costume, which also appears in the Mixtec, Borgia Group codices, and Maya clothing inventories, is usually found only on male deities. In the figure shown in example *20*, the kilt is worn by the Aztec rain god, Tlaloc.

CUEITL. The women's skirt, the *cueitl*, was a length of cotton, maguey, yucca, or palm-fiber cloth that was wrapped around the lower body and secured at the waist. It went to midcalf in length. This skirt was the basic lower-torso garment worn by all Aztec females. In varying degrees of elaboration, it is found associated with menial secular chores as well as solemn rituals. We can assume that the degree of decoration on the body of the garment, and particularly on its border, was a response not only to class and ritual context but also to age.

Molina defines *cueitl* as "*faldellin, faldillas, o naguas*"[79]

("overskirt or petticoats"). Two of the Aztec area 1577–89 *Relaciones geográficas*, from Coatepec and Chimalhuacán, mention the noble women still wearing richly embroidered skirts of delicate, thin cotton, with striped edges (hems) worked in colored trim made by combining finespun, dyed rabbit hair and feathers.[80]

Durán described the elegantly decorated noblewomen's clothing with their wide-bordered skirts woven or embroidered in different colors, designs, and feathers. He also mentioned apparel of other classes:

> [The clothes used by the ladies, wives of the lords and great chieftains were] splendid skirts of great price [which] were woven richly and with excellent skill. There was another type of female dress which was entirely white and this was used by the old and young women who served in the temples. There was yet another kind of clothing for women, made of maguey fibers, and this was worn by servant girls in the homes and was divided among them.[81]

Sahagún described the magnificent skirts worn at the ritual dances: *cueitl* with motifs of hearts, birds' gizzards, blanket designs, spirals, and leaves.[82] Another section tells of eight wide-bordered skirts of differing design: a skirt

[79] Molina 1970, fol. 26r.
[80] Cline 1972, census no. 29; Paso y Troncoso 1905, 6:55–56; 75–76.

[81] Durán 1967, 2:207; translation from Heyden and Horcasitas 1964, p. 129.
[82] Sahagún 1950–69, bk. 2, p. 93.

with an irregular design; a skirt with serpent skins; a skirt with square cornerstones; a skirt with thin, black lines; a white skirt like a bedcovering; an ocelot-skin skirt; a skirt with brown pendants; and a skirt with coyote-fur pendants.[83] In the *Florentine Codex, Book 8, Kings and Lords*, are illustrated six skirt patterns (fig. 12).

The first skirt (example 2*p*) in the *Cueitl* section of chart 2 is a type worn in ritual ceremonies. This figure is from a section of the *Codex Borbonicus* dealing with a harvest festival. A human impersonator of a fertility goddess has just been sacrificed in a temple richly decked with giant corncobs. Her body has been quickly flayed, and a male priest emerges from the temple wearing a portion of her headdress, her wraparound skirt, and her flayed skin. The flayed victim's hands dangle below the priest's, and he holds the symbolic double ears of corn. This skirt matches Fray Durán's descriptions cited above, for it is an elegantly decorated garment with a differentiated border. Since the women of the Valley of Mexico never went topless, this is the only illustration to be found in the Aztec codices that shows a skirt being worn without an upper-body garment.

The next skirt (example 2*q*) is worn by a woman who appears on a page devoted to mortuary practices. Aztec funerary procedure depended on the rank of the deceased and the manner of dying. The body of a high-status individual was wrapped in cloth, and the mummy bundle was decorated with the appropriate ritual paraphernalia. The woman depicted here stands in front of such a mummy bundle. The skirt shows the wraparound nature of the *cueitl*; the overlap of the material is clearly visible.

The third *cueitl* illustration (example 2*r*) from the tribute-tally section of *Codex Mendoza*, records 400 richly worked skirts and *huipilli*. This is the only pictograph in the entire tribute list that illustrates both the skirt (on the right) and the *huipilli*, or blouse (on the left). Both are superimposed on the pictograph for *manta* ("a large rectangle of cloth"). The notation records that Xilotepec gave 400 skirts of stepped-fret design and 400 women's blouses.[84] The *Matrícula de tributos* records only 1,200 skirts given in tribute every eighty days. Some of the textiles, however, are designated simply "*manta*" and could have been used as skirts.

The fourth *cueitl* (example 2*s*) is worn by a twelve-year-old girl going about her chore of sweeping the house and street before dawn. Her skirt is not a finished, bordered garment like the other two *cueitl* examples. The folio that includes this illustration (fig. 13) deals with the education of boys and girls ages eleven to fourteen. The eleven-year-old girl also wears a simple, unadorned skirt and *huipil*. The thirteen-year-old wears a bordered skirt but still wears the uneven-edged *huipil*. The fourteen-year-old, however, wears a finished, bordered skirt like that worn by her mother in all four scenes, It appears, then, that

EXAMPLE 20. Aztec kilt. *Codex Magliabechiano*, fol. 34r.

FIGURE 12. Six Aztec skirt patterns. Sahagún 1926, *lámina* 49, *libro* 8, plate 73.

[83] Ibid., bk. 8, pp. 47–48.
[84] Berdan 1975, p. 332.

EXAMPLE 2*p*. Aztec *cueitl*. *Codex Borbonicus*, p. 29.

EXAMPLE 2*r*. Aztec *cueitl*. *Codex Mendoza*, vol. 3, fol. 31r.

young girls wore a simplified version of their mothers' clothing and adopted the finished attire upon reaching womanhood.

The final *cueitl* (example 2*t*) is worn by a girl who appears as a participant in Pilauana, the feast involving children's ritual drinking. The end of her wraparound skirt is shown with stitching, as are a few other garments found in *Codex Magliabechiano*. There may be some connection between drinking and garments shown with crude stitching, as suggested by example 2*t*, the final *tilmatli* example, and the third *huipilli* (example 4*n*), to be dicussed in "Examples of Closed-sewn Garments" below.

Slip-on Garments

The first section of chart 3 is devoted to slip-on garments. Costumes of this class slip over the head through a neck opening, are worn hanging from the shoulders, and have no underarm seams. In the pan-Mesoamerican costume repertory only the *quechquemitl* falls into this category.

QUECHQUEMITL. The *quechquemitl* was a women's slip-on garment made of two rectangles of material joined so that when they were laid one atop the other they formed a square with a V at the neck. When the garment was put on and its points turned front and back, the sloped shoulders of the wearer gave the garment a triangular appearance. Among the Aztec pictorials the *quechquemitl* is seen only in ritual contexts and hence was special-purpose clothing.

EXAMPLE 2*q*. Aztec *cueitl*. *Codex Magliabechiano*, fol. 67r.

35

EXAMPLE 2s. Aztec *cueitl*. *Codex Mendoza*, vol. 3, fol. 6or.

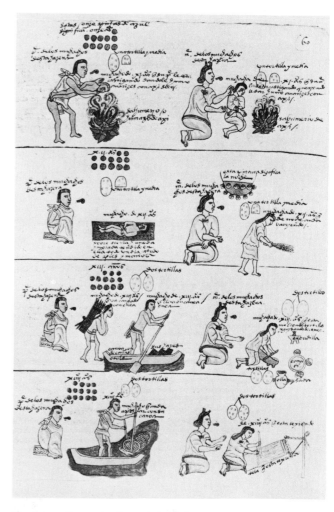

FIGURE 13. Stages in the training of Aztec children. *Codex Mendoza*, vol. 3, fol. 6or.

EXAMPLE 2t. Aztec *cueitl*. *Codex Magliabechiano*, fol. 41r.

The etymology of the term *quechquemitl* is of interest. The Nahuatl term *quechquemitl* probably comes from the word *quechtli* ("neck") and *quemi* ("to put on a manta or cape").[85] Seler described a *quemitl* as a biblike ritual garment[86] or a cape,[87] which in pre-Hispanic times the Indians tied around the necks of their idols. A garment meeting this description is worn by both men and women in the costume repertory of the Mixtecs and in the Borgia Group codices and by men in the Lowland Maya pictorials. The *quechquemitl*, however, appears to have been an entirely different sort of costume. Cordry and Cordry translated the term *quechquemitl* as "neck cape," although in their discussion of the modern examples they understandably objected to this terminology.[88] They pointed out that the garment is in no way "capelike," since it has no opening other than the single aperture for the head, and can be described as triangular only because of the effect it gives when worn. Figure 14 illustrates one way

[85] Molina 1970, 88v.
[86] Seler 1967, p. 359.
[87] Seler 1901–02, pp. 122, 130.
[88] Cordry and Cordry 1968, p. 81.

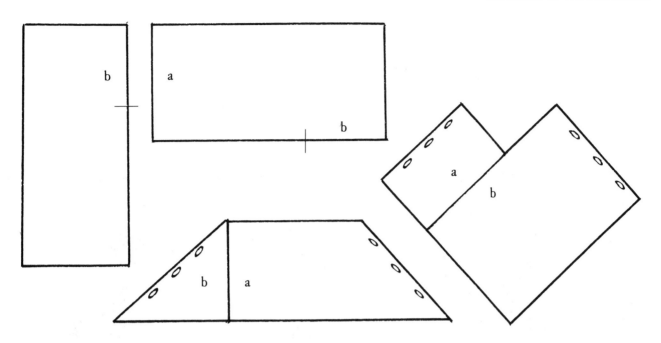

FIGURE 14. The most common way of constructing a modern *quechquemitl*. Cordry and Cordry 1968:83, fig. 10.

the modern *quechquemitl* can be constructed. This construction is by far the most common today and probably was in pre-Hispanic times as well.

In the Aztec costume repertory the *quechquemitl* is found only in ritual context; it does not appear as secular apparel. That was almost certainly not true, however, in other Mesoamerican costume repertories, as will be apparent in later discussion.

The *quechquemitl* could be worn either as the sole upper-body garment or over another costume. Figure 15 illustrates the costume as worn by a stone image of the goddess Chalchiuhtlicue. This garment is bordered by well-defined tassels, as is the first *quechquemitl* (example *3a*) in chart 3.

The first *quechquemitl* is seen on Mayahuel, a fertility goddess who is one of the pulque deities. This intoxicating beverage was brewed from the sweet fluid drawn from the heart of the maguey plant. Pulque played an extremely important part in Aztec ritual, ceremonial, and social feasting. The maguey plant itself was personified by the goddess Mayahuel. In an article on religion in pre-Hispanic Mesoamerica, Nicholson stated that the exuberant fertility of Mayahuel was often dramatized by her conception as a female with four hundred (that is, innumerable) breasts.[89] The human impersonator of Mayahuel (example *3a*) is dressed in ritual finery, wearing the *quechquemitl* over what appears to be a calf-length huipil.

The second *quechquemitl* (example *3b*) is worn as the sole upper-body garment. The deity is the goddess Ixnextli (Eye Ashes), from *Codex Telleriano-Remensis*. She was one of the youthful earth-mother goddesses particularly associated with flowers, lust, and pleasure and was also one of the patronesses of weaving. In this depiction Ixnextli has raised her right hand to wipe tears from her eyes, which have been blinded by ashes. Because of this gesture both the front and back points of the *quechquemitl* are visible.

The final quechquemitl (example *3c*), being worn in a harvest-festival ceremony, is from the same section of *Codex Borbonicus* as example *2p*—a priest wearing the flayed skin and wraparound skirt of a female sacrificial victim. Example *3c* is apparently the same male priest at a later stage of the ceremony. He is still holding the double ears of corn and wearing the sacrificial victim's flayed skin. Now he has added the towering *amacalli* headdress (see plate 3 for the full version of this headdress). The goddess whom the priest is impersonating is probably a fusing of Chicomecoatl, a corn deity, and Tlazolteotl, a fertility goddess associated with the abundance of the Gulf Coast "hot lands," as well as with flaying ceremonies. The *quechquemitl* is particularly the garment of Aztec fertility goddesses. These female deities have a bewildering propensity for fusing, blending, and melding.[90]

Open-sewn Garments

Open-sewn garments are constructed of several widths of material joined lengthwise by continuous sewn seams but worn open in front. Although costumes in this category sometimes have fasteners to secure the two front panels, they are still worn as open garments or jackets, and therefore exemplify the open-sewn principle.

[89] Nicholson 1971*b*, p. 420.

[90] Nicholson 1967*c*.

CHART 3
AZTEC COSTUME REPERTORY
Examples of Slip-on Garments

Male

- - - - - - - - - - - - - - -

Female

Triangular *Quechquemitl*

a

b

c

Examples of Open-sewn Garments

Male

Open *Ichcahuipilli*

d

e

f

g

h

Xicolli

i   j   k   l   m   n

Female

- - - - - - - - - - - - - - - -

SOURCES: (*a*) *Codex Magliabechiano*, fol. 58r; (*b*) *Codex Telleriano-Remensis*, fol. 11r; (*c*) *Codex Borbonicus*, p. 31; (*d*) *Codex Telleriano-Remensis*, fol. 29r; (*e*) *Codex Telleriano-Remensis*, fol. 37v; (*f*) *Codex Telleriano-Remensis*, fol. 38v; (*g*) *Códice Azcatítlan, planche* 2; (*h*) *Códice Azcatítlan, planche* 2; (*i*) *Codex Mendoza*, vol. 3, fol. 63r; (*j*) *Codex Magliabechiano*, fol. 63r; (*k*) *Códice Azcatítlan, planche* 12; (*l*) *Códice Xolotl, planche* 4 (León y Gama copy); (*m*) *Codex Magliabechiano*, fol. 70r; (*n*) *Codex Mendoza*, vol. 3, fol. 66r.

OPEN-SEWN ICHCAHUIPILLI. The open *ichcahuipilli* was a short, padded, quilted, jacketlike cotton armor that was worn by Aztec warriors in battle and hence was special-purpose clothing.

The word *ichcahuipilli* derives from the Nahuatl terms *ichcatl* ("cotton")[91] and (*h*)*uipilli* ("woman's shirt").[92] It is a cotton tunic, which agrees with Molina's definition, "cotton armor for war."[93] Sahagún described the garment's construction: "The padded shirt is made in this manner: fluffed up cotton is covered with cloth. On it is stitched a leather border. It also has leather thongs."[94]

The sleeveless, short, jacket-type armor with ties in front is amply illustrated in *Codex Telleriano-Remensis*, from which come three *ichcahuipilli* examples (*3d*, *3e*, and *3f*). The historical section of this pictorial manuscript contains repeated battle scenes, for it deals with the period 1193 to 1549, the years of Aztec migration, expansion, and subsequent Spanish conquest.

The first *ichcahuipilli* (example *3d*) is from a folio commemorating the first offensive campaign of the Mexicas in 1399 against Culhuacán. The warrior carries his shield and *maquilhuitl*, the wooden war club with insets of razor-sharp pieces of obsidian. He is wearing a version of the *ichcahuipilli* that comes to the upper thigh. The *maxtlatl* is visible below, as it is in all five examples of the *ichcahuipilli*.

The second warrior in the *ichcahuipilli* section (example *3e*) is from Tenochtitlán. This is an excellent example of pictographic writing. The Nahuatl term for "rock" is *tetl*, "cactus" is *nochtli*, and "the place of" is *tlan*. Therefore, Tenochtitlán is Place Where the Cactus Grows Out of the Rock. This warrior is engaged in the battle against Xiquipilco in 1478. He is wearing on his back a device or standard that probably designates his affiliation with a particular deity. His cotton armor differs from that of figure *d* in that it appears to fit closely at the waist and to have a lower section that comes down over the hips.

The third warrior (example *3f*) is also involved in a war, supposedly against Tzinacantépec in 1484 (the war is historical fact; nothing in the picture, however, identifies it as that particular engagement). The warrior is seen killing a woman by striking her with his war club. Like the preceding *ichcahuipilli*, this armor is fitted at the waist but ends in a feathered skirt rather than a band over the hips (skirts of this type, worn on martial attire, are discussed more fully in the *Ehuatl* section of chart 4).

A different kind of open-sewn *ichcahuipilli* appears in examples *3g* and *3h*, both from the *Códice Azcatítlan*, a pictorial manuscript that deals with early Aztec history. The warrior of example *3g* represents one of four territorial divisions of the Azcatítlan group.[95] He wears an open garment whose hatch marks no doubt indicate quilting—a

[91] Molina 1970, fol. 32r.
[92] Ibid., fol. 157v.
[93] Ibid., fol. 32r.
[94] Sullivan 1972, p. 159.
[95] Barlow 1949*b*, p. 104.

FIGURE 15. *Quechquemitl* worn by the Aztec goddess Chalchiuh-tlicue. Seler 1960 2:907, fig. 3.

EXAMPLE *3a*. Aztec *quechquemitl*. *Codex Magliabechiano*, fol. 58r.

type of representation that also appears in the *Codex Mendoza*. This garment and that of example *3b* (one of a crowd engaged in discussion) appear to have sleeves, but such is almost certainly not the case, as repeated costume examples demonstrate. This sleeve effect is a pictorial rendering of the fold created when a wide piece of material drapes over the shoulder and upper arm; other examples are illustrated in the following sections: *i, j, k, m, n*.

XICOLLI. The Aztec *xicolli*, a male garment, was a fringed, sleeveless jacket that tied in front. It is often found in association with a tobacco pouch, an incense bag, and an incense burner. The garment was sometimes (but not exclusively) worn in ritual, and was utilized in certain religious or civil observances rather than according to

EXAMPLE 3b. Aztec *quechquemitl*. *Codex Telleriano-Remensis*, fol. 11r.

EXAMPLE 3d. Aztec open *ichcahuipilli*. *Codex Telleriano-Remensis*, fol. 29r.

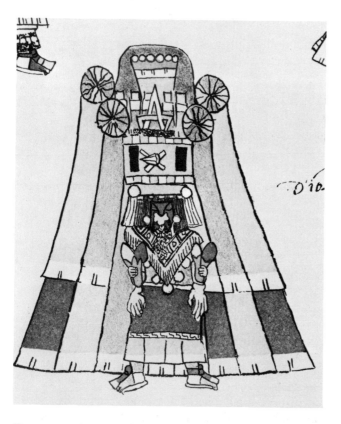

EXAMPLE 3c. Aztec *quechquemitl*. *Codex Borbonicus*, p. 31.

EXAMPLE 3e. Aztec open *ichcahuipilli*. *Codex Telleriano-Remensis*, fol. 37v.

EXAMPLE 3*f*. Aztec open *ichcahuipilli. Codex Telleriano-Remensis*, fol. 38v.

EXAMPLE 3*h*. Aztec open *ichcahuipilli. Códice Azcatítlan, planche* 2.

EXAMPLE 3*g*. Aztec open *ichcahuipilli. Códice Azcatítlan, planche* 2.

class. The *xicolli* was probably also worn as a badge of office, and among the Aztecs it was always special-purpose clothing.

The derivation of the word *xicolli* is unclear. No doubt the Nahuatl term for shoulder, *acolli*, is the second element.[96] The initial form *xi*, may be related in some way to the weaving term *xiotl* ("heddle for warping cloth and weaving it").[97]

The term *xicolli* does not appear in Molina's Nahuatl dictionary of 1571. The omission of an important costume of Indian religious life may reflect the Franciscan friar's efforts to stamp out idolatry, or its omission could simply be an error. The term is found in the 1885 Simeón dictionary, where it is defined as a short jacket of printed material that priests of the idol wore during their office.[98] Simeón credited Sahagún for this information, but a careful examination has determined that the garment was employed in a much wider ritual context than Simeón's definition would imply.[99] Before discussing how the costume was used, let us consider its construction.

My investigation of the *xicolli* revealed that an actual *xicolli* garment had been in the possession of the Museum für Völkerkunde in Berlin until 1945, when it was

[96] Molina 1970, fol. 2v.
[97] Ibid., fol. 159r.
[98] Simeón 1963, p. 694.
[99] Anawalt 1976.

41

destroyed by fire (fig. 16). In response to my inquiry, Immine von Schuler, of the museum, said that the garment, together with a feather mosaic and a deerskin belt, was collected by a man named Seiffort, the Prussian general counsel in Mexico from 1846 to 1850. He purchased the three items from an Indian who said that his three sons had recently found the objects in a cave on the escarpment of the *barranco* of Malinaltenango, between Zacualpán and Tenancingo in the state of Mexico. Seiffort believed that the artifacts dated from the time of the Conquest and had been hidden from the Spaniards by the Indians. He identified the material of the jacket as cotton and pita (agave- or yucca-fiber string or cord), but the Berlin Museum index card mentions only agave as the material.

As fig. 16 shows, this *xicolli* was a sleeveless jacket. Further confirmation that the garment was sleeveless is seen on the Churubusco Idol (figs. 17*a*, 17*b*, 17*c*); the draping of the fabric over the shoulders produces the sleevelike effect (this same effect is seen not only in many *xicolli* drawings in the codices but on other garments as well). Both fig. 16 and fig. 17*a*, 17*b*, and 17*c* demonstrate that the Aztec *xicolli* opened in front, was held closed with a string tie, and was fringed at the bottom. The Churubusco Idol also provides another example of the *tenixyo* border.

The *xicolli* played an interesting role in Aztec society. A careful examination of Sahagún's twelve books of the *Florentine Codex*, the most detailed source of information on Aztec life, reveals that the *xicolli* can be identified with

FIGURE 16. Catalog card from the Museum für Völkerkunde, Berlin, Germany.

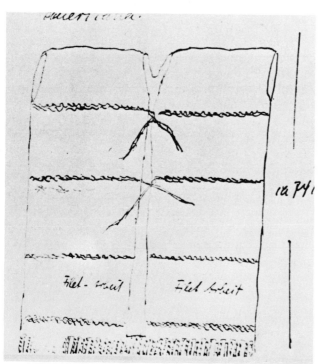

eight groups or categories: (1) idols,[100] (2) gods,[101] (3) god impersonators,[102] (4) merchants and their sacrificial slaves,[103] (5) pole decoration,[104] (6) priests,[105] (7) lords, chiefs, noblemen and constables,[106] and (8) metaphors.[107]

The appearance of the *xicolli* on idols, gods, and god impersonators demonstrates the connection of the costume with Aztec deities. The *xicolli* was also worn in certain ritual ceremonies by sacrificial slaves who at the time of sacrifice were physical reflections of the gods. The slaves' merchant sponsors also wore the garment. A *xicolli*, probably worn by a sacrificed prisoner of war, was used as a decoration atop a pole in the courtyard of the warrior who had offered his captive for sacrifice.

The *xicolli*, principally associated with priests, is regularly accompanied by three accessory items: the incense burner, the incense bag, and the tobacco container. The garment and the three accessories are evident in example *3i*. Because the priest is shown in side view, the opening of the jacket is not visible, but his accounterments; his long, bound hair; and the smear of blood at his temple from repeated autosacrifice give ample testimony to his vocation. On his back he wears a gourd containing tobacco pellets. According to Sahagún, the priests chewed these stimulants when they went about their penitential duties in the cold hours before dawn.[108] In one hand the priest holds an incense pouch filled with copal, which he is using in his incense burner.

The priest in example *3j* lacks the censer but is seen with the tobacco pouch and incense bag. Two sets of four dots on the body of his *xicolli* may represent ties that secure the garment in front. The same pattern of four dots also appears on the incense bag, however, and may be a version of the *tonallo* symbol for heat, sun, or light. No *maxlatl* shows beneath his *xicolli*, a strange omission for *Codex Magliabechiano*.

The same *xicolli* is found in what appears to be an initiation scene of an officeholder (fig. 18). Perhaps the scantily clad young man is about to be invested with a ceremonial *xicolli*. It is seen from the back, allowing a clear view of the tobacco pouch and cord. (Again the red *tenixyo* border appears, as in example *g* of the hip-cloth section and examples *i*, *k*, and *l* of the *tilmatli* section of chart 2.) The two priests on the right, their long hair bound with a leather cord, wear what appears to be the same type of garment pulled down over their knees (in a posture similar to that of example *j* in the *Tilmatli* section of chart 2).

Example *3k* is from a section of *Códice Azcatítlan* dealing with the founding of Tenochtitlán. In the entire manuscript only this figure and a companion directly to his left

[100] Sahagún 1950–69, bk. 2, p. 69.
[101] Ibid., bk. 7, p. 5; bk. 9, pp. 79–80; bk. 12, pp. 12, 15.
[102] Ibid., bk. 2, pp. 196–97, 199–200.
[103] Ibid., bk. 4, p. 69; bk. 9, p. 63.
[104] Ibid., bk. 2, p. 57.
[105] Ibid., bk. 2, pp. 75, 79–80, 82, 193, 198, 200; bk. 9, p. 66.
[106] Ibid., bk. 2, p. 151; bk. 8, p. 62; bk. 9, p. 4.
[107] Ibid., bk. 6, pp. 241–42.
[108] Ibid., bk. 8, p. 81.

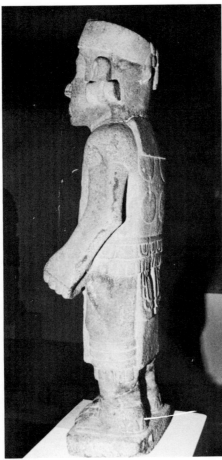

FIGURE 17. Three views of the Churubusco Idol. Museo Nacional de Antropología, Mexico City. Photographs courtesy of H. B. Nicholson.

wear very short jackets and carry incense bags. Although neither of the jackets has the diagnostic fringe, the presence of the incense bag, and in this instance the incense burner, define the costume as the "godly jacket." The companion figure carries a war club in addition to his incense bag, but his similarity to example *3k* indicates that his garment is a *xicolli* rather than an *ichcahuipilli*; the latter are depicted differently in *Códice Azcatítlan* (see examples *3g* and *3h*). The two figures are on a journey, and the name glyph indicates that this man is known as He of the Turquoise Sandal.[109]

The next *xicolli* (example *3l*) is from the section of *Códice Xolotl*[110] dealing with the history of the Chichimecs from the time of their leader Nopaltzin to the death of the ruler Quinatzin, a period of more than one hundred years.[111] This figure wears a very short garment that has a familiar *xicolli* feature, the fringed border, and he is carrying another *xicolli* diagnostic, an incense burner. The rabbit and circle on his left are, no doubt, the date 1 Tochtli (Rabbit), which in the fifty-two-year cycle could mean either 1298 or 1350, and refers to migrating Mexica leaders

at Chapultepec.[112]

Xicolli example *3m* is from the scene of human sacrifice shown in fig. 10. The two priests with their bound hair wear short, fringed *xicolli* while engaging in their ritual duty of extracting a human heart to be offered—still pulsating—as food to the gods.

To understand the final example (*n*), further information must be presented. The *xicolli*, in addition to being worn by full-time priests, was also worn by certain administrators when they performed particular ritual duties. In this category were members of the ruling class—chiefs, lords, nobles—and constables. This latter group deserves special attention.

Carrasco stated that a number of positions in the Aztec administrative hierarchy were filled by men of commoner origin.[113] In Tenochtitlán the executioners or *achcacauhtin* ("elders") were commoners. Sahagún, in discussing the council chamber of the warriors, spoke of the *achcauhcalli* as the meeting place of the constables—the ruler's executioners who carried out the death sentence on whomever the verdict had fallen.[114] The *achcacauhtin* are mentioned

[109] Barlow 1949*b*, p. 117.
[110] The *Códice Xolotl* (Dibble 1951) illustrations used in this study were photographed from the León y Gama copies (which are bound following each of the sixteenth-century originals) to obtain the clearest possible garment examples.

[111] Dibble 1951, p. 59.
[112] Nicholson, personal communication.
[113] Carrasco 1971, p. 354.
[114] Sahagún 1950–69, bk. 8, p. 43.

EXAMPLE 3*i*. Aztec *xicolli*. *Codex Mendoza*, vol. 3, fol. 63r.

EXAMPLE 3*k*. Aztec *xicolli*. *Códice Azcatítlan*, planche 12.

EXAMPLE 3*j*. Aztec *xicolli*. *Codex Magliabechiano*, fol. 63r.

EXAMPLE 3*l*. Aztec *xicolli*. *Códice Xolotl*, planche 4, León y Gama copy.

FIGURE 18. Aztec rite of initiation to office. *Codex Magliabechiano*, fol. 71r.

as wearing the *xicolli* in a description of these functionaries as part of the procession sent out by the ruler Ahuitzotl to welcome a merchant group returning after a four-year expedition and siege in the distant province of Soconusco.[115]

In two almost identical metaphors the important task the city gives the speaker, binding him to serve, is equated with the *xicolli*: "...my cord jacket [*mecaxicolli*], that is, when the city gave me a task, I thereby became a slave."[116] The jacket is referred to as being of cord; the verb *mecachiua* means "to make cord" (*mecatl*, "cord, rope").[117] The cord referred to is agave fiber or yucca rope; hence a cord jacket would not be the luxurious garment that Sahagún inferred was worn by higher-status men. Probably the Berlin Museum *xicolli* was an example of a cord jacket, and it may well have been the quality of *xicolli* the *achcacauhtín* wore. As mentioned earlier, the Aztec sumptuary laws are said to have been very explicit,[118] and cotton garments were supposedly the exclusive privilege of the upper classes.

EXAMPLE 3m. Aztec *xicolli*. *Codex Magliabechiano*, fol. 70r.

[115] Ibid., bk. 9, p. 4.
[116] Ibid., bk. 6, pp. 241–42.
[117] Molina 1970, fol. 55r.
[118] Durán 1967, 2:211–12.

FIGURE 19. Scenes from the *Codex Mendoza*. Six Aztec emissaries wearing *xicolli* are shown in the lower half. *Codex Mendoza*, vol. 3, fol. 66r.

EXAMPLE 3n. Aztec *xicolli*. *Codex Mendoza*, vol. 3, fol. 66r.

The final *xicolli* (example 3n) represents (according to the Spanish text on the folio) an Aztec emissary from the capital of the empire carrying a message of war and pending execution to the cacique of a rebellious village. On this page of the *Codex Mendoza* (see fig. 19) six figures are wearing this garment; four of them also carry the lance and fan of an ambassadorial mission. In addition to having the fringed hem, four of the costumes show a vertical line running from neck to hem in the middle of the garment, which must signify that it opens in front (three closed-sewn *ichcahuipilli* on the page give no indication of a front opening). All the *xicolli*-clad men have long, bound hair but lack the other diagnostics of the priests. One may speculate that, like the *achcacauhtín*, these men may be performing a special task for the state that calls for the wearing of such special-purpose clothing as the ritual-ceremonial *xicolli*.

Closed-sewn Garments

The first three rows of chart 4 present examples of closed-sewn garments. Costumes of this class were constructed of two or more widths of material joined lengthwise with continuous seams. Since such garments had no full-length opening in front or back, they were pulled on over the head. This category includes the women's *huipilli* and two martial costumes—the closed *ichcahuipilli* ("armor") and the *ehuatl* ("tunic").

CLOSED-SEWN ICHCAHUIPILLI. The etymology and basic construction of the *ichcahuipilli* have been considered in the discussion of the open-sewn quilted cotton armor. In addition to the jacket-type *ichcahuipilli*, there was also a closed-sewn-style *ichcahuipilli*.

The closed-sewn *ichcahuipilli* was of padded cotton armor made in two styles: (1) an undecorated, sleeveless garment that pulled on over the head, hugged the body, and reached to the top of the thigh and (2) a pull-on, sleeveless, flared costume that reached to midthigh and was decorated. The *ichcahuipilli* was worn by warriors of all levels of Aztec life and hence was special-purpose clothing serving as the basic martial garment.

Part 3 of the *Codex Mendoza* contains several depictions of *ichcahuipilli* worn by different segments of the population: (1) a number of enemy soldiers are shown wearing the closed-sewn *ichcahuipilli*;[119] (2) Aztec *tequihua* (warriors who have captured at least four enemy prisoners) are shown wearing the armor while reconnoitering enemy territory at night;[120] (3) the career of an Aztec warrior[121] (see fig. 9) and (4) the career of a priest-warrior[122] (see plate 3) are shown at six progressive stages of their adult lives. In the last two depictions only the initial drawings show the warriors wearing the short, slip-on *ichcahuipilli*, which is identical to that of their captives. The quilted

[119] *Codex Mendoza*, vol. 3, fols. 64r, 65r, 66r.
[120] Ibid., fol. 67r.
[121] Ibid., fol. 64r.
[122] Ibid., fol. 65r.

CHART 4
AZTEC COSTUME REPERTORY
Examples of Closed-sewn Garments

Male
Closed *Ichcahuipilli*

Ehuatl

Female
Huipilli

Examples of Limb-encasing Garments

Male
Tlahuiztli

Female

SOURCES: (*a*) *Codex Mendoza*, vol. 3, fol. 66r; (*b*) *Códice Xolotl*, planche 9 (León y Gama copy); (*c*) *Codex Magliabechiano*, fol. 86r; (*d*) *Códice Azcatítlan*, planche 5; (*e*) *Códice Azcatítlan*, planche 25; (*f*) *Codex Vaticanus A*, fol. 57v; (*g*) *Códice Matritense de la Real Academia de la Historia*, fol. 73r; (*h*) *Códice Matritense de la Real Academia de la Historia*, fol. 76r; (*i*) *Codex Telleriano-Remensis*, fol. 42v; (*j*) *Códice Xolotl*, planche 10 (León y Gama copy); (*k*) *Lienzo de Tlaxcala*, lámina 15; (*l*) *Codex Mendoza*, vol. 3, fol. 68r; (*m*) *Codex Mendoza*, vol. 3, fol. 49r; (*n*) *Codex Magliabechiano*, fol. 85r; (*o*) *Codex Mendoza*, vol. 3, fol. 61r; (*p*) *Códice Azcatítlan*, planche 26; (*q*) *Codex Mendoza*, vol. 3, fol. 65r; (*r*) *Códice Matritense de la Real Academia de la Historia*, fol. 53r; (*s*) *Codex Mendoza*, vol. 3, fol. 67r; (*t*) *Codex Mendoza*, vol. 3, fol. 27r; (*u*) *Codex Mendoza*, vol. 3, fol. 64r; (*v*) *Codex Mendoza*, vol. 3, fol. 54r.

Example 4a. Aztec closed *ichcahuipilli*. *Codex Mendoza*, vol. 3, fol. 66r.

EXAMPLE 4b. Aztec closed *ichcahuipilli*. *Códice Xolotl*, planche 9, León y Gama copy.

armor was also subsequently worn beneath the successful warriors' prestigious *tlahuiztli* (discussed below). A wide range of Aztecs wore the cotton armor, as shown by the examples illustrated in the *ichcahuipilli* section of chart 4.

The first example (4a) of the *ichcahuipilli* is worn by a warrior who has just mortally wounded a traveling Aztec merchant encountered on the road (see fig. 19). This soldier is a vassal of a cacique who is now doomed for having allowed interference with any representative of the powerful Triple Alliance Empire. On the aggressor's cotton armor are the hatch marks that indicate quilting. Like the open-sewn *ichcahuipilli*, this garment comes only to the upper thigh.

Example 4b of closed-sewn armor is a battle scene from *Códice Xolotl* showing the standard victory posture: the vanquished being pulled by his scalp lock. This portion of *Códice Xolotl* deals with the wanderings of the famous king of Tetzcoco, Nezahualcoyotl during the years the Tepanecas persecuted him.[123] It was rendered by a different artist, who made it longer than the same closed-sewn garment shown in example 4a.

Example 4c, from *Codex Magliabechiano*, is an enigma. The context in which this figure appears may be that of a pulque ceremony (probably an offering to fire, as suggested by the bowls of brew, flames, and smoke [fig. 20]). Questions arise: What is quilted armor doing in such an unlikely context? Could the costume be some other garment? The only two possibilities would be the *xicolli* or the *ehuatl*. It could not be the *xicolli*; the *Magliabechiano* contains twenty-three depictions of the "godly jacket," and each has its diagnostic fringed border. Nor could it be the *ehuatl*, which also has a diagnostic feature, the feathered skirt. Thus the garment must be the closed-sewn *ichcahuipilli*, but its role in such a context is unclear. The only other battle armor shown in *Codex Magliabechiano* (fig. 26) is the open-sewn jacket type, which also lacks any indication of quilting.

Example 4d, a closed-sewn *ichcahuipilli*, from *Códice Azcatítlan*, shows a warrior, lance and shield in hand, wearing quilted, somewhat flared, closed-sewn cotton armor. On the same folio an identical garment is seen from the back; it too lacks a full-length opening.

A more exaggerated version of a flared type of cotton armor is worn by another warrior in example 4e, from *Códice Azcatítlan*. The page on which he appears (fig. 21) depicts a battle between a Spaniard carrying a shield with the face of a sun on it (perhaps a depiction of Alvarado, whom the Indians called Tonatiuh [the Sun]), and the Indian warrior dressed in a decorated, flared *ichcahuipilli*. As Barlow's commentary explains, this is an aquatic scene involving a Spanish galleon and conquistadors wading ashore.[124] The *ichcahuipilli* shown in example *e* is decorated with whirlpoollike designs, the motif used in *planche* V of the same pictorial for a stylized river and in

123 Dibble 1951, p. 109.
124 Barlow 1949b, p. 130.

planche II to indicate a lake. The only other "decorated" *ichcahuipilli* in *Códice Azcatítlan* (fig. 22) has a "quilted" pattern and may indicate a deep type of quilting. Sahagún mentioned a whirlpool design on finely woven maguey capes.[125]

The last *ichcahuipilli* (example 4*f*), from *Codex Vaticanus A*, is of interest for two reasons. A Spanish text that appears on the same folio states that the Spaniards adopted this type of armor from the Aztecs because "it resists the arrows which could penetrate the strongest coat of mail and even some cuirass [but] could not penetrate these *escauiples*."

Certainly the Spaniards were wearing cotton armor by the time they were established in the Basin of Mexico. Aguilar described Cortés and a party of his conquistadors hurriedly leaving Tenochtitlán to confront Narváez in Veracruz: "We left Mexico then, all of us wearing cotton armor."[126] It was not from the Aztecs, however, that the Spaniards first learned the advantages of martial apparel. Bernal Díaz del Castillo, who accompanied Francisco Fernández de Córdoba in 1517 on the first voyage to reach Mesoamerica, mentioned that the conquistadors wore cotton armor when they first encountered the Lowland Mayas of Yucatán.[127] Therefore, the Spaniards had knowledge of these protective garments before they left Cuba. Again, Díaz del Castillo bears this out: "As in the country around Havana there is much cotton, we made well-padded armor for ourselves, which is most necessary when fighting Indians, on account of the great use they make of darts, arrows and lances, and stones which fall on one like hail."[128]

The second point of interest concerning the final closed-sewn *ichcahuipilli* (example 4*f*) is its appearance. It is a flared A-line garment reaching to midthigh, and it has a definite design on its surface. It is difficult to know exactly what this decorative quilted armor signifies. Since the garment is called an *ichcahuipilli* in the Spanish gloss on the folio and two similar decorated, closed-sewn *ichcahuipilli* are found in the *Códice Azcatitlán* (fig. 22, and example *e* in chart 4), the existence of such costumes cannot be denied. It is puzzling, however, that in the many references to the quilted armor by the early writers only Díaz del Castillo, commenting on the wealth of material in the armory of Moctezuma, referred to these cotton garments as being decorated: "There was also much quilted cotton armour, richly ornamented on the outside with many coloured feathers, used as devices and distinguishing marks."[129] The *ichcahuipilli*, whatever its degree of elaboration, was obviously so effective in withstanding arrows and lance thrusts that Cortés and his men adopted it.

EXAMPLE 4*c*. Aztec closed *ichcahuipilli*. *Codex Magliabechiano*, fol. 86r.

FIGURE 20. Aztec ritual scene involving the burning of copal incense. *Codex Magliabechiano*, fol. 86r.

[125] Sahagún 1950–69, bk. 10, p. 73.
[126] Aguilar 1954, p. 60.
[127] Díaz del Castillo 1967, 1:43.
[128] Ibid., p. 85.
[129] Ibid., 2:65.

49

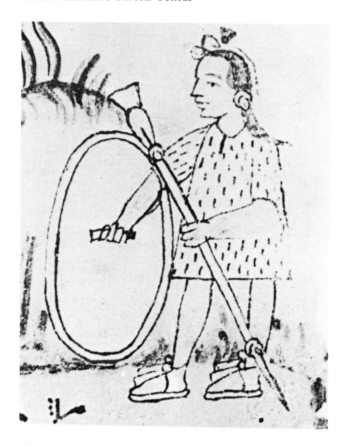

EXAMPLE 4d. Aztec closed *ichcahuipilli. Códice Azcatítlan, planche* 5.

EXAMPLE 4e. Aztec closed *ichcahuipilli. Códice Azcatítlan, planche* 25.

FIGURE 21. Aztec aquatic scene. *Códice Azcatitlán, planche 25.*

EHUATL. The *ehuatl* was a closed-sewn tunic made of feather-covered material, whose diagnostic feature was a short skirt. Made in various colors and kinds of feathers to indicate rank, it was worn by Aztec captains, lords, and rulers in a martial context. It was special-purpose clothing restricted to a specific cadre of warriors.

The term *ehuatl* is variously translated by modern scholars as "shirt,"[130] "doublet," [131] and "tunic."[132] Molina defined *ehuatl* as an animal pelt for tanning or as the peel and rind of fruit,[133] and Sahagún used the word *eoatl* with reference to human skin.[134] The meaning apparently is "outer layer," and according to Sahagún that is the role the garment played. His *Códice Matritense* presents a list of arms and insignia for the figures depicted.[135] The entire raiment of six noble warriors wearing the *ehuatl* is given; the first item mentioned for each lord is the padded cotton shirt (*ichcahuipilli*), followed by the tunic (*ehuatl*) and remaining accouterments.[136] The *ehuatl* itself was not a padded costume but an overgarment.

The *Matritense* also provides information on construction of the costume. In the descriptions of seven *ehuatl* it repeatedly states that the garment was made of a piece of cloth entirely covered with feathers.[137] Five color variations of the costume are mentioned: blue, yellow, white, dark violet, and red, as well as fine curly turkey-bird feathers.[138] The *ehuatl* had a hanging border of feathers, which may have been a separate feather "skirt." Sahagún

[130] Anderson and Dibble in Sahagún 1950–69, bk. 9, p. 89.
[131] Seler 1960, 2:545, etc.
[132] Sullivan 1972, pp. 156, 165, etc.
[133] Molina 1970, fol. 29v.
[134] Sahagún 1950–69, bk. 10, p. 95.
[135] The *Códices Matritenses* include the *Codex Primeros memoriales*, which Sahagún collected in Tepepulco between 1559 and 1561, at the outset of his ambitious project to record pre-Hispanic Aztec life. Tepepulco was not one of the great power centers of Central Mexico, and hence the information coming from it offers an interesting view of life in a populous but subordinate community (Nicholson 1973*b*, p. 208).
[136] Sullivan 1972, pp. 189–91.
[137] Ibid., pp. 165, 177.
[138] Seler 1960, 2:557, 580.

related how the rulers were arrayed when they went to war: "...and he puts on a red shirt made of the feathers of the red spoonbill, which is decorated with golden stone knives...and he wears a short skirt of sapote leaves, which is made entirely of green *quetzal* feathers."[139] Sahagún made another reference to the "little shirt of sapote leaves of Xipe," which was associated with the various colored *ehuatl*. Seler noted that this was the costume of the fertility god Xipe Totec (Our Lord the Flayed One), the red god, which the Mexican kings had worn into battle since the days of the emperor Axayacatl, who reigned between 1467 and 1481.[140]

In the attempt to determine the contexts in which the *ehuatl* appears, it is helpful to return to Sahagún's initial description of the garment and the men who wore it. An enumeration of the dress and insignia of the Aztec captains includes *ehuatl* made of red parrot feathers, bright red feathers, and turkey-hen feathers.[141] Sahagún's description of the arms and insignia of the lords, rulers, and nobles lists *ehuatl* of blue cotinga feathers, princely feathers, yellow parrot feathers, and white heron feathers.[142] A later manuscript tells of the kings of Mexico wearing a red spoonbill *ehuatl*[143] (mentioned in a discussion of the "skirt" of the costume). It is clear then that captains, lords, and rulers all wore the *ehuatl*, but their costumes were differentiated by both color and the kinds of feathers used in construction.

Aside from the pictorial evidence for the existence of the *ehuatl*, the descriptions of the garment in Sahagún, and the possible description of it by the Anonymous Conqueror[144] presented below, no further reference to the *ehuatl* has been found. In comparison, the other two types of martial attire are well documented; as noted above, the *ichcahuipilli* is repeatedly mentioned in the early colonial sources, as is the body-encasing warrior costume, *tlahuiztli*, to be discussed below.

The first *ehuatl* (example 4g) in chart 4, from the *Códice Matritense de la Real Academia de la Historia*, is worn by one of six noble warriors whom Sahagún illustrates. The construction of the costume is more clearly visible in example 4h, an unmodeled version from the same source.

Example 4i is from *Codex Telleriano-Remensis*. This warrior is shown involved in the 1512 Aztec war against the province of Quimichintepec, whose full place-name glyph, the Hill and Rat, is seen on chart 4.

A two-tiered version (example 4j) of the *ehuatl* skirt comes from *Códice* Xolotl which deals with the future king of Texcoco, Nezahualcoyotl, and his years of persecution. The skirt is similar to one worn by a Mexica warrior (example 4k) from the *Lienzo de Tlaxcala*, who wears the

FIGURE 22. Aztec warrior wearing what is probably quilted armor (*ichcahuipilli*). *Códice Azcatítlan, planche* 24.

EXAMPLE 4f. Aztec closed *ichcahuipilli*. *Codex Vaticanus A*, fol. 57v.

[139] Ibid., p. 594.
[140] Ibid.
[141] Sullivan 1972, p. 177.
[142] Ibid., p. 165.
[143] Sahagún 1950–69, bk. 8, p. 33.
[144] Anonymous Conqueror 1858, p. 372.

ehuatl with an animal-head insignia. The Anonymous Conqueror describes such an ensemble:

> The lords wear certain smock-like coats which among us are of mail but theirs are of gold or gilt silver, and the strength of their feathered garments is proportionate to their weapons, so that they resist spears and arrows, and even the sword. To defend the head they wear things like heads of serpents, or tigers, or lions or wolves, and the man's head lies inside the animal's jaws as though it were devouring him. These heads are of wood covered on the outside with feathers or incrustations of gold and precious stones, and are something wonderful to see.[145]

HUIPILLI. The Aztec (*h*)*uipilli* was a closed-sewn, sleeveless tunic or shift that came to a little below the hips or the top of the thighs. It was the basic woman's upper-body garment, and as such was worn by women of all classes. The *huipilli* often had a specially decorated rectangle over the chest that may have served the practical purpose of strengthening the neck slit and protecting it from tearing. There was also sometimes a differentiated area over each shoulder.

Molina described the (*h*)*uipilli* as an Indian woman's shirt,[146] and to the present day the term *huipil* is used to designate the closed-sewn, sleeveless tunic of whatever width or length worn by the Indian women of Middle America.

Durán wrote enthusiastically of the beautiful *huipilli* of the Aztec women:

> Women's clothing: blouses and skirts, as well finished and splendid as it is possible to make, all of them enriched with wide borders embroidered in different colors, and designs and feather work on the front. On the sides of the blouses were designs in colored thread, and on the back, embroidered flowers, imperial eagles or flowers embroidered and enriched with feather work. They were beautiful to see.[147]

Sahagún's description of fifteen elegant *huipilli* reflects the rich variety of color and design of these garments: orange-colored; yellow parrot-feather decoration; stamp device at the neck; flowers overspread; smoky color; large embroidered figures at the throat with designs of cut reeds; feathered; tawny-colored; coyote fur; duck feathers; dyed rabbit fur; gourd-and-thistle design; shift overspread with dahlias; eagle head in a setting done with flowers; border of flowers.[148] Sahagún illustrated some of the richly worked *huipilli* (fig. 23).

Many of the complex, detailed designs achieved on the *huipilli* were apparently carried out with a thread of fine-spun rabbit's fur from the soft underbelly of the animal. Motolinía praised this yarn, called *tochomitl*, for its ability to dye to rich hues, its lasting color, and its silklike sheen.[149] The *huipilli* were embroidered with particular

[145] Ibid.
[146] Molina 1970, fol. 157v.
[147] Durán 1967, 2:207; translation from Heyden and Horcasitas 1964, p. 128.
[148] Sahagún 1950–69, bk. 8, p. 47.
[149] Motolinía 1971, pp. 258–59.

EXAMPLE 4*g*. Aztec *ehuatl. Códice Matritense de la Real Academia de la Historia*, fol. 73r.

EXAMPLE 4*h*. Aztec *ehuatl. Códice Matritense de la Real Academia de la Historia*, fol. 76r.

EXAMPLE 4*i*. Aztec *ehuatl*. *Codex Telleriano-Remensis*, fol. 42v.

EXAMPLE 4*k*. Aztec *ehuatl*. *Lienzo de Tlaxcala*, *lámina 15*.

EXAMPLE 4*j*. Aztec *ehuatl*. *Códice Xolotl*, *planche* 10, León y Gama copy.

care at the throat and often on a rectangle at the nape of the neck as well.

The *huipilli* is repeatedly mentioned in the *Relaciones geográficas*. The *Relación* from Ichcateopan, Guerrero, refers to it as "a large shirt with neither sleeves nor collar."[150] A report from Coatepec, Mexico, gives more detail: "This costume is tasteful and costly, it is clothing of very thin cotton and the borders [of these garments] are of colored thread and feathers, woven and embroidered."[151]

Richly decorated *huipilli* were given in tribute, as is evident from the *Matrícula de tributos*, where 4,800 are listed as being given every eighty days and 25,200 annually.[152] The *huipilli*, translated "shift," also appears in a riddle in book 6, *Rhetoric and Moral Philosophy*, of the *Florentine Codex*: "What is it that has a tight shift? The tomato."[153]

The first *huipilli* (example 4*l*) is from *Codex Mendoza*. The figure is a newly married woman busily spinning cotton thread using a spinning whorl secured in a small pottery bowl atop a woven mat. In her left hand she holds a bank of fluffed-up cotton. Her *huipilli* is clearly visible with its decorated lower border and a rectangular worked panel at the neck.

Example 4*m*, from the tribute section of *Codex Mendoza*, shows a *huipilli* drawn over the pictograph for *manta*. The pine-tree-like sign at the top represents a

150 Cline 1972, census no. 52; Paso y Troncoso 1905, 6:91.
151 Cline 1972, census no. 29; Paso y Troncoso 1905, 6:56.
152 Berdan 1975, p. 367.
153 Sahagún 1950–69, bk. 6, p. 239.

53

FIGURE 23. Aztec women's array, *huipilli* and *cueitl*. Sahagún 1926, *lámina* 49, *libro* 8, plates 72, 74.

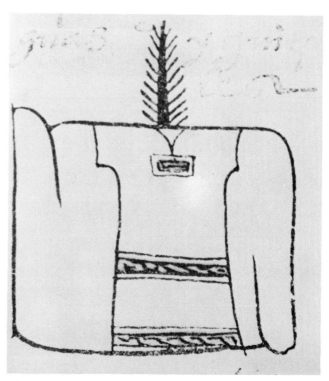

EXAMPLE 4*m*. Aztec *huipilli. Codex Mendoza*, vol. 3, fol. 49r.

EXAMPLE 4*l*. Aztec *huipilli. Codex Mendoza*, vol. 3, fol. 68r.

EXAMPLE 4*n*. Aztec *huipilli. Codex Magliabechiano*, fol. 85r.

EXAMPLE 4o. Aztec *huipilli*. *Codex Mendoza*, vol. 3, fol. 61r.

EXAMPLE 4p. Aztec *huipilli*. *Códice Azcatítlan*, planche 26.

human hair and is the symbol for 400, the number of *huipilli* given every eighty days from that particular province.

Example 4n is from a scene in *Codex Magliabechiano* depicting a feast of the pulque gods (see fig. 11). Like the *tilmatli* (example 2n) and the wraparound skirt (example 2s), this costume has crudely sewn seams, the only *huipilli* so depicted in all the Mesoamerican codices. Perhaps old, repaired clothing is being suggested. References to tattered garments reflecting the vicissitudes of life appear a number of times throughout the *Florentine Codex*. In addition to whatever symbolic connotations it may have, this outlining of the seams also illustrates that at least some of the *huipilli* were made of three joined webs of material.

The woman in example 4o is part of a wedding procession. She holds a pine torch to light the way for a matron, who is carrying the bride on her back to the home of the groom's parents. This figure illustrates that the Aztec *huipilli* came to a little below the hips. There appears to be an embroidered rectangle on the back of the garment.

Example 4p, from *Códice Azcatítlan*, shows five elegantly attired women impassively surveying a peaceful aquatic scene. Barlow speculated that this folio may represent the removal of some of the noblewomen from besieged Tenochtitlán in 1521.[154] Two of their *huipilli* clearly display the design square, carefully worked in intricate patterns, over the chest. All five of the garments show the specially worked band of close-set motifs that extended across the shoulders from the neckline to the edge of the shoulder.

Limb-encasing Garments

The fifth category in the analysis of the Aztec costume repertory is limb-encasing garments, the only classification that includes sleeves or trouser legs. The special-purpose warrior costume, *tlahuiztli*, is the sole example of this category.

TLAHUIZTLI. The *tlahuiztli* was a complete body-suit encasing the arms and legs. It was constructed of feather-covered cloth, made in a variety of colors and styles (plate 4). The basic shape of all these suits was probably the same; rank and status were indicated by the addition of various body colors, designs, headpieces, and attached insignia. It was a male garment, worn in varying colors and feather combinations by different grades of warriors and priest-warriors of high ascribed and achieved status. Since the *tlahuiztli* was worn only in martial or ritual contexts, it was special-purpose clothing.

This most spectacular type of Aztec military attire completely encased not only the limbs of the wearer but in some cases his head as well. Molina defined *tlahuiztli* as arms and insignia,[155] implying to the modern English-speaking reader that he was referring only to weapons and symbols of rank. Stevens's Spanish-English dictionary of 1726, however, defines *armas* as "arms, weapons, armour." This inclusion in the Spanish term *armas* of a garment for bodily protection coincides with the information presented in the *Matrícula de tributos*. There the Nahuatl term *tlahuiztli* is always associated with the entire warrior costume, including the fitted body suit, headdress, and shield. Previous discussion of the Aztecs' elaborate warrior regalia has focused primarily on descriptions of the headdresses and back devices,[156] but because these accouterments are marginal to my investigation, I have used the term *tlahuiztli* to refer to the body suit only.

Sahagún's *Códice Matritense*, which contains the section on battle garments from *Primeros memoriales*, provides most of the information available on the construction of the warrior costumes. It contains an illustration and writ-

154 Barlow 1949b, p. 130.
155 Molina 1970, fol. 145r.
156 Seler 1960, 2:509–619.

ten description of a yellow parrot-feather costume (example *r*, chart 4): "It is made in this manner: A frame is fashioned in the form of a coyote's head. It is covered with yellow parrot feathers. It has a crest of *quetzal* feathers."[157]

The construction of other warrior costumes is also described,[158] and it is clear that both the headdresses and the bodies of these suits were covered with feathers. Further data on construction of the costume comes from the *Lienzo de Tlaxcala* (fig. 24). This depiction of a Mexica warrior wearing a *tlahuiztli* shows that the garment, which fitted close to the body, opened in the back and was secured with ties.

The *tlahuiztli* displayed wide variety in both style and color. The coyote costumes were made in yellow, violet, white, black, red, flame-colored and starry-sky designs and combinations of these.[159] In addition to the coyote-type garments there were several other classes of *tlahuiztli*, including jaguar, death demons, and Huaxtec costumes. Other costume types emulated the gods, including Xipe Totec, Teteoinnan, Xochiquetzal, Chantico, and many of the pulque deities.[160]

Some of these warrior costumes were worn with a matching headdress, while others were in the form of a disguise, constructed so that the wearer's head was also encased by the suit and his face looked out from the gaping jaws of coyote, jaguar, or frightful specter. A further variant was the fitted body suit worn without a head covering, utilizing instead a complex form of insignia (often referred to in the literature as a "device") fastened to a ladderlike frame strapped to the back (fig. 25).

The Anonymous Conqueror provided evidence that the warrior costumes themselves were not padded garments but, like the *ehuatl*, were worn over the *ichcahuipilli*:

> The armor they use in warfare are certain shirts like jupons, of quilted cotton the thickness of a finger and a half and sometimes two fingers, which is very strong. Over these they wear suits all of one piece and of a heavy cloth, which they tie in back; these are covered with feathers of different colors and look very jaunty. One company of soldiers will wear them in red and white, another in blue and yellow, and others in various ways.[161]

The sharp divisions of the Aztec military hierarchy are reflected in the *tlahuiztli*. The warrior costume, complete with shield, headdress, and back device, functioned as the visual marker of achieved martial status. The privilege of wearing this regalia was hard won, for the Aztec warrior's career was advanced only on the field of battle. A man literally had to fight to wear the society's most prestigious clothing.

[157] Sullivan 1972, p. 167.
[158] Ibid., p. 187.
[159] Seler 1960, 2:580–81.
[160] Ibid., 2:509–619.
[161] Anonymous Conqueror 1858, p. 572.

FIGURE 24. Aztec warrior wearing a *tlahuiztli*, showing gusset in back and ties securing it. *Lienzo de Tlaxcala, lámina 15.*

FIGURE 25. Section of an Aztec tribute list showing a warrior suit and accompanying back-device frame. *Codex Mendoza*, vol. 3, fol. 20v.

FIGURE 26. A mock gladiatorial battle held during the Aztec monthly Feast of Tlacaxipehualiztli. *Codex Magliabechiano*, fol. 30r.

The *Codex Mendoza* pictorially records the gifts given to soldiers after they had captured enemy prisoners (see fig. 9).[162] A warrior who captured two prisoners was rewarded with a Cuextlán warrior costume; three prisoners, a "fire-butterfly" device and warrior costume; four prisoners, a jaguar costume; five or six prisoners, a *tlahuiztli* with a long feathered staff (which does not appear on the tribute rolls).

Priests who captured enemies in battle were also rewarded with *tlahuiztli*[163] (see plate 5). For the capture of five prisoners, a *momoyactli* ("dispersed-feather") costume was given; and for the capture of six of the enemy, a coyote-style costume was awarded.

It is logical to assume that there were greater numbers of costumes and *mantas* of the types awarded to persons who took only one or two captives; by far the most common costume given in tribute was the *cuextlán*, awarded for the capture of two prisoners. Beyond that, however, there is little correlation between numbers of certain types of costumes and numbers of prisoners captured.

Careful study of the components of the full battle regalia reveals that the same basic body garment was utilized by several warrior grades. The different colors for the limb-encasing suit, plus certain insignia, were the indicators of advanced rank. The coyote costume of the upper warrior categories was distinguished from those of the lower ranks by a bunch of *quetzal* feathers worn on the head.[164] That is also true of the back devices; it appears that the same device, made of more costly materials, was carried by the upper ranks of warriors, while less valuable versions were used by lower grades.[165]

The warrior costumes were also used in ceremonial contexts. In a description of the spectacular ceremony of Tlacaxipehualiztli ("The Flaying of Men"), Sahagún wrote of four costumed Mexica warriors who engaged in a ritualized gladiatorial combat with a doomed sacrificial victim (fig. 26).[166] The warriors were elegantly arrayed in their elaborate jaguar and eagle *tlahuiztli*.

Equally elegantly arrayed in example 4q, a priest-warrior who, having captured six prisoners, has been awarded a yellow-feather coyote-style costume. He holds his cotton-armor-clad captive by the hair in the standard

[162] *Codex Mendoza*, vol. 3, fol. 64r.
[163] Ibid., fol. 65r.

[164] Seler 1960, 2:580.
[165] Ibid., p. 582.
[166] Sahagún 1950–69, bk. 2, pp. 49–50.

Mesoamerican gesture of victory over an opponent.

A coyote costume (example 4*r*) made of yellow parrot feathers is from Sahagún's *Matritensis* (which contains the section of battle dress from the *Primeros memoriales*). A comparison of these two coyote costumes shows a difference in construction. The *Matritense* garment appears to be in a single unit, whereas the *Codex Mendoza* costume has a separate headpiece, as do the remaining four illustrations and all the warrior costumes in the *Mendoza* tribute list. The warrior suit with separate headpiece was probably the more common type. Durán's account tends to confirm this in a description of the battle headgear of one of the warriors: "On his head he placed a helmet, also of quilted cotton, in the form of a tiger or lion or eagle such as was customarily worn by warriors in battle."[167]

A *valiente* with the title Tlacochcalcatl (Master of the Spear House) is shown in example 4*s* wearing a *quetzal-tzitzimitl* ("the quetzal-feather frightful image") costume. The headpiece is a frame in the shape of a skull with the tangled hair of the death god, made of quetzal feathers. The costume has a design across the chest symbolizing the incision of the sacrificial cut, with the liver rather than the heart issuing forth.[168] Example 4*t*, from the tribute list of *Codex Mendoza*, is a different artist's rendition of the same costume.

Example 4*u*, also from *Codex Mendoza*, is a *valiente* wearing a jaguar costume, signifying that he has captured four prisoners. The final *tlahuiztli* example (4*v*) shows how this same costume appears in the tribute section.

SUMMARY

Most Aztec apparel was draped, worn just as it came from the loom, knotted over the shoulders as a cloak, tied about the waist as a hip-cloth, or wrapped around the body as a loincloth or skirt. The Aztecs' sewn garments were unfitted, created by simply joining the seams of two or three webs of material. With one exception none of this clothing had sleeves. The only class of apparel that encased the arms or legs was the warrior costume, worn only in highly specialized contexts by a small percentage of the population.

Each of the five principles of garment construction is manifested in the Aztec costume repertory, although there is only a single example of a closed-sewn garment, the *quechquemitl*. Both the female *quechquemitl* and the male open-sewn *xicolli* were worn solely as special-purpose clothing. The restriction of the two costumes to ceremonial-ritual contexts implies that they carried specific historical or religious significance.

The nature of Aztec society is linked to their costume repertory. They were an aggressive, militant people; their cultural focus is evident in the range of types and styles of

EXAMPLE 4*q*. Aztec *tlahuiztli*. *Codex Mendoza*, vol. 3, fol. 65r.

EXAMPLE 4*r*. Aztec *tlahuiztli*. *Códice Matritense de la Real Academia de la Historia*, fol. 53r.

---

[167] Durán 1967, 2:91; translation from Heyden and Horcasitas 1964, p. 63.
[168] Nicholson, personal communication.

EXAMPLE 4s. Aztec *tlahuiztli*. *Codex Mendoza*, vol. 3, fol. 67r.

EXAMPLE 4u. Aztec *tlahuiztli*. *Codex Mendoza*, vol. 3, fol. 64r.

EXAMPLE 4t. Aztec *tlahuiztli*. *Codex Mendoza*, vol. 3, fol. 27r.

EXAMPLE 4v. Aztec *tlahuiztli*. *Codex Mendoza*, vol. 3, fol. 54r.

battle attire. Aztec society was sharply stratified, as their clothing reflects: there were marked contrasts in the garments of the different classes, in the fibers used and in the degree of decoration.

In the Aztec clothing repertory the more elaborate costumes were special-purpose clothing; the more complex the context, the more elaborate and specialized the costume. The religious and military areas of Aztec life had the greatest elaboration of attire. The clothing depicted on deities and their impersonators in the context of the great ceremonials was indeed ornate and iconographically specialized (see plate 3). Military garb worn in battle was also ornate (see fig. 5 and plates 4 and 5), and much of it also depicted specific religious concepts.

All the above patterns observable in the Aztec costume repertory also existed in more modest form among their vigorous if impoverished neighbors on the east, the Tlaxcalans.

FIGURE 27. The conqueror of Mexico, Hernán Cortés, and his Tlaxcalan allies. *Lienzo de Tlaxcala, lámina* 47.

CHAPTER THREE

The Tlaxcalans of Central Mexico

 THE AZTECS were not the only independent political unit in the Mexican highlands. Across the mountains on the east lived their enemies the Tlaxcalans, who despite long-standing animosities were culturally "Aztecs."

The Tlaxcalans were one of the seven seminomadic tribes that came out of the mythical seven caves of the northern wilderness. Like the Mexicas of Tenochtitlán, the Nahuatl-speaking Tlaxcaltecans took a somewhat circuitous journey to their promised land, eventually establishing themselves in the highland basin just east of the Valley of Mexico. They became the dominant power in what is now known as the Puebla-Tlaxcala Valley. Earlier residents in the area, the historic Olmecs (not to be confused with the Preclassic–Formative period Olmecs of the southern Gulf Coast), were absorbed by the Tlaxcalans. Not so a neighboring people, the Otomís, who had a lower level of material culture and remained peripheral to the power structure of the Tlaxcalan state. The Otomís usually lived on the edge of Tlaxcalan territory, on the frontier, and often served as laborers and particularly as soldiers and buffer guards. Otomí warriors were formidable in battle, and the Aztecs prized them as captives.

The province of Tlaxcala, whose territory at the time of Spanish contact was somewhat smaller than that of the modern state of Tlaxcala, had a population of somewhere between 400,000 and 500,000 inhabitants.[1] Tlaxcalan political organization had developed along somewhat different lines from those of their Nahuatl-speaking neighbors in the adjoining Valley of Mexico. It appears from colonial sources that the Tlaxcalan governing council was really a confederation composed of the leaders of four semiindependent principalities, or *cabeceras*, of the area, each with its own political structure and leader. The conquistadors' accounts indicate that the autonomy of each division was clearly reflected in dress.

Although the eyewitness accounts do not specifically mention four rulers, both Cortés and Díaz del Castillo referred to several Tlaxcalan leaders, whereas in Tenochtitlán Moctezuma was the sole ruler with whom the Spaniards dealt. The government of Tlaxcala was an oligarchy, and the principle of heredity was firmly entrenched among its noble families. Colonial sources indicate that, when the head of one of the four *cabeceras* died, his oldest legitimate son by his principal wife succeeded him only if the successor was acceptable to the other three leaders. If not, another son was chosen.

The dominant feature of sixteenth-century Tlaxcalan life was the antagonistic relationship with the Aztecs of the neighboring Valley of Mexico. Relations between the two groups had been amicable up to the mid-fifteenth century, and until that time Tlaxcala prospered with a trade network extending from the Pacific to the Gulf Coast. As a result such lowland products as gold, cacao, cotton, multicolored feathers, wax and honey were part of the economy.[2] Salt also had to be imported, since there apparently were no salt mines within the Puebla-Tlaxcala basin in pre-Hispanic times.

Around 1450 life changed drastically for the Tlaxcalans. Under Moctezuma I the Aztec Empire's drive toward the Gulf Coast began threatening Tlaxcalan trade, and animosity between the peoples of the neighboring valleys began to build. Within a few decades the empire of the

---

[1] Dumond 1976, p. 20.

[2] Gibson 1967, p. 14.

Triple Alliance had virtually surrounded the province of Tlaxcala and in doing so had cut off access to the status items: cotton for garments, gold and silver for adornments, multicolored feathers for ceremonial and military dress, cacao for the status beverage, and salt for seasoning.[3]

Although never conquered, the Tlaxcalan state was completely hemmed in by the Aztec Empire, and the constantly recurring warfare between the foes became institutionalized. This was the famous "Flowery War," in which highly ritualized, protracted, and indecisive battles were periodically held. The war became a traditional and ceremonial rite whose purpose was not to destroy or defeat but to capture prisoners for sacrifice. Since the Tlaxcalans and the Mexicas shared the same culture, spoke the same language, and worshiped essentially the same gods, they were particularly desirable sacrificial victims for one another.

As the decades passed, the hostilities became increasingly bitter. Although crippling in other ways, the economic isolation of the Tlaxcalans did not prevent them from effectively equipping themselves for warfare, and they continued to remain formidable opponents. The long embargo, as well as battles and the need for constant military preparedness, produced a fierce hatred of the Aztecs. It also called forth a tremendous sense of internal loyalty and patriotism, which remained an outstanding trait of the Tlaxcalans. That was true not only throughout the Conquest period but also into modern times.[4]

The long years of resistance against the Aztec Empire effectively prepared the Tlaxcalans for the decisive role they were to play in the Spanish conquest: they became the indispensable auxiliary troops for Cortés and his conquistadors. The Spaniards, on their initial march from the coast to Tenochtitlán, first entered Tlaxcalan territory with the mistaken belief that they would be afforded a friendly reception. Only four months earlier the Europeans had landed in the area of the Totonac Indians (near present-day Veracruz). Cortés established a camp, reconnoitered, and consolidated his position in that region. He then turned his attention to the obvious center of power and wealth in the newly discovered lands, Tenochtitlán, the highland capital of the Aztec Empire. Some of the Gulf Coast Indians accompanied the Spaniards on their march inland. At a crucial junction on their advance toward the highlands the Spaniards were advised by their accompanying Totonac allies to take the route through Tlaxcalan territory, where they would be received peacefully. The conquistadors soon learned that nothing could have been further from the truth.

The Tlaxcalans quickly and accurately assessed the Spanish intrusion into their lands as threatening to their own independent existence, and their reply was full-scale war.[5] The strength of their military opposition astonished and dismayed the Spaniards. If this was the prowess of the impoverished Tlaxcalans, what would be the strength of the mighty Aztecs? The Tlaxcalan encounter was one of the most united oppositions to Spanish imperialism the Europeans were to experience. From long necessity the Tlaxcalans were formidable fighters, and defense of their territory was instinctive to them. On this occasion, however, they faced a different foe.

Cortés's first sight of the frontier of Tlaxcala was a forbidding wall, which indeed proved a harbinger of ill; sharp resistance followed soon after the invaders had marched into Tlaxcalan territory. The main engagements were fought during the first five or six days, and the Spaniards quickly found the Indians to be worthy opponents. However, it was unnerving to the Tlaxcalans to find such a small invading force capable of scattering and wreaking devastation on a vast horde of Indian warriors. In desperation some Tlaxcalan priests predicted that a night attack would be successful because the invaders lost their strength after dark. Díaz del Castillo notes that when this foray turned out badly the Indians sacrificed two of their priests.[6]

The fighting ability and staying power of the Spaniards greatly impressed the Indians; and, although one faction of Tlaxcalan leadership opposed it, they finally decided to make peace. The conquistadors welcomed a respite from hostilities, for many of them were wounded and sick. The Indians now welcomed the strangers and gave them an elaborate reception, presenting their new friends with whatever modest gifts they could assemble (plate 6). This sharing included providing the heretofore unknown horses with the same meat, tortillas, and turkeys consumed by their masters.

An alliance between the Tlaxcalans and the Spaniards was then forged, and when Cortés left Tlaxcala to continue his march toward Tenochtitlán, several thousand Tlaxcalan auxiliaries accompanied him. These Indian allies fought loyally alongside the Spaniards for two long years, including the final bitter siege and destruction of Tenochtitlán in 1521. This period included the near-fatal rout of Noche Triste in July, 1520, when the very survival of the Spaniards hung in the balance and depended on the continued support and succor of their Tlaxcalan allies. Despite pressure from one faction of Tlaxcalan leadership to turn against the Spaniards at this vulnerable time, the loyalty of the Indians held; and Cortés was thus able to recover, recoup, and return to bring about total victory. Without the Tlaxcalan refuge and native auxiliary troops in the ensuing decisive battles, the Spaniards' triumph would have been impossible. Following the Conquest, Cortés made a number of special concessions to the Tlaxcalans to show his gratitude. These privileges were to be

---

[3] According to the sixteenth-century Mexican historian Muñoz Camargo, the Tlaxcalans lost their taste for salt after sixty years of deprivation and consumed very little of it, even after the Conquest (Davies 1973, p. 228).

[4] Nutini 1976, pp. 124–34.
[5] Gibson 1967, p. 191.
[6] Díaz del Castillo 1967, 1:243.

held in perpetuity.

Thirty years later the Indians drew up the *Lienzo de Tlaxcala* to remind the Spaniards of their indispensable role as auxiliary troops.[7] Although the original has disappeared, a version of the pictorial has survived. It consists of a single sheet with a large main scene at the top showing Spanish and Tlaxcalan dignitaries and eighty-seven smaller scenes below. The latter group deals mainly with the participation of the Tlaxcalans as allies in the many battles of the Conquest. The clothing depicted in the *Lienzo de Tlaxcala* is informative, and a particularly interesting variety of martial garments is illustrated. Appropriately, the more affluent and powerful Aztec adversaries are shown having the greater variety of elaborate warrior costumes.

The *Lienzo* tends to misrepresent certain features of the Tlaxcalan past. It suggests an earlier and greater degree of accord between the Tlaxcalans and the Spaniards than was the case, and it exaggerates the promises of Cortés.[8] Nevertheless, this colonial source provides useful insights into certain phases of Tlaxcalan contact-period culture. Because it is drawn in a heavily Europeanized style, it is easily comprehensible to the twentieth-century viewer.

That is not the case with the only other major pictorial that depicts clothing worn in the Tlaxcalan area, the *Tonalamatl Aubin*,[9] a divinatory almanac painted on native paper and assembled in the screenfold manner. Although there are other minor Tlaxcalan documents, I have focused on the two most important for my purposes. The *Tonalamatl Aubin* is pre-Conquest and thus done in an early, unacculturated manner. The crudeness of the style of this ritual-calendrical document suggests it may have come from the mountainous eastern frontier area of Tlaxcala, which would indicate an Otomí origin.[10] The principal figures in this manual are deities. The crude style of the artist sometimes makes it difficult to determine the details of what is being worn, but illustrations from the document are nevertheless incorporated in this book because it is a religious pictorial from the Tlaxcalan region. Since the *Lienzo de Tlaxcala* is a historical account, reflecting the secular side of life, such special-purpose ritual garments as the Aztec *quechquemitl* would not be expected to appear in it. However, this female ceremonial costume is found in the *Tonalamatl Aubin*.

In comparison with the written material that documents Aztec life, the sources not only for Tlaxcala but for all the other Indian groups seem scant indeed. Moreover, only a few of the chronicles mention clothing. As a result,

any passing observation by an early writer is valued. One of the best sources for the pre-Conquest and early post-Conquest history of Tlaxcala was written by Diego Muñoz Camargo.[11] Born shortly after the Conquest, he was the son of a Spanish father and a Tlaxcalan mother of noble lineage.[12]

Since few of the chroniclers mention the clothing of Tlaxcala, the *Relaciones geográficas* of the area have been of particular help. Technically, there are no *relaciones* for the region covered by the modern state of Tlaxcala, but since the Puebla-Tlaxcala division is political, not cultural, and the two are culturally the same, it is possible to view them as a unit and use information from the sixteenth-century colonial bishopric of Tlaxcala.[13]

Drawing on all the above sources, I have compiled the following information regarding the Tlaxcalan costume repertory.

TLAXCALAN COSTUME REPERTORY

Draped Garments

MAXTLATL. The Tlaxcalan *maxtlatl* was a long, narrow garment that wrapped around the waist and tied in front. It was the basic garment for men of all classes and hence was general-purpose clothing. Since the garment was sometimes richly decorated, it also served to mark class difference.

As with the Aztecs, the *maxtlatl* was the essential male garment of the Tlaxcalans. It is mentioned frequently in the *Relaciones geográficas* under various spellings: *mastiles* in Tuxtla,[14] a village near Tlacotlalpa, a Nahuatl-speaking village; *maxtles* in Texaluca,[15] a Nahuatl-speaking village near Ahuatlán; *maxtla* in Cosastla (Cuetlaxtlán),[16] a subsidiary of Tlacotlalpa; *mastlatl* in Tepeaca, a Nahuatl-speaking community.[17] Motolinía defined it as a long piece of material that covered the wearers' "shameful parts."[18] The *Relación geográfica* of the Nahuatl-speaking community of Tlacotlalpa mentions that it was two *brazas* in length and tied at the waist.[19]

All the Tlaxcalan *maxtlatl* illustrated in the *Lienzo de Tlaxcala* are the short, both-ends-tied-in-front type like that of the Aztecs. With only a few exceptions[20] it is also the type the native artist shows on the Tlaxcalans' Indian adversaries in the many battle scenes. In the *Tonalamatl Aubin* twenty-four depictions of loincloths are clearly visible. Of these all but two are also the short, tied-in-front

[7] Glass and Robertson 1975, *Lienzo de Tlaxcala*, census no. 350.

[8] Gibson 1967, p. 194.

[9] Glass and Robertson 1975, *Tonalámatl Aubin*, census no. 15.

[10] Nicholson 1967b, pp. 81–82.

[11] Warren 1973, pp. 81–82.

[12] Muñoz Camargo's history was apparently written between 1576 and 1595. The modern scholar who has had fullest access to the original work of Muñoz Camargo is Charles Gibson, who in 1952 published *Tlaxcala in the Sixteenth Century*. I have utilized Gibson's work as well as that of the sixteenth-century writers Díaz del Castillo and Fray Motolinía, discussed in chapter 2. For the

ritual document, *Tonalamatl Aubin*, the pioneer work of the illustrious German scholar Eduard Seler is indispensable.

[13] Cline 1972, p. 211.

[14] Ibid., census no. 134; Paso y Troncoso 1905, 5:6.

[15] Cline 1972, census no. 3; Paso y Troncoso 1905, 5:87.

[16] Cline 1972, census no. 134; Paso y Troncoso 1905, 5:9.

[17] Cline 1972, census no. 110; Paso y Troncoso 1905, 5:28.

[18] Motolinía 1971, p. 339.

[19] Cline 1972, census no. 134; Paso y Troncoso 1905, 5:2.

[20] *Lienzo de Tlaxcala*, Cuezallan, p. 68; Tlaxichco, p. 72.

CHART 5
TLAXCALA COSTUME REPERTORY
Examples of Draped Garments

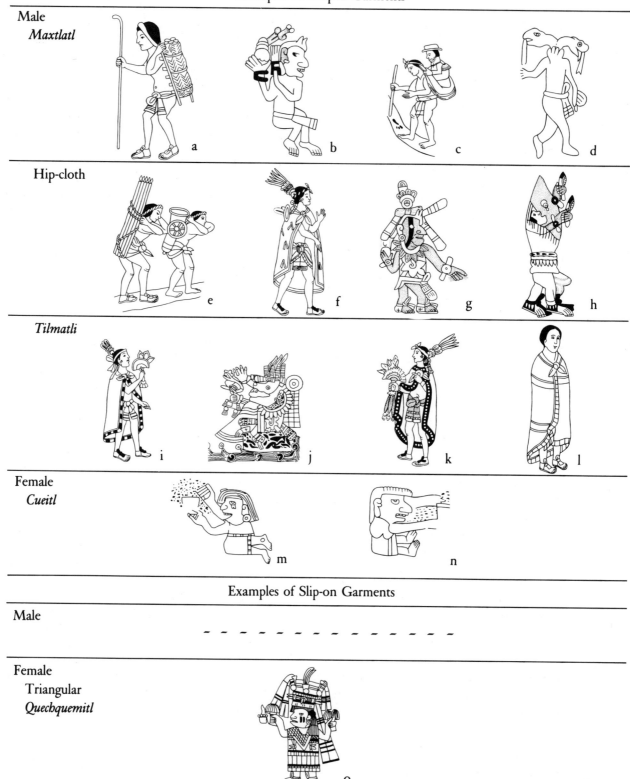

Male
Maxtlatl

a   b   c   d

Hip-cloth

e   f   g   h

Tilmatli

i   j   k   l

Female
Cueitl

m   n

Examples of Slip-on Garments

Male

– – – – – – – – – – – – – – – –

Female
Triangular
Quechquemitl

o

SOURCES: (a) *Lienzo de Tlaxcala, lámina* 10; (b) *Tonalamatl Aubin, lámina* 17; (c) *Lienzo de Tlaxcala, lámina* 30; (d) *Tonalamatl Aubin, lámina* 15; (e) *Lienzo de Tlaxcala, lámina* 30; (f) *Lienzo de Tlaxcala, lámina* 5; (g) *Tonalamatl Aubin, lámina* 3; (h) *Tonalamatl Aubin, lámina* 20; (i) *Lienzo de Tlaxcala,* *lámina* 4; (j) *Tonalamatl Aubin, lámina* 16; (k) *Lienzo de Tlaxcala,* first double folio; (l) *Lienzo de Tlaxcala, lámina* 8; (m) *Tonalamatl Aubin, lámina* 4; (n) *Tonalamatl Aubin, lámina* 8; (o) *Tonalamatl Aubin, lámina* 7.

type.[21] The shorter style must have been the accepted one in the Tlaxcala area.

The first man shown in the *Maxtlatl* section of chart 5 (example *5a*) wears a loincloth that ties in front and is without an end hanging down behind (this differs from the style of the Mixtec, the Borgia Group, and the Maya areas, where the knot of the *maxtlatl* is always seen in the back and the ends hang both in front and in back). The loincloth is white with a simple decoration on the ends. The individual is a *tameme* ("porter"), a native who accompanied the Spaniards on their first entry into Tenochtitlán.

In a discussion of modern Tlaxcala, Nutini mentioned such continuities with the colonial past as the custom of choosing certain positions for state government from three specific pueblos, which are three of the four former principalities of pre-Hispanic Tlaxcala.[22] Among these positions are porters. Díaz del Castillo wrote that the *tameme* porters were able to carry "fifty pounds weight on their back and march five leagues with it."[23]

Example *5b* is from the *Tonalamatl Aubin*, a divinatory calendar of 260 days, which embodied a system combining thirteen numerals with 20 day signs: twenty periods of 13 days each (these periods are referred to as *trecenas*, taking their name from the Spanish word for "thirteenth"). The 260-day ritual calendar played a vital role in Mesoamerican life: the number and sign of each day was associated with a given god; indeed, each day was itself a god and venerated as such. Children were often named with the number and sign of their day of birth.

Each of the twenty sections of the *Tonalamatl* was believed to be under the protection of the deity who was regarded as particularly influential for that time period. Each of the twenty *trecenas* is presented on a separate page with an illustration of the god and his attendants. The ruler of the seventeenth period was Chalchiuhtotolin, "the jeweled cock,"[24] who was regarded as an aspect of Tezcatlipoca. Facing the deity figure is a male attendant wearing only a loincloth. He is performing an act of autosacrifice, piercing his earlobe with a sharpened bone and allowing the blood to flow. With the other hand he is removing the blood, depicted as a flower. The purpose of this self-mortification was the removal of sin.

Another loincloth is worn by a porter from the *Lienzo de Tlaxcala* (example *5c*). Like that of example *a*, his *maxtlatl* is tied in front. The folio from which the figure comes portrays Cortés moving his supplies inland from the coast. Tlaxcalan porters were sent down to carry not only the conquistadors' equipment but also several of the invaders themselves, who weighed much more than the fifty pounds the *tameme* usually carried! In example *5c* a Spaniard is being carried over rough mountain passes on a

EXAMPLE *5a*. Tlaxcala *maxtlatl*. *Lienzo de Tlaxcala*, lámina 10.

EXAMPLE *5b*. Tlaxcala *maxtlatl*. *Tonalamatl Aubin*, lámina 17.

[21] *Tonalámatl Aubin*, pp. 4, 11.
[22] Nutini 1976, p. 24.
[23] Díaz del Castillo 1967, 1:166.
[24] Seler 1900–1901, p. 112.

porter's back. Díaz del Castillo mentions some of the older Tlaxcalan caciques as being transported in litters, in hammocks, or on men's backs.[25]

The final *maxtlatl* example (*5d*) is found in the *Tonalamatl Aubin* from the illustration of the fifteenth *trecena*, presided over by Itzpapalotl, "the obsidian butterfly."[26] The figure, an attendant to the god, wears a loincloth, which, like the three preceding examples, ties in front and has a simple decoration of three lines. From the neck wound of this decapitated male protrude two snake heads, symbolizing two streams of blood. Eduard Seler speculated that this is a sinner who in another context wears a two-headed snake coiled around his neck in the manner of a sacrificial yoke (the carved and curved wooden implement sometimes used to press down the head of the victim cast on the sacrificial stone).[27]

To concentrate attention on the loincloth, I chose for the *maxtlatl* section figures wearing only that garment. Individuals so attired are usually not the most prestigious of the society. It is of interest, then, that in the *tilmatli* section, where the loincloths of two very important individuals are shown, the figures wear the same type of plain *maxtlatl* as the four examples just discussed; hence this garment was not a social indicator.

HIP-CLOTH. The Tlaxcalan hip-cloth, often shown together with the loincloth, was worn over it. Since the hip-cloth is found on porters, lords, and deity figures, it must have been general-purpose clothing. As is repeatedly the case in the Mesoamerican costume repertories, the textual sources make no mention of the hip-cloth; however, frequent depictions make this garment's existence among the Tlaxcalans undeniable.

The first hip-cloth (example *5e*) comes from a folio of the *Lienzo de Tlaxcala* that depicts the moving of Cortés's equipment to the highlands. Two Tlaxcalan porters carry their burdens with the aid of a tumpline (the Mesoamerican carrying device that fits over the forehead to distribute the weight of the load). The porters are carrying a bundle of lances and a small cannon for Cortés. Díaz del Castillo mentioned that after peace had been made between the Spaniards and the Tlaxcalans the Indian leaders were most eager to supply porters to help carry Cortés's military supplies: "...in less than half an hour they provided over five hundred Indian carriers."[28]

Since it is questionable that one man could carry a small cannon, this representation is probably symbolic. Of the fourteen porters shown on this folio, half are wearing the *maxtlatl*, and the other seven are wearing hip-cloths. None of the fourteen figures wear both. This combination of loincloth and hip-cloth does occur in example *5f*, showing a male of high rank. A connection between high status and the wearing of the *maxtlatl* and hip-cloth combination is doubtful, however, because this correlation

EXAMPLE *5c*. Tlaxcala *maxtlatl*. *Lienzo de Tlaxcala, lámina 30.*

EXAMPLE *5d*. Tlaxcala *maxtlatl*. *Tonalamatl Aubin, lámina 15.*

[25] Díaz del Castillo 1967, 1:271.
[26] Seler 1963, 2:212.
[27] Seler 1900–1901, p. 106.
[28] Díaz del Castillo 1967, 1:272.

EXAMPLE 5e. Tlaxcala hip-cloth. *Lienzo de Tlaxcala, lámina 30.*

EXAMPLE 5f. Tlaxcala hip-cloth. *Lienzo de Tlaxcala, lámina 5.*

does not occur in the Aztec costume repertory, which is so similar.

Example 5f shows that the hip-cloth was worn knotted over the *maxtlatl*. The individual, one of the four principal lords of Tlaxcala, is Xicotencatl the elder who received Cortés on his initial entry into the city. The lord's son, also named Xicotencatl, was suspicious of the Spaniards. From the beginning he opposed making peace with them and he favored turning on them after Noche Triste. Fortunately for Cortés, Xicotencatl the younger was overruled by the other Tlaxcalan leaders. In this folio from the *Lienzo de Tlaxcala*, Cortés is shown embracing the elder Xicotencatl, but in the careful manner the conquistador always used: to protect his sword, he grasps the Indian's right hand while keeping his own sword arm free.

Example 5g is from the *Tonalamatl Aubin*. The figure, identified as Quetzalcoatl, stands facing the ruler of the third *trecena*, Tepeyollotli (Heart of the Mountain, God of the Caves) in the guise of a jaguar. With one hand Quetzalcoatl is holding a figure by the hair, presenting a victim to the jaguar.[29] In his other hand he holds the sign for *cuitlatl*, the emblem of human ordure, a symbol of sin. Quetzalcoatl's hair is divided into two locks that project from the crown of his head. Seler speculated that, while this coiffure could depict the style of some particular locality, it might also suggest a symbolic meaning, perhaps the space "between the mountains." The other accouterments of Quetzalcoatl suggest "a god in the rainy zone of the woodlands."[30] This corresponds with H. B. Nicholson's contention that the *Tonalamatl Aubin* may derive from the mountainous frontier area of Tlaxcala.[31]

The final hip-cloth (example 5h) is from the twentieth period of the *Tonalamatl Aubin*. The ruler of this *trecena*, the fire god, is faced by the "Iztapal Totec" version of the fertility deity, Xipe Totec (Our Lord the Flayed One). Xipe is here depicted as a stone, perhaps an allusion to the sacrificial knife used in the flaying ceremony. Seler said of this figure,

> Xipe Totec is draped in the typical way, in the human skin and face-mask of human skin, with the slit for the eye, the wide-open mouth...the face looks out from the open throat of a sacrificial stone knife...which forms a helmet mask [and] is somewhat awkwardly combined with the face of the god.[32]
>
> Xipe holds two sacrificial knives, and wears over the *maxtlatl* a form of hip-cloth that resembles a kilt or tiny skirt.

TILMATLI. The Tlaxcalan *tilmatli* appears to have been almost identical with its Mexica counterpart and, like it, could reflect varying degrees of rank and status. The many parallels between the Tlaxcalan capes and those of the Aztecs of the Valley of Mexico suggest that the Tlax-

[29] Seler 1900–1901, pp. 51–52.
[30] Ibid., p. 49.
[31] Nicholson 1967b, pp. 81–82.
[32] Seler 1900–1901, p. 125.

calans also used the *tilmatli* as the male general-purpose garment. To judge from examples found in the *Tonalamatl Aubin*, in the more provincial parts of the Tlaxcala region the Indians also wore some short capes similar to those seen in the Mixtec and Borgia codices.

The *tilmatli*, or "*tilmas*," are mentioned several times in the *Relaciones geográficas*. The *Relación* from the Nahuatl-speaking community Xonotla, connected with the town Tetela, likens them to the capes of Spain.[33] In another reference, from Nahuatl-speaking Chilapa, these Indian cloaks are also described as extending to the feet.[34]

The first *tilmatli* example (*5i*) is from the *Lienzo de Tlaxcala*. It is worn by one of the four Tlaxcalan leaders whose cloak has the Tlaxcalan red-and-white border. The cape is knotted in front. Although the *Relaciones geográficas* describe the garment as tying on the shoulder, no reference is made to the right shoulder, as was the case in the Aztec sources.

The folio of the *Lienzo* from which this example comes depicts the entry of Cortés into one of the four Tlaxcalan *cabeceras*. Díaz del Castillo mentioned that, after peace was declared, the Tlaxcalan Xicotencatl arrived at the Spanish camp "with many other caciques and captains, all clothed in white and red cloaks; half of the cloaks were white, the other half red, for this was the device and livery of Xicotenga."[35] The implication is that each *cabecera*, which no doubt was composed of a related lineage or *calpulli*, had its own distinctive dress. It must have seemed to the Spaniards almost like European heraldry.

Example *5j*, from the *Tonalamatl Aubin*, is worn by Xolotl, the ruler of the sixteenth period of the Tonalamatl; he is shown as a dog-headed deity. Seler equated Xolotl with the ball game.[36] Since this game was played in pairs, Xolotl was also the god of pairs and twins. In Mesoamerica twins were considered a monstrosity; Seler speculated that Xolotl was also the god of monstrosities. This deity was often depicted as a dog, and the native hairless dog was called *xoloitzcuintli*. In example *j*, Xolotl is depicted as the god of the ball game, but at the same time he also has many of the clothing attributes of Quetzalcoatl (in addition to meaning "snake," *coatl* also means "comrade and twin"). These include his collar of seashells, his breastplate sliced from a large seashell, and his ear pendant, cut longitudinally from a seashell.

Xolotl holds a bag of copal incense in his hand and wears a short cape tied around his throat, which Seler identifies as the *quemitl*.[37] This short cape, tied under the chin like a bib, also appears in ritual manuscripts from several of the other five groups discussed in this book. Although the garment is not as long as the *tilmatli*, it is nevertheless a cape and hence is included in this section.

The third *tilmatli* example (*5k*) is from the large initial

EXAMPLE *5g*. Tlaxcala hip-cloth. *Tonalamatl Aubin, lámina 3*.

EXAMPLE *5h*. Tlaxcala hip-cloth. *Tonalamatl Aubin, lámina 20*.

[33] Cline 1972, census no. 118; Paso y Troncoso 1905, 5:128–29.
[34] Cline 1972, census no. 22; Paso y Troncoso 1905, 5:179.
[35] Díaz del Castillo 1967, 1:265.
[36] Seler 1900–1901, pp. 109–10.
[37] Ibid., p. 112.

EXAMPLE 5*i*. Tlaxcala *tilmatli*. *Lienzo de Tlaxcala, lámina* 4.

EXAMPLE 5*k*. Tlaxcala *tilmatli*. *Lienzo de Tlaxcala*, first double folio.

EXAMPLE 5*j*. Tlaxcala *tilmatli*. *Tonalamatl Aubin, lámina* 16.

scene of the *Lienzo de Tlaxcala* showing the Spaniards meeting with twenty-four Tlaxcalan dignitaries (fig. 28). The Indians, all wearing the red-and-white headband of Tlaxcala, are divided into four groups, each with its leader standing in front. The dignitary shown in example *k*, like the other three rulers, wears more complex headgear than that of his followers. He is clad in a white *tilmatli* with red border and white dots; his *maxtlatl* is similarly decorated. As was also the custom for Aztec dignitaries on ceremonial occasions, all twenty-four nobles are carrying flower bouquets. Díaz del Castillo mentioned flower "cones made of sweet scented native roses of various colors," given by the Indians to Cortés and other soldiers they thought were captains, especially to the horsemen.[38]

An interesting variety of design motifs and border decorations is reflected in the twenty-four capes. To judge from what is known of the Aztec sumptuary laws, the designs could reflect the various warrior grades attained by the nobles, since the Tlaxcalans had a similar society. On the other hand, it may reflect lineage identity.

The final cape (example 5*l*) also comes from the *Lienzo de Tlaxcala* and is worn by one of the Tlaxcalan lords awaiting baptism to be administered by Díaz, the priest who accompanied Cortés. This depiction illustrates the width of the mantle and the manner in which it could

[38] Díaz del Castillo 1967, 1:275.

69

FIGURE 28. The twenty-eight lords of Tlaxcala. *Lienzo de Tlaxcala*, first folio.

envelop the body to offer protection against the elements. According to Díaz del Castillo, all of this clothing was made of henequen, the maguey-plant fiber, "for there was no cotton to be obtained, [but the cloaks] were very fine and beautifully embroidered and painted."[39] Moctezuma's ambassadors commented contemptuously that there was not a decent cotton cloak in all of Tlaxcala.[40] The historian Charles Gibson, however, drawing on a number of primary Tlaxcalan documents, argued that there may have been exceptions to this general poverty:

> [The chief lords] were accustomed to a degree of personal luxury that was denied to commoners. Thus even in the periods of hardship and want occasioned by the Tlaxcalan-Aztec wars, it was possible for nobles to connive with the enemy and to receive cloth, cacao, salt, gold, and other products.[41]

CUEITL. As in all other parts of Mesoamerica, the wraparound skirt was worn in the Tlaxcala area. Like the Aztec *cueitl*, it displayed varying degrees of decoration, especially at the hem, and was undoubtedly the basic lower-body garment for women.

The skirt—*nabuas* or *naguas*—is mentioned frequently in the Tlaxcalan *Relaciones geográficas* (for example, in the Nahuatl-speaking communities of Tepeaca).[42] Unfortunately, little more descriptive information is given than the following from Coyatitlanapa pueblo, a subsidiary of

EXAMPLE 5*l*. Tlaxcala *tilmatli*. Lienzo de Tlaxcala, *lámina* 8.

[39] Ibid., p. 274.
[40] Ibid., p. 270.
[41] Gibson 1967, p. 12.
[42] Cline 1972, census no. 110; Paso y Troncoso 1905, 5:28.

EXAMPLE 5*m*. Tlaxcala *cueitl. Tonalamatl Aubin, 1981,* 4.

EXAMPLE 5*n*. Tlaxcala *cueitl. Tonalamatl Aubin, 1981,* 8.

Nahuatl-speaking Ahuatlán: "From the waist down [the women wore] a *manta* in the style of a skirt."[43]

Only two examples (5*m* and 5*n*) of the wraparound skirt as the sole lower-body garment are to be found from the Tlaxcalan area. Both come from the *Tonalamatl Aubin.* The first (*m*) is from the fourth *trecena,* presided over by Huehuecoyotl, (Old Coyote God of the Dance).[44] Eduard Seler associated this deity with the Otomí territory,[45] a connection mentioned earlier in regard to the provenience of the *Tonalamatl Aubin* manuscript. The deity of example 5*m* is identified as the goddess Ixnextli[46] (discussed in the Aztec *quechquemitl* section of chart 3), shown topless and weeping from eyes blinded by ashes. She is kneeling and strewing ashes from a bowl. Although the details of Ixnextli's skirt are faint, it is patterned with a series of small squares with dots in the center.

The other skirt (example 5*n*) is from the eighth *Tonalmatl* period, presided over by Mayahuel, the goddess of the maguey plant, from whose juice the intoxicating liquor pulque is distilled. Example 5*n* is the female half of a pair of pulque drinkers. Seler referred to pulque as the drink of the warriors,[47] but in this scene the female is also imbibing. She is topless, and her skirt has a border of contrasting color.

Slip-on Garments

QUECHQUEMITL. The *quechquemitl* apparently existed in the Tlaxcala area and, as among the Aztecs, was restricted to ritual use. Although the *Lienzo de Tlaxcala*—a document concerned with secular, historical matters—contains no depiction of the garment, what is probably the *quechquemitl* appears in the ritual *Tonalamatl Aubin: lámina 7* (example 5*o*). Seler identified this figure as Chicomecoatl,[48] who along with the rain god Tlaloc was patron of the twenty-day period. The corn goddess is wearing the same enormous square headdress decked with rosettes at the four corners that is illustrated in the Aztec costume repertory (see plate 3 and chart 3, example *c*). Both Chicomecoatl depictions show the goddess's distinctive emblem, the double ears of corn.

Although iconographically Chicomecoatl is repeatedly identified with the *quechquemitl* in both the codices and sculpture, Seler noted that this garment is the "*axochiauipilli*" ("rosy-water *huipilli*").[49] Despite Seler's identification, I accept the garment as a *quechquemitl* in accord both with its appearance and with the well-established association between the costume and the fertility and maize goddess Chicomecoatl.

[43] Cline 1972, census no. 3; Paso y Troncoso 1905, 5:91.
[44] Seler 1963, 2:183.
[45] Seler 1900–1901, p. 53.
[46] Ibid., pp. 54–55.
[47] Ibid., p. 69.
[48] Seler 1900–1901, *lámina* 7.
[49] Molina 1970, fol. 160r.

EXAMPLE 50. Tlaxcala *quechquemitl. Tonalamatl Aubin, lámina* 7.

Open-sewn Garments

Chart 6 contains no examples of open-sewn garments, but it is known from Motolinía that the Tlaxcalans wore the *xicolli*. In his discussion of the great Teoxihuil ceremony as celebrated by the Tlaxcalans, he noted that many capes, *xicoles*, and *tecuxiculli* were given as offerings. He described the *xicolli* as a vestment similar to a mantle or cape. He defined the *tecuxiculli* ("lord's jacket") as "a cloak or long gown, such as [are used] by [the Spaniards] in mourning, open in the front and very elegantly worked with trimming which felt like silk, made of cotton and spun rabbits' fur."[50]

Closed-sewn Garments

CLOSED-SEWN ICHCAHUIPILLI. The Tlaxcalan *ichcahuipilli* was a closed-sewn, padded armor that was made in two styles: a garment with a wide-scalloped hem below which the loincloth usually did not show and an even-hemmed garment below which the *maxtlatl* did show. The costume was utilized by warriors and was special-purpose clothing.

The Tlaxcalan *Relaciones geográficas* contain several references to cotton armor: ". . . the defense of their person was a sewn corset of cotton," from the Nahuatl-speaking community Coatzinco, a subsidiary of Ahua-

tlán;[51] and ". . . the habit and dress that they wore was to go nude, except the captains and *caciques*, who wore armor made of mantas and cotton 'stitched,'" from the Nahuatl-speaking town Chilpa.[52]

The question arises: Where did the Tlaxcalans obtain this cotton if the Aztecs' economic embargo was so effective? There are two possibilities. The first has already been mentioned: the upper classes were able to barter for luxury goods, and cotton would have been among them. Whether or not this scarce commodity would have been made up into cotton armor is questionable. Alternatively, henequen could have been used for that utilitarian purpose, saving the scarce and valuable cotton for more prestigious, status-linked garments.

A likely source of supply not only for cotton armor but even more for the prestigious feathered martial apparel would have been the battlefield. From eyewitness accounts of conquistadors, we know that the Tlaxcalans went into combat magnificently arrayed.[53] Díaz del Castillo reported the panoply of the Tlaxcalan troops: ". . . fields crowded with warriors with great feathered crests and distinguishing devices"[54] If the Tlaxcalans were cut off from a steady supply of the multicolored feathers and gems necessary to construct the warrior suits and magnificent standards, they certainly had a ready stock of such martial apparel from their war captives. A small section of one of the folios from *Códice Xolotl* (fig. 29) indicates that the battlefield may have been a source of supply. A complete set of warrior attire is laid out on the ground at the side of an authoritative-looking individual, who seems to be lecturing a companion at his feet, perhaps indicating the martial axiom, "To the victor go the spoils." Whatever the source, the Tlaxcalans went into battle wearing costumes resembling those of their arch foes, the Aztecs.

All the figures in the closed-sewn *ichcahuipilli* section of chart 6 are from the *Lienzo de Tlaxcala*. Example *6a* illustrates the quilting of the garment, which creates a diamond-like pattern, and the *maxtlatl*, which is visible hanging beneath the even-hemmed costume. The warrior, like examples *b*, *c*, and *d*, carries what Díaz del Castillo called a "two-handed sword . . . made with stones which cut worse than knives so cleverly arranged that one can neither break nor pull out the blades . . . they are as long as broadswords."[55] The Tlaxcalan warrior is from a section of the *Lienzo* dealing with Córtes's attack on Narváez, the Spaniard sent by the governor of Cuba to usurp the conquistador's authority.

Example *6b* is from a folio that relates the Spaniards' disastrous flight from Tenochtitlán on Noche Triste. The warrior is one of the four Tlaxcalans marching close beside the mounted Cortés. The warrior's costume appears to have an uneven hem, and his *maxtlatl* does not

[50] Motolinía 1971, pp. 78–79.
[51] Cline 1972, census no. 3; Paso y Troncoso 1905, 5:96.
[52] Cline 1972, census no. 22; Paso y Troncoso 1905, 5:178.

[53] E.g., Cortés 1971, p. 58.
[54] Díaz del Castillo 1967, 1:237.
[55] Ibid., p. 229.

CHART 6
TLAXCALA COSTUME REPERTORY
Examples of Open-sewn Garments

| Male | – – – – – – – – – – – – – – – – – |
| Female | – – – – – – – – – – – – – – – – – |

Examples of Closed-sewn Garments

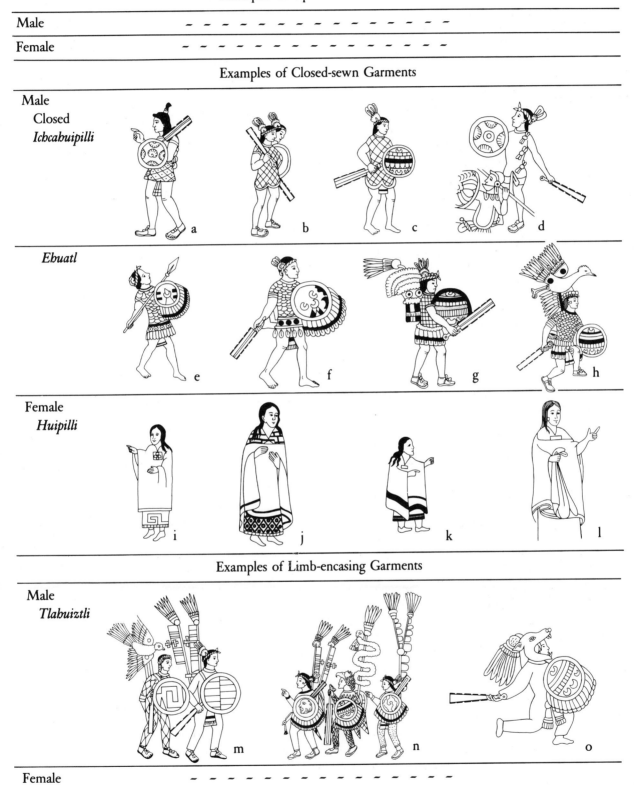

Male
Closed
Ichcahuipilli

a   b   c   d

Ehuatl

e   f   g   h

Female
Huipilli

i   j   k   l

Examples of Limb-encasing Garments

Male
Tlahuiztli

m   n   o

| Female | – – – – – – – – – – – – – – – |

SOURCES: (*a*) All from *Lienzo de Tlaxcala*: lámina 13; (*b*) lámina 18; (*c*) lámina 18; (*d*) lámina 9; (*e*) lámina 21; (*f*) lámina 35; (*g*) lámina 37; (*h*) lámina 52; (*i*) lámina 9; (*j*) lámina 19; (*k*) Antón 1965; (*l*) lámina 7; (*m*) lámina 43; (*n*) lámina 48; (*o*) lámina 34.

FIGURE 29. Scene perhaps depicting a vanquished warrior's battle attire being presented to the victor. *Códice Xolotl, planche* 7.

EXAMPLE 6*a*. Tlaxcala closed *icbcabuipilli. Lienzo de Tlaxcala, lámina* 13.

EXAMPLE 6*b*. Tlaxcala closed *icbcabuipilli. Lienzo de Tlaxcala, lámina* 18.

Tolteca acalotlí
ypan ōcāmicovac.

EXAMPLE 6c. Tlaxcala closed *ichcahuipilli. Lienzo de Tlaxcala,*
lámina 18.

EXAMPLE 6d. Tlaxcala closed *ichcahuipilli. Lienzo de Tlaxcala,*
lámina 9.

show below. On the same folio, however, another Tlaxcalan wears a similar garment (example 6c) that does show
the end of the loincloth extending below the armor.

These first three examples of the cotton armor seem to
be tuniclike garments that pulled on over the head; it appears that there was still another style. It is mentioned in a
written reference to cotton armor in a *Relación geográfica*
from Tuxtla, a village near Tlacotlalpa, in the Tlaxcala
region: "...and for their defensive arms they wore some
'*ychcagueipilis*,' which are a kind of leather jacket buttoned
from behind."[56] This raises the question of the construction of the garment. The armor probably had an opening
that extended partway down the back and fastened with
ties, creating a closed-sewn garment.

The *Lienzo de Tlaxcala* illustrates such a garment, the
ichcahuipilli (example 6d), which shows three ties on the
front left side. This costume is included though it does
not resemble the other cotton-armor examples, lacking
both their diagnostic quilting and slightly flared line.
Since the garment is shown on a Tlaxcalan warrior, however, it is obviously another variant of battle apparel. The
dangling piece of cloth at the crotch may indicate a loincloth, which is almost always shown on the full-length
warrior costumes. The warrior is shown fighting alongside the Spaniards in the battle at Cholula.

EHUATL. The Tlaxcalans, like the Mexicas of Tenochtitlán, wore the *ehuatl* into battle. It was the same closed-
sewn short tunic made of feather-covered cloth with a
short skirt of feathers. Since it was a martial garment, it
was special-purpose clothing.

Although the *ehautl* is not mentioned in the Tlaxcalan
Relaciones geográficas there can be no doubt that the garment existed in the Tlaxcalan repertory. The four *ehuatl*
examples of chart 6 (*e, f, g,* and *h*) are exact depictions of
the Aztecs' short, feathered tunic with its diagnostic
feather skirt. They are so similar that they could have
been procured on the battlefield.

The first example (6e) comes from one of the folios of
the *Lienzo de Tlaxcala* devoted to the exodus from
Tenochtitlán after Noche Triste. The figure shown is the
guide who led Cortés and his men back to the haven of
Tlaxcala. Since this costume so resembles the Mexica
model, it can be assumed that padded armor was worn
beneath it, as was the *maxtlatl*. The warrior carries a
javelin, "barbed and fire-hardened, which could pierce
any armor and could reach the vitals where there is no
protection."[57]

The second *ehuatl* (example 6f) is from a folio showing
the Tlaxcalans aiding the Spaniards in the conquest of
Tecamachalco. The feathered skirt is sparse but nonetheless distinguishable as the *ehuatl* hallmark.

The third example (6g), also from the *Lienzo de Tlaxcala,* illustrates a further variant of the *ehuatl's* diagnostic
skirt. The warrior wears on his back what appears to be

[56] Cline 1972, census no. 134; Paso y Troncoso 1905, 5:6.
[57] Díaz del Castillo 1967, 1:238.

the device of the pulque god: "...a frame shaped like a pot is covered with feather mosaic and prince's feathers and heron feathers stuck in."[58]

Another *ehuatl*-clad warrior (example 6*b*) is wearing a back device in the shape of a bird. Each of the *cabeceras* of Tlaxcala had a specific device. Díaz del Castillo mentions a "white bird with the appearance of an ostrich, with wings outstretched, as though it wished to fly, and each company had its own device and uniform, for each *cacique* had a different one, as do our dukes and counts in our own Castille."[59] Díaz del Castillo's white bird was probably a heron, the device of the young Xicotencatl, the leader of the Tizatla (Place of the White Earth) *cabacera* of Tlaxcala. The bird on the device is yellow rather than white and is not a heron. The yellow bird may represent another of the three Tlaxcalan *cabeceras*.

HUIPILLI. The Tlaxcalan *huipilli* was a closed-sewn, sleeveless tunic of unusual width and length, extending to the ankles. It was the basic woman's upper-body garment. As can be seen from examples *i, j, k,* and *l,* the Tlaxcalan variant was an extremely full garment and somewhat longer than its Aztec counterpart.

The *huipilli* is mentioned repeatedly in the Tlaxcala area *Relaciones geográficas* from the Nahuatl-speaking communities of Tepeaca[60] (*huipiles*) and Coyatitlanapa, a village near Ahuatlán[61] (*huypil*), but never with a detailed description.

Example 6*i*, from the *Lienzo de Tlaxcala*, is Marina, Cortés's interpreter, adviser, and mistress, giving advice and aid to Cortés during the battle at Cholula. In the *Lienzo de Tlaxcala* her *huipil* is striped with pale–orange lines against a white ground, creating a plaid effect. Her skirt is white. The extension of her arm reveals the fullness of the garment.

Although Marina spoke Nahuatl, she was not from central Mexico. She was probably born in the Isthmus of Tehuantepec area and was sold into slavery by her mother, who supposedly wanted the daughter's inheritance for a younger son by a new husband. Marina was among the women given to Cortés by the ruler of a community at the mouth of the Río de Grijalva at the time the conquistador was sailing north toward the Veracruz landing.[62]

Example 6*j*, also from the *Lienzo*, is either Marina or Doña Luisa of Tlaxcala (Chavero's text is ambiguous). The very full *huipilli* is tan with a pink-and-white-decorated shoulder area. The richly decorated skirt is in a pink-and-white design. Doña Luisa was the daughter of Xicotencatl and was given in marriage to Pedro de Alvarado, Cortés's fiery lieutenant.

EXAMPLE 6*e*. Tlaxcala *ehuatl. Lienzo de Tlaxcala, lámina* 21.

EXAMPLE 6*f*. Tlaxcala *ehuatl. Lienzo de Tlaxcala, lámina* 35.

[58] Seler 1960, 2:575.
[59] Díaz del Castillo 1967, 1:236.
[60] Cline 1972, census no. 110; Paso y Troncoso 1905, 5:28.
[61] Cline 1972, census no. 3; Paso y Troncoso 1905, 5:91.
[62] Wagner 1969, pp. 68–79.

EXAMPLE 6g. Tlaxcala *ehuatl. Lienzo de Tlaxcala, lámina* 37.

EXAMPLE 6i. Tlaxcala *huipilli. Lienzo de Tlaxcala, lámina* 9.

EXAMPLE 6b. Tlaxcala *ehuatl. Lienzo de Tlaxcala, lámina* 52.

EXAMPLE 6j. Tlaxcala *huipilli. Lienzo de Tlaxcala, lámina* 19.

77

EXAMPLE 6k. Tlaxcala *huipilli. Lienzo de Tlaxcala*, Antón 1965.

EXAMPLE 6l. Tlaxcala *huipilli. Lienzo de Tlaxcala, lámina 7.*

The third *huipilli* (example 6k) is from another pictorial related to the *Lienzo de Tlaxcala* that contains only four scenes, all done on native paper.[63] Like 6j, it demonstrates the fullness of the garment, as does example 6l, from the scene in which the Tlaxcalans present to Cortés and his companions jewels, fine clothing, and many beautiful young women (plate 6). This maiden wears a "plaid" *huipilli* with orange lines on a light-orange ground; her skirt is a diamond pattern. It is not clear what sort of cloth she holds in her hand.

Limb-encasing Garments

TLAHUIZTLI. The range of Tlaxcalan warrior costumes may have included some jaguar and eagle suits, but most of their limb-encasing martial garments appear to have been of a more generalized nature. Some of these costumes appear to have been made of feather-covered material, and all are similar in design. As with the Aztecs, most of the rank and status differentiation appears to have been conveyed through back devices and shield emblems. Warrior costumes were, of course, special-purpose garments.

There is no mention of the fitted warrior costumes in the Tlaxcalan *Relaciones geográficas*, although Motolinía reported that experienced and honored Tlaxcalan warriors were known as "eagles, lions, jaguars."[64] In the *Lienzo de Tlaxcala* the eagle and jaguar costumes appear far more frequently on Aztecs than they do on Tlaxcalans. The latter are shown wearing limb-encasing warrior costumes, but they are not made in the semblance of a bird or animal. As compared with the Mexica *tlahuiztli*, the less elaborate fitted warrior costumes of the Tlaxcalans may reflect their poorer economic condition.

The lack of elaborate warrior costumes is an intriguing puzzle. If the Tlaxcalans were obtaining some of their flamboyant military apparel from the battlefield, why are no Azteclike jaguar or coyote costumes shown? The Tlaxcalan back devices are very ornate. What was the source of the valuable feathers? Perhaps the gleanings of the battlefield were reworked into the more critical back devices. Some of the Tlaxcalan warrior suits could have been made of henequen.

The first *tlahuiztli* example (6m) is from a folio of the *Lienzo de Tlaxcala* that tells about the bringing of the brigantines, which Cortés constructed in Tlaxcala, to Tenochtitlán for the final siege of the city. The two Tlaxcalan warriors wear limb-encasing martial apparel, but it is not as detailed as that of the Aztecs. The back device of the left-hand figure is similar to one accompanying the Azteclike *ehuatl*, example *b* (see plate 7). The companion warrior wears the banner of the fertility god, Xipe Totec (Our Lord the Flayed One). The latter device is made of red spoonbill feathers.

The second warrior group (example 6n) comes from a

[63] Anton 1965.

EXAMPLE 6*m*. Tlaxcala *tlahuiztli*. *Lienzo de Tlaxcala, lámina* 43.

EXAMPLE 6*n*. Tlaxcala *tlahuiztli*. *Lienzo de Tlaxcala, lámina* 48.

folio depicting the surrender of the Aztec emperor Cuauhtemoc and other Mexica lords after the final siege and fall of Tenochtitlán. Despite the appearance of the red-and-white Tlaxcalan headband on the first and third figures, they may be Mexica nobles. There is reason to believe that the artist or artists of the *Lienzo de Tlaxcala* used the device of the royal headband to denote aristocracy, both Tlaxcalan and Mexican.[65] It is therefore possible that all three of the figures in *n* are Mexica lords, a contention further supported by the accouterments of the middle warrior. The text does not comment on his distinctive back device, a standard seen in the Aztec tribute roll that appears in the cognate manuscripts *Matrícula de tributos* and *Codex Mendoza*.[66] The device was called the "yellow-twisted-to-and-fro." It was made of yellow parrot feathers with red feathers at the top and was sent to Tenochtitlán as tribute from the Mixteca area. Seler suggested that it represents the wavy contour by which the wrinkled skin of a flayed sacrificial victim was indicated,[67] particularly on certain depictions of the god Xipe Totec (fig. 30) and the goddess Tlazolteotl (fig. 31). The warrior on the left in example *n* wears the same back device as that of the left-hand warrior of example *m*, that of Xipe Totec.

The final warrior costume (example 6*o*) shows a Tlax-

[64] Motolinía 1971, p. 339.
[65] Nicholson 1967*b*.
[66] *Codex Mendoza*, vol. 3, fol. 43r.
[67] Seler 1960, 2:587.

EXAMPLE 6*o*. Tlaxcala *tlahuiztli*. *Lienzo de Tlaxcala, lámina* 34.

calan wearing one of the few completely encasing "animal" *tlahuiztli*. The folio relates the exploits of the Tlaxcalans against the community of Tepeyacac. As with all the other body-encasing warrior costumes of the *Lienzo de Tlaxcala*, the knot of the loincloth is shown in place over the crotch. The Aztec *tlahuiztli* are also shown with the *maxtlatl* knot; hence it is possible that these garments were constructed with a fly front, which would account for the presence of the *maxtlatl* knot in the unmodeled Aztec tribute-list warrior costumes. Since the knot is always shown on these garments, it could be considered a symbolic, stylized element. Even if this is true, the consistency of appearance of the *maxtlatl* knot indicates that it was actually used. Inasmuch as the loincloth was the basic, indispensable male garment, it had a masculine and hence virile association.

SUMMARY

Although the Tlaxcalan costume repertory lacked the open-sewn *ichcahuipilli*, the other clothing types represented are identical to those of the Aztecs. In both groups the same styles of the four basic Mesoamerican draped garments appear: loincloth, hip-cloth, cape, and wraparound skirt. The same simply constructed clothing of the slip-on, closed-sewn, and limb-encasing categories is also duplicated. The only principle of garment construction not pictorially represented is the open-sewn category, but this probably reflects lack of data. Like the Aztecs, the Tlaxcalans wore the open-sewn *xicolli* in ritual contexts, as Motolinía made clear.[68] Although some of the Tlaxcalan clothing may have been made of less extravagant materials than that of the Aztecs, it was identical in its manifestation of the five principles of garment construction. A correlation no doubt also existed between the extent of costume elaboration and the degree of ceremonial complexity.

The close similarity between the two costume repertories is not surprising, considering that the Aztecs and the Tlaxcalans were almost identical culturally and linguistically. If more Tlaxcalan pictorial data were available, the resemblance of clothing types would no doubt be heightened. Such is definitely not the case, however, with the Aztecs' neighbors on the west, the Tarascans.

[68] Motolinía 1971, pp. 78–79.

FIGURE 30. The Aztec god Xipe Totec wearing the flayed skin of a sacrificial victim. *Codex Borbonicus*, p. 14.

FIGURE 31. The Aztec goddess Tlazolteotl wearing the flayed
skin of a sacrificial victim. *Codex Borbonicus*, p. 13.

FIGURE 32. The Michoacán market where the founder of the
Tarascan state, Tariacuri, found his lost mother and nephews.
Relación de Michoacán, lámina 12.

CHAPTER FOUR

The Tarascans of Michoacán

DIRECTLY WEST OF THE VALLEY of Mexico was the Tarascan kingdom, a politically independent realm whose capital, Tzintzuntzan, was situated at Lake Patzcuaro, near the western edge of the central plateau. At the time of Spanish contact, Tarascans controlled most of present-day Michoacán and an adjacent area that extended from the southern side of Lake Chapala in present-day Jalisco to south of the Balsas River and from slightly west of the Tepalcatepec River into part of Guanajuato.[1]

The name Tarascan was probably given the Indians of Michoacán by the Spaniards as a result of a misunderstanding. The word in question was *tarascue* ("son-in-law"), which reflected the conquerors' propensity for taking over the Indian girls. The Spaniards misunderstood the term and thought the Indians were Tarascues; thus the name Tarascan came into use.[2]

The Indians referred to themselves as Purépechas, a non-Nahuatl term.[3] By the time of the Conquest, Tarascan culture had undergone strong acculturation from the invading Chichimecas. According to the primary source on native history, *Relación de Michoacán*, the entire leadership of the ancient peoples of the lakes was Chichimecan.[4] The origin of the Purépecha Tarascans remains an enigma. According to one interpretation they emerged from the "seven caves of the west" with their contemporaries the Aztecs.[5] Most anthropologists, however, generally discount this idea of a common origin with the Nahuas because of the language differences. Not only is Nahuatl distinct from Tarascan but it has been suggested that there is some remote link between Tarascan and Quechua, one of the Peruvian Indian languages.[6] Some Tarascan religious concepts, together with certain social and political institutions, appear to be unique in Mesoamerica.

Contact-period Tarascan culture is perhaps best described as eclectic. Some of the archaeological material could be interpreted as having an intriguing flavor of the west coast of South America because of the presence of stirrup-handled ceramic containers and excellent, advanced metallurgy.[7] Tarascan mastery of such metalwork processes as cold-hammering, casting in the lost-wax process, soldering, and gold plating allowed the Michoacán craftsmen to produce magnificent copper masks, as well as copper awls, bracelets, and needles; copper bells in the shape of turtles; and such virtuoso pieces as fish with gold bodies and silver fins. Members of the Tarascan aristocracy were easily identified by the beautifully carved obsidian earplugs and delicate lip plugs of laminated gold and turquoise. Tarascan craftsmen also produced excellent ceramics, rock-crystal beads for necklaces, anthropomorphic and spiraled clay pipes, spiraled spindle whorls, silver tweezers, gold rings, and brightly colored featherwork.[8] The Tarascans produced highly desirable luxury goods; little wonder the Aztecs on the east viewed them covetously.

At the time of the Spanish conquest the Tarascans' culture was flourishing. They had created what might be termed a "rural empire" that included areas of the adjoin-

[1] Beals 1969, p. 725.
[2] Craine and Reindrop 1970, p. 237.
[3] Corona Nuñez 1958, 1:49.
[4] Glass and Robertson 1975, *Relación de Michoacán*, census no. 213.
[5] Durán 1967, 2:30.
[6] Swadash 1967, pp. 92–93.
[7] Chadwick 1971.
[8] Ibid., pp. 690–91.

ing *tierra caliente*. From these "hot lands" came copper, gold, honey, wax, cinnabar, cacao, cotton, feathers, hides, and skins. Most of the Tarascans, however, lived in or near the mountainous region of coniferous forests of pine and fir trees. The role of these forests in Tarascan religious life is apparent in the colonial document *Relación de Michoacán*. There is a constant preoccupation by pious individuals with gathering wood for the temples and building huge fires on lofty mountain tops to honor their god, the fire deity Curicaveri.

The Aztecs held the Michoacán area in high regard. Sahagún's informants described it as "an esteemed place—salubrious, a place to grow old in, a cool place, in some places warm. The people of Michoacán are prudent, able; they are weavers of designs."[9] The wealthy—and unconquered—Tarascan state just two hundred miles west of Tenochtitlán was a source of frustration for the Aztecs, who regularly tried to expand into the area. As a result the Tarascans, like the Tlaxcalans, spent a great deal of their energy maintaining strong military outposts to hold off their avaricious neighbors, the members of the Triple Alliance. It was only through the prowess of the Michoacán warriors who defeated the Aztec emperor Axayacatl in the prolonged and bloody war of 1469–78 that the Tarascans retained political and cultural independence in the face of the expanding Aztec Empire.

Although the Tarascans had a rich, desirable kingdom, their culture was not as complex as the Aztecs'. There is no evidence of truly urban centers in Michoacán. Unquestionably, however, they had a stratified society, with craft specialization and well-developed commercial interests, particularly with the western coastal lands.

The real founder of the Tarascan nation was Tariacuri, who reigned in the first half of the fifteenth century. His mother was the daughter of a local fisherman, and his father was a Tarascan Chichimec noble. Tariacuri was aided in the forging of the state by his son Hiquingare and his two nephews, Hiripan and Tangaxoan I. The final Tarascan ruler was the weak Tangaxoan II, who was reigning when the Spaniards arrived. Bewildered by omens and myths about the coming of "new" men and distracted by a plague that had swept through his kingdom, the Indian ruler failed to send his powerful armies against the Spaniards who arrived, led by Cristóbal de Olid, in 1522. Tangaxoan II finally surrendered himself and his kingdom in 1530 at the Spanish camp on Río Lerma, north of Puruandiro. He was strangled, and his body was tied to a stake and burned.[10] The native Tarascan state collapsed and was never rebuilt.

Despite this act of cruelty, the conquest of the Tarascan region was relatively peaceful compared with that of many other areas of Mesoamerica. That may explain why no proud colonial Tarascan wrote with nationalistic fervor of the extent and composition of the former Tarascan state, an unfortunate circumstance since the Michoacán area also lacks pre-Conquest codices and historical records.

The primary source for pre-Conquest cultural history, the *Relación de Michoacán*, was recorded by a Spanish missionary, probably the Franciscan Fray Jerónimo de Alcalá, in the Tarascan capital of Tzintzuntzan between 1539 and 1541. Although the document was produced about twenty years after the Spaniards arrived in the New World, it nevertheless appears to present a valid picture of indigenous Tarascan life. The author obtained his material from Indian informants and endeavored to present it in their idiom as much as possible, which makes certain sections somewhat difficult to follow. The Spanish priest admitted to finding "among these people . . . no virtue other than generosity" and "hardly a single moral virtue, . . . rather recriminations, idolatries, drunkenness, death and war."[11] These themes run throughout the *Relación de Michoacán*.

The manuscript is illustrated with forty-four colored drawings depicting the history of the Tarascan people. Since these scenes show the Indians in both secular and religious contexts, they are helpful in understanding the costume repertory because many of the same garments are shown worn in a number of different situations. It is therefore possible to make repeated comparisons of the illustrations to understand some confusing garments. For example, it can be determined that the strange Tarascan woman's neck garment was a tiny *quechquemitl* worn on the shoulder and that the Tarascan man's garment, the *cicuilli*, which appears to be full length when seen on a seated figure, actually reached only to the knees.

The text and accompanying drawings of the *Relación de Michoacán* contain a great deal of historical, ethnographic, and genealogical information. Unfortunately, this lone manuscript constitutes the entire pictorial evidence of the pre-Hispanic Tarascan clothing repertory. This information is supplemented by whatever relevant clothing references exist in the Michoacán region *Relaciones geográficas*. Nevertheless, there is still not sufficient variety in garment depiction to make possible a detailed costume inventory such as that of the other Mesoamerican Indian groups. Instead, only a summary chart of the Tarascan clothing can be offered. To present as full a picture as possible of Tarascan culture, I will discuss in some detail the contexts in which these figures are found.

As is true for many other aspects of Tarascan culture, several facets of the clothing repertory of these particular Indians are unique in Mesoamerica. The most notable difference, about which their enemies never tired of commenting, was that the Tarascan men did not wear the loincloth. As though this were not aberrant enough, the men of Michoacán often dressed in a full, tuniclike garment called a *cicuilli* ("a woman's *huipilli*," scoffed the

---

[9] Sahagún 1950–69, bk. 11, p. 256.
[10] Scholes and Adams 1952.

[11] *Relación de Michoacán* 1956, p. 4.

Aztecs). Others are depicted wearing a tightly wrapped garment that covered the hips but revealed the buttocks.

Durán, relating the migration of the Aztecs from their mythical homeland of the seven caves, explained why the Tarascan men did not wear the loincloth. According to the friar, when the migrating band reached the peaceful, pleasant Lake Pátzcuaro, they implored their god to allow at least a part of the group to remain there. Huitzilopochtli consented, ordering that while some of the men and women were bathing in the lake others of the band were to steal their clothing. While the bathers were enjoying the water, the others broke camp and left, following the route indicated by their god.

The bathers, naked and forsaken, decided to settle beside the lake. Durán concludes:

> Those who tell this story say that they remained dressed only in their own skins, men as well as women, and as they were there a long time they came to lose shame and leave their private parts uncovered. These people did not previously use loincloths nor mantles, but rather long tunics.[12]

The clothing of the women in the mountainous Tarascan area was also unusual for the central plateau: they went about all but topless. Either they did not wear an upper-body garment at all or they wore a *quechquemitl* so small, and in such a manner, that it often served to cover little more than the neck and one shoulder. The Tarascans, however, resembled their Mesoamerican brothers in the predictable presence of the ubiquitous cotton armor, the feathered warrior tunic, and that pan-Mesoamerican priestly accouterment, the tobacco gourd worn on the back. They also had a version of the *xicolli*.

TARASCAN COSTUME REPERTORY

Draped Garments

The first example (*a*) of chart 7 shows a *carcelero*, "jailer." In this instance "executioner" would be a better translation, for he has just dispatched an adulterous woman by striking her on the back of the head with his club. The illustration from which this figure is taken deals with the administration of justice to those who had been rebellious or disobedient. In addition to "bad women," the condemned group also included subjects who had four times failed to bring wood for the ritual temple fires, doctors who had let someone die, workers who had neglected the seedbeds of the *cazonci* ("ruler"), workers who had damaged the maguey, and victims of diseases of the genitals.

Each day for twenty days before the Feast of the Arrows, court was held and justice meted out. The *petamiti* ("chief priest") heard the cases. On the day of the feast all the offenders were gathered in the *cazonci's* patio, together with the *principales* (wise old men who had

EXAMPLE *7a*. Tarascan draped garment. *Relación de Michoacán, làmina 2.*

served the community), chiefs, and common people. After the head priest had told the gathered throng the entire history of their ancestors, the executioner administered justice to the offenders.[13]

The executioner shown in example *7a* is wearing what looks like a variant of the traditional Mesoamerican loincloth. It is not a loincloth, however. After carefully studying his strange apparel, I have concluded that the force of the executioner's turning movement has caused the two ends of material on his costume to stand out from his body. Since this item of dress does not occur again in the *Relación de Michoacán*, little more can be said about it. Because it is a single example, I have not included it on the final summary chart in chapter 9.

Examples *7b* and *7c* illustrate the front and back of the Tarascan male garment that was the equivalent of the loincloth. Note that it wrapped around the body in such a way that the buttocks were exposed. The *Relación geográfica* of 1579 from Jilquilpán states that the Tarascan men wore "chamarras [a short, loose jacket] without another thing and without '*masteles*' of cotton."[14] Similar descriptions are repeated in other *Relaciones geográficas* from Otomí-speaking Necotlán.[15] and Tarascan-speaking

---

[12] Durán 1967, 2:30; translation from Heyden and Horcasitas 1964, p. 16.
[13] *Relación de Michoacán* 1956, p. 12.

[14] Cline 1972, census no. 60; Corona Nuñez 1958, 1:12.
[15] Cline 1972, census no. 72; Corona Nuñez 1958, 1:43.

CHART 7
TARASCAN COSTUME REPERTORY
Examples of Garments Reflecting
the Five Basic Principles of Garment Construction

Draped Garments

a

b

c

d

e

Slip-on Garments

f

g

Open-sewn Garments

h

i

j

Closed-sewn Garments

k

l

m

Limb-encasing Garments

SOURCES: (a) *Relación de Michoacán, lámina* 2; (b) *Relación de Michoacán, lámina* 18; (c) *Relación de Michoacán, lámina* 25; (d) *Relación de Michoacán, lámina* 38; (e) *Relación de Michoacán, lámina* 38; (f) *Relación de Michoacán, lámina* 19; (g) *Relación de Michoacán, lámina* 37; (h) *Relación de Michoacán, lámina* 37; (i) *Relación de Michoacán, lámina* 25; (j) *Relación de Michoacán, lámina* 44; (k) *Codex Telleriano-Remensis,* fol. 33v; (l) *Relación de Michoacán, lámina* 41; (m) *Relación de Michoacán, lámina* 30.

Acámbaro, a village near Celaya.[16] The claim in two of the *Relaciones geográficas* (from the Tarascan-speaking communities Chocondiram[17] and Perivan,[18] associated with Jilquilpán)[19] that the loincloth was used is cancelled out by a statement by Sahagún in his book *The People*: "...they [the men of Michoacán] wore no breech clouts, but went bare, covering themselves only with their *cicuilli*, the so-called sleeveless jacket."[20]

Example 7b of the Tarascan male garment is from an illustration of an episode in the life of Tariacuri, founder of the Tarascan state. He has ordered his one worthy son and two outstanding nephews to kill another of his sons, Curatame, because the latter is a drunkard. One of the nephews, the future ruler Tangaxoan I, wields the bloody club that slays his drunken cousin. The frightened servants who witness the act are reassured by the murderers that the commoners have nothing to fear; it is a matter between the "masters." The servants are then told to be about their business of gathering wood for the temples that honor the Tarascan fire god, Curicaveri.[21]

In example 7c a back view of the Tarascan lower torso is shown in a scene concerning the manner in which the ruler Tariacuri dealt with those who disobeyed him. Another of the ruler's sons, Tamapucheca, had been captured when very young and subsequently ransomed for very rich feather plumage. In later years the young man was again captured by enemies who intended to sacrifice him. His father, Tariacuri, was very pleased to learn of this, believing that through his son's sacrifice the father himself would provide nourishment to the sun and gods of the heavens, having begotten the head and heart they would receive.

The boy's captors, however, were uneasy about sacrificing the son of such a powerful ruler. They urged the boy to return to his village, but he refused, knowing that custom decreed that a promised sacrificial victim would be killed if he returned to his home. The boy's governesses, who were determined to save him, waited until he was drunk and then ransomed him with long green plumes and, with the aid of assistants, carried him home in a hammock. As the son had anticipated, his father was furious and ordered not only his son's death but also that of the governesses and those who had aided them (fig. 33; example 7c).[22]

The woman shown sweeping in example 7d is wearing the Tarascan wraparound skirt. Sahagún gave a succinct description of the garment: "The women [of Michoacán] wore only a skirt; they lacked a shift. Their skirts were neither full nor long; they reached only to above the knees."[23] The *Relación de Michoacán* also describes the skirt, stating that the dress of the Tarascan women con-

EXAMPLE 7b. Tarascan draped garment. *Relación de Michoacán*, *lámina* 18.

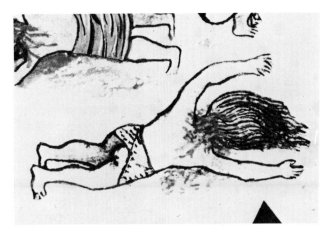

EXAMPLE 7c. Tarascan draped garment. *Relación de Michoacán*, *lámina* 25.

sisted of a skirt of a square of material tied at the waist with the torso left bare.[24] It was called a *siríhtaqua*.[25] Another page speaks of *"naguas de yerbas."*[26] which has been translated as skirts decorated with vegetal fiber and as "weed skirt."[27]

16 Cline 1972, census no. 18; Corona Nuñez 1958, 2:61.
17 Corona Nuñez 1958, 1:19.
18 Ibid., p. 33.
19 Cline 1972, census no. 60; Corona Nuñez 1958, 1:19, 33.
20 Sahagún 1950–69, bk. 10, p. 189.
21 *Relación de Michoacán* 1956, pp. 131–34.

22 Ibid., pp. 159–60.
23 Sahagún 1950–69, bk. 10, p. 189.
24 *Relación de Michoacán* 1956, p. 91.
25 Ibid., p. 201.
26 Ibid., p. 134.
27 Ibid., p. 136.

FIGURE 33. The execution of a disobedient Tarascan servant.
Relación de Michoacán, lámina 25.

FIGURE 34. Scene showing the family duties of members of the
Tarascan lower class. *Relación de Michoacán, lámina 38.*

The illustration from which example *d* comes (fig. 34) deals with the manner of marriage of the lower classes, specifically a man marrying for a second time. After the new wife entered his house, it was customary for him to spend four days gathering wood for the temple before he approached her. During those days she would sweep not only the house but also the road approaching it for some distance. In that manner the couple prayed for a successful marriage; the sweeping was symbolic of the life they were to have in the future.[28]

Another female (example 7*e*) from the same illustration is shown walking down the path swept by (*d*) the bride; it may be the same married woman, before shown topless, now bundled up. The nature of her wrap is perplexing. She is wearing what appears to be a type of shawl, a colonial garment. The costume occurs only once in the *Relación de Michoacán*, and, although it is in a section that is supposed to deal with pre-Contact history, the garment is suspect. No other apparel resembling it appears in the entire Mesoamerican costume repertory. Because it appears in the *Relación de Michoacán*, it is included on the Tarascan chart; but since it is an aberrant garment that was probably colonial, and appears only once, I have not used it on the summary chart of chapter 9.

Slip-on Garments

Two women shown in the slip-on-garment section (examples 7*f* and 7*g*) are wearing variants of the same costume, a very small *quechquemitl*. As mentioned in chapter 2, the *quechquemitl* is sometimes difficult to identify because of the many ways it can be arranged around the shoulders (for a more ample version of the Tarascan style of the garment, see fig. 35). There is no mention of the costume in the *Relación de Michoacán*, the *Relaciones geográficas*, or Sahagún, but an authority on modern Mexican Indian costume, Irmgard Johnson, who has done ethnographic field work in *quechquemitl*-wearing areas, suggests that the garments seen in examples *f* and *g* are a tiny version of that costume being worn with the triangular point resting on the left arm.

In light of what is known about the association between the Aztec *quechquemitl* and female deities, it is of interest that example *f* is indeed a goddess. She is seen in a dream by the future Tarascan ruler Tangoxoan I. He was preparing to do battle with a neighboring people, and to propitiate the gods, he built a huge fire on a high mountaintop. While he slept near the fire, the goddess Xaratanga appeared to him. She came in the guise of an old lady: "Her hair was grey in spots, she wore a weed skirt and a coarse manta and another manta she wore draped."[29] Since she appears to be wearing only two garments, the description is confusing; however, from a comparison with the other *quechquemitl* in the *Relación de Michoacán*,[30] it does seem that a tiny version of the same

[28] Ibid., pp 214–15.
[29] Ibid., p. 136.
[30] Ibid., p. 64, *lámina* 15; p. 160, *lámina* 26; p. 207, *lámina* 37.

EXAMPLE 7*d*. Tarascan skirt. *Relación de Michoacán, lámina 38.*

EXAMPLE 7*e*. Tarascan shawl. *Relación de Michoacán, lámina 38.*

garment is being worn by the goddess. Unlike the Aztecs, however, the Tarascans did not restrict the use of the garment to deities.

Example *g* shows a young noblewoman wearing a *quechquemitl* on the way to her wedding (see plate 8). The *Relación de Michoacán* reports that "the lords marry among themselves; they always marry their relatives and take wives of the stock they sprang from."[31] Obviously the

[31] Ibid., p. 213.

lineages were endogamous, a social practice that may be very old in Michoacán. Chadwick notes that Chupicuaro pottery from the Preclassic period displays a drawing of a six-fingered hand, a trait sometimes caused by inbreeding in rigidly endogamous groups.[32]

Open-sewn Garments

Examples *b* and *i* in the open-sewn garments section of chart 7 are male Tarascans wearing the *cicuilli*, which Sahagún referred to as "the so-called sleeveless jacket."[33] The word "jacket" is translated from the Nahuatl term *xicolli*; hence I have classified this costume as an open-sewn garment.

Eduard Seler defined the *omicicuilli* as a short, sleeveless, bodicelike garment that enveloped the rib cage and was covered with "little balls that hang."[34] He also discussed the *cicuilli* in relation to the Tarascans, referring to Sahagún's statement that they wore only a knee-length shirtlike garment, called *cicuilxicolli* by the Aztecs.[35]

It seems that the Aztecs, encountering a male garment with which they were not familiar, gave it the name of one of their own costumes that it resembled. Perhaps the Nahuatl word *xicolli*, when it passed into Tarascan, became *cicuilli*, the term thereafter used by Nahuatl-speakers for the unusual male costume of the Michoacán area. Molina, either through oversight or because of his sensitivity to anything connected with the pagan religion, excluded from his dictionary the ritual *xicolli* but included the secular *cicuilli*. He defined it as *cuerpezuelo*,[36] a small body-encasing garment or waistcoat (vest), a definition that would also apply to the *xicolli*.

The *Relaciones geográficas* provide further confirmation of the *cicuilli's* construction as an open-sewn garment (that is, having a full-length opening, in this case in the front). Repeatedly the *Relaciones geográficas* refer to the male Tarascan garment as resembling the *chamarro*,[37] which Stevens's 1726 dictionary defines as "a long coat or garment made of sheep skins with wool on, and properly called camarro." In the *Relación de Michoacán* the costume is usually seen on seated individuals (as in example *i* of chart 7). The few standing figures illustrate that the garment came to just below the knees, as in example *7b*.

Sahagún wrote of the garment that "they wore it just like a shift."[38] It does have the enveloping quality of the *huipil*, which caused the Aztecs and other Mesoamerican groups to ridicule the Tarascans for wearing "women's clothes."

The *cicuilli*-clad male of example *7b*, like the preceding *quechquemitl* figure (example *7g*), is from the illustration showing the manner of marriage among the lords (see plate 8). The bride (example *7g*) is escorted to her wedding by the older man (example *7b*). Although the full-length front opening of his *cicuilli* is not apparent in the

illustration, I have classified example *7b* as an open-sewn garment in deference to the sixteenth-century sources.

The seated figure in example *7i* is the ruler Tariacuri, who has ordered the slaying of a disobedient servant who rescued the ruler's son from his fate as a sacrificial victim (see fig. 33). Tariacuri, dressed in his *cicuilli*, is seated on the low stool used by the *cazonci*. On his head he wears a cloverleaf wreath.

The final example of an open-sewn garment (example *7j*) is a male wearing a feathered warrior costume with a band of alternating red and blue feathers at the hem. This feather border resembles the Aztec *ehuatl*, except that the Aztec costume was a pull-on, closed-sewn garment, whereas the full-length front opening of this Tarascan garment is clearly visible. The individual wearing this warrior garb is the worried and ill-fated Tangaxoan II, the *cazonci* who was ruling when the Spaniards arrived. In anticipation of the appearance of the conquerors in Michoacán, the Tarascan ruler was about to weight himself down with heavy copper on his back and drown himself in the lake so that he would not have to face the Spaniards, who he feared would enslave him and his people. His brother-in-law, called Don Pedro by the Spaniards, persuaded the *cazonci* to reconsider. The garment shown in example *7j* may be the costume he donned to dance with plume-bedecked chiefs and *principales* on the eve of the fateful Tarascan-Spanish encounter (see plate 9).[39]

Closed-sewn Garments

The initial figure in the closed-sewn section of chart 7 (example *7k*) comes from the Aztec pictorial *Codex Telleriano-Remensis*. It is a depiction of a Tarascan warrior of Michoacán (Place of the Fish, noted by the fish glyph above the figure's head) wearing battle dress. The Tarascans were extremely effective warriors, and the Aztecs had repeated cause to show respect for the prowess of Michoacán in battle. When Moctezuma was preparing to withstand the Spaniards, he asked the Tarascans to aid him, believing that his Aztec forces combined with those of the Tarascans could certainly defeat the invaders and their Tlaxcalan allies. Moctezuma reportedly said to the Tarascan emissaries, "Why should we not be successful when everyone flees from you people of Michoacán who are such great archers?"[40] Unfortunately for the Tarascans their ingrained distrust of the Aztecs precluded providing the requested aid:

> Let the strangers kill the Mexicans because for many days they have not lived right for they do not bring wood to the temples but instead, we have heard, they honor their gods only with songs. What good are songs alone? How are the gods to favor them if they only sing songs?"[41]

The costume worn by figure *k* (an Aztec rendering of a

---

[32] Chadwick 1971, p. 673.
[33] Sahagún 1950–69, bk. 10, p. 189.
[34] Seler 1960, 2:438.
[35] Ibid., 4:428.
[36] Molina 1970. fol. 22r.

[37] E.g., Corona Núñez 1958, 1:19, 25, 33, etc.
[38] Sahagún 1950–69, bk. 10, p. 189.
[39] *Relación de Michoacán* 1956, pp. 253–56.
[40] Ibid., p. 243.
[41] Ibid., p. 244.

Relación de Michoacán, lámina 8._

FIGURE 35. Four Tarascan women wearing *quechquemitl.*
Relación de Michoacán, lámina 8.

EXAMPLE 7f. Tarascan *quechquemitl. Relación de Michoacán,*
lámina 19.

EXAMPLE 7g. Tarascan *quechquemitl. Relación de Michoacán,*
lámina 37.

Tarascan warrior) may be the closed-sewn *ichcahuipilli*. Such a garment is mentioned in the Michoacán *Relaciones geográficas* from Cuitzeo, a village near Necotlán, as a "doublet stuffed with cotton,"[42] and from Chilchotla as a "loose garment of *manta* and cotton that they call *escuaypiles*."[43] The *Relación de Michoacán* also mentions "doublets of cotton" being worn in battle by "all of the valiant men."[44] It was called *cherenguequa*.[45] It is possible that the Michoacán warrior's garment is the full "robe" of the Tarascans, also depicted in the *Lienzo de Tlaxcala* (see plate 7).

The same passage in the *Relación de Michoacán* mentions that in battle the lords and valiant men put on doublets of rich feathers. The second warrior (example 7*l*) wearing a closed-sewn garment may be clad in such a costume. The individual is one of three captains dressed in blue-striped tunics. The captains are presenting a group of captives for sacrifice to a newly ordained ruler.[46] No doubt such feathered garments as those of example 7*l* were worn over the *ichcahuipilli* by warriors of high status, who thereby displayed their high rank but still ensured their protection by the use of the cotton armor. As already discussed, the Aztecs utilized the *ehuatl* and *tlahuitzli* over the *ichcahuipilli* in the same manner.

The final figure (example 7*m*) wearing a closed-sewn garment is from an illustration depicting the priests of the temple. The individual is the greatly revered chief priest, called *petamuti*, who ruled over all the other priests. The *Relación de Michoacán* makes several references to his costume,[47] many facets of which are illustrated. His official regalia was a tunic made of feathers placed in a stepped design, called *ucata-tararenguequa*;[48] a necklace of miniature golden tweezers around his neck; a wreath of fiber or plumage on his head in a womanlike braid of hair; a gourd set with turquoise on his back; and a lance set with a flint point. Only the high priest wore this distinctive garment; his assistants wore open-sewn costumes like examples *h* and *i* in chart 7.

SUMMARY

The outstanding feature of the Tarascan costume repertory is its dramatic divergence from the pan-Mesoamerican pattern. While four of the five principles of garment construction are manifested—only limb-encasing apparel is lacking—several of the Tarascan garments are unique.

Whereas all other Mesoamerican males wore some style of loincloth, the Tarascans girded their loins in a completely different manner. The usual Mesoamerican

EXAMPLE 7*b*. Tarascan *cicuilli*. *Relación de Michoacán*, *lámina* 37.

EXAMPLE 7*i*. Tarascan *cicuilli*. *Relación de Michoacán*, *lámina* 25.

---

42 Cline 1972, census no. 72; Corona Nuñez 1958, 1:52.
43 Cline 1972, census no. 23; Corona Nuñez 1958, 2:22.
44 *Relación de Michoacán* 1956, p. 192.
45 Ibid.
46 Ibid., p. 226.
47 Ibid., pp. 13, 223.
48 Ibid., p. 13.

EXAMPLE 7*j*. Tarascan feather warrior costume. *Relación de Michoacán, lámina* 44.

EXAMPLE 7*l*. Tarascan feather warrior costume. *Relación de Michoacán, lámina* 41.

EXAMPLE 7*k*. Tarascan *ichcahuipilli. Codex Telleriano-Remensis,* fol. 33v.

EXAMPLE 7*m*. Tarascan ceremonial costume. *Relación de Michoacán, lámina* 30.

cape was also absent from the Michoacán area; in its place the men wore a tuniclike costume, a garment type elsewhere identified with women. The same style was used for the warrior costumes, the more prestigious of which were brightly patterned with feathers. The women either went about topless (a surprising custom in an often-cold mountainous area), or were clad in a *quechquemitl* so small and worn in such a manner that it could have afforded little protection from the elements.

The very limited pictorial corpus for the Tarascan area has made it impossible to compile charts with multiple examples of their clothing. Fortunately the sole pictorial Tarascan source, *Relación de Michoacán*, contains enough illustrations to allow garment comparisons and hence afford an understanding of the *sui generis* Tarascan costume repertory. It differed not only from that of the neighboring Aztecs, but from all other Mesoamerican groups as well, including the Mixtecs on the southeast.

FIGURE 36. A Mixtec place sign, one component showing a Mixtec noblewoman spinning a cotton fillet into thread. *Codex Vindobonensis*, obverse p. 9.

CHAPTER FIVE

The Mixtecs of Oaxaca

 SOUTHEAST OF THE VALLEY of Mexico is the region known as the Mixteca. This geographically diverse area is the homeland of the Mixtec-speaking Indians whose language was early recorded both in a dictionary by Fray Francisco de Alvarado (1593)[1] and in a grammar by the sixteenth-century Dominican friar Antonio de los Reyes.[2] To deal with the geographic and dialectic diversity of the Mixteca, which includes the western portion of the state of Oaxaca and adjoining sections of the present-day states of Guerrero and Puebla, Fray Reyes divided the region into three subareas: Alta, Baja, and Costa. These designations are still in use today. The Mixteca Alta is the mountainous region of high, fertile valleys west of the state capital, Oaxaca. North of the Alta is the Mixteca Baja, extending into southern Puebla and eastern Guerrero. The Mixteca de la Costa borders the Pacific Ocean along the southeastern coastal lowlands of Oaxaca and adjoining Guerrero.[3]

In the Late Postclassic period the Mixteca region was comprised of small independent states, each controlled by a hereditary ruling family. Although certain lineage ancestors were venerated by families from several different areas, each of these kingdoms was nonetheless a distinct political entity. While there was never an area-wide imperial unification in the Aztec or even the Tarascan sense, marital alliances between royal houses provided a loose social, political, and economic network that linked the many communities and political domains ranging from highland valleys to tropical lowlands.[4] The focus of Mixtec culture, however, was mainly in the Mixteca Alta area.

As was true throughout the rest of Mesoamerica, warfare appears to have been well developed among the Mixtecs. Local skirmishes were fought between neighboring communities over disputed boundaries—probably in instances of contested royal succession—to achieve extensions of tributary dominion and to take slaves for sacrifice.[5] Among the Mixtecs martial enterprise appears to have been a matter of raiding rather than the highly institutionalized warfare characteristic of the Aztecs and Tlaxcalans. In this, as in other social institutions, Mixtec culture was not as complex as that of the Aztecs. There appears to have been no Mixtec territorial residence group analogous to the Aztec *calpulli*, the kin-based land-holding unit. No great center of urban life such as Tenochtitlán emerged, nor have any extensive ceremonial centers been found. The Mixtec kingdoms were neither urban nor occupationally specialized in craft production.[6]

Ronald Spores estimated that at the time of Spanish contact the Mixtec-speaking population was probably around 500,000.[7] It appears that none of the communities was very large. In the Mixteca Alta the settlements were along the fertile river valleys, and each of the politically independent groups had its main center, or *cabecera*, in a separate mountain enclave. Population was moderately dense in the broader valleys (an estimated 50,000 in some twenty settlements in the Nochixtlán valley) and sparse in the more rugged areas.[8]

As was common throughout Mesoamerica, at least half

---

[1] Alvarado 1962.
[2] Reyes 1890.
[3] Smith 1973, p. 3.
[4] Spores 1974, p. 297.

[5] Spores 1967, p. 14.
[6] Spores 1974, p. 301.
[7] Spores 1967, pp. 72–75.
[8] Spores 1974, p. 299.

of the Mixtec *cabeceras* had small satellite communities nearby. Only a few of the states numbered more than ten thousand persons, and most of that population was dispersed throughout dependent hamlets at varying distances from the main center. In the Mixteca Alta, 80 percent of the land surrounding the *cabecera* and attendant hamlets consisted of the sharply sloping flanks of rugged mountains.[9] Unlike other mountainous areas of Mesoamerica, where small cornfields were cultivated on even the steepest hillsides, only the valleys and terraced lower slopes were used for agriculture; the Mixtecs lived and worked in their valleys. Spores suggested that this restriction of agricultural potential could have had a pronounced effect in limiting the direction and development of Mixtec culture,[10] particularly considering the size of many of those tiny kingdoms, whose holdings could be traversed on foot in a day.[11]

The Mixtec *cabecera* was the civic and commercial center; the royal family resided there, and the most important market was regularly held there. The Mixtec ceremonial centers were situated apart from, though near, the head towns. The ceremonial zone was usually established in association with some unusual natural configuration: on a mountain or hilltop, in a cave, or at a spring.

Neither the *cabeceras* nor the ceremonial centers were decorated with large-scale architecture or sculpture. The Mixtec artistic gift was for superb art in miniature, including carving and working metal, stone, bone, and wood; producing magnificent pottery; and creating spectacular small ornaments of gold, jade, crystal, and turquoise. The Mixtecs emphasized the decorative and precious, and they developed careful and painstaking techniques to bring their craftsmanship to a high level. Although the Mixtecs' creative efforts may have stopped short of attaining the urban stage of development with its political and architectural complexity, they were unsurpassed in the delicacy, refinement, and finesse of their craftsmanship. The small, precious, transportable objects from the Mixteca were renowned throughout Late Postclassic Mesoamerica.

The wealth of the Mixtec kingdoms made them prime targets for the economically ambitious Aztecs, and by the early years of the sixteenth century the greater part of the Mixteca had fallen to the forces of Aztec imperialism.[12] In keeping with the Triple Alliance policy of continuing local rule, the native rulers of the Mixteca were allowed to retain their power, but a periodic heavy tribute in luxury goods had to be sent to Tenochtitlán.

Just as the Aztecs were drawn to the Mixteca because of its riches, so too Spaniards first came into the area looking for gold. In 1520, at Cortés's insistence during the

months he held Moctezuma prisoner in one of the palaces of Tenochtitlán, the Aztec emperor assigned certain of his tax collectors to guide a few of the conquistadors to some of the gold-producing provinces of the empire to ascertain the potential of these particularly lucrative regions. The Europeans, like the Aztecs before them, recognized the political and economic advantage of encouraging the continuity of local rule and, from that point on, Mixtec royal succession depended on proving direct, legitimate descent from a line of native rulers. By 1540 the court records were full of litigation revolving around disputed titles, property, and privileges. Spores noted that the energy that had once gone into warfare was now diverted into litigation,[13] the machinery for which was amply supplied by the Spanish judicial system (whose slow-moving apparatus embodied all the elements of eternity).

At least two of the Mixtec codices played a role in these colonial power struggles. Since the pictorials represented the charters of the Mixtec royal families, they were presented as evidence in some of the interminable lawsuits. The Mixtec pictorial codices were created as dynastic histories, recording the genealogies and activities of the royal families. Collectively the documents record the history of rulers whose lives covered a span from the tenth to the mid-sixteenth century. The eight major animal-skin screenfolds chronologically record the births, marriages, conquests, and deaths of the royal lines of specific towns. With one exception (the obverse of *Codex Vindobonensis*), the histories relate actual events, although sometimes the accounts are obscured by mythology.

The Mixtec pictorials represent the art of the ruling class; hence they deal only with matters participated in by that segment of Mixtec society. As Elizabeth Smith has noted, there are no genre scenes or "spear bearers" in the Mixtec screenfolds;[14] all the personages depicted are members of the royalty, priests (in Mesoamerica rulers were usually both), or deities.

Since a number of the Mixtec ruling families claimed certain famous lineage ancestors, there are sometimes local and contradictory versions of the same story. That is particularly true of the famous culture hero 8 Deer (Jaguar Claw), the eleventh-century ruler of the kingdom of Tilantongo in the Mixteca Alta.[15] His was the most prestigious of the royal Mixtec lines, and because of the luster associated with this vaunted ruler, many of the royal families were intent on demonstrating descent from him. All but two of the extant Mixtec pictorials relate some aspect of 8 Deer's epic. Although 8 Deer was from the Mixteca Alta, even the pictorial that probably comes from Tututepec—in the Mixteca de la Costa—recounts an aspect of his story. At some point in 8 Deer's fifty-year

[9] Spores 1967, p. 182.
[10] Ibid., p. 100.
[11] Spores 1974, p. 302.
[12] Barlow 1949*a*, pp. 100–25.
[13] Spores 1967, pp. 119–20.
[14] Smith 1973, p. 21.
[15] Caso 1960, p. 80. I have discussed 8 Deer's dates with Emily Rabin, who is

working on a revision of the early segment of Caso's Mixtec chronology. As of this writing Rabin accepts Caso's dates for 8 Deer. Her changes in Caso's chronology occur in the early segments of Mixtec history. By the time 8 Deer appears on the scene, Caso's dates fit into Rabin's chronological revision. There is the probability that Rabin's later research may necessitate moving 8 Deer's date of birth ahead by one 52-year cycle.

reign Tilantongo apparently controlled Tututepec.[16]

Although two of the Mixtec codices, *Codex Bodley* and *Codex Selden*, were compiled after the Conquest, they are completely in the native tradition and pre-contact in nature. As is the case with most of the major Mixtec pictorials (six of the eight), the reading sequence in *Bodley* and *Selden* is arranged in a meander or boustrophedon pattern. The reader is led by red guidelines; a zigzag from bottom to top passes from one band to another at the place the red line separating the bands is interrupted.[17]

Each of the eight pictorials is painted in color on an animal-skin screenfold sized with white slip made of a mixture of lime and clay, and each displays the identifying features of the Mixtec art style. Elizabeth Smith summarized the idiom with the observation that the Mixtecs made little attempt to represent an illusion of three-dimensional space.[18] Like Egyptian painting, Mixtec art is based on convention. The human body is represented as a compendium of separable parts: profile legs and a profile head may be connected to a front-facing torso. Occasionally there is a front-facing head, and some seated figures are shown with front-facing crossed legs (see chart 9, example *b*).

Although most of the personages who appear in the pictorials actually lived, there is no attempt at portraiture. In the Mixtec manuscripts individuals are identified by their names, not by their physical features. Aside from a conventional tear that is sometimes shed by a captive or sacrificial victim or the baring of teeth as a warrior goes into battle, the protagonists express little emotion. There are, however, a few stereotyped postures and gestures that convey a degree of expression. Example *d* in Chart 8 shows the body of a conquered figure bending forward as his captor holds him by the hair, a traditional depiction of victory over a foe.

In recent years exciting breakthroughs have been made in the understanding of the Mixtec codices. One example concerns the hand gestures made by some of the individuals in the pictorials. Nancy Troike has investigated the gestures and is convinced that meaning is conveyed not by the position of the fingers or by pointing or using the whole hand but by the location of the hands.[19] All gestures occur within the 180-degree arc in front of the figure, with directions ranging from straight up to straight down. The gestures are clustered in only three areas of the arc, and the areas are separated from one another by buffer zones. Gestures of command, request, or offer (the difference depends on the status of the individuals) are made by a horizontal or slightly downward motion. Acceptance or agreement is shown by the hand held upward.[20] I have referred to Troike's work in discussions of

individuals on the Mixtec costume charts.

Of the eight major Mixtec codices only six are helpful to this book. A detailed analysis of clothing depends both on the clarity of costume depiction and the possibility for comparison presented by repeated examples of the same or similar garments. As a result, two pictorials are unsuitable: *Codex Becker II*, which consists of only four sheets, is too brief, and *Codex Edgerton*, sometimes referred to as *Codex Sanches Solis*, is eroded, and the painted outline of the figures is too indistinct for use on the clothing charts.

I have used the six major Mixtec codices remaining— *Zouche-Nuttall*,[21] *Vindobonensis*,[22] *Colombino*,[23] *Becker I*,[24] *Bodley*,[25] and *Selden*,[26]—in varying degrees for costume study, depending on the appropriateness of their clothing data.

Of the forty-eight depictions in the three Mixtec costume charts (8, 9, and 10), twenty-five come from *Codex Zouche-Nuttall* because of their clarity of line and wide range of garment types and styles. The pictorial is a carefully detailed and magnificently crafted pre-Hispanic manuscript that contains a biography of part of the life of 8 Deer on one side and a series of genealogies on the other. The pictorial is known to have been in the Dominican monastery of San Marco, in Florence, Italy, in 1859, when it was sold to an Englishman and taken to Britain.

About thirty years after the codex had left Italy, Zelia Nuttall, an American pioneer in ancient Mexican historical studies, learned of the pictorial's existence while she was doing research in Florence. Intrigued by a description of the manuscript, she finally traced it to its last owner, the fifteenth Earl of Zouche. He consented to her request to publish a facsimile of the manuscript in 1902, through the Peabody Museum of Harvard University. In 1917 the original manuscript, which now bears the name of both its last owner, Zouche, and its modern discoverer, Nuttall, was acquired by the British Museum, where it is presently housed.

Zelia Nuttall considered the pictorial to be the most superb "ancient Mexican historical manuscript" she had seen.[27] She believed that *Codex Zouche-Nuttall* and *Codex Vindobonensis* (discussed below) were the two documents Hernán Cortés sent from Veracruz along with the famous "Moctezuma treasure," to Charles V in July, 1519. While it is extremely doubtful that they are the two famous "books" (the Spaniards did not enter the Mixteca until 1520), it is believed that both *Zouche-Nuttall* and *Vindobonensis* were taken from Mexico soon after the Conquest. Nicholson has suggested that they may have gone as part of a second gift shipment that Cortés sent back to the crown from Veracruz in March, 1520, with Alonzo de Mendoza and Diego de Ordás.[28] Only if the two books

---

[16] Smith 1973, p. 68.

[17] Caso 1960, p. 12.

[18] Smith 1973, p. 11.

[19] Troike 1974*a*, 1974*b*, 1975.

[20] Troike 1975, p. 4.

[21] Glass and Robertson 1975, *Codex Zouche-Nuttall*, census no. 240.

[22] Glass and Robertson 1975, *Codex Vindobonensis*, census no. 395.

[23] Glass and Robertson 1975, *Codex Colombino*, census no. 72.

[24] Glass and Robertson 1975, *Codex Becker I*, census no. 27.

[25] Glass and Robertson 1975, *Codex Bodley*, census no. 31.

[26] Glass and Robertson 1975, *Codex Selden*, census no. 283.

[27] Nuttall 1902, p. 4.

[28] Nicholson MS, p. 18.

were taken to Europe at that time does an otherwise enigmatic inscription on one of the pictorials became understandable. *Codex Vindobonensis* contains a short Latin text stating that it was given to Pope Clement VII by King Manuel of Portugal, who died in December, 1521, indicating that it was in Europe by that date. Unfortunately the inscription is somewhat suspect because the pope did not become pontiff until almost two years after Manuel's death.[29]

In addition to the confusion over when and how *Zouche-Nuttall* and *Vindobonensis* reached Europe, there is also disagreement over the age and dating of the historical sequence represented in the Mixtec codices. Tremendous strides have been made in recent years in understanding the chronology of those pictorials. One of the greatest scholars of the Mixtec codices was the eminent archaeologist-ethnohistorian Alfonso Caso. He was the first to recognize and demonstrate the genealogical content of the documents; by tracing back the royal family lines, he developed the first chronology. He believed that events related in the codices began as early as A.D. 692 and that *Codex Zouche-Nuttall* was compiled in 1330.[30]

In recent years the Mixtec scholar Emily Rabin has reassessed the early portion of Caso's chronology. Taking a biological approach (that human beings must conform to human limitations), she has pointed out such anomalies as women being in their seventies and older by Caso's chronology when they give birth and a man being nearly 200 years old when he marries. She suggested that at least 156 years (three cycles of 52 years) need to be cut from the early segments of Caso's chronology dealing with the early period of Mixtec history. Nancy Troike thinks that recent research places all the Mixtec pre-Hispanic codices at mid- to late fifteenth century, within 50 to 100 years before the Conquest.[31]

Codex Vindobonensis, also known as *Codex Vienna* because of its present repository, the National Library in Vienna, closely resembles *Codex Zouche-Nuttall* in figural style and draftsmanship, but the obverse of this pictorial differs markedly from the other Mixtec pictorials. Whereas they include some representation of a religious nature, they are primarily historical documents that present detailed genealogies of rulers who actually lived. The obverse of *Vindobonensis*, however, primarily contains mythological material that relates the creation of the Mixtec world, the manner in which the gods were originally assigned to specific cosmic duties, and geographic areas of the Mixteca. Jill Furst views this codex as a highly mythologized land document that depicts both actual locales, particularly pertaining to the Mixteca Alta town of Apoala, and mythological places.[32]

The many deities included in *Vindobonensis* carry Mixtec-style calendric names, but in many instances their accouterments reveal that they are Mixtec versions of personalized supernaturals worshiped throughout central and southern Mexico at the time of Spanish contact. The status of the *Vindobonensis* personages as deity figures in no way negates the value of the information conveyed by their clothing. Human beings may or may not create gods in their own image, but they usually clothe them from their own costume repertoires. In some cases the garments of the gods may be archaic, but they definitely are a reflection of the culture from which they come.

The obverse sheets of *Codex Vindobonensis* and those of *Codex Zouche-Nuttall* are the most colorful and elaborate of all the Mixtec screenfolds. Nine of the forty-eight figures on the Mixtec costume charts are from *Codex Vindobonensis*. The back of the screenfold is very different from the front, however. Elizabeth Smith has noted that it "almost seems to be the 'poor stepchild' of Mixtec history painting, principally because of its draftsmanship, which is more slovenly than that of any other known example of pre-Columbian Mixtec painting."[33] The content sets forth genealogies, and the probable provenience of the manuscript is Tilantongo.[34]

The next two pictorials to be discussed, *Codex Colombino*, presently in Mexico City in the National Museum of Anthropology, and *Codex Becker I*, housed in the Museum für Völkerkunde, Vienna, are probably both part of the same original screenfold. In addition to the stylistic features that they share, both manuscripts were annotated during the colonial period with glosses in the Mixtec language. The annotations have nothing to do with the pictorials' content—the biography of 8 Deer and 4 Wind—but refer almost exclusively to boundaries within the sphere of influence of the coastal town of Tututepec (the matching of the glosses with the place-name glyphs of the codices has been a major factor contributing to a growing understanding of Mixtec pictographic writing).[35] In 1717 the native ruler of that town presented the *Codex Colombino* in court for a land-claim case; there is also evidence that as early as 1541 the pictorial was owned by the ruling house of Tututepec.

Codex Becker was annotated two times. The first set of glosses was scraped off, but a faint trace remains of the names of several Mixtec coastal towns. The earliest post-Conquest notice of the document was in 1852, when it appeared in a lawsuit in Puebla.

Internal evidence indicates that *Colombino* and *Becker I* were originally one manuscript and were owned by the ruling house of Tututepec. Whether the pictorial was actually painted there is still unknown.

Besides being the same size and in the same figural style, the screenfolds also deal in detail with part of the life of 8 Deer, but at no point is there an overlap in the story. The *Colombino-Becker I* biography of 8 Deer is similar to that

---

[29] Nicholson 1966*b*, p. 148.
[30] Smith 1973, p. 19.
[31] Troike 1978, p. 554.
[32] Furst 1978.

[33] Smith 1973, p. 12.
[34] Glass 1975, p. 235.
[35] Smith 1973.

narrated on the back of *Codex Zouche-Nuttall*, but the painting style is very different. Only two examples from *Codex Colombino-Becker I* appear on the Mixtec clothing charts because the paint is badly eroded on the manuscripts and the clothing is standardized.

The last two Mixtec pictorials used in this study are *Codex Bodley* and *Codex Selden*, both now in the collection of the Bodleian Library of Oxford University. *Codex Bodley* deals with genealogies of several dynasties of the still-flourishing Mixtec towns of Tilantongo and Teozacoalco. *Codex Selden* presents the genealogies of rulers of the town now known as Magdalena Saltepec, in the Nochixtlán valley.[36] Its pre-Hispanic Mixtec place-sign is usually described as "Belching Mountain." Apparently the pictorial was acquired from the literary estate of John Selden, who lived from 1584 to 1654 and collected manuscripts of all kinds.[37]

The *Codex Bodley* reached the Bodleian Library sometime between 1603 and 1605. Sir J. Eric S. Thompson thought it possible that the screenfold might previously have been in the library of the bishop of Faro, Hieronymus Osorius. In a raid on the coasts of Spain and Portugal, the Earl of Essex, the favorite of Elizabeth I of England, ransacked the bishop's library and, upon his return to England, presented the books to his friend Sir Thomas Bodley. Whether *Codex Bodley* was among them is unknown. Caso attempted to confirm Thompson's supposition but was unable to do so. Nevertheless, Caso agreed that *Codex Bodley* might have reached England in that manner.[38]

Both *Codex Bodley* and *Codex Selden* represent the human figure with great simplicity. In some cases that is advantageous for the understanding of the costume, but it also creates standardization of dress. Seven of the forty-eight clothing examples were taken from *Selden*, five from *Bodley*.

In addition to the six Mixtec pictorials, I also used sixteenth-century Spanish documents to reconstruct the Mixtec costume repertory. The greatest written source of data has been the extant *Relaciones geográficas* for the Oaxaca area dealing with the Mixtec-speaking communities. Because the Amusgo and Cuicatec speakers are so closely allied,[39] information from those areas has also been included, along with relevant information from neighboring Zapotec communities, which is enlightening from a comparative standpoint. Because the *Relaciones geográficas* were written in 1579–1580, over fifty years after the Conquest, they provide a colonial view of postcontact Indian costume that raises some interesting questions, as do the accounts of the missionaries.

In the mid-seventeenth century Fray Francisco de Burgoa wrote of the work of the Dominican order among the Mixtecs.[40] His chronicles contain little costume data,

and those that exist are presented with almost no descriptive detail. Despite its paucity all the early colonial clothing information is included.

Some costume information exists in Fray Francisco de Alvarado's Spanish-Mixtec dictionary.[41] Because of the close proximity of the neighboring Zapotecs, I have also consulted Fray Juan de Córdoba's Zapotec dictionary for cognate words and supporting information.[42] There is a linguistic interrelationship between Mixtec and Zapotec because they were originally one language. Over a long period of time they separated into two distinct units, but because of their original affiliation it is possible, with careful extrapolation, to benefit from consulting the Zapotec material. Although neither of the dictionaries contains many garment terms, the appearance of the few that are listed is irrefutable proof that the Indians were still wearing, or at least remembered, some of the pre-Hispanic garments in the last quarter of the sixteenth century.

MIXTEC COSTUME REPERTORY

As with Aztec, Tlaxcalan, and Tarascan costumes, I have classified and presented the Mixtec data according to the principle of garment construction each exemplifies. The Mixtec material contains a unique additional feature that is both intriguing and frustrating: many of the figures found in those codices "wear" their names. It is intriguing to a student of costume that individuals are identified by the incorporation of certain items of their clothing in various kinds of appellative glyphs. They appear to be personal names, including calendar names, family names, and personal or dynastic titles. Frustration arises with the realization that, while it is often possible to recognize a particular individual by characteristics of his clothing, it is sometimes impossible to tell which class of appellative glyph is being incorporated in the dress. There is the additional problem whether the depictions in the codices should be understood as representing actual costumes worn or regarded as merely glyphic devices.[43]

Since this investigation of Mesoamerican costume is based on the premise that the clothing shown in the codices reflects garments that actually existed in the pre-Hispanic Indian world, I have accepted Mixtec costumes as representations of reality except for such obviously impossible costume as Eagle Ballcourt's attire (fig. 37). Personal names that Caso attached to individuals who appear on the costume charts are included.[44] In all other instances the figures are discussed only in the context in which they are found.

Since the Mixtec codices are histories and genealogies of the ruling class, the garments depicted are more elaborate that those of the lower classes. However, the

[36] Smith 1974.
[37] Caso 1964, p. 61.
[38] Caso 1960, p. 11.
[39] Harvey 1972, p. 281.
[40] Burgoa 1934*a*; 1934*b*.

[41] Alvarado 1962.
[42] Córdoba 1942.
[43] Kelly 1973.
[44] Caso 1960, 1964, 1966.

FIGURE 37. A Mixtec nobleman, Eagle Ballcourt, shown "wearing" his name. *Codex Selden*, p. 9.

EXAMPLE 8a. Mixtec *maxtlatl*. *Codex Zouche-Nuttall*, p. 50.

apparel of the common people apparently was a simple version of some of the same styles, made in maguey fiber and almost devoid of decoration.

Draped Garments

MAXTLATL. The Mixtec loincloth, the basic male garment, was a long narrow length of cotton or maguey fabric worn wrapped around the lower torso, passed between the legs, and tied at the back in such a manner that the two ends fell in front and back. Among the Mixtecs the garment does not appear to have been highly decorated, although certain types of loincloths were diagnostic costume elements of particular deities.

In his *Vocabulario de lengua Mixteca*, Fray Alvarado listed the loincloth, *bragas*, as "*satu, sainino saha*."[45] For this book the Nahuatl term *maxtlal* seems more appropriate because it appears constantly in the Oaxacan sixteenth-century textual sources, as well as in the contemporary literature.

The usual Spanish word for loincloth is *braguero*, but Alvarado used *bragas*, which also occurs in the Spanish glosses of the Aztec pictorial *Matrícula de tributos*. Fray Juan de Córdoba gives both in his Zapotec dictionary: "*bragas o braguero*."[46] Equating the two terms defines *bragas* as "loincloth."

In his general observations of Mixtec culture Caso referred to the loincloth by its Nahuatl word, *maxtlatl*.[47] It is also mentioned repeatedly by that term in the Oaxaca *Relaciones geográficas* (for example, in the Chinantec-speaking communities of Usila,[48] and the Zapotec-speaking communities of Ocelotepec,[49] a village associated with Chichicapa[50]). The descriptions indicate that the Mixtec loincloth was essentially the same garment as one of the two types worn by the Aztecs. The following description of a loincloth comes from Amatlán, a Zapotec-speaking village associated with Chichicapa: "... their [the Oaxaca Indians'] '*maxtles*,' that is a long narrow strip of cloth of the width of eight inches which was placed between both [legs] and brought [around] to tie at the waist, in such a manner that their shameful parts were hidden and the rest of the body remained uncovered."[51]

The first section of chart 8 presents three examples of Mixtec loincloths. The first figure (example 8a), from the side of *Zouche-Nuttall* dealing with the biography of 8 Deer, is a priest who holds a lighted torch of bound branches in his hand. His blackened body accentuates his white loincloth, which was probably made of cotton. The knot of the *maxtlatl* is clearly visible at the priest's back. The Mixtec loincloth is longer than that of the Aztecs and Tlaxcalans; the front end of the *maxtlatl* of the figure

[45] Alvarado 1962, 38r.
[46] Fray Córdoba 1942, 60v.
[47] Caso 1960, p. 14.
[48] Cline 1972, census no. 138; Pasy y Troncoso 1905, 4:49.
[49] Paso y Troncoso 1905, 4:140.
[50] Cline 1972, census no. 21.
[51] Ibid., census no. 21; Paso y Troncoso 1905, 4:121.

CHART 8
MIXTEC COSTUME REPERTORY
Examples of Draped Garments

Male
Maxtlatl

a   b   c

Hip-cloth

d   e   f   g   h

Cape

i   j   k   l   m

Kilt

n   o   p

Female
Skirt

q

Cape

r   s   t   u   v

SOURCES: (a) *Codex Zouche-Nuttall*, p. 50; (b) *Codex Zouche-Nuttall*, p. 70; (c) *Codex Vindobonensis* obverse, p. 48; (d) *Codex Zouche-Nuttall*, p. 83 (e) *Codex Zouche-Nuttall*, p. 63; (f) *Codex Zouche-Nuttall*, p. 67; (g) *Codex Vindobonensis* obverse, p. 1; (b) *Codex Bodley*, p. 31; (i) *Codex Zouche-Nuttall*, p. 82; (j) *Codex Becker I*, p. 16; (k) *Codex Vindobonensis* obverse, p. 8; (l) *Codex Colombino*, p. XIII; (m) *Codex Vindobonensis* obverse, p. 34; (n) *Codex Vindobonensis* obverse, p. 26; (o) *Codex Vindobonensis* reverse, p. III; (p) *Codex Vindobonensis* reverse, p. VI; (q) *Codex Zouche-Nuttal*, p. 30; (r) *Codex Zouche-Nuttall*, p. 12; (s) *Codex Zouche-Nuttall*, p. 30; (t) *Codex Bodley*, p. 35; (u) *Codex Selden*, p. 1; (v) *Codex Vindobonensis* reverse, p. 1.

EXAMPLE 8b. Mixtec *maxtlatl*. *Codex Zouche-Nuttall*, p. 70.

EXAMPLE 8c. Mixtec *maxtlatl*. *Codex Vindobonensis* obverse, p. 48.

hangs down to the ankles, and the garment is knotted in the back.

The calendric name of the figure in example 8b appears to be 6 Vulture; he is also covered with the black body paint of the priest, in the standard practice among the Aztecs. The blackening may have been done with soot. The *Relación de Michoacán* refers to pious individuals covering themselves with a piece of material and holding a smoking torch under this "tent" to blacken their bodies.[52] On the Mixtec priest's back is the priestly accouterment the tobacco pouch, and he holds in his hands what may be two hearts topped with flint knives. The figure is found directly above a scene in which 8 Deer and 4 Tiger perform self-sacrifice at the Temple of the Quetzal-Feather Headdress.[53]

The third *maxtlatl* (example 8c) comes from the ritual side of *Codex Vindobonensis*. The figure is one of a group of sixteen males, each of whom wears a *maxtlatl* of the same type: the end of the loincloth is rounded and colored either red or tan. The Mixtec scholar John Pohl points out that that type of loincloth, as well as those ending in a scallop or swallowtail design, are costume diagnostics of certain deities; hence their presence conveys ritual meaning.[54] In example 8c the deity represented is Quetzalcoatl.

Only codices *Selden* and *Bodley*, in which the clothing is otherwise standardized, consistently show decorated loincloths. Almost all other breechclouts in the other Mixtec codices are without ornamentation.

HIP-CLOTH. The Mixtec hip-cloth covered the hips and ranged in length from just below the buttocks to just above the knee. Many examples are fringed, some are plain, and others have a multicolored striped border. The ends of the *maxtlatl* often appear to have been pulled up over the hip-cloth; indeed, the loincloth almost seems to hold it on. In some examples the loincloth is not visible. Whether that is a result of the artist's carelessness it is impossible to know. It is also impossible to tell from the context in which the hip-cloth is found whether or not it was special-purpose clothing; to judge from its ubiquitous presence in Mesoamerica, it probably was not.

The Mixtec name for the hip-cloth is not known, nor is there any mention of it in Burgoa, Alvarado, or the Oaxaca *Relaciones geográficas*. As the five examples of chart 8 demonstrate, however, it apparently was not an uncommon item of apparel.

The first hip-cloth (example 8d) is worn by a famous ruler whose calendric name is 4 Wind. As his posture demonstrates, he has been taken captive by 8 Deer. The site of the capture is known as Red and White Bundle, from a ritual offering that is part of that community's name glyph. The end of 4 Wind's *maxtlatl* has been

[52] *Relación de Michoacán* 1956, pp. 78–79.
[53] Caso 1966, p. 133.
[54] Pohl 1978, pp. 63, 106.

pulled over the fringed hip-cloth, and the knot is clearly visible.

The second hip-cloth (example 8e) is also fringed, but no *maxtlatl* is visible. It is worn by 10 Dog, one of the 112 lords attending the great conference or assembly of rulers called by 8 Deer and his half brother 12 Movement. Three-fourths (eighty-one) of the attending lords are wearing hip-cloths. Of these, twelve are shown with hip-cloth but no *maxtlatl*.

The eighty-one hip-cloths depicted in the scene described above vary in length from just covering the buttocks to just above the knee. The third figure (example 8f), whose name is 4 Rabbit, is wearing the longer type. Examples 8e and 8f are making a hand gesture that Troike has suggested is one of command or request, depending on the status of the individuals involved.[55] Since the two lords, as well as the other 110 rulers attending the conference, are dealing with the mighty 8 Deer, their gesture probably more likely indicates a request than a command.

The fourth figure wearing a hip-cloth (example 8g) is from the ritual side of *Codex Vindobonensis*. He is one element in a place-name glyph and is wearing his fringed hip-cloth in a unique, apronlike manner. The object over the small of his back may be a mirror, a ritual accouterment that is sometimes part of Mesoamerican ceremonial costumes.

The final individual (example 8b) in the hip-cloth section is a member of the procession that accompanied the ruler 4 Wind home after he had been made a *tecuhtli* ("lord"). Caso referred to the figure as "the bearer of the skin strips."[56] His hip-cloth has a dark gold border and the end of his *maxtlatl* is decorated with two lines. The hip-cloth is found in all the Mixtec codices used in this study except *Codex Selden*.

CAPE. Although there is no doubt that capes were worn by some of the males in the Mixtec codices, they are the least common garments in those pictorials. No more than thirty examples have been identified.[57] The male capes were short garments that do not appear to have extended farther than the base of the torso. They were worn as a cover for either the back or the chest. The capes often appear to have been fringed and may have had ornamented ties.

EXAMPLE 8d. Mixtec hip-cloth. *Codex Zouche-Nuttall*, p. 83.

EXAMPLE 8e. Mixtec hip-cloth. *Codex Zouche-Nuttall*, p. 63.

[55] Troike 1975, p. 4.

[56] Caso 1960, p. 62.

[57] Male capes in the Mixtec codices (Roman numerals indicate row numbers): *Codex Selden*: none. *Codex Bodley*: 8, IV (back cape); 9, I, II (3?) (back capes); 14, II (back cape); 32, III (2) (back capes); merchants (Caso 1960:62). *Codex Colombino*: IX, middle band, bottom band (back capes); X, middle band (chest cape, down ball); XI, middle band, bottom band (back capes); XIII, middle band (back cape); XVI, top band (2 chest capes, both with down balls). *Codex Becker I*: 5, bottom band (chest cape); 14, bottom band (back cape); 15, middle band (chest cape, down ball); 16, middle band (chest cape, down ball). *Codex Zouche-Nuttall*: 5 (front cape); 8 (front cape? 2); 23 (back cape); 25 (back cape); 39 (front?); 44 (back cape); 80 (2 front capes, one with a down ball). *Codex Vindobonensis* reverse: VI, top band (front cape). *Codex Vindobonensis* obverse: 34 (knot shows on one of these two back capes); 8 (knot shows on this front cape).

Problems arise in attempting to reconcile the short capes shown on males in the Mixtec codices with Spanish sixteenth-century documentation. The references from the Oaxaca area repeatedly mention the use of *mantas*, particularly as worn by the Indian men as cloaks. There are confusing discrepancies between the illustrations in the codices and the Spanish texts. Certainly there is no question about the presence of *mantas* in the Mixteca in the 1570s, when the *Relaciones geográficas* were compiled. Burgoa wrote that they were given in tribute[58] and as sacrificial offerings[59] and that they were made of fine thread and beautifully decorated.[60] He also noted the materials with which two of the capes were dyed: red from brazilwood and purple from sea mollusks, and he said that "they called [the capes] *huazontecas*."[61]

Although Fray Alvarado did not list *manta* or *capa* in his Mixtec dictionary, the *Relaciones geográficas* of 1579 to 1581 for Mixtec–speaking communities mention the wearing of both cotton and henequen *mantas* (for example, Tilantongo[62] and its dependency Mitlantongo,[63] Texupa,[64] Cuahuitlán,[65] and Nochistlán[66]). The question, then, is not the use of the capes in the Mixteca but the frequency with which they were worn and their nature, length, and elaboration. They may have been clothing of a bygone era that represented the powerful elite and appeared in the codices as symbolic of an entire class.

The sixteenth-century Spanish descriptions of *mantas* in the Oaxaca area sound suspiciously like those of the Nahuatl-speaking Valley of Mexico. That is true not only of costume data from the Mixteca but also of *Relaciones geográficas* from Zapotec-speaking communities. According to the report from Taliztaca, the *mantas* tied at the shoulder and came to the knee;[67] the report from Tlacolula refers to the distinction between cotton clothing for the upper classes and maguey fiber for the common people.[68] Fray Juan de Córdoba's Zapotec dictionary presents thirteen *manta* entries, the general word for *manta* being *làati*.[69] The friar listed the following types of *mantas*: curly silk plush cape; net capes; Indian "painted cape"; clean unworked capes; Indian cape with some ribbons; capes like those with which the Indians cover themselves; capes of little cords like this *mena* (?); cape of dyed wool without cords; cape with some worked roundels, or similar clothing; feathered cape.

These descriptions, together with statements from the Cuicatec-language *Relaciones geográficas* from Atlatulauca

EXAMPLE 8f. Mixtec hip-cloth. *Codex Zouche-Nuttall*, p. 67.

EXAMPLE 8g. Mixtec hip-cloth. *Codex Vindobonensis* obverse, p. 1.

[58] Burgoa 1934a, 2:221.
[59] Ibid., p. 267; Burgoa 1934b, p. 229.
[60] Burgoa 1934a, 1:272, 2:232.
[61] Ibid., 2:406.
[62] Cline 1972, census no. 127; Paso y Troncoso 1905, 4:74.
[63] Paso y Troncoso 1905, 4:79, 84.
[64] Cline 1972, census no. 124; Paso y Troncoso 1905, 4:55.
[65] Cline 1972, census no. 33; Paso y Troncoso 1905, 4:158.
[66] Cline 1972, census no. 74; Paso y Troncoso 1905, 4:208.
[67] Cline 1972, census no. 94; Paso y Troncoso 1905, 4:170.
[68] Cline 1972, census no. 133; Paso y Troncoso 1905, 4:146.
[69] Córdoba 1942, 258r.

EXAMPLE 8*h*. Mixtec hip-cloth. *Codex Bodley*, p. 31.

FIGURE 38. Mantas worn in the Mixtec *Códice de Yanhuitlán*. Spores 1967:188.

that the *manta* tied on the right shoulder and extended to the ankles,[70] indicate that the cloaks worn in Oaxaca in the 1570s were not the small chest and back capes of the Mixtec codices. This impression is further confirmed by an illustration (fig. 38) from the colonial Mixtec document *Códice Yanhuitlán*, which dates from 1545–50 and contains an illustration of two Indian men wearing what looks like the Valley of Mexico *manta*.

All of this evidence indicates that by the mid-sixteenth century the capes of the Mixtec codices had been supplanted by the Aztec-style *tilmatli*. The impetus behind such a style change needs far more research. Two possible explanations are particularly intriguing. The early Spanish priests, insisting that the Indian men adopt more modest attire, may have attempted to impose a standardized dress requirement over all of Mesoamerica: European pantaloons and shirt covered with a cloak of the Valley of Mexico type. Fifty years after the Conquest the memory of a different, shorter type of cape could have disappeared. The other possibility is that the penetrating influence of the pre-contact Triple Alliance included a change in clothing style. Certainly that appears to be true of Late Postclassic Oaxaca ceramics, which clearly reflect the prevailing style of the Mixteca-Puebla horizon.[71] The result of adoption of the Aztec clothing style would be that the Conquest-period Mixtecs were actually wearing Valley of Mexico–type garments but in the Mixtec codices continued to depict their ancestors in archaic costumes. Additional evidence for the latter argument appears in the discussion of the Mixtec women's garments below.

The initial example (8*i*) in the male-cape section of chart 8 is a short chest cape, which Seler referred to as an apronlike garment called a *quemitl* (the garment is also discussed in chapter 3).[72] He stated that the Indians used to tie such a garment around the necks of their idols,[73] which suggests that the chest capes may have had a particular religious significance. In example 8*i* the chest cape is worn by 8 Deer, who is sitting on a jaguar-skin stool, a symbol of power. In a standing position his short, white, fringed cape probably would have covered only his chest; in the illustration it is pulled over his knees. The ties that must have secured the garment at the back of the neck are not visible.

The next example (8*j*) confirms the short length of the chest cape. It is worn by a standing figure whose blackened body indicates that he may be a priest. He holds in his hand a maguey spine, usually associated with autosacrifice. The design on his chest cape is a ball of feather

[70] Cline 1972, census no. 11; Paso y Troncoso 1905, 4:170.
[71] Nicholson 1957.
[72] Seler 1901–1902, p. 130.
[73] Ibid., p. 122.

down, which in Aztec iconography is associated with human sacrifice.[74]

The third cape (example 8*k*) is worn by a male who comprises one component of a place glyph. Since he comes from the ritual side of *Codex Vindobonensis*, the locale referred to may well be mythological. The individual's chest cape, which clearly illustrates the knot at the back of the neck, is the largest cape illustrated in the Mixtec codices.

The fourth cape (example 8*l*) is worn by an individual who appears next to the depiction of the great nose-piercing ceremony in *Codex Colombino*. The septum of 8 Deer's nose is perforated, indicating that he is a *tecuhtli* ("lord"). The individual in example 8*l* may be the vanquished ruler of Acatepec, whose name was 1 Movement. He was captured by 8 Deer and became the conqueror's sacrificial offering at the time of the hero's elevation to power. At that time 8 Deer's nose was pierced to commemorate the event. From the woebegone demeanor of the figure, he seems indeed to be a prisoner. He wears a chest cape that appears to tie in front and extends to the base of his torso.

The final cape example (8*m*), from the ritual side of *Codex Vindobonensis*, is one partner of seven pairs of males who appear on that sheet. Each of the seven couples face one another and exchange hand signals. The personage whose hand is raised in the gesture that Troike has equated with acceptance wears only a short black cape with its knot clearly visible. He is one of the few male figures in the Mesoamerican codices shown without a loincloth.

KILT. The Mixtec pictorial *Codex Vindobonensis* obverse contains a scene showing eight depictions of a short, waist-encircling men's garment that can only be likened to a kilt. There is one example of the costume on page 39 of *Codex Zouche-Nuttall*. This garment also occasionally appears in other Mixtec codices. For example, in *Codex Colombino* (page II, middle band), both a human and a deity figure wear kilts while playing ball. Apparently, then, not only gods but also human beings wore the costume, at least when interacting with gods in some circumstances. There is no mention of a kiltlike garment in any of the Spanish documentation, but since it occurs in the Mixtec pictorials, it is included in this book.

An individual (example 8*n*) named 7 Snake is one of eight male figures on sheet 26 of the ritual side of *Codex Vindobonensis*. All their bodies are stained red, and each wears the same type of headgear and round-eyed Tláloc mask, but the lower parts of their faces differ. The gar-

ment worn around the waist of 7 Snake appears to be a short pleated kilt held in place by a belt with a chevron design, the symbol of warfare. A plain white *maxtlatl* hangs below the skirt.

Example 8*o* is from the reverse side of *Codex Vindobonensis*, in a section dealing with genealogical matters of the Mixtec town Tilantongo. The individual's name is 3 Monkey, and, like that in the preceding example, his body is stained red. The cords of his belt are clearly visible, and the pleats of his kilt appear to be separate pieces of material. The *maxtlatl* hangs almost to the ground.

The last kilt (example 8*p*) is also from the reverse side of *Codex Vindobonensis*. His blackened body indicates that he may be a priest. He wears a kilt with the same multicolored "fringe" seen on many of the Mixtec *xicolli* (discussed in a following section) and a belt with a fret design. Below his kilt both ends of his plain white *maxtlatl* extend to his sandals.

SKIRT. Although Burgoa made no mention of the Indian women's skirts, Alvarado offered a minimal definition: "Skirts, which the Indian women use, *dziyo*."[75]

As in the Aztec costume repertory, it is difficult to find an example of a Mixtec skirt worn without an upper-body garment. Example 8*q*, from *Codex Zouche-Nuttall*, is the unnamed child of 13 Eagle's third marriage, to 8 Reed.

Although there is only brief reference in a Mixtec *Relación geográfica* (Tilantongo) to "little skirts,"[76] the *Relación geográfica* of the nearby Cuicatec-speaking community Atlatlauca describes the wraparound skirt as tying at the waist and reaching to the ankles,[77] which many of the adult skirts appear to have done (see chart 9, the *quechquemitl* section, and chart 10, the *huipil* section). *Relaciones* of another Cuicatec-speaking community, however—Papaloticpac,[78] and of a Zapotec town, Ixtepexic[79]—speak of cotton and maguey-fiber skirts coming only to a little below the knee. The length may have varied by region and group, as is the case today.[80]

FEMALE CAPE. The Mixtec female cape was a draped garment that covered the upper torso and was secured by ties. Although it is sometimes drawn to resemble a "bolero" (that is, the arms appear to extend from the armholes of a short, sleeveless jacket), comparative evidence suggests that such erroneous depictions may be the result of native artistic convention. The cape appears to have been a general-purpose garment.

The woman's cape is not mentioned in Burgoa, Alvarado, or the Oaxaca *Relaciones geográficas*, but examples (*r–v*) in chart 8 are evidence that such a garment existed in

---

[74] In regard to down-feather balls, Caso (1958, pp. 12–13) relates: "According to legend, Coatlicue, the old goddess of the earth, had become a priestess in the temple, living a life of retreat and chastity after having given birth to the moon and the stars. One day while sweeping, she found a ball of down which she tucked away in her waistband. When she finished her tasks, she looked for the ball of feathers, but it had disappeared. Then she suddenly realized that she was pregnant...." Her child was the sun, Huitzilopochtli.

[75] Alvarado 1962, 154v.
[76] Cline 1972, census no. 127; Paso y Troncoso 1905, 4:75.
[77] Cline 1972, census no. 11; Paso y Troncoso 1905, 4:170.
[78] Cline 1972, census no. 78; Paso y Troncoso 1905, 4:90–91.
[79] Cline 1972, census no. 57; Paso y Troncoso 1905, 4:18–19.
[80] Cordry and Cordry 1969, pp. 100–14.

EXAMPLE 8*i*. Mixtec male cape. *Codex Zouche-Nuttall*, p. 82.

EXAMPLE 8*k*. Mixtec male cape. *Codex Vindobonensis* obverse, p. 8.

EXAMPLE 8*j*. Mixtec male cape. *Codex Becker I*, p. 16.

EXAMPLE 8*l*. Mixtec male cape. *Codex Colombino*, p. XIII.

the pre-Hispanic Mixtec costume repertory. It is, however, extremely difficult to be certain of several aspects of women's clothing because of the stylized nature of depictions.

There is confusion in the contemporary literature regarding the proper pre-Conquest Indian terminology for the Mixtec upper-body garments and for other women's costumes. Caso mentioned the women in the Mixtec codices as wearing "the overblouse or *huipil*

EXAMPLE 8*m*. Mixtec male cape. *Codex Vindobonensis* obverse, p. 34.

EXAMPLE 8*n*. Mixtec kilt. *Codex Vindobonensis* obverse, p. 26.

(*xique*)...and...a wrapped skirt (*dziyo*)."[81] While the sixteenth-century Mixtec dictionary of Alvarado gives the same word for skirt, "Naguas que usan las indias, *dziyo*,"[82] there is disagreement on the term for *buipil*. Alvarado's definition reads: "Camissa que usan las yndias que llaman *buipil. Dzico*."[83]

According to Dahlgren, among the Amuzgo-Mixtecs and in the general Mixtec area, the word for *buipil* is *xiqhu* (*siqhu, sighu*).[84] *Xiqhu* has not been found in Alvarado's sixteenth-century dictionary.

It is interesting that there should be such a disparity regarding the proper pre-Conquest Mixtec term for *buipil* because the costume seldom occurs in the pre-Hispanic Mixtec codices. The garment that Caso considered a *buipil* is interpreted differently by others, including me.

In his commentary on the *Selden Roll*, Cottie Burland referred to the Mixtec upper-body garment as a kind of "poncho" or "tunic,"[85] and to some extent Smiley Karst,[86] in her study of the female garments in the Mixtec codices, followed him in the classification. It is my contention, however, that the poncho effect is in reality a large, full *quechquemitl*, which when viewed from the side gives a "rounded" effect (see *quechquemitl* section of chart 9). Caso's *buipil* in my opinion is a short cape[87] also viewed from the side. As Karst[88] pointed out, the codex figures are not always anatomically credible; portions of a torso may be in opposition, with the lower half facing front or back and the upper part presented in profile. Arms are portrayed as extending from the body in unnatural if not impossible angles. The codices' artists used whatever presentation best displayed those features that they wanted to show with clarity. As a result, many details of attire are shown in front view, even when the individual is in profile, and vice versa. Such problems are particularly evident when the Mixtec women's capes are considered.

The first cape example (8*r*) is worn by Lady 2 Flower. She wears a fringed cape that covers her shoulders and back and appears to fasten under her chin, as shown by the two ties. Since the ties hang in front, it is doubtful that they belong to her necklace; in the Mixtec codices the ties securing necklaces usually extend out from the back of the neck as seen in (*s*) the second cape example. She has two sets of ties, one for her necklace, the other for her cape.

Example 8*s* (presented in a three-quarter view) is seen on Lady 10 Deer, who wears a cape that hangs from the shoulders down the back to just below the waist and ties in front. *Codex Zouche-Nuttall* contains another example in

[81] Caso 1960, p. 14.
[82] Alvarado 1962, 154v.
[83] Ibid., 42v.
[84] Dahlgren 1954, pp. 114–15.
[85] Burland 1955, p. 12.
[86] Karst 1972, pp. 10–16.
[87] Caso 1960, p. 14.
[88] Karst 1972, pp. 5–6.

Jnic v. parrapho ipan mitoa imʒqujtla
manfli minechichioaya mjlatoque ioã
jncioapipilfm.

(2)

(1)

PLATE I. Examples of the colorful cotton clothing worn by the
Aztec nobility. *Codex Primeros memoriales*, vol. 3, *estampa* 21.

PLATE 2. Nezahualpilli, ruler of Texcoco, one of the three cities that controlled the Aztec Triple Alliance Empire. *Codex Ixtlilxochitl*, fol. 108r.

PLATE 3. An Aztec priest impersonating the maize goddess
Chicomecoatl-Tlazolteotl. *Codex Borbonicus*, p. 30.

PLATE 4. A page from the tribute list of the Aztec Empire, *Codex Mendoza*, vol. 2, fol. 29r.

PLATE 5. Six grades of Aztec priest-warriors and their captives.
Codex Mendoza, vol. 3, fol. 65r.

PLATE 6. Cortés and Marina with Tlaxcalan lords and ladies. *Lienzo de Tlaxcala, lámina 7.*

PLATE 7. The Tlaxcalans and Spaniards in battle against the
Tarascans of Michoacán. *Lienzo de Tlaxcala, lámina 52.*

papas a ahora aon quinto dias y quatro noches y despues y baçon
todala gente por leña paralos griec y dava al sacerdote aquelles
Dia puesto enel senorio manias y çirioles y guirnaldas de
hilo que usavan lues sacerdotes y bolbiase ala abdad de mechuacan con
el hacalo sal al sacerdote mayor comole avia puesto enel senorio
y el sacerdote mayor los hapasa balençonia y deziale el caçonçi sea
en or priesse aqs ynolo hiziere bien quitallo emos del officio y proba
ra otro ensulugar aqs comolo hazes

Odamancia que secasavan los señores

ponese aqui comose caso don pedro ques ahora governador porq
desta maneza se casava todos.

PLATE 8. A Tarascan noblewoman being escorted to her wedding. *Relación de Michoacán, lámina 37.*

PLATE 9. The Spanish arrival in Michoacán. *Relación de
Michoacán, lámina* 44.

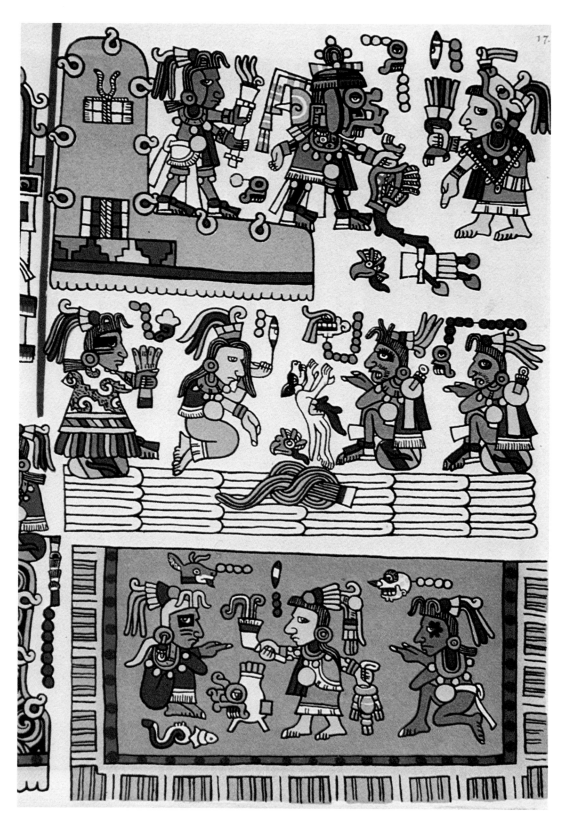

PLATE 10. A section of the history of a Mixtec noblewoman, Lady 3 Flint. *Codex Zouche-Nuttall*, p. 17.

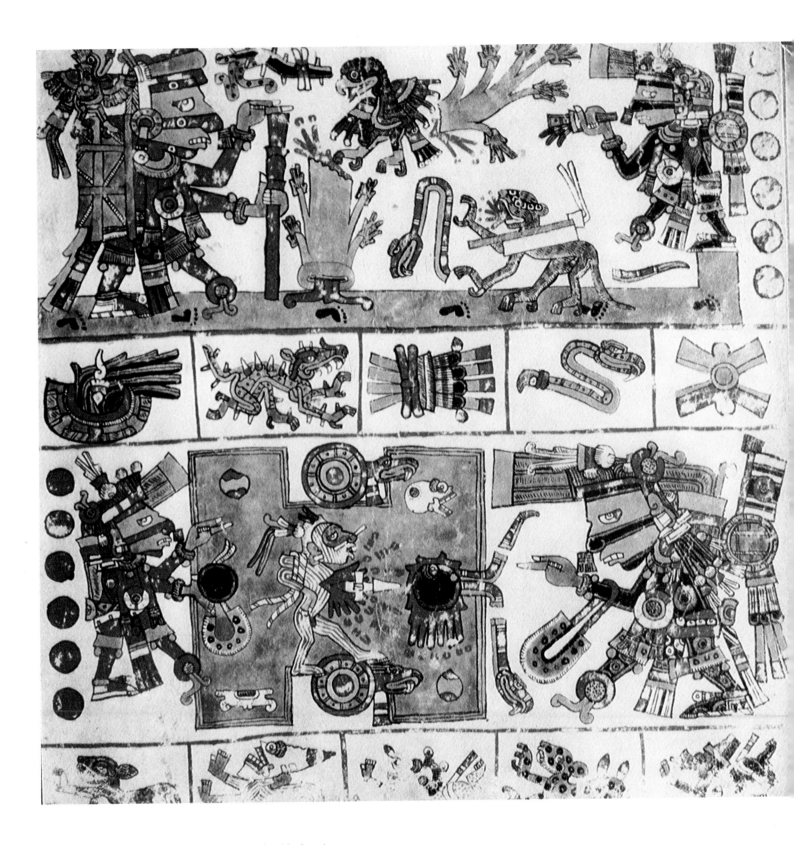

PLATE II. Tezcatlipoca in both his red and his black guises as merchant, warrior, and ballplayer. *Codex Borgia*, p. 21.

PLATE 12. A scene showing a section of the six celestial wonders
and the six heavens. *Codex Fejérváry-Mayer*, p. 35.

PLATE 13. The goddess Tlazolteotl wearing both the female skirt
and the male loincloth. *Codex Laud*, p. 6D.

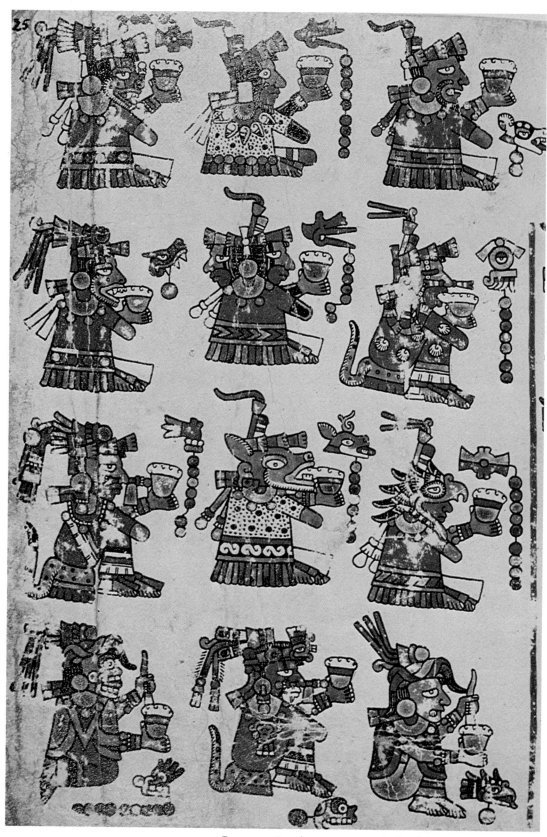

PLATE 14. A pulque ceremony depicted in a Mixtec pictorial.
Codex Vindobonensis obverse, p. 25.

PLATE 15. The lowland Mayas' youthful god. *Codex Dresden*, p. 49.

PLATE 16. A lowland Maya depiction of a torrential downpour.
Codex Dresden, p. 74.

EXAMPLE 8*o*. Mixtec kilt. *Codex Vindobonensis* reverse, p. III.

EXAMPLE 8*p*. Mixtec kilt. *Codex Vindobonensis* reverse, p. VI.

EXAMPLE 8*q*. Mixtec skirt. *Codex Zouche-Nuttall*, p. 30.

EXAMPLE 8*r*. Mixtec female cape. *Codex Zouche-Nuttall*, p. 12.

FIGURE 39. A Mixtec noblewoman, Lady 7 House, with ties on her cape. *Codex Zouche-Nuttall*, p. 29.

EXAMPLE 8s. Mixtec female cape. *Codex Zouche-Nuttall*, p. 30.

which two sets of ties are visible on Lady 7 House (fig. 39).

The third cape (example 8t) is worn by Lady 6 Monkey (War *Quechquemitl*) shown taking a prisoner. Although her arm extends from her upper-body garment as though it were an open-sewn costume with an armhole (that is, a bolero), it is my contention—based on comparative analyses—that the costume, like the two preceding examples, is probably a cape that was secured in front with ties.

In the fourth cape example (8u), Lady 7 Eagle (Head-Wall-Jade) is wearing a garment similar to that in example 8t. The costume appears to be a cape covering the shoulders and back and falling a little below the waist. Karst has suggested that the line above the elbow may represent a sleeved undergarment.[89] If this were true, the garment would encase a section of the limbs, a style generally used only in the Mesoamerican warrior-ceremonial costume. Since the sleeve effect occurs regularly only in *Codex Selden* and occasionally in *Codex Bodley*,[90] it may be an artistic convention of those two pictorials, which are very similar in style. A sleeved undergarment is out of keeping with the fundamental canons of the pan-Mesoamerican costume repertory.

[89] Ibid., pp. 15–17.
[90] E.g., *Codex Bodley*, pp. 3–5.

EXAMPLE 8t. Mixtec female cape. *Codex Bodley*, p. 35.

EXAMPLE 8u. Mixtec female cape. *Codex Selden*, p. 1.

The final cape example (8v) is seen on the Lady 1 Skull, who is wearing a cape that logically should tie in the front. The ties, however, are shown on her right shoulder and may be those of her necklace. Although her body is in profile, her cape is presented from a front view.

Slip-on Garments — Quechquemitl

There is no mention of the *quechquemitl* in Burgoa or in the Oaxaca *Relaciones geográficas*, nor does the word for the garment appear in either Fray Alvarado's or Juan de Córdoba's dictionary. The *quechquemitl* is not worn by the Mixtecs today, which is surprising in view of its many appearances in the Mixtec codices. As in the case of the Mixtec short male capes, either the early Spanish missionaries abruptly ended the wearing of the *quechquemitl* or its appearances in the Mixtec codices reflect an archaic style of clothing.

The contemporary *quechquemitl* distribution is of interest. Johnson has demonstrated that in modern Mexico today the *huipil* is found in the south in Oaxaca, Veracruz, Yucatán and Chiapas and also in Michoacán and Jalisco.[91] The *quechquemitl* is found in the north in Hidalgo, Toluca, and among the Coras, Huichols, and Tepecanos. It is also worn in the San Luis Potosí region by the Huastecs and the Mazahuas. It is from the latter groups that modern ethnographic examples can be drawn to clarify some of the misunderstandings regarding the upper-body female costume of the Mixtec codices.

Cordry and Cordry's chapter on the *quechquemitl* describes modern examples of the garment in a great variety of sizes ranging from two 24×4¾″ rectangles joined end to side to form a 14½″ square (fig. 40) to a 29″ square (fig. 41) (see fig. 14 for the construction of the

EXAMPLE 8v. Mixtec female cape. *Codex Vindobonensis* reverse, p. 1.

modern *quechquemitl*).[92]

The *quechquemitl* data from the Mixtec codices can best be understood by separating the larger type of garment from the smaller. The larger, fuller *quechquemitl* is presented in a category termed "rounded *quechquemitl*," reflecting the appearance of the garments in the pictorials. There they are often viewed from one side, which gives a rounded effect to the two triangular points. The smaller garments, always depicted with the points center front and back, are termed "triangular *quechquemitl*," reflecting

[91] Johnson 1953.

[92] Cordry and Cordry 1968, pp. 81–99.

CHART 9
MIXTEC COSTUME REPERTORY
Examples of Slip-on Garments

Male

- - - - - - - - - - - - - - - - - -

Female
  Rounded
  Quechquemitl

a   b   c

Triangular
Quechquemitl

d   e   f   g   h

Examples of Open-sewn Garments

Male
Xicolli

i   j   k   l   m

SOURCES: (a) *Codex Zouche-Nuttal*, p. 9; (b) *Codex Zouche-Nuttall*, p. 7; (c) *Codex Vindobonensis* obverse, p. 1; (d) *Codex Zouche-Nuttal*, p. 20; (e) *Codex Selden*, p. 5; (f) *Codex Bodley*, p. 4; (g) *Codex Zouche-Nuttall*, p. 19; (h) *Codex Selden*, p. 6; (i) *Codex Bodley*, p. 14; (j) *Codex Bodley*, p. 21; (k) *Codex Selden*, p. 8; (l) *Codex Selden*, p. 14; (m) *Codex Zouche-Nuttall*, p. 70.

the sharp triangular appearance the rectangular garment assumes when worn.

ROUNDED QUECHQUEMITL. The first rounded *quechquemitl* (example 9*a*) is worn by Lady 9 Rain. She wears a large *quechquemitl* with the points center front. Where the garment falls over the shoulder and arm, the lower border is raised.

The next example (9*b*) is seen on Lady 3 Eagle. Unlike the figure in example 9*a*, she wears her *quechquemitl* with the points over the shoulder. The *quechquemitl* is still worn in this fashion among the Mazahuas in the area of Iztlahuaca and San Felipe del Progreseo in the state of Mexico (fig. 42).

Lady 13 Flower (example 9*c*), like Lady 9 Rain (*a*), wears her garment with the points center front. The sides of the full costume cover her arms almost to the elbow.

TRIANGULAR QUECHQUEMITL. The small, narrow triangular *quechquemitl* is always depicted with its point center front. It is sometimes worn as the sole upper-body garment, but more often it is seen over a cape. The garment occurs both on historical women and on goddesses, and it may have been a symbol of aristocracy. Doris Heyden considers the triangular *quechquemitl* to have been a ceremonial garment, in some cases serving as a political status indicator. The rounded *quechquemitl* she views as used for warmth.[93]

It is the triangular *quechquemitl* that occurs as the glyph used in the codices to designate a woman's name. It is found in many combinations: Flint Quechquemitl,[94] Quechquemitl of White Rhombs (a rhomb being a white square with a black dot),[95] Bloody Quechquemitl,[96] Quechquemitl Jewel,[97] Quechquemitl of Venus,[98] Jaguar Quechquemitl,[99] Sun Quechquemitl,[100] and War Quechquemitl.[101]

The goddess 9 Grass (example 9*d*), to whom all the Mixtec kings paid homage,[102] wears a fringed *quechquemitl* over a "matching" fringed cape. Her skirt has a border of white *xonecuilli* on a black ground, a characteristic symbol of the goddess.[103] The border also occurs in example *b*.

The second figure (example 9*e*) is Lady 9 Wind (Flint *Quechquemitl*), a founding member of the second dynasty of Belching Mountain. She provides an excellent example of portraits of individuals wearing their names. She is making an offering of copal in front of the temple of the sacred bundle of Belching Mountain. Under her *quechquemitl*, which is bordered with depictions of flint knives, she wears a cape that covers only her back, leaving one breast showing.

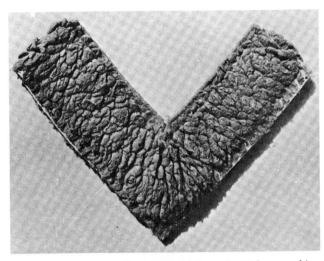

FIGURE 40. A very small *quechquemitl* (from the Nahua-speaking town Sasaltitla, Veracruz), the type referred to in this book as triangular *quechquemitl*. Cordry and Cordry 1968:88, fig. 57.

FIGURE 41. A large *quechquemitl* (from the Huichol-speaking town Alta Vista, Nayarit). Cordry and Cordry 1968:208, fig. 163.

---

93 Heyden 1977.
94 *Codex Bodley*, p. 6.
95 Ibid., p. 12.
96 Ibid., p. 4.
97 Ibid., p. 15.
98 Ibid., p. 16.

99 Ibid., p. 18.
100 Ibid.
101 *Codex Zouche-Nuttall*, p. 44.
102 Caso 1960, p. 39.
103 Caso 1964, p. 82.

EXAMPLE 9a. Mixtec rounded *quechquemitl*. *Codex Zouche-Nuttall*, p. 9.

EXAMPLE 9b. Mixtec rounded *quechquemitl*. *Codex Zouche-Nuttall*, p. 7.

The third triangular *quechquemitl* (example 9f) is seen on another depiction of the goddess 9 Grass (Skull), who wears the small triangular *quechquemitl* over a bordered cape.

The fourth example (9g) is worn by the deity 13 Flower, who appears to wear her fringed, triangular *quechquemitl* as the sole upper-body garment. The final figure (example 9h) wears the triangular *quechquemitl* over a cape. She too is the goddess 9 Grass (Skull), here giving advice to 10 Wind and his wife 6 Monkey. The goddess's *quechquemitl* is bordered with one of her symbols, the white *xonecuilli* on a black ground.

Open-sewn Garments

XICOLLI. The Mixtec *xicolli* was a short, sleeveless, fringed garment that opened in the front and had two long cords attached at the back of the neck. The cords apparently were for decorative purposes only. Unlike the Aztec *xicolli*—a special-purpose costume worn only for ceremonial occasions—the Mixtec *xicolli* was a class-related garment apparently worn regularly by aristocratic males and priests. It also occurs in the Mixtec pictorials in personal names and place-names and as sacrificial offerings and gifts.

Neither Burgoa nor Alvarado mentioned the *xicolli*, although the term occurs in Córdoba's Zapotec dictionary: "*Xicolli, manta vestidura antigua. Ià ti yàba.*"[104] The Mixtecs were still wearing the garment in the colonial period; it appears in the *Relación geográfica* from the Chocho-Mixtec–speaking community Texupa.[105] The

FIGURE 42. A large, full *quechquemitl* (from the Mazahua-speaking town San Felipe del Progreso, Mexico), the type referred to in this book as rounded *quechquemitl*, worn with the points to the side. Cordry and Cordry 1968:90, fig. 59.

104 Fray Córdoba 1942, 429v.
105 Cline 1972, census no. 124; Paso y Troncoso 1905, 4:55.

EXAMPLE 9c. Mixtec rounded *quechquemitl*. *Codex Vindobonensis* obverse, p. 1.

EXAMPLE 9d. Mixtec triangular *quechquemitl*. *Codex Zouche-Nuttall*, p. 20.

gicoles are referred to as "painted" whatever color the owner wished.

As with some other costume items from the Mixtec pictorials, there is confusion in the contemporary literature regarding the construction of the *xicolli*. In discussing the clothing worn by male figures in the Mixtec codices, Caso spoke of the *xicolli* as a "kind of long shirt with sleeves, which was tied behind with two cords ending in tassels."[106] Knowledge gained through an examination of the Aztec *xicolli* counsels caution regarding Caso's definition. The Aztec garment came only to the knees. It had no real sleeve; instead the material of the garment fell over the shoulders creating a sleevelike effect, and it tied in front, not behind. Apparently the Mixtec *xicolli* was a similar costume, as Dahlgren has shown.

In her book *La Mixteca* Dahlgren discussed the Mixtec *xicolli* in a chapter on dress and adornment.[107] With information gathered from the sixteenth-century Spanish documentation of the area, she demonstrated that the garment was short, sleeveless, and open in the front. To have this last fact verified is fortunate because, like so many of the Aztec *xicolli* depictions, the Mixtec *xicolli* are usually not drawn showing their front opening. *Codex Colombino* offers pictorial proof of the jacketlike construction of the Mixtec *xicolli* (figs. 43a and 43b). This male personage car-

[106] Caso 1960, p. 14.
[107] Dahlgren 1954, pp. 109–10.

EXAMPLE 9e. Mixtec triangular *quechquemitl*. *Codex Selden*, p. 5.

EXAMPLE 9*f*. Mixtec triangular *quechquemitl*. *Codex Bodley*, p. 4.

EXAMPLE 9*h*. Mixtec triangular *quechquemitl*. *Codex Selden*, p. 6.

EXAMPLE 9*g*. Mixtec triangular *quechquemitl*. *Codex Zouche-Nuttall*, p. 19.

ries an incense bag, which, together with the front opening of the garment and the diagnostic fringe at the hem, proves the Mixtec *xicolli* to be very similar to its Aztec counterpart. A puzzling added feature is the pair of long cords that appear to be attached to the back of the garment. If the *xicolli* opened in the front, why are long tassels in the back? *Codices Bodley, Zouche-Nuttall,* and *Vindobonensis* contain illustrations that help explain this enigma.

A *xicolli* offering is seen in *Codex Bodley* (fig. 44), which has two cords hanging from the center of the neck. Similar cords are seen on *xicolli* in *Codex Zouche-Nuttall*

and *Codex Vindobonensis*, including *xicolli* held up by tabs, no doubt being presented as offerings (figs. 45 and 46). The *xicolli* are shown with the two cords hanging from the neck of what must be the back of the garments. If that is the case, perhaps the tabs the men are holding are the ties that secure the garment in front. There is further evidence in *Codex Selden* that the area of elaboration on the *xicolli* was the back, not the front.

The *xicolli* had many associations with the ruling class. The red *xicolli* was a symbol of royalty,[108] and in *Codex Selden*, sheet 7, two red *xicolli* are given as marriage gifts to 11 Wind and 6 Monkey (fig. 47). Caso described the gifts:

> . . . a white *huipil* with undulating lines, red dots, and snail symbol; two small cloths similarly decorated with red lines; other black dotted cloths with red border and fringe, one of them having a red bow and the other what appears to be a knotted feather; a *xicolli* or red tunic, with feathered fringe and cords to tie it, ending in pearls; a similar *xicolli*, decorated besides with an ear of corn, which seems to be a symbol of royal power, as represented in other codices; and finally two feather headdresses.[109]

The two red *xicolli*, particularly the one with the ear-of-corn decoration, must have been shown from the back; otherwise, since the Mixtec *xicolli* opened in the front, the ear-of-corn decoration would have been split in half. A rear view of the garment is not without precedent in the codices. *Codex Magliabechiano,* folio 71*r*, illustrates an un-

---

[108] Caso 1960, p. 34.
[109] Caso 1964, p. 82.

FIGURE 43. Above: Mixtec *xicolli* showing the front opening. *Codex Colombino*, p. IX. Below: Drawing based on figure above. Dahlgren 1954:110, fig. 4.

FIGURE 44. Mixtec *xicolli* presented as an offering. *Codex Bodley*, p. 7.

modeled Aztec *xicolli* (see fig. 18), presenting the garment from the back, the better to show one of its most frequent accouterments, the tobacco pouch.

In light of the above arguments it would seem logical to assume that the Mixtec *xicolli* was very similar in construction to the Aztec costume, with the added feature of the two long cords. The Mixtec *xicolli* apparently sometimes had a design applied to the center of the back.

The problem of determining which classes and social types wore the Mixtec *xicolli* is more complex than that encountered when investigating its Aztec counterpart.

FIGURE 45. Mixtec *Xicolli* offering. *Codex Zouche-Nuttall*, p. 81.

FIGURE 46. Two Mixtec *xicolli* offerings. *Codex Vindobonensis* obverse, p. 22.

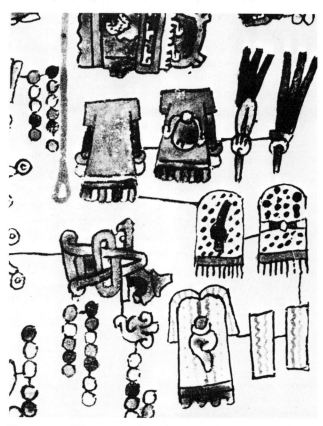

FIGURE 47. Gifts presented at the time of a Mixtec wedding. *Codex Selden*, p. 7.

Because of the wealth of Spanish documentation for the Valley of Mexico, it is possible to demonstrate the Mexica range of contexts and classes in which the *xicolli* was utilized. Since a comparable corpus of pre-Hispanic ethnographic data is not available for the Mixtec area, we must investigate those points by contrasting information that exists within the codices themselves.

As noted, all the major Mixtec pictorials are historical-genealogical manuscripts with the exception of the obverse of *Codex Vindobonensis*. The fifty-two sheets depict hundreds of individuals, but only fourteen are wearing the *xicolli*, and almost all of the jackets are red. Seven of the fourteen figures wearing the jacket appear in a single ceremonial scene dealing with gods involved in a pulque ritual (plate 14).[110] Their *xicolli* are easily identified by the costume's two tassels and its diagnostic fringe of what appears to be feathers, portrayed in alternating yellow, green, blue, and tan; similarly colored fringe appears on almost all the Mixtec jackets.

The remaining seven *xicolli*-clad figures of the obverse side of *Codex Vindobonensis* are found in a section of the manuscript which lists a series of sites,[111] perhaps mythological locations, and no doubt the *xicolli* wearers serve as elements of the place-name glyphs. In addition to the modeled jackets, there are four occurrences of pairs of individuals holding up one red and one striped *xicolli* by

[110] *Codex Vindobonensis* obverse, p. 25.
[111] Ibid., pp. 9, 39, 41, 42, 42, 42, 43.

the tabs, as though presenting them for offerings[112] (see fig. 46). There is one incidence of an element of a place glyph including a male pair holding up a red *xicolli*.[113] Two similar *xicolli* are also depicted in a group of offerings.[114] Two white *xicolli* draped in the doorways of temples are part of the place glyphs, as is another white *xicolli* that hangs—as though on a clothes line—between two poles[115] (see fig. 61). An unmodeled *xicolli* is shown as part of the god 9 Wind's attire.[116]

Aside from the above examples, the *xicolli* is shown depicted in the ritual-calendrical obverse of *Codex Vindobonensis*, and yet it is found in profusion in the historical-genealogical Mixtec documents, utilized by what appears to be a diverse cast of characters. In all of those codices the jacket is worn by bridegrooms and ancestors. The *xicolli* also appears on figures whom Caso designated as "warriors," males carrying weapons;[117] on individuals carrying staffs, whom Caso termed "ambassadors";[118] on musicians playing instruments;[119] and on intended victims who are carrying sacrificial flags[120] (also see example *k*). Almost all of those *xicolli* are red, a color Caso associated with the ruling class.[121]

Obviously there is something special about the red *xicolli*, or it would not have been used predominantly in the religious-calendrical *Vindobonensis* obverse to denote gods, place-names, and offerings. If red *xicolli*-clad individuals are found in such a wide range of contexts in the historical-genealogical documents, it is doubtful that the costume could have been special-purpose clothing as it was among the Mexica. The Aztec *xicolli*, always worn for a particular ceremony or purpose, is found in association with a wide range of social groups: gods, priests, nobles, sacrificing warriors and their sacrificial captives, sacrificing merchants and their sacrificial slaves, and administrators.

Since in Mesoamerica it is plausible that even so high-born a lord as the ruler himself might be in the course of his life not only bridegroom, warrior, musician, and ancestor but also sacrificial victim, it would seem that the Mixtec red *xicolli* was not a special-purpose garment in the Aztec sense of restriction to specific context but rather a costume of a special *class*. One more type of *xicolli* to be considered before any final conclusion can be reached is a white-with-black-dots version of the jacket which Caso[122] implied was worn exclusively by the priests.

In Mesoamerica, where religion so permeated every aspect of life, it is all but impossible to differentiate com-pletely between sacred and secular. This difficulty becomes particularly apparent when one is endeavoring to understand the Mixtec priestly jacket. According to Caso, males wearing white-with-black-dots *xicolli* are priests.[123] Aztec priests depicted in the *xicolli* are often shown with an incense bag and an incense burner (as on chart 3, examples *i*, *k*, and *l*). Similarly attired individuals also appear in the Mixtec codices (chart 9, example *l*). A further identifying attribute of the Aztec priest is a smear of blood in front of the ear, a symbol of repeated autosacrifice; that priestly diagnostic is also found in the Mixtec codices.[124] In neither the Aztec nor the Mixtec codices is the wearing of the *xicolli* restricted to the priestly class, however.

On the dedication stone of the Templo Mayor of Tenochtitlán, the Aztec emperors Tizoc and Ahuitzotl appear attired in the *xicolli*, which indicates that they were serving in their priestly guise. The dual role of ruler-priest also existed among the Mixtecs. The depiction of the saga of 5 Alligator in *Codex Bodley* shows the ruler in eleven episodes.[125] In four of them, 5 Alligator is receiving goods that indicate the bestowing of rank, and he wears the white-with-black-dots *xicolli*. The garment is also worn by a ruler whom 5 Alligator visits, 7 Movement, Lord of Mountain of Malinalli. In two subsequent scenes 5 Alligator is shown as a bridegroom wearing the red *xicolli*. The same pattern occurs throughout the Mixtec codices: where males are depicted as bridegrooms or ancestors, they almost always wear some variant of the red *xicolli*; sometimes stripes or dots are added.

Considering the above information, it would appear that the priestly *xicolli* was indeed restricted to a ritual context. Having stated this, I must hastily add the disclaimer "mainly" because the jacket is also found on Lord 10 Flint at the great gathering called by 8 Deer[126] and on a spear-carrying figure[127] Caso described as a "warrior."[128]

The Aztec *xicolli* is found in association with emissaries who carry staffs.[129] As mentioned earlier, Mixtec *xicolli*-clad figures carrying staffs can also be found, but unfortunately not much importance can be given to the Aztec-Mixtec similarity of *xicolli*-associated accouterments because the red *xicolli* the figures wear are the same garments they also don as warriors or as sacrificial victims.

The red *xicolli* also occurs in association with the playing of musical instruments. *Codex Becker I* contains a group of six musicians;[130] the five men all wear the ubiquitous red jacket and the lone woman has the same cos-

[112] Ibid., pp. 17, 22, 30, 35.
[113] Ibid., p. 46.
[114] Ibid., p. 18.
[115] Ibid., pp. 42, 46, 43.
[116] Ibid., p. 48.
[117] E.g., *Codex Colombino*, pp. i, iv, v.
[118] E.g., *Codex Selden*, p. 7.
[119] E.g., *Codex Becker I*, pp. 8–9.
[120] E.g., *Codex Becker I*, pp. 10–11.
[121] Caso 1960, p. 34.

[122] Caso 1960, e.g., 24, 33.
[123] Ibid., p. 33.
[124] E.g., *Codex Zouche-Nuttall*, p. 84.
[125] *Codex Bodley*, p. 6–8.
[126] *Codex Zouche-Nuttall*, p. 56.
[127] *Codex Colombino*, p. v.
[128] Caso 1966, p. 124.
[129] *Codex Mendoza*, vol. 3, fol. 66.
[130] *Codex Becker I*, pp. 8–9.

FIGURE 48. *Xicolli* being worn and utilized in a ritual performed by Mixtec musicians. *Codex Becker I*, p. 8.

tume hanging from the stand supporting the wind instrument she is playing (fig. 48). Again, musicians have no monopoly on the wearing of the jacket; theirs is the same costume seen throughout the codices.

An unmodeled *xicolli* utilized as an offering is connected with the office of ruler. Caso mentioned a combination of symbols that occur as offerings in the codices and are always connected with a king's ascent to the throne: a kind of feather fan, a lump of copal, a jade bead, and a red *xicolli*.[131] In the *Codex Bodley* the "red" *xicolli* include red with white stripes, red with white designs, and white with red dots. They also display a variety of designs on the decorative band above the fringe.[132]

The red-*xicolli* offerings could be considered badges of office except that they are the same costume worn by all the high-status Mixtec males so far discussed: gods, bridegrooms, ancestors, warriors, ambassadors, musicians, and sacrificial victims. It appears that the red *xicolli* was found in association with almost the full range of male ranks depicted in the Mixtec codices. If that is true, the ubiquitous garment was not distinctive enough to serve as a badge of office but was the accepted apparel of the class associated with all those positions.

The variety of pictorial and textual sources available for research on the Aztec costume repertory is large enough

to permit the differentiation between the dress of commoners and nobles. For example, the *xicolli* of the lower classes was made of maguey fiber; cotton garments were restricted to nobility. The Aztec *xicolli* was an event-associated rather than a class-associated garment. Because a similar corpus does not exist for the Oaxaca area, such a class differentiation cannot be made. Since it is doubtful that any commoners are depicted in the Mixtec codices, it is impossible to know whether or not they wore some modest version of the *xicolli*. What is obvious from the foregoing analysis of the Mixtec *xicolli* is that males of the ruling class wore the red jacket in so wide a range of contexts that it must have been their principal item of apparel. Unlike the Aztecs, for whom the wearing of the costume connoted a special occasion, the Mixtecs must have seen the *xicolli* as associated with class rather than event. Since the *xicolli* was the garment of the aristocracy, it is not surprising that it should also occur as part of personal and place-names, for example, Cloud Xicolli[133] and Hill of *Xicolli*.[134]

The first *xicolli* (example 9i) is worn by 2 Movement (Shining Serpent, as his headpiece implies). He was the sixth king of the second dynasty of Tilantongo. Here he is seen leaving the Temple of the Bag. He wears his red *xicolli* over a loincloth decorated with black dots.

[131] Caso 1960, p. 24.
[132] *Codex Bodley*, e.g., pp. 7, 25, 28.

[133] Caso 1960, p. 64.
[134] Caso 1966, p. 134.

The second *xicolli* example (9*j*) is seen on 8 Grass (Tláloc Sun; note the Tláloc mask and sun disk). He is shown at his marriage ceremony. His *xicolli*, which has red dots and a long cord hanging down the back, is pulled down over his knees in a manner reminiscent of the two seated Aztec priests in fig. 18. Such a depiction may have caused Caso to consider the *xicolli* a "long" garment that tied in back.

The third example (9*k*) is worn by 6 Lizard (Twisted Hill-Cotton?), who is carrying the sacrifice flag. The following scene of the folio shows him, clad only in his loincloth, stretched out on the sacrificial block with his heart cut out (fig. 49). His red *xicolli* has unusually long cords that end in fat tassels.

The next example (9*l*) wears a white *xicolli* with black dots, the garment associated with priests in the Mixtec codices.[135] This figure is 10 Monkey (Celestial Rain), the eleventh king of the third dynasty of Belching Mountain. He is making an offering of copal and carrying an incense bag and incense burner, two of the classic accouterments of the Aztec "priestly jacket."

The final example (9*m*) is also a priest, 9 Alligator, wearing a white *xicolli* with black markings. He holds a burning torch and has a red ear, which perhaps signifies the autosacrifice of the priests. The cord of his *xicolli* hangs down his back.

EXAMPLE 9*i*. Mixtec *xicolli*. *Codex Bodley*, p. 14.

Closed-sewn Garments.

ARMOR. The Mixtecs had a closed-sewn, sleeveless cotton armor that was quilted in vertical lines and reached only to the base of the torso. They also made use of jaguar skin for a type of body-protecting armor. Both cotton and skin garments were special-purpose clothing.

Fray Alvarado listed "*armas de la guerra: dai yecu, tatnu yufa, duvuacufifafaitninódodzo*"; and "*armas pitadas: dzononuuyecu, dzo no yecunuu*."[136] Stevens's 1726 Spanish-English dictionary defines *pita*: "An herb in the Indies, of which they make fine thread, as we do of flax." The *armas pitadas* may therefore refer to maguey- or henequen-fiber war jackets. The Mixtecs also had cotton armor; that is verified in the *Relaciones geográficas* from Tilantongo: ". . . their armor were *esquapiles* which are a kind of small clothing of *manta* cloth stuffed with cotton."[137]

Similar cotton armor was used throughout the Oaxaca region. The Zapotec dictionary of Fray Juan de Córdoba lists both "*Armas para la guerra todo genero: Lecàna quelaye*" and "*Armas de algodón: Piàga xilla que layè nunaquiné quelayè*."[138] The Zapotec *Relaciones geográficas* also verify that quilted armor was used; it is referred to as *ychca-huipiles* in the Zapotec-speaking community of

EXAMPLE 9*j*. Mixtec *xicolli*. *Codex Bodley*, p. 21.

---

[135] Caso 1960, p. 33.
[136] Alvarado 1962, 25v.
[137] Cline 1972, census no. 127; Paso y Troncoso 1905, 4:79.
[138] Fray Córdoba 1942, 37v.

EXAMPLE 9*l*. Mixtec *xicolli*. *Codex Selden*, p. 14.

EXAMPLE 9*k*. Mixtec *xicolli*. *Codex Selden*, p. 8.

FIGURE 49. Sacrifice of the Mixtec nobleman Lord 6 Lizard.
Codex Selden, p. 8.

Iztepexic.[139] From its description in the 1579 *Relaciones geográficas* from Zapotec-speaking Nexapa it is the same type of armor the Aztecs used:

> . . . among them the principal men and the captains used some short military jackets in the form of corslets quilted and stitched, which are [the types] the conquistador adopted to be the cotton armor with which they conquered the land.[140]

The few depictions of armor in the Mixtec codices also bear out the description.

Example 10*a* is a depiction of Lord 13 Rabbit, attending the famous meeting of the 112 lords. He wears white-cotton armor that is quilted in a vertical fashion, and he holds his shield and arrows in his hand.

The second example (10*b*) is 9 Flint (Xiuhcóatl from Hill of the Toztli and Blood).[141] He is armed with an odd-shaped stone weapon that Caso speculated may have been used by the Mixtecs and Zapotecs of the Valley of Oaxaca.[142] The armor of 9 Flint is red (as are most of the male garments in the *Codex Selden*), with the vertical quilting shown in white.

Caso made no mention of 9 Flint's opponent, who also wears a type of armor, a jaguar skin. The use of jaguar hide for a defensive garment is again illustrated in the final example in the armor section (10*c*).

All the figures in examples 10*b* and 10*c* of the armor section are in a posture that Nancy Troike calls "combat position":

> The weapon being used is usually a spear, *atlatl*, or ax, although the spear predominates in the great majority of cases. . . . this position is used for all *armed* figures involved in battle or conquest scenes, regardless of whether they are attacking or defending.[143]

ROBE. The robe appears to have been a full-length, body-encasing garment. It is found worn by a priest, an old man, a ruler at his marriage ceremony, and male deities seated on jaguar-covered stools, symbols of royal power.

The robe category has been a challenge. Of the five Mixtec codices utilized in this study, only *Zouche-Nuttall* and the obverse of *Vindobonensis* show the robe. Since no robes are shown on the side of *Codex Zouche-Nuttall* that deals with the life of 8 Deer, the garment is probably a religious-ritual garment. Robes appear only on seated figures. The possibility therefore exists that, where it is certain that the figure is male, the garment could be a *xicolli* or a long cape pulled down over the knees. If it is a female figure—and often it is extremely difficult to differentiate between the sexes—it could be a long *huipil* pulled down. After careful study I set aside such uncertainties and established a category to accommodate the garments.

EXAMPLE 9*m*. Mixtec *xicolli*. *Codex Zouche-Nuttall*, p. 70.

The *Codex Zouche-Nuttall* contains eight depictions of robes.[144] Two of them, examples *d* and *e* in the robe section of chart 10, are undoubtedly male figures because their *maxtlatl* are shown.

The first robed figure (example 10*d*) is named 5 Alligator. He may be a priest because his body is blackened and clothed in a white garment with black dots, a combination associated with priests in the Mixtec codices.

The second example (10*e*) is worn by 1 Flower, who is an aged deity as his single tooth testifies. The third robe (example 10*f*) is seen on 10 Dog. Though no *maxtlatl* is showing, he is no doubt a male because he is found in a seated position confronting a female, a convention generally agreed upon as designating a marriage ceremony.[145]

Example 10*g* is from the obverse side of *Codex Vindobonensis*, which contains the only three robe depictions in the pictorial. In a ceremonial scene dealing with pulque (plate 14) the Mixtec version of the god Xipe (second row from the bottom, right-hand side), and two others (first row, middle, and second row, left-hand side) are part of a group of twelve figures. Seven of the individuals are unquestionably male, since they wear *xicolli* and *maxtlatl*. Two are female, since they wear women's apparel, a triangular *quechquemitl*, a rounded *quechquemitl*, and a skirt. The remaining three figures are seated on jaguar-covered stools and are wearing what appear to be robes. In addition the figure on the second row left, appears to be wear-

[139] Cline 1972, census no. 57; Paso y Troncoso 1905, 4:18.
[140] Cline 1972, census no. 73; Paso y Troncoso 1905, 4:35.
[141] Caso 1964, p. 90.
[142] Ibid.

[143] Troike 1975, p. 6.
[144] *Codex Zouche-Nuttall*, pp. 5, 10, 11, 11, 17, 24, 36, 40.
[145] Smith 1973, p. 29.

CHART 10
MIXTEC COSTUME REPERTORY
Examples of Closed-sewn Garments

Male
Armor

a

b

c

Robe

d

e

f

g

Female
Huipil

h

i

j

k

Examples of Limb-encasing Garments

Male
Ceremonial Costume

l

m

n

o

p

SOURCES: (*a*) *Codex Zouche-Nuttall*, p. 66; (*b*) *Codex Selden*, p. 17; (*c*) *Codex Colombino*, p. VI; (*d*) *Codex Zouche-Nuttall*, p. 40; (*e*) *Codex Zouche-Nuttall*, p. 36; (*f*) *Codex Zouche-Nuttall*, p. 11; (*g*) *Codex Vindobonensis* obverse, p. 25; (*b*) *Codex Zouche-Nuttall*, p. 5; (*i*) *Codex Vindobonensis* obverse, p. 20; (*j*) *Codex Zouche-Nuttall* reverse, p. 9; (*k*) *Codex Vindobonensis* reverse, p. IV; (*l*) *Codex Zouche-Nuttall*, p. 32; (*m*) *Codex Zouche-Nuttall*, p. 10; (*n*) *Codex Zouche-Nuttall*, p. 45; (*o*) *Codex Vindobonensis* obverse, p. 4; (*p*) *Codex Selden*, p. 3.

ing a chest cape over his robe; the individual in the bottom row wears only the robe. The third individual (*g* in the robe section of chart 10) wears a garment with a decoration on it identical to that of two robed figures of the Borgia Group costume repertory (examples *b* and *d* of chart 13). The design is that of the down-feather ball, which was used as an offering and to decorate certain sacrificial victims.

Choosing a name for the robelike garments has been a difficult decision. Dahlgren refers to them as *camisones* ("long, wide shirts").[146] Alvarado does not list the term, nor does Juan de Córdoba. The latter, however, lists "Camisa de hombre o vestidura assi, Piàga, latipiaga-taceni, xiàga ya, mia.l.xipiàgaya."[147] For the purpose of this book *camisones* ("shirts") is not a good term for the garments because the western shirt is a sleeved garment, and it is doubtful that those costumes had sleeves (again, the sleevelike effect is probably caused by the material across the shoulder draping over the upper arm). The best word for the costumes seems to be "robe," which implies a long, enveloping garment, not necessarily with sleeves.

The Mixtec robe could have been similar to the full, enveloping garment worn in Michoacán. Perhaps it is only the convention of the artist that renders it so sleek and slim-fitting. Since the robe is seen only in a sitting position, it is difficult to know how long it was.

HUIPIL. The Nahuatl term for the Mesoamerican female blouse, *huipilli*, occurs as the shortened form *huipil* in the sixteenth-century Spanish documents that deal with non-Nahuatl-speaking peoples. In the interest of consistency, and because of its prevalence in the colonial and modern literature, the term *huipil* is used when discussing this garment among the four remaining Indian groups.

Although Burgoa did not mention the woman's *huipil*, Alvarado did.[148] He defined "*Camisa que usan las yndias que llaman huipil*" as "*dzico*." The *Relaciones geográficas* also refer to the use of the woman's blouse in the Mixtec-speaking community of Tilantongo: ". . . and the women with their . . . *guaypiles*, which resemble a surplice without sleeves."[149] A *Relación geográfica* from Cuicatec-speaking Papaloticpac describes the "*guaypil*" as reaching from the chest to below the thigh.[150] The examples of the woman's *huipil* in the Mixtec codices bear out these descriptions.

The Mixtec *huipil* was a closed-sewn, sleeveless tunic that extended to midthigh. Although the *huipil* does not occur in the Mixtec codices as frequently as the cape and the *quechquemitl* do, a few depictions of it exist in these pictorials.

The first example (10*b*) is worn by a female from the genealogical side of *Codex Zouche-Nuttall*; she is named 2 Serpent. Her *huipil* falls to the middle of her thigh, as

EXAMPLE 10*a*. Mixtec armor. *Codex Zouche-Nuttall*, p. 66.

EXAMPLE 10*b*. Mixtec armor. *Codex Selden*, p. 17.

---

[146] Dahlgren 1954, p. 110.
[147] Fray Córdoba 1942, 69r.
[148] Alvarado 1962, 42v.
[149] Cline 1972, census no. 127; Paso y Troncoso 1905, 4:75.
[150] Cline 1972, census no. 78; Paso y Troncoso 1905, 4:90–91.

EXAMPLE 10*c*. Mixtec armor. *Codex Colombino*, p. VI.

EXAMPLE 10*e*. Mixtec robe. *Codex Zouche-Nuttall*, p. 36.

EXAMPLE 10*d*. Mixtec robe. *Codex Zouche-Nuttall*, p. 40.

EXAMPLE 10*f*. Mixtec robe. *Codex Zouche-Nuttall*, p. 11.

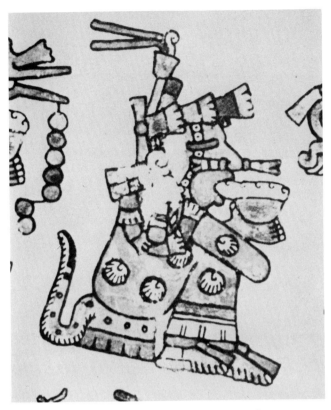

EXAMPLE 10g. Mixtec robe. *Codex Vindobonensis* obverse, p. 25.

EXAMPLE 10b. Mixtec *huipil. Codex Zouche-Nuttall*, p. 5.

does the *huipil* of the second example (10*i*), from the ritual side of *Codex Vindobonensis* obverse. She must represent a sacrifice by decapitation, for her head is thrown back in an unnatural manner and blood is flowing from her neck. In her hands she holds bowls (of blood?) topped by flint knives. Both her *huipil* and her skirt are fringed with a decorative border arranged to look like flint knives.

Jill Furst has suggested that this figure may be the personification of the maguey plant. She interprets the goddess as not only decapitated, but also with her heart cut out. This is analogous to the maguey plant in that the plant is similarly treated when its juice is extracted to make intoxicating beverages.[151]

The calendric name of the next example (10*j*) is 6 Rain. Her *huipil* is somewhat shorter than that of example 10*k*, the final figure, 4 Rabbit, who comes from the genealogical side of *Codex Vindobonensis*. It appears that 4 Rabbit is wearing a small, triangular *quechquemitl* over her multicolored *huipil*. To date this is the only such combination found in the Mixtec codices.

Limb-encasing Garments

CEREMONIAL COSTUMES. In the Mixtec codices appear three styles of a type of limb-encasing garment: jaguar, puma, and eagle costumes. Since the garments encase the entire body, we can assume that at least portions of the garments were woven, man-made facsimiles of the actual

[151] Troike 1978, p. 558.

EXAMPLE 10*i*. Mixtec *huipil. Codex Vindobonensis* obverse, p. 20.

EXAMPLE 10*j*. Mixtec *huipil*. *Codex Zouche-Nuttall*, p. 9.

EXAMPLE 10*l*. Mixtec ceremonial costume. *Codex Zouche-Nuttall*, p. 32.

EXAMPLE 10*k*. Mixtec *huipil*. *Codex Vindobonensis* reverse, p. IV.

skins. Unlike the Aztec limb-encasing garments, the Mixtec costumes do not occur in a martial context; they appear to be associated with ceremonial activities.

Since the individuals in the Mixtec codices sometimes are depicted wearing various elements of their names,[152]

the question arises whether these ceremonial outfits actually existed and were worn. Since jaguar, puma, and eagle costumes occur too repeatedly in the Mixtec codices to be merely examples of individuals wearing their names,[153] it seems logical to consider them a legitimate part of the Mixtec costume repertory.

In example 10*l*, worn by 8 Flint, the jaguar costume completely encases the body, with neither hands nor feet showing. In example 10*m*, 2 Lizard wears a jaguar costume with the feet and one hand exposed.

Example 10*n* shows 8 Deer wearing what is probably a puma costume with one hand exposed. The eagle costume also sometimes reveals a human hand and human feet, as in example 10*o*. In example 10*p*, which portrays the birth of 10 Reed, the eagle costume encases the body completely.

[152] Kelley 1973.
[153] *Codex Becker I* contains 2 jaguar costumes and 1 puma costume: Jaguar, page 2. Puma, page 7. *Codex Bodley* contains 47 jaguar costumes and 6 eagle costumes. Jaguar, 1, 3, 3(?), 5, 5, 5, 5, 5, 5, 6, 6, 6, 7, 8, 8, 8(?), 9, 9, 9, 9, 10, 10, 13, 13, 15, 15, 16, 16, 17, 17, 18, 19, 20, 22, 24, 24, 25, 28, 30, 30, 34, 34, 35, 36, 36, 37, 38. Eagle, 13, 28, 29, 30, 31, 39. *Codex Colombino* contains 7 jaguar costumes and 2 eagle costumes. Jaguar, ii, iii, iv, iv(?) (this is a black-and-white variant; Caso [1960, p. 28] sometimes referred to these black-and-white feline costumes as "lion"), iv, ix, xii. Eagle, iv, iv. *Codex Selden* contains 11 jaguar costumes, 23 eagle costumes, and 14 puma costumes. Jaguar, 10, 10, 10 (an unfinished garment that most closely resembles the jaguar costume), 11, 11, 12, 12, 13, 13, 13, 15. Eagle, 3, 3, 3, 4, 4, 4, 5, 8, 9, 10, 10, 10, 11, 12, 12, 16, 17, 18, 18, 18, 19, 19. Puma, 5, 6, 8, 9, 10, 10, 12, 12, 13, 13, 14, 14, 19, 20. *Codex Vindobonensis* contains 9 jaguar costumes and 11 eagle costumes. Jaguar, iii, v, xi, 9, 28, 28, 29, 29, 33. Eagle, 1, 4, 28, 28, 28, 29, 29, 29, 29, 35, 36. *Codex Zouche-Nuttall* contains 14 jaguar costumes, 9 eagle costumes and 2 puma costumes. Jaguar, 8, 10, 11, 13, 22, 26, 27, 32, 32, 41, 43, 52, 54, 68. Eagle, 3, 5, 5, 11, 12, 19, 25, 27, 19. Puma, 45, 77.

EXAMPLE 10*m*. Mixtec ceremonial costume. *Codex Zouche-Nuttall*, p. 10.

EXAMPLE 10*o*. Mixtec ceremonial costume. *Codex Vindobonensis* obverse, p. 4.

EXAMPLE 10*n*. Mixtec ceremonial costume. *Codex Zouche-Nuttall*, p. 45.

EXAMPLE 10*p*. Mixtec ceremonial costume. *Codex Selden*, p. 3.

SUMMARY

All five principles of clothing construction are manifest in the Mixtec costume repertory. In comparison with other Mesoamerican groups, the Mixtecs appear to have had a wider range of clothing available to them; theirs is the most extensive repertory yet considered. The draped-garment category has been extended to include the woman's cape. Among the Mixtecs, the *quechquemitl* and *xicolli* were not restricted to ceremonial wear but were the principal garments worn by the lords and ladies of the Mixtec codices. This may be related to the existence of two types of Mixtec *quechquemitl* and a number of design patterns and colors seen in the *xicolli*.

The *ichcahuipilli* occurs in the Mixtec repertory along with a leather battle jacket. The closed-sewn-garments category also includes the robe, which appears to have been restricted to ritual use. The fifth category of clothing construction, limb-encasing garments, is also present in the repertory; unlike the Aztecs, however, the Mixtecs wore these garments only in ceremonials. Examples of these garments indicate that the extent of their elaboration was a measure of the complexity of the ceremonial in which they were worn.

Close examination of the codices and colonial documents suggests that a hallmark of Mixtec clothing was its beauty and refinement, a reflection of the Mixtec cultural focus on fine craftsmanship. The same attention to detail is also evident in the apparel found in a similar group of ritual pictorials, the Borgia Group codices.

FIGURE 50. Tlazolteotl holding a spindleful of cotton thread. *Codex Laud*, p. 16D.

CHAPTER SIX

The Borgia Group Codices

of Unknown Provenience

 IN THIS CHAPTER the clothing repertory to be considered is that appearing in the ritual books known collectively as the Borgia Group: *Borgia*,[1] *Vaticanus B*,[2] *Cospi*,[3] *Fejérváry-Mayer*,[4] and *Laud*.[5] Although many classifiers also include two additional pieces, the single folio *Fonds Mexicain 20* and *Porfirio Díaz Reverse*, I believe that only the five core members of the group are pertinent for this costume analysis.

This distinctive collection of precontact religious pictorials is named after its most spectacular member, *Codex Borgia*. The manuscripts probably originally served as manuals for Indian priests and diviners and may also have been utilized as teaching aids. Their early history is obscure. They were first noted in Europe at different times ranging from the sixteenth to the nineteenth centuries and in different places—Italy, England, and Hungary. No completely reliable information on when or how they reached the Old World has ever come to light. *Codex Borgia* is known to have been in Italy since the sixteenth century, and was part of the private collection of Cardinal Stefano Borgia in the second half of the eighteenth century. Since 1814 it has been in the collection of the Biblioteca Apostolica Vaticana in Rome.

Codex Vaticanus B has been in the Vatican Library since the sixteenth century; there is no information on how it arrived there. In the library's inventory it is mentioned early among the Latin manuscripts.[6]

The origin of *Codex Cospi* was at first misunderstood. Its seventeenth-century cover shows that it was first considered Chinese: the word "Messico" is written over "la China." The inscription on the cover states that the codex was given as a Christmas present to Ferdinando Cospi by Valerio Zani in 1665. Nothing is known of the history of the pictorial before this date. Today it is in the Biblioteca Universitaria, Bologna, Italy.

Codex Laud was presented to the Bodleian Library in the 1630s by its last private owner, William Laud, archbishop of Canterbury and chancellor of the University of Oxford. The binding case of the pictorial described it as "Egyptian"; and Archbishop Laud may have come by it as a result of his involvement in Arabic studies. It is possible that *Codex Laud* was taken to England from the Continent. It may have been given to Charles, prince of Wales, or to George Villiers, duke of Buckingham, while he was on a mission to Spain in 1623 in an unsuccessful negotiation to obtain the hand of a Spanish princess for the heir to the English throne.[7] There is also the possibility that it came from some part of the central European region of the Hapsburg dominions. It must be remembered that, at the time of the Spanish conquest of Mexico, Vienna was the capital of the Hapsburg Empire, headed by Charles V of Spain. Soon after it reached Spain, much of New World treasure was sent on to Vienna, which may explain why the fifth member of the Borgia Group was first noted in nearby Hungary.

Codex Fejérváry-Mayer came to light in the first quarter

[1] Glass and Robertson 1975, *Codex Borgia*, census no. 33.
[2] Glass and Robertson 1975, *Codex Vaticanus B*, census no. 384.
[3] Glass and Robertson 1975, *Codex Cospi*, census no. 79.
[4] Glass and Robertson 1975, *Codex Fejérváry-Mayer*, census no. 118.

[5] Glass and Robertson 1975, *Codex Laud*, census no. 185.
[6] Anders 1972, p. 44.
[7] Burland 1966, pp. 5–6.

of the nineteenth century. At that time it was in the collection of the Fejérváry family, an eminent Hungarian noble family in the Hapsburg dominions.[8] In 1828 the Fejérváry family sent the pictorial to Paris to be copied by an artist employed by Lord Kingsborough. Since the Englishman was interested in publishing all the extant Mesoamerican codices, he apparently sent his Italian artist abroad to make copies of them.[9]

When Gabriel Fejérváry died in 1815, the codex passed to his nephew Franz Pulszky, who because of political disruptions in Hungary was living in exile in London. To relieve financial problems he sold the pictorial to Joseph Mayer, a noted citizen of Liverpool and collector of rare and exotic treasures. In 1897, Mayer consigned all of his collection to the Liverpool museum, where the codex is now housed.

Like the Mixtec pictorials *Zouche-Nuttall* and *Vindobonensis*, the *Codex Fejérváry-Mayer* and *Codex Laud* have been suggested as the two native books listed in the inventory of gifts Cortés sent back to Spain from Veracruz in July, 1519. Nicholson at first thought that they might have been acquired by the conquistadors in the area of Cuetlaxtlán on their initial voyage along the Gulf Coast.[10] In a later article, however, he summarized the scanty evidence available concerning the pictorial style of the region in late pre-Hispanic times and concluded that it was not particularly close to the two manuscripts.[11] Therefore, while it is not inconceivable that *Fejérváry-Mayer* and *Laud* were the two books of the 1519 inventory, some evidence argues against it.

In addition to the mystery of the Borgia Group codices' post-Conquest peregrinations, confusion over their place(s) of origin has surrounded the manuscripts. Unlike the Mixtec codices, whose historical and genealogical content can be used to place them in time and space, the ritual nature of the Borgia Group precludes specific attributions. Not only does religion change notoriously slowly, but the same religious concepts can be shared over wide geographic areas. A further problem is the absence of any colonial Spanish annotations on the Borgia Group manuscripts. Whereas all the ritual pictorials from the Nahuatl-speaking areas of the Valley of Mexico bear some sixteenth-century glosses, the members of the Borgia Group carry no such helpful aids. The result has been recurring efforts by scholars to determine the provenience of these important codices; in recent decades differing opinions have inspired interesting, lively debate.

It was the great German scholar Eduard Seler who first formally noted the similarity of style and content of the five core members of the group. He was the first to make a detailed analysis of the pictorials. Between 1887 and 1923 his learned treatises were published on *Codex Fejérváry-*

Mayer (1901–1902), *Codex Vaticanus B* (1902–1903), and *Codex Borgia* (1904–1909). The emphasis of the studies was almost entirely on interpretation. Seler speculated only briefly on provenience, considering first the Gulf Coast and then a highland area straddling the Puebla-Oaxaca border. From the beginning he was convinced, because of certain correlations between pictorial symbols and linguistic metaphors, that the Borgia Group had been produced by Nahuatl-speakers.

In 1927, in a significant development, a buried temple was excavated at Tizatlán, in Tlaxcala. Within the temple were discovered two plaster-covered altars with polychrome paintings. The Mexican archaeologist Alfonso Caso noted the close resemblance in style between the paintings and the *Codex Borgia*, particularly in a representation of Tezcatlipoca, the omnipotent, capricious god of the Nahuatl-speakers. Caso declared that the same culture had produced both the paintings and the screenfold. This conclusion, and the absence from the Mixtec pictorials of Tezcatlipoca, who is so important in manuscripts with religious content, made a Mixtec provenience seem doubtful. Furthermore, the resemblance of the Borgia Group manuscripts to the polychrome pottery of the Nahuatl-speaking pilgrimage center Cholula, near Tlaxcala, caused Caso to suggest the Puebla-Tlaxcala region as the probable place of origin of the pictorial manuscripts. For many years the views of both Seler and Caso were quoted, and the provenience problem remained unsolved.

In the past two decades Nicholson, archaeologist and ethnohistorian,[12] and Donald Robertson,[13] the art historian, have been considering the question of the provenience of the Borgia Group. Robertson, working especially with *Codex Borgia* and basing his argument on stylistic criteria, strongly espouses the Mixtec region as the point of origin for the manuscripts.[14] He views the Borgia Group pictorials as the Mixtecs' ritual documents — the religious counterpart to their historical-genealogical books. He emphasizes the presence of a variant of the *A–O* year symbol in *Codex Borgia* and thinks it significant that, unlike the codices on native paper of the Nahuatl-speakers, the Borgia Group manuscripts are all of animal skin, as are the Mixtec pictorials. As for the absence of the capricious god Texcatlipoca from the Mixtec histories, Robertson thinks that it simply reflects one of that deity's diagnostic qualities: chance.[15] Since the histories deal primarily with the secular world of human beings and hence do not emphasize the full Mixtec pantheon, the absence of one particular deity is neither surprising nor important.

Since Robertson credits an influx of Mixtec artists and artisans as the source of the high art on display in Tenochtitlán when Cortés arrived there, he dismisses the

---

[8] The Fejérváry family probably supported the Hapsburgs in the disturbed days of the Turkish invaders, who retreated in 1532 and again in 1552 (Burland 1971, p. 13).

[9] Nicholson, personal communication.

[10] Nicholson 1966a, p. 261.

[11] Nicholson MS, pp. 88–89.

[12] Nicholson 1957, 1966a, 1966b, 1967a, 1967b, 1967c, 1971b, 1971c, 1973a, 1973b, 1973c, 1974.

[13] Robertson 1959, 1963, 1966, 1968.

[14] Robertson 1963.

[15] Ibid., p. 161.

theory of a Puebla-Tlaxcala origin for the Borgia Group. From his standpoint the Tizatlán altar paintings were provincial and derivative, and he relegates Cholula, the center for the much-cited pictorial-style polychrome pottery, to "a station along the way" in the diffusion of artistic influence from the Mixteca to the Valley of Mexico.[16]

Nicholson disagrees with Robertson. He believes that, although the five major members of the Borgia Group share many fundamental features when compared with other Mesoamerican ritual books, their stylistic differences suggest the likelihood of diverse proveniences.[17] Basing his argument primarily on representations of a symbolic-ritual character, Nicholson thinks that the god Tezcatlipoca presents a special problem. Although the obverse of *Codex Vindobonensis* is irrefutably a Mixtec pictorial containing a broad range of deities, Tezcatlipoca is absent. Yet the god appears fairly regularly in the Borgia Group codices and repeatedly in *Codex Borgia*, appearances that argue that at least *Borgia* must have been produced in an area where Tezcatlipoca was a paramount god. Nicholson thinks that this fact definitely points away from the Mixteca. Impressed by the *Borgia's* stylistic similarity to Cholula polychrome ceramics, Nicholson favors that pre-Conquest religious and manufacturing center as *Borgia's* probable place of origin, or at least the general Puebla area, although he does not completely rule out the Mixteca or even the Gulf Coast, especially Cempoallan.

The archaeologists Robert Chadwick and Richard MacNeish have presented evidence that they interpret as suggesting that *Codex Borgia* was executed in the Tehuacán Valley, approximately 125 air miles southeast of Tlaxcala. They point to the similarities, which Nicholson also noted,[18] in the house types from the Tehuacán area as well as the close resemblance between Tehuacán's Venta Salada Phase ceramic vessels and containers that appear in *Codex Borgia*.[19] In essence their interpretation is a return to Eduard Seler's final views on the provenience of *Codex Borgia*. Now, however, Seler's position is considerably reinforced by recently uncovered archaeological data.

Of the fifty costume depictions used in the Borgia Group costume charts (charts 11 to 13) only eight come from *Codex Borgia*. The very profusion of detail that causes this manuscript to be treasured as an outstanding artistic expression makes it difficult to analyze some of the depicted clothing.

Codex Vaticanus B is regarded by Nicholson as a "problem child." While it resembles *Borgia*, it is much sketchier in both content and style. Aesthetically it is definitely inferior, with a much looser delineation of line. (For that reason only seven of the fifty clothing examples on the three clothing charts come from that screenfold.) Nicholson has attributed *Vaticanus B* to the Puebla-Tlaxcala or Gulf Coast area and pointed out that, if the

Mixteca is to be considered, certainly it would have to be a peripheral, provincial portion of that area, removed from the demanding artistic canon of codices *Zouche-Nuttall* and *Vindobonensis* obverse.

Codex Cospi is a brief manuscript with many blank pages. Stylistically, it is closest to *Borgia*, but it is not as impressive; only four of the fifty costume examples have come from that pictorial. Noting that *Cospi* resembles the Tizatlán altar paintings even more than does *Codex Borgia*, Nicholson has attributed it to the Puebla-Tlaxcala region.

Because the two are virtually identical in style, *Fejérváry-Mayer* and *Laud* can be considered together. Of all the members of the group they are closest to the Mixtec pictorials stylistically, but they are much more "streamlined," stripped to essentials, with less clutter of detail. That makes their costumes easier to interpret for use in the clothing charts; thirteen of the fifty depictions come from *Fejérváry-Mayer*, and eighteen come from *Laud*.

Of the five core members of the Borgia Group, *Codex Laud* is the least clearly understood: seven of its eleven sections have no known cognates. *Fejérváry-Mayer*, however, has sections cognate with other members of the group. Nicholson has suggested that certain tantalizing hints in the pictorials suggest the southern Gulf Coast as their place of origin: the emphasis on the mother goddess Tlazolteotl-Ixcuinan; the frequency of bare-chested females; the occurrence of armbands and axes; resemblances in universe diagrams in *Fejérváry-Mayer* and the *Codex Madrid*.[20]

The continuing uncertainty about the provenience of the Borgia Group makes it impossible to give a precise location in which the accompanying Mesoamerican costume repertory was worn. The question then arises, Can an analysis of the clothing from the Borgia Group aid in determining the pictorials' origin(s)? If the books are indeed the religious counterparts of the Mixtec histories, as Robertson contends, will there be marked garment similarities in the two costume repertories? Are the two repertories sufficiently analogous to make a valid comparison? Since the content of the Borgia Group pictorials is unquestionably religious, almost all the personages depicted are gods and goddesses wearing deity attire. That poses no problem in my investigation, since my policy has been to view clothing of Mesoamerican deities as reflecting local costume repertories. The garments are perhaps archaic, but they definitely mirror the culture from which they come.

THE BORGIA GROUP COSTUME REPERTORY

Draped Garments

MAXTLATL. The *maxtlatl* worn in the Borgia Group codices resembles the Mixtec loincloth; the knot of the

[16] Ibid., p. 164.
[17] Nicholson 1966b.
[18] Ibid., p. 150.
[19] Chadwick and MacNeish 1967.
[20] Nicholson 1966b, p. 155.

costume is worn at the back, with the front and back ends of the garment reaching well below the knees (as opposed to one type of *maxtlatl* — a much shorter loincloth knotted in front — worn by the Aztecs and Tlaxcalans). There are also some differences. Far more examples of decorated loincloths exist in the Borgia Group codices than are to be found in the Mixtec pictorials. That could be explained by the religious nature of the Borgia Group: deities wear more elaborate attire. If that is true, a good point of comparison is provided by *Codex Vindobonensis* obverse, the Mixtec pictorial that contains a considerable range of Mixtec deities or their impersonators.

There is a difference in the religious subjects covered by *Codex Vindobonensis* obverse and the Borgia Group codices. The content of the latter revolves around rituals, divinatory calendars, pantheons, and general religious ideologies, whereas the *Codex Vindobonensis* obverse is a telling of the Mixtec creation myth. The use of the latter pictorial as the Mixtec point of comparison is valid, however, because in both cases it is the clothing of ritual that is depicted. It is this point of union that justifies utilizing *Codex Vindobonensis* obverse as the Mixtec source with which to contrast and compare the garments from the Borgia Group.

The obverse side of *Vindobonensis* contains approximately 371 full depictions of loincloths (that is, depictions in which at least one full end of the garment is visible). Of these only 55 (15 percent) are decorated. In some codices of the Borgia Group the percentage of decorated loincloths is higher: *Borgia*, 55 percent (335 loincloths, 185 decorated); *Vaticanus B*, 68 percent (167 loincloths, 114 decorated); *Cospi*, 11 percent (56 loincloths, 6 decorated); *Fejérváry-Mayer*, 68 percent (81 loincloths, 55 decorated); *Laud*, 18 percent (93 loincloths, 17 decorated).

Chart 11 shows examples of draped garments in the Borgia Group. The first example (11a) in the *maxtlatl* category, from *Codex Laud*, shows the knot of the loincloth at the back of the body. Like seventy-six of the ninety-three breechclouts in the *Laud*, it is plain white and unadorned.

The second figure wearing a loincloth (example 11b) was identified by Seler (in the "explanatory tables" of his commentary on the *Vaticanus B*) as "the dancer," who comes from a *tonalamatl* section of the codex.[21] His *maxtlatl* is the most elaborate of all the loincloths portrayed in the Mesoamerican pictorials. I have found no other example that has a similar row of tabs along one edge of the garment. The waist section of the loincloth is unadorned, however. A portion of the knot at the back is visible, and it, too, is plain white. Of the approximately 167 *maxtlatl* in *Codex Vaticanus B* only 53 are unadorned.

The next example (11c) is from *Codex Fejéváry-Mayer*. The figure is the "Pinocchio nose god," a deity who occurs only in this pictorial of the Borgia Group. The god

carries a fan, a rattle stick as his traveling staff, and a carrying pack on his back — all diagnostics of the Nahuatl-speakers' merchant god Yacatecuhtli, who is sometimes compared to the Maya God M.[22] His white loincloth is unadorned, as are only twenty-six of the approximately eighty-one that appear in *Codex Fejérváry-Mayer*.

The fourth example (11d) of chart 11 is from the third *trecena* of the *tonalamatl* of *Codex Borgia*, presided over by Quetzalcoatl as the wind god. The male figure is kneeling in adoration before the god. The worshiper's loincloth, white and unadorned, appears to have been wrapped twice around his waist before being tied with a knot in the back. While this loincloth is plain, 55 percent of the deity figures in the *Codex Borgia* (185 of 335 apparent depictions) wear other clothing over their loincloths, and it is difficult to use them as examples.

The final example (11e) is from *Codex Laud*. The figure's *maxtlatl* appears to have been wrapped twice around his body and then tied in back. Of the five Borgia pictorials *Laud* has the lowest number of decorated loincloths: 18 percent (17 of 93 apparent depictions). As in the other four Borgia pictorials, personages who wear only a loincloth usually also lack other accessories.

HIP-CLOTH. The hip-cloths shown in the Borgia Group codices range in length from just below the buttocks to midthigh. In almost all cases the knot and ends of the *maxtlatl* have been pulled over the hip-cloth. The garment is worn by both gods and subsidiary helpers in the *Borgia Codex*; hence it was probably a general-purpose garment in the culture.

In comparing the elaboration of the Borgia Group hip-cloths with *Codex Vindobonensis* obverse, proportions differ within the group. *Vindobonensis* itself contains approximately 165 examples, none of which is a simple, unadorned white hip-cloth. Most are two colors, and several display a carefully drawn fringe. The same description applies to the approximately 172 hip-cloths of *Codex Borgia*, all of which are decorated, and of the 21 examples found in *Codex Cospi*. In *Codex Vaticanus B*, 48 of the 71 hip-cloths — 68 percent — are decorated, and the remaining 23 are white, adorned with white fringe. In *Codex Fejérváry-Mayer* only 17 percent are decorated, and in *Laud*, 18 percent. Most of the hip-cloths in the two pictorials are white (43 of 52 in *Fejérváry-Mayer*, 14 of 17 in *Laud*) and are adorned with only a fringed border. Thus the latter two pictorials, which most closely resemble *Codex Vindobonensis* in style, differ most markedly from it in the portrayal of the hip-cloth.

The first hip-cloth example (11f) is from the section of *Codex Fejérváry-Mayer* dealing with the Six Heavenly Wanderers, merchant deities. Seler identified the deer-headed god as the fourth of the Four Wandering Gods, the Priest of the Olden Time, the primeval time.[23] The

---

[21] Seler 1902–1902, fol. 52.
[22] Nicholson 1966b, p. 155.

[23] Seler 1901–1902, p. 160.

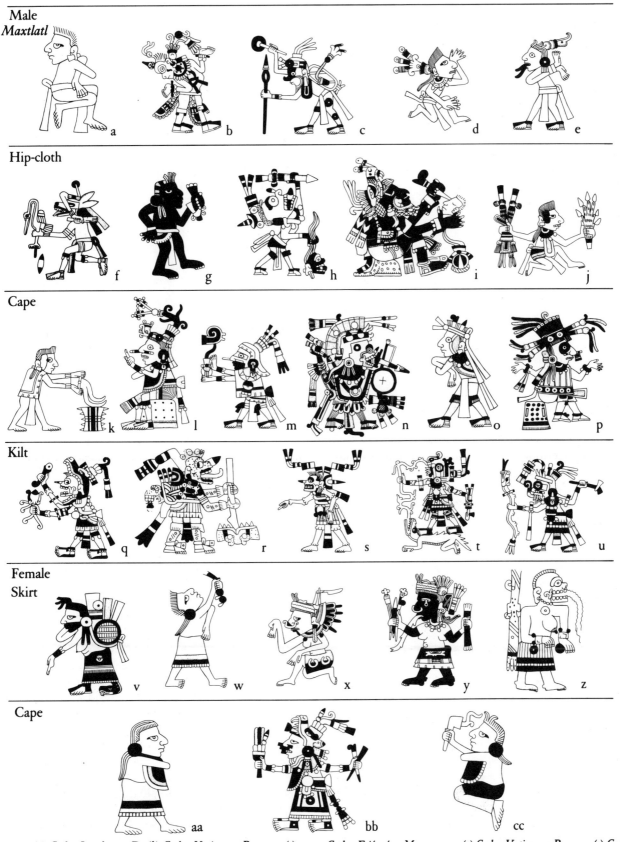

Male
Maxtlatl

Hip-cloth

Cape

Kilt

Female
Skirt

Cape

SOURCES: (a) *Codex Laud*, p. 15D; (b) *Codex Vaticanus B*, p. 52; (c) *Codex Fejérváry-Mayer*, p. 36; (d) *Codex Borgia*, p. 62; (e) *Codex Laud*, p. 20; (f) *Codex Fejérváry-Mayer*, p. 32; (g) *Codex Vaticanus B*, p. 33; (h) *Codex Cospi* recto, p. 1; (i) *Codex Vaticanus B*, p. 33; (j) *Codex Borgia*, p. 67; (k) *Codex Laud*, p. 3D; (l) *Codex Fejérváry-Mayer*, p. 36; (m) *Codex Laud*, p. 3; (n) *Codex Cospi* recto, p. 9; (o) *Codex Laud*, p. 4; (p) *Codex Borgia*, p. 69; (q) *Codex Fejérváry-Mayer*, p. 3; (r) *Codex Vaticanus B*, p. 12; (s) *Codex Laud*, p. 7D; (t) *Codex Fejérváry-Mayer*, p. 4; (u) *Codex Laud*, p. 4; (v) *Codex Fejérváry-Mayer*, p. 30; (w) *Codex Laud*, p. 12D; (x) *Codex Borgia*, p. 23; (y) *Codex Borgia*, p. 48; (z) *Codex Vaticanus B*, p. 41; (aa) *Codex Laud*, p. 15D; (bb) *Codex Fejérváry-Mayer*, p. 3; (cc) *Codex Laud*, p. 11D.

EXAMPLE 11a. Borgia Group *maxtlatl. Codex Laud*, p. 15D.

EXAMPLE 11b. Borgia Group *maxtlatl. Codex Vaticanus B*, p. 52.

EXAMPLE 11c. Borgia Group *maxtlatl. Codex Fejérváry-Mayer*, p. 36.

EXAMPLE 11d. Borgia Group *maxtlatl. Codex Borgia*, p. 62.

152

god, whose staff is a white heron, wears a white fringed hip-cloth that extends to midthigh. In the deity's hand is a human forearm. We know from Sahagún that the left forearm of a woman dying in childbirth was much sought after by Aztec wizards.[24] It was reputed to have magic power. When a gang of malicious wizards used it to knock on the door of a house, the inhabitants immediately became crippled, paralyzed, or overcome by sleep. The gang could then enter to steal from the residents or take advantage of them. The body of a woman dying in childbirth had to be protected not only from wizards but also from warriors. The latter group coveted both her hair and the middle finger of her left hand. They would attach these trophies to their shields to ensure courage and success in battle.[25]

The second figure of the hip-cloth section (example 11g) is from *Codex Vaticanus B*. Seler identified him as Xochipilli, one of the twenty-five divine pairs.[26] His white-fringed, gray hip-cloth is shorter than example *f* but, like it, gives the impression of being held in place by the *maxtlatl*. The Austrian scholar Karl A. Nowotny contended that the series of twenty-five male-female pairs from which the figure comes constitutes a section of the codex that the Indian priests used for prognosticating the success or failure of impending marriages.[27]

The third example (11h) is from the section of *Codex Cospi* devoted to the *tonalamatl* and, according to Seler, is a *temani*, "he who has captured a prisoner."[28] His plain gray hip-cloth comes to midthigh, and the knot of his white *maxtlatl* has been pulled over it.

The fourth hip-cloth (example 11i) is worn by a figure in *Codex Vaticanus B*. One of the "four times five guardians of the Venus periods," he was specifically identified by Seler as God of the East,[29] although this identification has been questioned.[30] The deity's white fringed hip-cloth has a decorated border of two black lines and one red line and is held in place by a wide, wine-colored *maxtlatl* with a blue border and a white fringe. Seler speculated that the little head the god is holding and "jabbing with the bone dagger" is his symbol.[31] In another context Seler mentioned that among the Mexicas eye gouging was a symbol of mortification—bloodletting in honor of the gods.[32]

Example 11j, the last hip-cloth example of chart 11, is from the thirteenth *trecena* of the *tonalamatl* of *Codex Borgia*, presided over by the rain god Tlaloc.[33] The figure, who may be a priest, judging from the smear of

EXAMPLE 11e. Borgia Group *maxtlatl*. *Codex Laud*, p. 20.

[24] Sahagún 1950–69, bk. 4, pp. 101–06.
[25] In *The Golden Bough* Sir James Frazer (1959, p. 55) points out that burglars of all ages and many lands have made use of such imitative magic in the belief that people can be rendered blind, deaf, and dumb by the use of a dead person's body or anything tainted with the infection of death.
[26] Seler 1902–1903, fol. 33.
[27] Nowotny 1961, p. 38.
[28] Seler 1902–1903, p. 25.
[29] Seler 1901–1902, p. 100.
[30] Nicholson, personal communication.
[31] Seler 1901–1902, p. 95.
[32] Ibid., p. 47.
[33] Seler 1963, *Códice Borgia, láminas explicativas*, p. 67.

EXAMPLE 11f. Borgia Group hip-cloth. *Codex Fejérváry-Mayer*, p. 32.

EXAMPLE 11g. Borgia Group hip-cloth. *Codex Vaticanus B*, p. 33.

EXAMPLE 11h. Borgia Group hip-cloth. *Codex Cospi* recto, p. 1.

blood at his temple and the incense bag in his hand, kneels before Tlaloc. His hip-cloth is dark green with a red border and a white fringe.

CAPE. The men's capes found in the Borgia Group codices are either worn over the chest or cover the back and shoulders. None extend below the torso, and most come only to the waist. While it seems impossible that the capes could stay on the body without being secured in some fashion, no ties are visible. Since the garments are worn by deity figures, the cape was obviously a high-status garment.

Capes do not appear frequently in the Borgia Group codices, and identifying them is sometimes a problem. The richly detailed style of *Codex Borgia* makes it difficult to determine what is or is not a cape in that pictorial. The male figures wear such elaborate necklaces and pectorals, plus ornate headdresses that often extend down their backs, that it is impossible to identify the fabric of the body garment. The only depictions about which I feel fairly certain are the male chest capès in figure 51 and example *p* of chart 11 and the chest capes placed over mummy bundles shown in figure 52). Since *Codex Vindobonensis* obverse, the Mixtec pictorial showing the fullest range of deities or their impersonators, has only two capes (see chart 8, examples *j* and *k*), it is similar to *Borgia* in this facet of costume repertory.

Codex Cospi shows five figures wearing chest capes[34] (see chart 11, example *n*). *Fejérváry-Mayer* has twelve examples,[35] and *Laud* has eight.[36] *Laud* also has the only two back capes of the Borgia Group[37] (see examples *k* and *o* of chart 11).

The first cape example (11*k*), one of the back capes from *Codex Laud*, is worn by an individual who appears to be making an offering in front of a temple where the death god officiates.[38] The cape comes only to the end of his torso and has a fringed border. There is no visible means of securing it to the shoulders, but a narrow edge of the other side of the garment can be seen.

The second example (11*l*) is from a section of *Codex Fejérváry-Mayer* dealing with the six heavens;[39] the figure illustrated is the maize god, who wears a flowering maize plant on his head.[40] The god's cape covers only his chest, and appears to extend a little below his waist. It is dark green with a red border and narrow white-beaded trim. There is no evidence of the ties that must have secured the garment around the neck.

The chest cape is probably the same apparel that is shown in *Codex Fejérváry-Mayer* worn over long robes

[34] *Codex Cospi*, recto, pp. 9, 9, 10, 10, 11.
[35] *Codex Fejérváry-Mayer*, pp. 24, 25, 25, 30, 30, 32, 33, 33, 34, 35, 36, 36.
[36] *Codex Laud*, pp. 6, 7, 20, 23, 17D, 20D, 20D, 21D.
[37] Ibid., pp. 3D, 4.
[38] This man may be a priest; note the stylized smear of blood in front of his ear.
[39] Seler 1901–1902, p. 182.
[40] Ibid., p. 188.

EXAMPLE 11*i*. Borgia Group hip-cloth. *Codex Vaticanus B*, p. 33.

EXAMPLE 11*j*. Borgia Group hip-cloth. *Codex Borgia*, p. 67.

(see chart 13, examples *b* and *c*). Seler referred to the garment as "an apron-like garment,...the *quemitl*."[41] In another section he defined the *quemitl* as "a long apron-like garment which was fastened around the neck of idols."[42] The same chest cape is depicted in *Codex Borgia*, tied around the necks of the four mortuary bundles (see fig. 52).

The deity wearing the third cape example (11*m*) was identified by Seler as Tezcatlipoca,[43] although that identification is now considered doubtful.[44] The god is bringing an offering of a rubber ball topped by a single *quetzal* feather to the yawning mouth of the earth monster. The extension of the deity's arms displays the fullness of his white, wide-fringed cape with its gray horizontal stripe. Over the cape he wears a collar or pectoral. Again no securing device for the garment is visible. It is difficult to determine whether it is a back or chest cape. From the position of the arms the cape appears to cover the back and shoulder; however, since anatomical fidelity is not a strong feature of the pictorials, the costume could be a chest cape.

The fourth cape example (11*n*) is worn by a skull-faced god identified by Seler as the "deity of the evening star."[45] In one hand he holds an atlatl, the native spear-thrower, with a spear in place. In the other hand he holds a shield, a hand flag, a bundle of spears, and a hunter's net bag. His chest cape is green banded in red with a white border. Over it he wears the white ring (*anauatl*) associated with Tezcatlipoca (the deity is also wearing a kiltlike garment, discussed below).

The next cape (example 11*o*), from *Codex Laud*, shows a

FIGURE 51. A central Mexican deity wearing a male chest cape. *Codex Borgia*, p. 24.

deity wearing a white fringed back cape. His blue pectoral with round balls is an accessory repeatedly seen in both *Laud* and *Fejérváry-Mayer*. A similar adornment is also worn with a cape in example *p*. It is regrettable that more information cannot be presented regarding many of the examples from *Codex Laud*. Much of its context is not fully understood at the present time.

The last cape (example 11*p*) was identified by Seler as

[41] Ibid., p. 130.
[42] Ibid., p. 122.
[43] Seler 1902–1903, p. 47.
[44] Nicholson, personal communication.
[45] Seler 1902–1903, p. 318.

FIGURE 52. Chest capes worn on mummy bundles. *Codex Borgia*, p. 26.

the "god of the planet Venus, the morning star."[46] His chest cape is white with a border of two tones of gray. The red tie visible at the back of the neck apparently secures the red, gold, and gray pectoral, rather than being a fastener for the cape.

EXAMPLE 11*k*. Borgia Group male cape. *Codex Laud*, p. 3D.

KILT. It has been mentioned that the Mixtec pictorial *Codex Vindobonensis*, obverse and reverse, contains a few depictions of kilts. Several kilts can also be found in three of the Borgia Group codices: *Vaticanus B*, *Fejérváry-Mayer*, and *Laud* (and possibly also in *Cospi*). There is a correlation between skeleton depictions and the wearing of the kilt. A caped figure (*n*) from *Codex Cospi* shown in chart 11 seems to have a kilt beneath his long chest cape. A similar kilt is found on certain Tlaloc figures (see chart 2, example *o*, and chart 8, example *n*).

The first kilt (example 11*q*) is the death god, Mictlantecutli (Lord of the Underworld), whose skull head looks out of a reptile's open jaws. In one hand he holds a gouged eye, and in the other a rendered heart.

The next example (11*r*) is wearing a similar kilt. He too is Mictlantecutli, and Seler speculated that he is thrusting a pointed staff into the open throat of the earth monster to signify the digging of a hole in the earth, possibly in connection with two nearby bodies done up in mummy bundles.[47] The third example (11*s*) is also the death god and wears a similar skirt.

The rain god Tlaloc (example 11*t*) wears a similar skirt;

[46] Seler 1963, *Códice Borgia, Láminas explicativas*, sheet 69.
[47] Seler 1902–1902, p. 74.

EXAMPLE 11*l*. Borgia Group male cape. *Codex Fejérváry-Mayer*, p. 36.

EXAMPLE 11*m*. Borgia Group male cape. *Codex Laud*, p. 3.

EXAMPLE 11*n*. Borgia Group male cape. *Codex Cospi* recto, p. 9.

EXAMPLE 11*o*. Borgia Group male cape. *Codex Laud*, p. 4.

EXAMPLE 11*p*. Borgia Group male cape. *Codex Borgia*, p. 69.

EXAMPLE 11*q*. Borgia Group kilt. *Codex Fejérváry-Mayer*, p. 3.

EXAMPLE 11*r*. Borgia Group kilt. *Codex Vaticanus B*, p. 12.

EXAMPLE 11*s*. Borgia Group kilt. *Codex Laud*, p. 7D.

his entire array of attributes resembles that of the Mixtec Tlaloc in *Codex Vindobonensis* (see chart 8, example *n*). Similar garments are worn by five Tlaloc depictions in *Codex Vaticanus B*.[48] Example 11*u*, another Tlaloc, displays a similar skirt.

[48] *Codex Vaticanus B*, pp. 43, 44, 45, 46, 47.

SKIRT. The wraparound skirts found in the Borgia Group codices vary from knee to ankle length. Unlike examples in the Mixtec codices, in which a skirt is almost never worn without an upper-body garment, these Borgia Group skirts are often the only clothing worn. That is

EXAMPLE II*u*. Borgia Group kilt. *Codex Laud*, p. 4.

EXAMPLE II*t*. Borgia Group kilt. *Codex Fejérváry-Mayer*, p. 4.

EXAMPLE II*v*. Borgia Group skirt. *Codex Fejérváry-Mayer*. p. 30.

one of several reasons why Nicholson includes the southern Gulf Coast as a possible place of origin of the Borgia Group.[49]

The skirts found in the Borgia Group codices give no indication that they are wraparound garments, but what we know of the Mixtec skirts and those of other Mesoamerican groups strongly suggests that the Borgia Group skirts are also wraparound.

The first wraparound skirt (example II*v*) is worn by Tlazolteotl,[50] the goddess associated with the coastal Huaxtec region, who carries on her back a warrior's shield and bundle of darts. A red-snake head has been substituted for one of her feet. Tlazolteotl's skirt, which comes to her ankles, is red with a white fringe, a green-and-red band, and a white-beaded border.

The second skirt (example II*w*) is worn by one of a pair of "lords and ladies of the third night hour and of the north."[51] She is dancing with her male partner, holding one end of a garland. Her skirt is white with a blue-and-red band and a white-beaded border. It is shorter than the skirt in example *v*, coming only to midcalf.

The next example (II*x*) is worn by Tlazolteotl, "goddess of filth, goddess of the earth,"[52] one of a series of twenty deities. Her skirt, which comes to just above the knee, is red and black and has two crescent-shaped designs. Her nose ornament, a Huaxtec symbol, indicates her place of origin. An unspun cotton fillet encircles her head, and a

spindle is arranged in her hair.

A similar skirt is found on example II*y*, one of the Cihuateteo, deceased women transformed into goddesses. Her skirt is black with yellow, white, red, and green bands and a wide fringed border. It is decorated with a design of a leg bone.

The final skirt (example II*z*) is worn by a deity who is

[49] Nicholson 1966*b*, p. 155.
[50] Seler 1963, 2:130.

[51] Ibid., p. 154.
[52] Seler 1963, *Códice Borgia, Láminas explicativas*, p. 23.

EXAMPLE 11w. Borgia Group skirt. *Codex Laud*, p. 12D.

EXAMPLE 11x. Borgia Group skirt. *Codex Borgia*, p. 23.

wearing the death's-head mask. Her skirt is white with narrow vertical brown lines and two wider, horizontal brown stripes. Like (*y*) the preceding skirt, it comes to midthigh.

FEMALE CAPE. The problem of classifying certain women's upper-body garments that appear in the Borgia Group codices is as perplexing as it is for the Mixtec codices. At least some of the capelike costumes in the Mixtec codices have visible ties that give an indication of how the garments might have been secured on the body; the Borgia Group illustrations all too often lack such clues. The female chest cape is shown in only three of the five Borgia Group codices: *Fejérváry-Mayer*,[53] *Laud*,[54] and *Vaticanus B*.[55] It appears to have tied at the neck and to have extended just below the waist. Since the women shown wearing it are goddesses, it may have been a high-status garment; the women in the three codices are also sometimes depicted topless or wearing *quechquemitl*.

The first female cape (example 11*aa*) poses no identification problem, for, although the garment displays no visible ties, it is obviously a chest cape analogous to example 11*l*, the male cape that Seler referred to as a *quemitl*.[56] He identified the female figure as Tonacacihuatl, "goddess of life," in the Nahuatl-speaker's paradise, Tamoanchan.[57] She and her male counterpart function as the lords of a section of the divinatory manual Seler called the "sixth nocturnal hours and of the upper region."

The second cape (example 11*bb*) was identified by Seler as Chalchiuhtlicue, "she of the jeweled robe, the water goddess, the lady of the flowing water."[58] Her helmet mask combines the upper jaw of a snake and a jaguar's ear (behind the snake's eye). In one hand she holds a receptacle made of feathers, in the other a bone dagger and an agave-leaf spine, implements that served for autosacrificial bloodletting. The goddess's white, green, and red skirt has a round-jewel decoration in the center. Her blue cape is a *quemitl* type (like example 11*aa*), and both her cape and necklace have a white beadlike border.

A similar chest cape is seen on example 11*cc*, the final example. It is also blue with a white, beaded fringe. No garments analogous to these *quemitl*-type female capes appear in the Mixtec *Vindobonensis* or the other Mixtec codices.

Slip-on Garments

ROUNDED QUECHQUEMITL. The rounded *quechquemitl* of the Borgia Group range in size from full garments that come below the waist (similar to those of the Mixtec codices, particularly *Vindobonensis* obverse) to shorter costumes that appear to fall just across the rib cage. None of

---

[53] *Codex Fejérváry-Mayer*, pp. 3, 35(?), 37.
[54] *Codex Laud*, pp. 10D, 11D, 13D, 13D, 15D, 15D.
[55] *Codex Vaticanus B*, p. 39.
[56] Seler 1901–1902, pp. 122, 130.
[57] Seler 1963, 2:159.
[58] Seler 1901–1902, p. 37.

EXAMPLE 11y. Borgia Group skirt. *Codex Borgia*, p. 48.

EXAMPLE 11z. Borgia Group skirt. *Codex Vaticanus B*, p. 41.

EXAMPLE 11aa. Borgia Group female cape. *Codex Laud*, p. 15D.

EXAMPLE 11bb. Borgia Group female cape. *Codex Fejérváry-Mayer*, p. 3.

EXAMPLE 11cc. Borgia Group female cape. *Codex Laud*, p. 11D.

EXAMPLE 12a. Borgia Group rounded *quechquemitl*. *Codex Fejérváry-Mayer*, p. 25.

the latter type appears in the Mixtec pictorial corpus. The shorter-style *quechquemitl* are sometimes worn in such a way as to give them a decidedly capelike appearance.

The first rounded *quechquemitl* (example 12a) is worn by a goddess whom Seler identified as one of the deities of the six quarters.[59] She is an old woman, as her sole tooth indicates. She is sitting before a spider and holding a portion of its web in her hand. She wears a full, rounded blue *quechquemitl* with a white fringe.

The second example (12b) is worn by the maize goddess, companion to the *quemitl*-cape-wearing god in example *l* of chart 11. She wears a large, dark-green rounded *quechquemitl* with a red band and a beaded border. The garment is pulled over her knees, giving it an apronlike appearance.

The third example (12c) shows the ambiguities involved in classifying many of the female upper-body garments. She is Chantico, the goddess of fire,[60] who presides over the sixth *tercena* of the *tonalamatl*. She is wearing a short, red rounded *quechquemitl* that appears to be fringed with feathers. At first glance the two ties hanging down her back suggest that her garment may be a cape, but closer inspection shows that the cords are part of her headdress. The undulating border of the upper-body garment identifies it as a *quechquemitl*.

The fourth example from *Codex Laud* (12d) is also a short, rounded *quechquemitl*, white with a red border. As in the preceding examples the elevated section of the border at the area that would ordinarily fall over the arm argues against identifying the garment as a cape.

Example 12d is one of a number of figures with undeniably feminine diagnostics who also wear the quintessential male garment, the *maxtlatl*. These bisexual figures, with their blended, melded, and fused iconography of several deities, are the challenge of Mesoamerican scholars' lives. These androgynous personages are usually associated with the involved and esoteric earth-death-fertility complex.[61] To date such examples have been found in only three of the Borgia Group: *Laud*,[62] *Fejérváry-Mayer*,[63] and *Vaticanus B*.[64] Analogous figures are not found in the Mixtec corpus, but occur once in *Codex Telleriano-Remensis*, from the Nahuatl-speaking Valley of Mexico,[65] and also once in the *Tonalamatl Aubin*, from the neighboring Puebla-Tlaxcala valley.[66]

The final *quechquemitl* (example 12e) is the most capelike of all. It comes from the section of *Codex Fejérváry-Mayer* dealing with the "four times five guardians of the Venus period." Seler classified the goddess as one of the five female deities identified with suckling infants,[67] which he

[59] Ibid., pp. 132–33.
[60] Seler 1963, *Códice Borgia, Láminas explicativas*, p. 63.
[61] Nicholson 1967c, p. 85.
[62] *Codex Laud*, pp. 17, 18, 20, 24.
[63] *Codex Fejérváry-Mayer*, pp. 28, 28.
[64] *Codex Vaticanus B*, pp. 30, 77, 78, 78, 79, 79, 89.
[65] *Codex Telleriano-Remensis*, fol. 18v.
[66] *Tonalamatl Aubin*, fol. 13.
[67] Seler 1901–1902, p. 94.

CHART 12
THE BORGIA GROUP COSTUME REPERTORY
Examples of Slip-on Garments

Male - - - - - - - - - - - - - -

Female
Rounded
Quechquemitl

a   b   c   d   e

Triangular
Quechquemitl

f   g   h   i   j

Examples of Open-sewn Garments

Male
Xicolli

k   l

Female - - - - - - - - - - - - - - - - -

SOURCES: (a) *Codex Fejérváry-Mayer*, p. 25; (b) *Codex Fejérváry-Mayer*, p. 36; (c) *Codex Borgia*, p. 63; (d) *Codex Laud*, p. 20; (e) *Codex Fejérváry-Mayer*, p. 28; (f) *Codex Borgia*, p. 59; (g) *Codex Laud*, p. 17; (h) *Codex Vaticanus B*, p. 89; (i) *Codex Fejérváry-Mayer*, p. 8; (j) *Codex Laud*, p. 16D; (k) *Codex Fejérváry-Mayer*, p. 27; (l) *Codex Laud*, p. 8.

EXAMPLE 12*b*. Borgia Group rounded *quechquemitl*. *Codex Fejérváry-Mayer*, p. 36.

EXAMPLE 12*d*. Borgia Group rounded *quechquemitl*. Codex Laud, p. 20.

associated with nursing the gods with blood symbolized by the smearing of the idol's mouth with a dishful of sacrificial blood. Each of the five goddesses has her *quech-quemitl* pushed back in the manner of example *e* so that the breasts are exposed.[68] Three of the goddesses are nursing infants.

TRIANGULAR QUECHQUEMITL. The small, narrow triangular *quechquemitl* of the Borgia Group codices is identical to its Mixtec counterpart. When worn with the points front and back, the garment extends just slightly beyond the shoulders with the front point coming only to the waist or slightly below. It is usually shown as the sole upper-body garment.

The first triangular *quechquemitl* (example 12*f*) is worn by a figure identified by Seler as Xochiquetzal (goddess of love),[69] one of the lunar deities of *Codex Borgia*. She wears a very short triangular *quechquemitl* with blue and red stripes and a border of white *xonecuilli* on a black-ground design, also seen on a Mixtec *quechquemitl* (example *b*, chart 9).

Example 12*f*, one of the few overtly erotic depictions in the Mesoamerican codices, represents Xochiquetzal in her guise as amorous companion to the warriors; in the same scene she is also depicted as representing the conjugal union (fig. 53). A second Xochiquetzal is vigorously pulling the hair of the fertility god Xochipilli, who is ardently admiring the courtesan Xochiquetzal seen in example *f*.

The triangular *quechquemitl* seen in example 12*g* is a larger garment. It is dark red with a wide white border, and is worn as the sole upper-body costume. That is not the case with the following example (*b*), a goddess who—like example 12*g*—is wearing the male *maxtlatl*.

EXAMPLE 12*c*. Borgia Group rounded *quechquemitl*. *Codex Borgia*, p. 63.

[68] *Codex Fejérváry-Mayer*, pp. 28, 29.
[69] Seler 1963, 1:77.

Seler identified the deity in example 12*b* as Mayauel, the "agave plant goddess."[70] She is wearing a tan-and-wine-colored *quechquemitl* over a striped, fringed, bolerolike cape which is similar to those seen in the Mixtec codices. It is the only such combination found in the Borgia Group codices.

The next figure (example 12*i*) is Xochiquetzal in her guise as the goddess of flowers, patroness of female artistic work. Her *quechquemitl* is white with a white band and she wears it as the sole upper-body garment. According to Seler, "...she shows a chain of gems which hangs down from the rosette attached to the loins, the so-called *cuitlatezcatl*, the 'back mirror.'"[71]

The final example (12*j*), the goddess Tlazolteotl, also wears the triangular *quechquemitl* as her sole upper-body garment. Her red-and-gray *quechquemitl* has a wide-fringed border. She has spindles filled with cotton thread arranged in her hair and held in her hand.

Open-sewn Garments

Xicolli. The *xicolli* is depicted in only two of the five Borgia Group codices, *Fejérváry-Mayer* and *Laud*, and in both examples the jacket is worn by individuals whose accouterments and environment identify them as priests. Since the *xicolli* occurs in no other context, it may have been exclusively special-purpose clothing (in the Mixtec region the costume was the regular upper-class garment). We must remember, however, that the Borgia Group codices are all ritual-divinatory manuscripts and hence would not be as likely to reflect the secular side of their culture, as do the Mixtec genealogies and histories.

Approximately 455 male figures are depicted in the Mixtec mythological pictorial *Codex Vindobonensis* obverse. Only seven seated males (shown in one scene; see plate 14) wear the *xicolli*. It also occurs as an element in place-name glyphs.[72] The *xicolli* on the obverse side of the manuscript are offerings, either held up[73] or presented flat.[74]

The two *xicolli* depicted in the Borgia Group codices appear on chart 12 (examples *k* and *l*). Example 12*k* comes from a section of *Codex Fejérváry-Mayer* dealing with the most positive aspects of life; Seler referred to it as the "day side" of the manuscript.[75] The priest, whose body is blackened, wears the short white jacket with yellow fringe and in one hand holds a *xicolli* accouterment, the incense burner. In the other hand he presents a burnt offering, a bundle of firewood, and a rubber ball topped by a *quetzal* feather. Another feature often associated with the *xicolli* is also present: the smear of blood at the priest's temple extending down to the ear. In this highly stylized depiction the blood is shown as white.

---

[70] Seler 1902–1903, p. 89.

[71] Seler 1901–1902, p. 64.

[72] *Codex Vindobonensis* obverse, pp. 9, 39, 41, 42, 43, 43.

[73] Ibid., pp. 17, 22, 30, 35.

[74] Ibid., p. 18.

[75] Seler 1901–1902, p. 136.

EXAMPLE 12*e*. Borgia Group rounded *quechquemitl*. *Codex Fejérváry-Mayer*, p. 28.

EXAMPLE 12*f*. Borgia Group triangular *quechquemitl*. *Codex Borgia*, p. 59.

FIGURE 53. The central Mexican goddess Xochiquetzal representing both conjugal union and amorous companionship to the warriors. *Codex Borgia*, p. 59.

EXAMPLE 12g. Borgia Group triangular *quechquemitl*. *Codex Laud*, p. 17.

The second *xicolli* of the Borgia Group (example 12*l*) is found in *Codex Laud*. The garment is white with pale-yellow lines and nine circular dots.[76] What would be the fringe area at the hem of the costume is plain white. The individual also has the blood smear at the temple, depicted in brown. The priest is performing a human sacrifice, an activity that further identifies his garment as the *xicolli*.

Closed-sewn Garments

ROBE. The robe appears to have been a long garment that reached from neck to ankles (it is impossible to be certain of its length because all the robed figures are seated). The robe is sometimes shown covered by a chest cape. The costume was a male garment worn by deity figures; thus it may have been a status garment.

Seler's commentary on *Codex Fejérváry-Mayer* makes reference to "the long robe falling down to the feet" worn by several male deities among the gods of the six quarters.[77] The garments are identical to those encountered in the Mixtec codices *Zouche-Nuttall* and *Vindobonensis* obverse.

The first robe (example 13*a*) was identified by Seler as one of the "lords of the seventh night hour, and of the upper regions."[78] The individual is holding an incense pouch

[76] The Churubusco Idol in the Museo Nacional de Antropología, Mexico City, also has a decoration of circles on his *xicolli* (see fig. 17).
[77] Seler 1901–1902, p. 130.
[78] Seler 1963, 2:161.

EXAMPLE 12*h*. Borgia Group triangular *quechquemitl*. *Codex Vaticanus B*, p. 89.

EXAMPLE 12*i*. Borgia Group triangular *quechquemitl*. *Codex Fejérváry-Mayer*, p. 8.

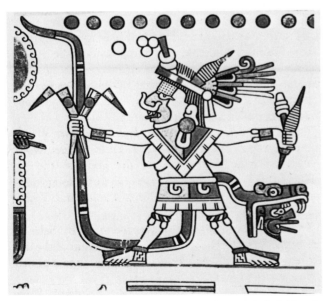

EXAMPLE 12*j*. Borgia Group triangular *quechquemitl*. *Codex Laud*, p. 16D.

EXAMPLE 12*k*. Borgia Group *xicolli*. *Codex Fejérváry-Mayer*, p. 27.

167

EXAMPLE 12*l*. Borgia Group *xiciolli*. *Codex Laud*, p. 8.

EXAMPLE 13*a*. Borgia Group robe. *Codex Laud*, p. 15D.

in his hand but displays none of the other diagnostics of the priest. *Codex Laud* also contains six other robes; four are similar to example *a*, and the other two are covered by chest capes,[79] as is example 13*b*.

The next figure (example 13*b*) wears a blue robe with white designs of feather-down balls used to adorn sacrificial offerings (a motif also found on a Mixtec robe, example *g* of chart 10). A red chest cape with a wide red band and a white fringe is worn over the robe, and the red band and white fringe are repeated on the hem of the robe.

As noted, Seler mentioned chest capes, or *quemitl*, as being tied around the necks of idols.[80] Of the thirteen robes found in the *Codex Fejérváry-Mayer*,[81] eleven are covered with matching chest capes. Many of the robes give the impression of having sleeves that extend below the elbow; again, this is probably a depiction of the material of the garment draped over the shoulders.

The third example (13*c*), from *Codex Vaticanus B*, is the god Tezcatlipoca as one aspect of Xipe Totec.[82] The deity holds the lower section of a severed left arm. His robe has a design of feather-down balls identical to Mixtec robe example *g* in chart 10 and example *b* in chart 13. Fourteen other garments in the *Codex Vaticanus B* are probably also robes.[83]

Although no robe depictions have yet been identified in *Codex Borgia*, all nine males depicted on the reverse of *Codex Cospi* appear to be wearing robes.[84] Example 13*d* is a deity whose red robe and matching headgear also bear the feather-down-ball motif. The god is holding a spear-thrower with a spear in place.

HUIPIL. As is the implication in the Mixtec costume repertory, the *huipil* must have been rare in the area from which the Borgia Group comes; there are few depictions of it in these pictorials. The three examples in chart 13 (*e*, *f*, and *g*) suggest that the garment ranged in length from just above the waist to midhip. I have found no other examples of the *huipil* in the Borgia Group codices. Because of the ambiguous nature of the codices' garment depictions, an argument could be made that the *huipil* illustrated here are really some form of cape. Because the costumes resemble *huipil* more than any other type of garment, I have assigned them to that category.

The first example (13*e*) comes from a section of *Codex Cospi* that presents the *tonalamatl*. Each of the calendric

[79] In *Codex Laud* most of the seated women have their knees pulled under their bodies; the men sit with their knees pulled up in front of their bodies. By this criterion all the *Laud* figures wearing robes are men. The plain white robes are found on pp. 23, 4D, 14D, 15D, 16D; the two robes covered by chest capes are found on pp. 23, 9D.

[80] Seler 1901–1902, p. 130.

[81] The robe examples in *Codex Fejérváry-Mayer* appear on pp. 23, 24, 25, 25, 30, 30, 32, 33, 33, 34, 35, 36, 37. The robes with chest capes over them are on folios 24, 25, 25, 30, 32, 33, 33, 34, 35, 36, 37.

[82] Seler 1902–1903, *tonalamatl*, fol. 30.

[83] *Codex Vaticanus B*, pp. 1, 2, 2, 4, 4, 5, 6, 6, 7, 8, 8, 8, 9, 30.

[84] *Codex Cospi*, verso, pp. I, II, III, IV, VII, VIII, IX, X, XI.

CHART 13
THE BORGIA GROUP COSTUME REPERTORY
Examples of Closed-sewn Garments

Male
Robe

a   b   c   d

Female
Huipil

e   f   g

Examples of Limb-encasing Garments

Male
Ceremonial Costume

h   i

SOURCES: (*a*) *Codex Laud*, p. 15D; (*b*) *Codex Fejérváry-Mayer*, p. 25; (*c*) *Codex Vaticanus B*, p. 30; (*d*) *Codex Cospi* verso, p. 9; (*e*) *Codex Cospi* recto, p. 1; (*f*) *Codex Laud*, p. 12D; (*g*) *Codex Laud*, p. 15D; (*b*) *Codex Laud*, p. 13D; (*i*) *Codex Borgia*, p. 60.

EXAMPLE 13*b*. Borgia Group robe. *Codex Fejérváry-Mayer*, p. 25.

EXAMPLE 13*c*. Borgia Group robe. *Codex Vaticanus B*, p. 30.

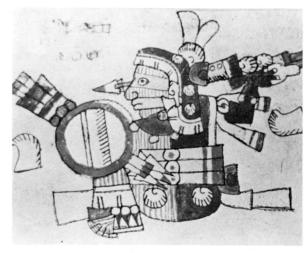

EXAMPLE 13*d*. Borgia Group robe. *Codex Cospi* verso, p. 9.

quarters is divided into thirteen divisions. The female figure shown in example *e* heads the fourth column of the first quarter. Her *huipil* is gray with a white fringed border, and her skirt is the same combination.

The second example (13*f*) is worn by a kneeling female, confronting a creature with a bird beak and a human body painted red. The goddess wears a white *huipil* with a red border, and her skirt is blue and red with a blue band at the white-bordered hem. Her *huipil* appears to be a shorter garment than example *e*.

Example 13*g* is the female goddess who, according to Seler, is companion to the Lord of the Seventeen Night Hour and of the Upper Regions (example *a*, chart 13). The deity is wearing a solid-white *huipil* and a red skirt with a white border (because she is kneeling, her skirt reaches the ankles; on figures in a standing position in *Codex Laud* the skirts come only to midcalf). Her *huipil* is longer than those of examples 13*e* and 13*f*.

Limb-encasing Garments

CEREMONIAL COSTUMES. Whereas the Mixtec codices have a total of 116 limb-encasing garments (only 7 from the obverse side of *Codex Vindobonensis*), the entire Borgia Group shows only 2 garments that encase the limbs of the body. Since all the Borgia pictorials are religious documents, the costumes appear in a ritual context.

The first example of a limb-encasing garment (13*b*) is from *Codex Laud*. The figure appears in one of the twenty-five male-female confrontation scenes dealing with the twenty-five divine pairs. The example is a jaguar costume similar to those seen in the Mixtec codices.

The second example (13*i*) is from a section of *Codex Borgia* that also deals with the twenty-five divine pairs. Seler identified him as "Tonacatecuhtli, Lord of Life, as Tlacaocelotl, as jaguar."[85] His ceremonial costume encases the body but reveals a hand and the feet. It is reminiscent of some of the Mixtec jaguar costumes.

[85] Seler 1963, *Códice Borgia, Láminas explicativas*, p. 60.

EXAMPLE 13e. Borgia Group *huipil*. *Codex Cospi* recto, p. 1.

EXAMPLE 13f. Borgia Group *huipil*. *Codex Laud*, p. 12D.

EXAMPLE 13g. Borgia Group *huipil*. *Codex Laud*, p. 15D.

EXAMPLE 13h. Borgia Group ceremonial costume. *Codex Laud*, p. 13D.

EXAMPLE 13*i*. Borgia Group ceremonial costume. *Codex Borgia*, p. 60.

SUMMARY

The costume repertory of the Borgia Group codices resembles that of the Mixtecs in many ways. All five principles of clothing construction are manifest in both inventories, and the same types of garments are presented, with a single exception: the pictorials of the Borgia Group contain no examples of military attire. This might seem consonant with ritual documents, except that in Mesoamerica religion and warfare often went hand in hand.

The contrasts between the two repertories are particularly intriguing. The female chest cape, the ritual-connected *quemitl*, occurs only in the Borgia Group. Three of the pictorials are unique in their depiction of bisexual deities, who wear both the female *quechquemitl* and the male loincloth.

There are two further differences. Whereas there is only one topless female figure (a child) in the Mixtec pictorials, the Borgia Group contains a number of such depictions, which suggests the possibility of a lowland homeland for these codices. The relative occurrence of the *xicolli* is a further contrast. The jacket is ubiquitous in the Mixtec historical-genealogical codices because it was the usual attire of the aristocracy, but the garment occurs only twice throughout the five Borgia Group pictorials.

The implications of the contrasts are discussed at length in chapter 8. Before it is possible to assess the question whether the clothing reflects the culture for the whole of Mesoamerica, the sixth costume repertory, that of the Lowland Mayas, must be considered.

FIGURE 54. A lowland Maya goddess weaving on a backstrap loom. *Codex Madrid*, p. 79.

CHAPTER SEVEN

The Lowland Mayas of Yucatán

 THE LOWLAND MAYAS OF YUCATÁN are the sixth Mesoamerican group whose costume repertory is presented here. Although the name Maya conjures up the elaborate art styles of such great Classic period sites as Copán, Palenque, and Tikal—all of which date between A.D. 300 and 900—the clothing data from those impressive centuries of Maya achievement cannot be used in this book. They reflect a time too far removed from the era being discussed, the Late Postclassic period which terminated in the Spanish conquest.

In the centuries between the collapse of the Classic period around 900 and contact with the Spaniards of the Córdoba expedition in 1517,[1] Maya culture shifted from the jungles of the Petén at the base of the Yucatán Peninsula to the dry scrub forests of its northern plains. In those six hundred years the Mayas of northern Yucatán absorbed many influences from central Mexico, and those influences were reflected in their culture. As a result, only Late Postclassic Yucatecan data can be used to reconstruct their costume repertory. To understand the period, we must place it in historical perspective. The Late Postclassic Mayas were uniquely the result of earlier diverse influences.

By the time of sixteenth-century Spanish contact, the great achievements of the preceding periods had generally dissipated. The dramatic Classic-period collapse in the tenth century produced a rapid and drastic population drop in the Petén. In the northeastern portion of the Yucatán Peninsula such Maya centers as Uxmal in the Puuc Hills survived another one hundred years. Its people

may have finally succumbed to the same combination of natural and cultural factors that brought down the southern sites, or intruding military forces from central Mexico may have spelled their demise. In any event it was not the Puuc area to which invaders were drawn but rather a site in the center of the northern end of the peninsula, Chichén Itzá: mouth of the Itzá well.

Chichén was a desirable location in which to settle because the area contained a number of cenotes—natural water reservoirs. Yucatán is a dry, low-lying limestone plain covered with scrub forest. It has almost no surface rivers or streams; nearly all of the water seeps through the thin soil and rock to the water table. The limestone crust has broken through in many areas, providing access to the underground water. Two large cenotes at Chichén were a critically important feature of the site. They provided a water supply that was much more secure than the supplies of the northern plains. One cenote was also the focus of a rain-god cult; hence Chichén was a pilgrimage center. For several reasons, then, it was a logical area in which intrusive groups would settle.

Early in the ninth century the so-called Itzás, a ruling group of Mexican derivation, moved into the area (the later Mayas had scant respect for the Itzás and claimed that they introduced all manner of evils into Yucatán: lewdness, promiscuity, incest, and perversion; in an additional indication of contempt, the Mexicanized Itzás were also reported to speak broken Maya).[2] It appears that the incursive Itzás were the Chontals (Putúns) who originally controlled the lowland Tabasco area at the bottom of the Gulf Coast. There they served as middlemen in trade be-

---

[1] It is possible that Ponce de León discovered Yucatán in 1513 on the homeward voyage from Florida, where he had tried and failed to find the Fountain of Youth. Unfortunately, there is no record that he made contact

with the Mayas (Closs 1976).

[2] Adams 1977, p. 240.

tween Mexico and Yucatán. Because of those contacts, they were familiar with the resources of the peninsula, which contained the largest salt fields in Mesoamerica plus a dense, exploitable population.[3] Despite the Chontal-Itzá military and political intrusion, apparently their relationship with the native Mayas was relatively harmonious. That changed with the coming of a second foreign group.

The establishment of a Toltec center at Chichén Itzá in northern Yucatán constitutes one of the most intriguing episodes in Mesoamerican prehistory. The colonization may have been tied to political dissension in the Toltec capital of Tula in central Mexico. Such speculations are hypothetical.[4] In one reconstruction[5] it is conjectured that in the latter part of the tenth century Tula was under the leadership of a historical figure named Topiltzin, also known as Quetzalcoatl because he was the high priest of that cult. The ruler became involved in a power struggle with the Tezcatlipoca religious and political faction. The chronicles report that Topiltzin Quetzalcoatl was defeated by trickery and forced into exile. The exiled leader and his entourage are said to have left Tula in A.D. 987. One version of the Quetzalcoatl legend relates that he traveled east, down to the coast. There he disappeared into the sea, vowing someday to return in an anniversary year of his birth, Ce Acatl (1 Reed). It was in that prophetic year of the recurring fifty-two-year "century" that Cortés sailed out of the east to land on the beach he named Veracruz.

Maya history reports that the Toltec invasion of Yucatán was carried out under the leadership of Kukulcán, the Maya name for Quetzalcoatl. As a result of the takeover the center at Chichén was greatly enlarged and embellished to become an architectual blend of Toltec and Maya cultures. The Itzás and their Toltec colleagues ruled Chichén and dominated all of the peninsula for about two hundred years.

In 1187 the head of the nearby center Mayapán, infuriated by the abduction of his bride by the ruler of Chichén, took vengeance and sacked the city. At about that time the Toltec capital of Tula in central Mexico fell; Chichén was thus set adrift without the Mexican support it had once enjoyed. By 1250 the Toltec era in Yucatán had come to an end, and Chichén and its Mexicanized Itzás had lost their primacy.

During the two hundred years of Toltec-Itzá control the east coast of Yucatán preserved a more strictly Maya tradition. After the Toltec colony fell, the Maya influences flowed back into the northern plains. The reestablishment of the more native tradition took its most vigorous form at Mayapán, yet in every way Mayapán represents a cultural decline from the Classic and Toltec periods. It reflects an incomplete fusion of two traditions, and the ideological fragmentation may have been one

reason it could not hold together. For a period a unified government was established with local lords required to reside in the center to guarantee political control. Then dissension arose, followed by the destruction of the urban center in 1446. It was abandoned and had become a ruin by the time of Spanish conquest about a hundred years later.[6]

In 1517, when the Spanish expedition of Fernández de Córdoba landed on the coast of Yucatán, centralized government no longer existed on the peninsula. It was divided into sixteen separate states, each competing for prestige and constantly warring over any local issue. Most of the states were dominated by a capital city or center that was the seat of a provincial ruler called the *balach uinic*. Each town was ruled by a *batab*, who was administrator, judge, and commanding officer.

It is difficult to estimate the population of the Yucatán Maya area at the time of Spanish contact. From the 1549 tax lists, Roys speculated that it contained well over 300,000 inhabitants.[7] The subsistence base was provided by corn, beans, and squash grown in fields cleared by cutting and burning the scrub forest. Such fields can be planted profitably for only a year or two; they must then be allowed to lie fallow for seven years or more before being reused. The recurrent shifting of fields caused the common people to live scattered throughout the area in clusters of houses near their crops.

The elite upper classes and their slaves resided in town centers, where the nobles filled all the important political and military offices and monopolized the priesthood. After the Toltecs' fall the new Maya rulers were the merchant class. Commerce was a highly honored pursuit, and the Mayas were great traders, with every level of their stratified society represented in their trading ventures. The nobles controlled the prestige goods, whereas commoners acted as peddlers of less valuable wares, carried in packs on their backs. Slaves served the nobles both as carriers of long-distance goods and as merchandise themselves, for Yucatán was an established source of slaves. Although the area lacked precious metals, it was rich in other exportable goods: honey, beeswax, salt, and cotton cloth.

The Maya rulers apparently controlled the long-distance trade, and commerce by sea was on an extensive scale, with well-established routes. They occupied the center of a vast commercial empire that reached from northern Honduras to Tabasco, and the large trading canoes of the Mayas appear early in the accounts of the Spanish conquest. Columbus and his sailors witnessed one on their fourth voyage;[8] Thompson speculated that the merchants and crew were Chontal Mayas, the Phoenicians of Mesoamerica.[9]

Preoccupation with the sacred permeated all levels of

[3] Ibid., p. 236.
[4] Nicholson 1979.
[5] Jiménez-Moreno 1941; 1966.
[6] Adams 1977, p. 263.

[7] Roys 1965, p. 661.
[8] Las Casas 1951, 2:274.
[9] Thompson 1970, pp. 126–27.

Maya life. The activities of each class were highly religious. The day-to-day religion of the rank and file centered primarily on agricultural aspects—the wind and rain gods on whose favor the crops depended. The priesthood had a large membership and, like the society as a whole, was arranged in a hierarchy. Many rituals involved the burning of copal and offerings of animals, birds, and human blood. Some human sacrifice was practiced, particularly of children to the agricultural gods.

The most striking intellectual achievement of the Lowland Mayas was the calendar, which was basically agricultural in purpose. Connected with the calendar were associated systems of writing and notations. The Classic-period Mayas' knowledge of mathematics, chronology, and astronomy was advanced, but the architectural decline that marked the end of the Classic period was accompanied by an intellectual deterioration as well. Today it is impossible to say how much of the earlier knowledge still existed at the time of the Conquest. Certainly hieroglyphic writing was in use, and, although the long count of the Classic period had disappeared, the fifty-two-year calendar was still utilized. Since that esoteric knowledge was controlled by the priests, much of the information disappeared when they died.

The three Maya codices upon which I based most of the Maya clothing study probably predate the Spanish conquest by at least a century. Each is known by the name of the city in which it is now housed: Dresden, Madrid, and Paris. All are similar in format and content. Each is composed of a single sheet of native paper folded like a screen so that each page is twice as tall as it is wide. Each of the three manuscripts is made of the pounded inner bark of the wild fig tree (*ficus*), and covered with a sizing of lime. On both sides of each of the codices are painted pictorial representations interspersed with explanatory glyphic texts. The three books are also similar in content, dealing primarily with divinatory, calendric, and ritualistic matters.

Among the Mayas, whose preoccupation with the measuring of time has often been noted, the days themselves were divine. Each day was personified as a god and conceived as a bearer who carried a specific division of time on his back. The burden that each god carried signified the expected good or ill fortune according to the benevolent or malevolent aspect of the bearer-god. As a result of those concerns, the three Maya codices are largely filled with divinatory almanacs giving information on the aspects of the gods of particular days, identifying which were favorable and unfavorable for sowing crops, hunting, fishing, and beekeeping. There are also passages on astronomy, but they too emphasize the comings and goings of the gods.

Of the three extant Lowland Maya codices, *Codex Madrid* is the longest,[10] fifty-six leaves painted on both sides. *Codex Dresden* has thirty-nine leaves[11] but only seventy-four pages of text; the rest are blank. *Codex Paris* is a fragment of what was probably a much longer document;[12] it contains only eleven leaves—twenty-two pages—of text. *Dresden* is probably the earliest codex and may be a later edition of an even earlier original. Estimates for the date of *Dresden* vary between A.D. 1200 or 1250 and 1350. Whether or not the earlier date accounts for its superiority to the other two is difficult to say. Thompson thought that the *Dresden* was probably produced to Chichén Itzá early in the thirteenth century because the document contains strong stylistic signs of central Mexican influence,[13] which was strongest in Yucatán during occupation of that site by the Toltecs. It has been speculated that *Dresden* was one of the Indian pictorial manuscripts sent by Cortés to the emperor Charles V in 1519.[14] The emperor's residence was normally in Vienna, and in 1739 the book first appeared in Austria. It was purchased in Vienna by the director of the royal library of Dresden,[15] where it has remained.

Codex Madrid is crude in workmanship and is thought to be no earlier than the fifteenth century. Its exact place of origin in the Lowland Maya territory is still in dispute, although the east coast of Yucatán near the Late Postclassic site of Tulum has been suggested.[16]

Nothing is known of the route by which *Codex Madrid* reached Europe. The manuscript, also known as *Codex Tro-Cortesianus*, first appeared as two separate parts. In 1866 the Abbé Brasseur de Bourbourg, a Middle-American-prehistory enthusiast, was visiting in Madrid when he recognized the Maya character of a manuscript in the possession of a professor of Spanish paleography, Juan Tro y Ortolano. In 1869 the owner permitted the abbé to publish the document, which appeared under the name *Manuscript Troano*. In 1888 it was acquired by the Museo Arqueológico of Madrid, now called the Museo de América.

In 1867 another codex was offered for sale by a Spaniard. The second pictorial was at first regarded as a fourth Maya manuscript, and after some years, in 1872, it was acquired by the Museo Arqueológico in Madrid. At the time it was suggested that it might have come from Estremadura, having been brought to Spain by Cortés. The manuscript was therefore called *Codex Cortesianus*. Later the first half of the document was also tied to Cortés through the suggestion that Tro y Ortolano might have been a descendent of the conquistador.[17] In 1880, Léon de Rosny discovered that both the codices in Madrid were parts of a single manuscript, and by 1883 both parts of the *Codex Madrid* were combined. It remains today in the Museo de América.

Codex Paris, also known as *Codex Peresianus*, is a frag-

---

[10] Glass and Robertson 1975, *Codex Madrid*, census no. 187.
[11] Glass and Robertson 1975, *Codex Dresden*, census no. 113.
[12] Glass and Robertson 1975, *Codex Paris*, census no. 247.
[13] Thompson 1972*b*, p. 16.

[14] Ibid.
[15] Glass 1975, p. 125.
[16] Thompson 1950, p. 26.
[17] Anders 1967, p. 51.

ment of what no doubt was originally a much longer manuscript. It is of better workmanship than *Codex Madrid*, although the portraits are somewhat crude. The date and source of the acquisition of the manuscript by the Bibliothèque Nationale Paris are unknown, though, according to J. F. Ramírez, its acquisition was verified by purchase in 1832. Its discovery has been widely credited to Léon de Rosny, who reported finding it in a basket in the Bibliothèque Nationale in Paris in 1859 together with other Mexican manuscripts. Attached to it was a slip of paper with the name Pérez, from which one of its synonyms derives.[18] De Rosny's claim of discovery is considered suspect.[19]

Researching the Late Postclassic Lowland Maya costume repertory is difficult because the available pictorial material is very limited. To broaden the data base, I have included costume depictions found on frescoes at two Late Postclassic archaeological sites on the east coast of northern Yucatán: Tulum, in Quintana Roo, and Santa Rita, in Belize. Fortunately, reproductions of the murals have been published; both sites have suffered severe deterioration since their discovery.[20]

In varying degrees the frescoes of Tulum and Santa Rita resemble the depictions found in the Maya codices. The Tulum murals used in this book come from the Temple of the Diving God and the Temple of the Frescoes and are considered to date from A.D. 1500 or later. Several Maya scholars have commented on how much these frescoes and those at Santa Rita resemble the pictures in the Maya codices.[21] Thompson[22] and Miller[23] in particular have seen marked similarities to the distinctive style of *Codex Paris*; a strong Mexican or Mixteca-Puebla influence is observable in the depiction of the human body in both the murals and the pictorial.

R. L. Roys has also likened the style of the Tulum murals to that of the *Madrid Codex*.[24] The so-called diving gods in the frescoes over the doorway niches are now considered to be bee deities and bear a striking resemblance to the honeybees depicted in the pictorial. This resemblance, plus an emphasis on beekeeping, is one reason for believing that the *Madrid Codex* may have originated in that area, which was famous for its honey, a valuable export item. Tulum was on an important pre-Hispanic trade route, close to the pre-Conquest pilgrimage island of Cozumel (today still a free port).

The Santa Rita frescoes are notably Mexican in style, sharing what Donald Robinson has called the "International Style" of Late Postclassic times in Mesoamerica.[25] Nevertheless, the murals are set in the context of the Maya calendar. At the time of their discovery they con-

tained a long glyphic text, which, sadly, has been destroyed. The frescoes featured a rare Maya glyph that appears elsewhere only in the *Codex Paris*.[26]

Further recognition of Maya elements in the Santa Rita murals comes from the Mesoamerican art historian Jacinto Quirarte.[27] He points out that there are distinctive Maya treatments of the subject matter, which involves deities or their impersonators engaged in sacred actions. Chac, the rain god, and other deities resemble their images on Mayapan-style incense burners that were found in association with the murals.

Since Santa Rita and Tulum, both Late Postclassic sites, are located on the east coast of the peninsula—an area that E. W. Andrews IV suggested preserved the more strictly Maya traditions even through the earlier Toltec period[28]—the sites probably reflect what was worn by the dominant class of that region at the time the Spaniards arrived. I therefore think it appropriate to include clothing examples from their frescoes in the Lowland Maya costume repertory.

In addition to the pictorial data used to analyze the costume repertory, I consulted Spanish documents. The richest secular sources for costume data on the Lowland Mayas are the more than fifty extant *Relaciones geográficas* for the region. Further information on the area can be found in the work of the Franciscan missionary Bishop Diego de Landa, whose *Relación de las cosas de Yucatán* contains valuable ethnographic data.[29] Landa arrived in Yucatán in 1549, learned to speak Maya, and for many years was active in work toward the conversion of the Indians. His proselytizing zeal resulted in his ordination as a bishop in 1562. He wrote his *Relación* in 1566, basing it on information from the codices of the Indians (which the bishop subsequently ordered destroyed), Indian informants—some of them native priests—and personal observations of the Indians. Landa's work covers practically every phase of Maya life and is particularly informative regarding the indigenous religion and rituals.

The writings of Bernal Díaz del Castillo are also useful in reconstructing the Lowland Maya costume repertory.[30] The writings of that old conquistador are without peer for forthrightness and charm. His account must be used with great care, however; he often handled the truth carelessly. Among other self-aggrandizements he claimed to have been a part of all three of the early voyages of discovery from Cuba to Mesoamerica: Córdoba's in 1517, Grijalva's in 1518, and Cortés's in 1519. The eminent historian Henry R. Wagner was skeptical of Díaz del Castillo's claim to have accompanied Grijalva but accepted his Córdoba-expedition claim.[31]

[18] Glass 1975, p. 179.
[19] Nicholson, personal communication.
[20] Lothrop 1924; Gann 1900.
[21] Miller 1972, p. 467; Proskouriakoff 1965, p. 492; Robertson 1968, p. 85; Thompson 1965, p. 638.
[22] Thompson 1965, p. 638.
[23] Miller 1972, p. 467.
[24] Adams 1977, p. 264.

[25] Robertson 1968.
[26] Thompson 1965, p. 638.
[27] Quirarte 1975.
[28] Andrews 1965.
[29] Landa 1941.
[30] Díaz del Castillo 1967.
[31] Wagner 1969, pp. xix–xxiv.

Accounts of the 1517 and 1518 voyages are also included. Those reports are particularly important to the study of Lowland Maya costume because they contain some interesting observations about the clothing of the Lowland Mayas in the Cape Catoche region, at the northeastern tip of the Yucatán Peninsula. Since Córdoba's 1517 voyage was the first recorded one to reach Mesoamerica, it probably constituted the initial contact between the Spanish invaders and the Lowland Mayas (see note 1). Because the chronicler Fernández de Oviedo had access to firsthand reports from both the Córdoba and the Grijalva voyages, his writing is a particularly valuable source.[32]

All the clothing examples in charts 14 and 15 are taken from pictorial depictions or frescoes that deal with religious or divinatory matters; hence the personages involved are all deities. Since it is my contention that costumes of gods and goddesses reflect the most prestigious clothing of the society they serve, deity garments are an appropriate part of this book.

LOWLAND MAYA COSTUME REPERTORY

Draped Garments

MAXTLATL. The best description of the Lowland Maya loincloth comes from the *Relación geográfica* of the village of Mutul: "...a band of material the width of a hand which was wrapped around the waist, passed between the legs and knotted in such a way that the ends of the material fell in front and behind."[33] Other *Relaciones* of the area (such as those of Chunchuchu,[34] Mama,[35] and Valladolid[36]) frequently refer to the garment. Bishop Landa reported that the Maya women decorated the ends of the loincloths "with a great deal of care and with feather work."[37] Díaz del Castillo, referring to the first contact with the Lowland Mayas at Cape Catoche in February, 1517, mentioned that the Indians "covered their persons with a narrow cloth which they call *mastlels*."[38] Reference to the word *maxtlatl* indicates that in retrospect the conquistador attributed a Nahuatl term to Yucatecan Maya speakers.

Describing the loincloths worn by the Indians of coastal Yucatán, Oviedo stated:

> Around the middle of their bodies they wore many fillets or bands of cotton as wide as a hand. (When twisted they were as thick as a thumb.) They wore these wrapped around the waist twenty or thirty times. From this belt hung down an end which covered their privates, so that by loosening the end they could easily take out their members in order to urinate or to evacuate their bowels, as the end which they use for breeches passes

through the fork between the thighs from the shoulders to the belly, to make a turn or tie with the other turns around the body. The Christians thought they wore this in place of a breastplate or defensive armor but it is only their habitual costume. The young gentlemen among these Indians wear in the manner mentioned more turns of the belt.[39]

The top row of chart 14 presents illustrations of the *maxtlatl*, called *ex* in Yucatecan Maya; it was the basic, indispensable male garment. The first example (14*a*) is from the *Codex Madrid*. The figure is God M, the merchant deity; he has the projecting lower lip that is one of his characteristics in the Maya codices. His loincloth (and all the others from the Lowland Maya region) has the knot in the back, as do those of the Mixtec and Borgia Group codices.

The second loincloth (example 14*b*) is worn by a Chac figure. He is a rain god whose *maxtlatl*, like that of example 14*a*, has multiline horizontal decoration on the ends. The example also has decoration on the waistband, where some sort of ornament has been added in front.

A similar decoration appears on the loincloth waistband worn by the third example, 14*c*, from a farmer's almanac of *Codex Dresden*. He too is a Chac; he holds a vomiting dog in one hand and an ax in the other. The indication of the almanac seems to be that those particular days are associated with bad weather for the crops.[40]

The last *maxtlatl* (example 14*d*) is from *Codex Paris*. The deity, whose body is partly encased in what appears to be a huge conch shell, wears a white loincloth with decorated ends that reach to his ankles. The horizontal multiline decoration again appears; because of the conch shell, the knot of the garment does not show.

HIP-CLOTH. All the examples of Maya hip-cloths have a triangular shape that is probably the result of a square of material being folded diagonally and then tied or in some way secured around the body. There is no mention of the hip-cloth in either Landa's *Relación* or the Yucatán *Relaciones geográficas*; but, as is true for the other five costume repertories, repeated depictions of the garment are undeniable proof of its existence in the Lowland Maya area. There are no hip-cloth examples, however, in *Codex Madrid*.

In some instances, the hip-cloth appears to be held in place by a padded belt, as can be seen in example 14*e*, a figure from an almanac portion of *Codex Dresden* dealing with the problems of farmers. That section is dominated by the *chacs*, the rain gods; here one of the deities is standing with raised fist. His hip-cloth appears to be held in place by a padded belt. A similar combination occurs in example *f*.

[32] Córdoba 1942; Grijalva 1942.
[33] Cline 1972, census no. 69; Asensio 1898, 1:82.
[34] Cline 1972, census no. 27; Asensio 1898, 1:149.
[35] Cline 1972, census no. 63; Asensio 1898, 1:162.
[36] Cline 1972, census no. 139; Asensio 1898, 2:29.

[37] Landa 1941, p. 89.
[38] Díaz del Castillo 1967, 1:15.
[39] Grijalva 1942, pp. 101–02.
[40] Thompson 1972*b*, p. 94.

CHART 14
LOWLAND MAYA COSTUME REPERTORY
Examples of Draped Garments

Male
Maxtlatl

a   b   c   d

Hip-cloth

e   f   g   h

Cape

i   j   k   l   m

Kilt

n

Female
Skirt

o   p   q   r   s

Hip-cloth

t   u

Sources: (a) *Codex Madrid*, p. 95; (b) *Codex Madrid*, p. 6; (c) *Codex Dresden*, p. 31; (d) *Codex Paris*, p. 6; (e) *Codex Dresden*, p. 33; (f) *Codex Paris*, p. 4; (g) mural, north wall of Mound 1, Santa Rita, Belize; (h) *Codex Dresden*, p. 14; (i) *Codex Dresden*, p. 23; (j) *Codex Dresden*, p. 27; (k) mural, north wall of Mound 1, Santa Rita; (l) mural, Structure 5, Temple of the Diving God, Tulum, Quintana Roo, Mexico; (m) mural, Structure 5, Temple of the Diving God, Tulum, Quintana Roo; (n) *Codex Dresden*, p. 28; (o) *Codex Dresden*, p. 39; (p) *Codex Madrid*, p. 30; (q) *Codex Madrid*, p. 10; (r) *Codex Madrid*, p. 93; (s) *Codex Madrid*, p. 95; (t) *Codex Dresden*, p. 22; (u) *Codex Dresden*, p. 16.

178

In example 14f, the god's hip-cloth also appears to be secured by a padded belt, as do the other eight examples that are discernible in the *Codex Paris*.[41] The hip-cloth has a notched hem, a feature that occurs frequently in the Lowland Maya costume repertory.

The third hip-cloth (example 14g) is from one of the murals at Santa Rita, Belize (fortunately published in 1900 by Thomas Gann; they were subsequently badly damaged). The figure is from the east half of the north wall of mound 1. He is apparently a victor who has taken seven or eight captives, for he appears to be holding a rope that connects them. As with all the other Santa Rita figures the deity wears an elaborate costume that includes a striped green, white, yellow, and orange hip-cloth. Like example 14f, the second Maya hip-cloth example, the garment is folded into a triangular shape. The right front of the victor's cape is obscured by the top of his *maxtlatl*, and it cannot be determined whether is is knotted in front or in back.

The deity who wears the last hip-cloth (example 14h) was referred to by Thompson as God H.[42] The designation by letter indicates that he is one of several gods whose identity is still in question.[43] The hip-cloth worn by the deity reaches almost to the knee and has a version of the notched hem. Like the preceding two examples, it appears to be held in place by a padded belt.

CAPE. Lowland Maya capes appear to have been short garments, none longer than just below the knee. Some of them were back capes, covering only the shoulders and back. Others were chest capes, apparently fastening behind the neck and covering only the shoulders and chest, though sometimes extending to below the knee. A third type has a poncholike appearance.

Referring to the first Córdoba voyage in 1517, Díaz del Castillo wrote that the Lowland Maya Indians of Campeche were "clad in good cotton mantles."[44] While the Spaniards were investigating the temple precinct of that town, the conquistador was approached by a group of Indians carrying reeds to the temple; the carriers were all wearing "ragged mantles." Shortly after that, ten priests appeared, "with their long hair reeking with blood, and matted together, that it could never be parted or even combed out again, unless it was cut." They were "clad in long white cotton cloaks, reaching to their feet."

Oviedo relates that on the Grijalva expedition in 1518 the Indians presented to Captain Francisco de Montejo "many very pretty painted mantles." The chronicle also mentions dyed-cotton mantles and two "hair cloths."[45]

Landa mentioned that the Maya men wore "large square *mantas* and they tied them over their shoulders."[46]

[41] *Codex Paris*, pp. 2, 3, 5, 7, 8, 9, 10, 11.
[42] Thompson 1972b, p. 37.
[43] Ibid., p. 31.
[44] Díaz del Castillo 1967, 1:19–20.
[45] Grijalva 1942, p. 115.
[46] Landa 1941, p. 89.

EXAMPLE 14a. Lowland Maya *maxtlatl. Codex Madrid*, p. 95.

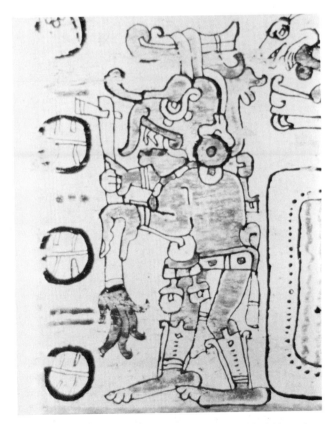

EXAMPLE 14b. Lowland Maya *maxtlatl. Codex Madrid*, p. 6.

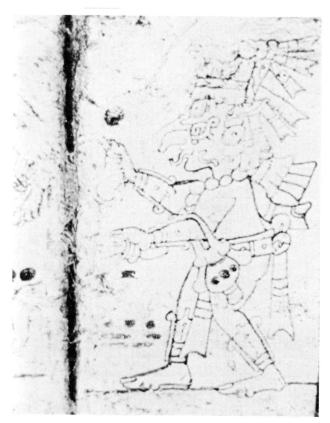

EXAMPLE 14*c*. Lowland Maya *maxtlatl*. *Codex Dresden*, p. 31.

EXAMPLE 14*d*. Lowland Maya *maxtlatl*. *Codex Paris*, p. 6.

The *Relación geográfica* from Chunchuchu states that "they cover themselves in place of a cape with some square *mantas* of a *braza* [in width], woven of thread of white and colored cotton [and] tied over the shoulder."[47] Another *Relación geográfica*, from Mama, describes such garments in this manner: "...and [they wore] a towel that served them as [a] cape which was tied with the two edges at the chest [hanging] from a shoulder [and] coming from underneath the upper arm."[48]

The *Relación geográfica* of Chunchuchu says, "...and for a cape a painted *manta* that covered the body, with a knot at the left shoulder."[49] As with the Mixtecs, there is a discrepancy between the short capes pictured in the Maya codices and the Spanish descriptions, which sound like a colonial, Valley of Mexico garment. The description can only partly be construed to coincide with the illustrations found in the Maya pictorials.

The first cape (example 14*i*) is from an almanac section of *Codex Dresden* that deals with the moon goddess. It is worn by a world directional god called a Bacab, who sits facing a moon-goddess-type woman. The god wears what Thompson referred to as "a flashy cloak and the *tun* headdress, one of his attributes."[50] The tie, which is visible on his back, apparently is attached to the beads he wears.

The second cape (example 14*j*) is also from *Codex Dresden* in a section that deals with new year ceremonies. A death god is making an offering of a decapitated turkey.[51] The deity's fringed cape covers the shoulders and the front of his body, extending to slightly below the knee. Again, the ties at the back of the neck apparently secure the necklace; from the position of the cords on the body it seems obvious that the cape too must have tied at the back of the neck.

The third cape (example 14*k*), from the Santa Rita murals, is a figure from the east half of the north wall of mound 1.[52] It is the remaining portion of one of a group of figures involved with the victor shown in example *g*. The cape has an orange border in front outlining an intricately designed multicolored back panel. The garment covers the shoulders and back and probably extended only to the waist. The cape may have been fastened by utilizing the narrow band of material that extends over the left shoulder. The notched hem, which occurs repeatedly among the Lowland Maya costume examples, is visible.

The final two examples (14*l* and 14*m*) are from Structure 5 of the Temple of the Diving God in Tulum, Quintana Roo.[53] Both figures are male, as shown by their *maxtlatl*, although each of them wears an upper-body garment that from its side view, curved configuration is reminis-

[47] Cline 1972, census no. 27; Asensio 1898, 1:82.
[48] Cline 1972, census no. 63; Asensio 1898, 1:163.
[49] Cline 1972, census no. 27; Asensio 1898, 1:150.
[50] Thompson 1972*b*, p. 60.
[51] Ibid., p. 93.
[52] Gann 1900, plate 29.
[53] Miller 1972, p. 466.

EXAMPLE 14e. Lowland Maya hip-cloth. *Codex Dresden*, p. 33.

EXAMPLE 14f. Lowland Maya hip-cloth. *Codex Paris*, p. 4.

EXAMPLE 14g. Lowland Maya hip-cloth. Mural, north wall, Mound 1, Santa Rita, Belize.

EXAMPLE 14h. Lowland Maya hip-cloth. *Codex Dresden*, p. 14.

EXAMPLE 14*i*. Lowland Maya male cape. *Codex Dresden*, p. 23.

EXAMPLE 14*j*. Lowland Maya male cape. *Codex Dresden*, p. 27.

cent of the Mixtec women's rounded *quechquemitl*. At first the costumes appear to be a similar, poncholike apparel, pulled on over the head. I have decided, however, to classify the two garments as capes because of the long piece of material that extends from the back of the shoulder. The Santa Rita cape immediately preceding (*k*) has a similar "tie," perhaps showing how the latter two "wraparound" capes were secured. A further argument against identifying these costumes as slip-on garments is the lack of other male apparel of that type in any of the Maya codices, or for that matter in the entire Mesoamerican costume repertory.

MALE KILT. *Codex Dresden* contains a section (sheets 25 to 28) that deals with the ceremonies for the incoming year. The rites took place during the unlucky five-day period just before new year. On the upper section of each of the sheets are four Bacabs, world directional gods, disguised as opossums. Each is a bearer and wears a carrying frame upon which is perched the patron of a forthcoming year. The Bacab example (14*n*) bears on his back the death god as the burden or fate of the incoming year. The Bacab is carrying a fan, an incense pouch, and a staff that terminates in a human hand; he is walking across a symbol that denotes a hollow in the ground, perhaps a cenote.[54] Each of the four Bacabs wears an identical kiltlike garment that appears to be made of individual panels of supple woven or plant material. Perhaps it is some sort of grass. To date, these are the only male kilts I have found in the late Postclassic Maya data.

SKIRT. The Maya skirt was called *pyq* (*pic*, in *Relación geográfica* from the community of Mama),[55] and the *Relación geográfica* of Valladolid describes this basic garment of the Maya women: "The Indian women wore their kind of petticoat, which is like a sack open on both ends, and these, tied at the waist, covered their private parts."[56] The definition may refer to a length of fabric sewn together end to end, creating a wide tube that was draped to the body and secured. Tubular skirts are known throughout present-day Mesoamerica.[57]

The *Relación geográfica* of Motol states that "the women went about covered from the waist to the middle of the leg with a *manta* of colored threads."[58] While the last three of the five skirt examples (*q*, *r*, and *s*) conform to the above descriptions (the skirt extending to the middle of the leg), the first two are either too long (*o*) or too short (*p*).

The first skirt (example 14*o*) is from the section of *Codex Dresden* concerned with farmers' almanacs. Thompson identifies the figure as "the old goddess of weaving with snake headdress pours rain from an inverted jar. Her

[54] Thompson 1972*b*, p. 90.
[55] Cline 1972, census no. 63; Asensio 1898, 1:163.
[56] Cline 1972, census no. 139; Asensio 1898, 2:29.
[57] I am indebted to my colleague Anne-Louise Schaffer for calling this matter of tubular skirts to my attention.
[58] Cline 1972, census no. 69; Asensio 1898, 1:82.

snake headdress may show her connection with rain-making."[59] Her skirt, with its notched hem, reaches to the ankles, and over it she appears to be wearing a triangular hip-cloth similar to example *t* in chart 14.

The next skirt (example 14*p*) is worn by a goddess who has some connection with water. Her breasts are bare, and her upper body appears to be tatooed. Landa mentions that the women "tatooed their bodies from the waist up, except their breasts for nursing, with more delicate and beautiful designs than [those of] men."[60] Her skirt is richly decorated, including a stepped-fret motif.

The next skirt (example 14*q*) is not as intricately worked as the preceding example (14*p*), but it too has several design motifs. It is of the length described in the sixteenth-century sources, extending from the waist to the middle of the leg. The hair style is of interest. Landa wrote that the Mayas "dress the hair of the little girls, until they reach a certain size, in four or two horns, which are very becoming to them."[61] While the "horn hair style" description applies to the figure, her sole surviving tooth testifies that she has long since left the "little girl" category.

On the back of the woman wearing the fourth skirt (example 14*r*) is a carrying cloth that supports two Maya hieroglyphs; on the head of the woman wearing the fifth skirt (example 14*s*) is perched an inquisitive-looking bird. Both skirts show a cross-hatch pattern in the central section of the garment. The skirts also have the same distinctive hem as those of the preceding three examples. The same notching is visible on the skirts from the Tulum murals, worn in examples *b* and *e* in chart 15 below.

FEMALE HIP-CLOTH. As with the male Maya hip-cloth, there is no mention of the female hip-cloth in any of the Maya sources. Repeated depictions of it in the *Dresden Codex*, however, leave little doubt that it existed in the pre-Hispanic Maya costume repertory.

The first hip-cloth (example 14*t*) comes from a section of *Codex Dresden* dealing with the effect of certain deities on crops: all three figures depicted in the passage carry maize signs. Thompson identified the figure shown in example 14*t* as "seated Goddess I, with coiled snake in hair."[62] Her fringed hip-cloth bears a striking resemblance to that worn over Maya skirt example *o*. Like the hip-cloth of the "old goddess," this garment has a triangular look, no doubt the result of a square of material being folded diagonally.

The second hip-cloth (example 14*u*) is also from *Codex Dresden*. Thompson described the female as a "seated moon goddess without distinguishing attributes"[63] Her hip-cloth is unadorned but no doubt is a variant of the same garment worn by example *t*.

[59] Thompson 1972*b*, p. 100.
[60] Landa 1941, p. 126.
[61] Ibid.
[62] Thompson 1972*b*, p. 61.
[63] Ibid., p. 57.

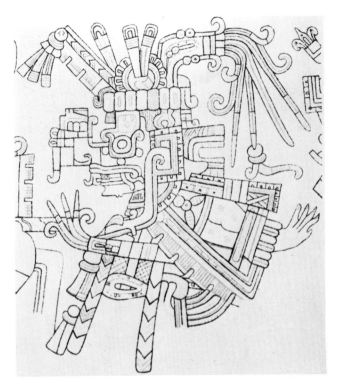

EXAMPLE 14*k*. Lowland Maya male cape. Mural, north wall, Mound 1, Santa Rita, Belize.

EXAMPLE 14*l*. Lowland Maya male cape. Mural, Structure 5, Temple of the Diving God, Tulum, Quintana Roo, Mexico.

EXAMPLE 14*m*. Lowland Maya male cape. Mural, Structure 5, Temple of the Diving God, Tulum.

EXAMPLE 14*o*. Lowland Maya skirt. *Codex Dresden*, p. 39.

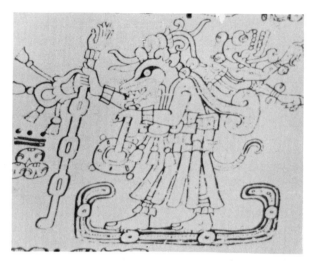

EXAMPLE 14*n*. Lowland Maya kilt. *Codex Dresden*, p. 28.

Slip-on Garments

ROUNDED QUECHQUEMITL. The Spaniards of the Córdoba expedition described the Indian women's heads and breasts as being covered.[64] A large *quechquemitl* may have been one of the garments described by the Yucatán *Relaciones geográficas* and by Bishop Landa as covering the upper body. According to the *Relación geográfica* of Motul, the Indian women wore "some little sleeveless shirts that covered them to the navel ['asta la boca del estomago'], the chests and back being covered."[65] Landa says of the women of the coast and the province of Bacalar and of Campeche:

> ...they covered their breasts, tying a folded *manta* underneath their armpits. All the others did not wear more than one garment like a long and wide sack, opened on both [sides], and drawn in as far as the hips, where they fastened it together with the same width as before. And they had no other garment except the *manta* which they always used in sleeping.[66]

Landa mentioned female idols that "had their breasts covered, as is the custom of Indian women."[67]

The *Relación geográfica* from Chunchuchu refers to upper-body garments: "...in front of the breasts a small net which on some extends down to the elbow."[68] Another reference, the *Relación geográfica* from Mama, adds, "...and on the (upper) body a sack-like garment of the type worn by San Benito which only covers the breast and is not big enough to extend from one side of the waist at the elbow to the other."[69]

The consensus seems to be that the Maya Indian women went about with their breasts covered, but the exact shape of their "small net" or "sack-like garment" re-

[64] Córdoba, Fernández de 1942, pp. 37, 40, 41.
[65] Cline 1972, census no. 69; Asensio 1898, 1:82.
[66] Landa 1941, p. 126.
[67] Ibid.
[68] Cline 1972, census no. 27; Asensio 1898, 1:150.
[69] Cline 1972, census no. 63; ibid., 1:163.

EXAMPLE 14*p*. Lowland Maya skirt. *Codex Madrid*, p. 30.

EXAMPLE 14*q*. Lowland Maya skirt. *Codex Madrid*, p. 10.

EXAMPLE 14*r*. Lowland Maya skirt. *Codex Madrid*, p. 93.

EXAMPLE 14*s*. Lowland Maya skirt. *Codex Madrid*, p. 95.

EXAMPLE 14*t*. Lowland Maya female hip-cloth. *Codex Dresden*, p. 22.

EXAMPLE 14*u*. Lowland Maya female hip-cloth. *Codex Dresden*, p. 16.

mains unclear. To judge from example 15*a*, a large "rounded" *quechquemitl* may have been one of the garments referred to. It is the only such costume in the Maya codices.

TRIANGULAR QUECHQUEMITL. The smaller, triangular *quechquemitl*, worn with the points center front and back, was also present in the Late Postclassic Lowland Maya area. Whether or not it was confined to ritual occasions is impossible to know; no specific mention of it is made in the sixteenth-century sources, nor are there many extant depictions of it. All four examples shown (*b*, *c*, *d*, and *e*) are from the murals at Tulum, Quintana Roo. Examples 15*b* and 15*e* are from structure 5, Temple of the Diving God.[70] The other two examples (15*c* and 15*d*) were traced[71] from enlarged photographs of the mural on the west passage of the Temple of the Frescoes, building 16.[72] Each of the goddess figures is wearing a narrow triangular *quechquemitl* with a notched border like those shown in the skirt section. Three of the four figures also appear to have notched hems on their skirts.

Open-sewn Garments

XICOLLI. The Lowland Maya males wore the *xicolli*, which is described in the Yucatán *Relaciones geográficas* as a colorful, short sleeveless jacket that fastened in front. Díaz del Castillo mentioned that a garment meeting the *xicolli* description was worn in the Cape Catoche region of northern Yucatán in 1517: "These Indians were clothed in cotton shirts made like jackets."[73]

The Maya *xicolli* was worn by the ruling class, and from the written sources and a depiction in the *Madrid Codex*, it seems that its use and construction resembled that of the Mixtec *xicolli*, which not only was an important part of the costume repertory but also was used for gifts and offerings.

The *Relación geográfica* of Valledolid states that "all the Indians of these provinces of Chiquinchel, Tacees, and Cochua and Copules went clothed; the lords in certain *xicoles* of cotton and feathers woven into a kind of many colored jacket of two flaps."[74] The *Relación geográfica* from Tiquibalon refers to *xicoles*, "which are a kind of *chamarretas*."[75] Further reports (such as those from Motul[76] and Cuicuil[77]) confirm the existence of a short, sleeveless, cotton jacket of many colors that fastened in front.

The Maya codices contain no depiction of an individual wearing a garment like the *xicolli*. There is,

[70] Miller 1972, fig. 2.

[71] The tracing of the two triangular *quechquemitl* figures from Lothrop 1924, plate 7, was done by Jean Cuker Sells, of the Graphics, Geophysics Department, University of California, Los Angeles.

[72] Lothrop 1924, plate 7.

[73] Díaz del Castillo 1967, 1:15.

[74] Cline 1972, census no. 139; Asensio 1898, 2:29.

[75] Cline 1972, census no. 129; Asensio 1898, 2:154.

[76] Cline 1972, census no. 69; Asensio 1898, 1:81.

[77] Cline 1972, census no. 36; Asensio 1898, 1:245.

CHART 15
LOWLAND MAYA COSTUME REPERTORY
Examples of Slip-on Garments

Female
Rounded
Quechquemitl

a

Triangular
Quechquemitl

b   c   d   e

Examples of Open-sewn Garments

Male
Xicolli

f

Female — — — — — — — — — — — — —

Examples of Closed-sewn Garments

Male
Quilted Armor

g   h   i

Female — — — — — — — — — — — —

Examples of Limb-encasing Garments

Male — — — — — — — — — — — —

Female — — — — — — — — — — — —

SOURCES: (*a*) *Codex Madrid*, p. 11; (*b*) mural, Structure 5, Temple of the Diving God, Tulum, Quintana Roo, Mexico; (*c*) mural, Building 16, Temple of the Frescoes, Tulum; (*d*) mural, Building 16, Temple of the Frescoes, Tulum; (*e*) mural, Structure 5, Temple of the Diving God, Tulum; (*f*) *Codex Madrid*, p. 84; (*g*) *Codex Madrid*, p. 50; (*h*) *Codex Madrid*, p. 51; (*i*) *Codex Madrid*, p. 79.

EXAMPLE 15a. Lowland Maya rounded *quechquemitl*. *Codex Madrid*, p. 11.

EXAMPLE 15b. Lowland Maya triangular *quechquemitl*. Mural, Structure 5, Temple of the Diving God, Tulum.

however, one group of three figures in the *Madrid Codex* (fig. 55) showing each personage holding up an offering that looks very much like similar depictions in the Mixtec codices, where ceremonial gifts of what must be *xicolli* are offered (see fig. 48 and 49). The most detailed of the three individuals (example 15f) is presented as the sole example of a *xicolli*. The costume, like the other two of fig. 55, has the notched hem so prevalent on the Maya garments.

Closed-sewn Garments

QUILTED ARMOR. From the sixteenth-century written sources it is clear that the Lowland Mayas, like the Aztecs, Tlaxcalans, Tarascans, and Mixtecs, used quilted-cotton armor in battle. They were wearing it in 1517, when the Spanish conquistadors of Córdoba's voyage first came in contact with them at Cape Catoche. Díaz del Castillo wrote, "These [Indian] warriors wore armor made of cotton reaching to the knees and carried lances and shields, bows and arrows, slings and many stones."[78]

In discussing the quilted armor, Tozzer pointed out that Landa mistranslated when he spoke of "jackets made strong with salt and cotton."[79] The friar confused *tab* ("salt") with *taab* ("twisted cord"). The garment was, of course, the Mesoamerican *ichcahuipilli*, first seen by the Spaniards in 1517.

The *Relación geográfica* of Dohot states, "The defensive arms which they wore on the body were twisted *mantas* made into small rolls and cotton in the middle, and some were so strong that the arrows did not go through them."[80] Other *Relaciones geográficas* confirm the existence of cotton armor (Mérida,[81] Motul[82]). The *Relación geográfica* of Campocolche and Chochola refers to the sturdy quilted armor as *euyub*.[83]

It is difficult to determine whether examples 15g, 15h, and 15i, the three figures presented in the cotton-armor section of chart 15, are really wearing the *ichcahuipilli*. All three examples come from *Codex Madrid*. The first two figures, both of whom may be depictions of God L, the "black god," carry spears, which seems to indicate that this apparel is a martial costume. The close cross-hatching on the garment could very well depict quilting.

The third armor (example 15i) is enigmatic. The garment appears to be thick, perhaps even made in "rolls," as mentioned in the *Relación geográfica* of Dohot; but it may be a ceremonial version of the costume because there is too large an area of the bare chest exposed for it to be practical battle garb. The figure wears a mask of God M, the "merchant god," as a chest pendant. To date, the three examples shown are the only garments found in the Maya codices that could be construed as cotton armor.

[78] Díaz del Castillo 1967, 1:16.
[79] Landa 1941, p. 35.
[80] Asensio 1898, 2:209.
[81] Cline 1972, census no. 64; Asensio 1898, 1:41.
[82] Cline 1972, census no. 69; Asensio 1898, 1:81.
[83] Cline 1972, census no. 15; Asensio 1898, 2:186.

EXAMPLE 15c. Lowland Maya triangular *quechquemitl*. Mural, Building 16, Temple of the Frescoes, Tulum.

EXAMPLE 15d. Lowland Maya triangular *quechquemitl*. Mural, Building 16, Temple of the Frescoes, Tulum.

EXAMPLE 15e. Lowland Maya triangular *quechquemitl*. Mural, Structure 5, Temple of the Diving God, Tulum.

EXAMPLE 15f. Lowland Maya *xicolli*. *Codex Madrid*, p. 84.

FIGURE 55. A lowland Maya offering of three *xicolli*. *Codex Madrid*, p. 84.

EXAMPLE 15g. Lowland Maya quilted armor. *Codex Madrid*, p. 50.

EXAMPLE 15h. Lowland Maya quilted armor. *Codex Madrid*, p. 51.

SUMMARY

The Lowland Maya costume repertory contains only four of the five principles of clothing construction. All the basic Mesoamerican draped garments are represented: the male loincloth, the hip-cloth, the cape, and the female wraparound skirt. In addition—as in the inventories of the Mixtec and Borgia Group codices—the male kilt is present. The Lowland Maya pictorials, however, contain no female capes, although the only Mesoamerican female hip-cloths to be found in the codices are present. The slip-on *quechquemitl* was worn in the Lowland Maya area, as was the open-sewn *xicolli*. Not only is the jacket referred to in the Spanish sources, but three examples of it, used as offerings, are illustrated. There are also three garments that are probably open-sewn cotton armor.

The most striking departure from the Mesoamerican norm is the lack of elaborate ritual costumes. Since none are shown pictorially, it is impossible to know whether there was a correlation between extent of ceremonial complexity and degree of garment elaboration. It is of particular interest that no limb-encasing warrior ceremonial costumes are shown; there is no trace of these garments in the Maya pictorials, nor are they mentioned anywhere in the Spanish sources dealing with the Yucatán Peninsula. Considering the strong Mexican influence on the Postclassic Lowlands, the absence of those garments is strange. The matter is discussed at greater length in chapters 8 and 9.

EXAMPLE 15i. Lowland Maya quilted armor. *Codex Madrid*, p. 79.

FIGURE 56. Aztec warriors carrying their back devices in a procession. Prescott 1922, 1:332–33.

the Clothing as a Reflection of the Culture:
A Comparative Analysis of the Six Costume Repertories

 A SAMPLING OF THE PICTORIAL clothing data from the Late Postclassic Meso-american cultures for which there is information has been presented. We can now compare and contrast those six groups, looking at their unique qualities, their similarities, and their differences. We thus can begin to assess the degree to which each costume repertory reflects the culture from which it came.

To compare the apparel of the six groups, I have summarized each of their repertories on a single chart. A chart of this type has already been presented for the Tarascan costume repertory (chart 7), and a duplicate (chart 18) appears in this chapter. The other five charts (16, 17, 19, 20, 21) have been compiled by using the initial example from each clothing category in the costume analysis; thus each garment type in a costume repertory is represented.

AZTEC COSTUME REPERTORY

When considering the Aztec costume repertory summarized on chart 16, one is struck by the degree of variation among the principal status-garment types. Certainly this is true of the *tilmatli*, which ranged from the short maguey- or palm-fiber cloaks of the lower classes to the magnificent, long, richly worked cotton mantles of the notables and successful warriors. The same wide variation is evident in the wraparound skirts and *huipilli*. The garments varied dramatically both in material and in design; hence they could be used to reflect all levels of social stratification. Despite the reputedly rigid Aztec sumptuary laws, Fray Bernardino de Sahagún's informants reported that a colorful range of maguey-fiber capes, usually associated with the lower classes, existed in the society. It is a tribute to Aztec artistic creativity that, no matter how prescribed their dress, it was never controlled to the point of monotony. Indeed, the sumptuary laws appear to have been more vaunted than effective. Recent research indicates that it was really only ceremonial and ritual costumes that were controlled. The everyday clothing was apparently far more varied than the sources indicate.[1]

Aztec armor is particularly striking in its variety, form, and decoration of basic costume type. Not only were there two different kinds of quilted armor—open- and closed-sewn—but a range of variation existed for each. Style diversity is also evident in the flamboyant Aztec feathered garments, which served as the martial status markers. The fitted warrior suits were made in many designs, including eagle, ocelot, and coyote costumes. Within each category the level of military rank was defined by the type and color of feathers used in the costume and its accouterments.

The most surprising aspect of the Aztec costume repertory is the limited range of secular-garment types recorded in the codices and mentioned in the Spanish texts. It might be anticipated—because of the wealth and complexity of the Aztec empire—that there would be less standardization in their costume repertory and that it would contain the largest number of different garment forms for everyday wear. With the exception of the *sui generis* Tarascan clothing, however, the other Indian groups utilized the same four basic draped garments (loincloth, hip-cloth, cape, and wraparound skirt), as well as some of the other Aztec apparel.

The Lowland Maya, the Borgia Group, and the Mixtec

[1] Anawalt 1980.

codices include an interesting diversity of men's and, in the latter two groups, women's capes. The Borgia Group and Mixtec codices display a variety of *quechquemitl*, and the Mixtecs and Lowland Mayas wore the *xicolli* as both a secular and a ceremonial garment.

It is noteworthy that the Aztecs, a group so open to the incorporation of the religious ideas of other peoples, absorbed two "foreign" garments only in a ceremonial context. While it is true that the Aztec costume repertory contains the *quechquemitl*, apparently only the triangular type was represented, and it was utilized solely for religious purposes. In contrast, the *quechquemitl* is the prevalent female upper-body garment repeatedly seen in the Mixtec and Borgia Group codices, some of which date from the fifteenth century. The same situation applies to the *xicolli*, a secular-religious status garment among the Mixtecs but solely a ritual costume among the Aztecs.

Acculturation studies have demonstrated that it is not uncommon for a foreign trait to become highly specialized when it is absorbed into a more complex context.[2] Foreign traits usually are absorbed in clusters; it is probable, therefore, that the presence of the *quechquemitl* and the *xicolli* in the Aztec costume repertory is a visual reminder of the earlier absorption of religious concepts originating in another region. That probability will be discussed in chapter 9, which deals with the cultural and historical implications of the various garments.

The Aztec costume repertory clearly reflects the culture from which it came. The sharply stratified nature of the complex society is evident in the degree of elaboration of the basic garment types that served the society as visual status markers. The Aztecs' tolerance of the religious preferences, practices, and pantheons of their subject provinces is manifest in the absorption of certain "foreign" garments for ritual purposes only. The variety of military garments mirrors a culture whose principal emphasis was on aggressive expansion. Since in the Aztec world a man literally had to fight to wear the status garments of his society, the coveted apparel served as a reinforcing mechanism that encouraged young men to put forth their greatest effort on the field of battle.

TLAXCALAN COSTUME REPERTORY

Since the Tlaxcalans were also Chichimec-derived, it is not surprising that their costume repertory (chart 17) is similar to that of their cultural and spiritual neighbors, the Aztecs. The Tlaxcalan and Aztec loincloths, capes, skirts, and *ehuatl* and the general construction of the warrior costumes are nearly identical. However, the Tlaxcalans wearing the *maxtlatl* are shown only in the short style that tied in front. There is a minor difference in the manner of wearing the hip-cloth: the Aztecs tied it on the right side; the Tlaxcalans tied it in front. The Tlaxcalan

huipil was a longer, much wider garment than its Aztec counterpart, and the warrior costumes were not as elaborate in detailing or variety as those of the Aztecs. Although there is no extant illustration of the Tlaxcalan *xicolli*, Motolinía's description of it matches exactly that of the Aztec ritual garment.[3]

The *ichcahuipilli* of the Tlaxcalans do not precisely duplicate those of the Aztecs. Such differences could reflect the style of the native artist, or the lack of cotton, which may have caused the Tlaxcalans to use a henequen version of the garment. Whatever the material, the Aztec and Tlaxcalan garments were similar. Since the two repertories were alike in other respects, it is doubtful that they would vary greatly in such a practical matter as the general construction of battle armor.

The effect of the strong provincial style of the *Tonalamatl Aubin* on the illustration of the triangular *quechquemitl*, as well as the other six draped garment examples from the same source, has been mentioned. No doubt the highly stylized *quechquemitl* from the *Tonalamatl Aubin* was the same type as those worn by the Aztecs. In both groups the *quechquemitl* appears as part of the traditional attire of the maize goddess Chicomecoatl, further suggesting that the two versions were probably identical. No other *quechquemitl* in the Mesoamerican costume repertory resembles the Tlaxcalan example.

Although pictorial data for the Tlaxcalan costume repertory is limited, the martial focus of their culture is nonetheless reflected in the clothing examples pictured. Like their traditional foes the Aztecs, the Tlaxcalans had a disproportionate variety of warrior garments. Although the *Lienzo de Tlaxcala* was drawn up as a self-promoting propaganda document, the early battle scenes show the Mexicas wearing the more detailed and elaborate martial attire. But in the latter thirty or so folios, where Tlaxcalan auxiliaries are shown aiding the Spaniards in further conquests (following the fall of Tenochtitlán), the Indians' fitted warrior costumes and towering back devices are elaborate indeed. It is difficult to know what is reflected here, the spoils of war or self-aggrandizement.

Although the style of the *Tonalamatl Aubin* is obviously provincial, the apparel and accouterments of the highly stylized deity portrayals demonstrate how strongly the inhabitants of the Puebla-Tlaxcala valley and adjoining mountainous area were influenced by the Aztecs of the Valley of Mexico.

TARASCAN COSTUME REPERTORY

In the sense that Tarascan culture displays more puzzling non-Mesoamerican traits than any of the other Late Postclassic groups, the Tarascan clothing repertory indeed reflects the milieu from which it comes (chart 18). The absence of the elsewhere ubiquitous Mesoamerican loincloth is unusual enough. In addition to that aberration the

---

[2] Keesing 1953; Redfield, Herskovitz, Linton 1936.

[3] Motolinía, 1971, pp. 78–79.

CHART 16
AZTEC COSTUME REPERTORY
Example of Garments Reflecting
the Five Basic Principles of Garment Construction

Draped Garments

a   b   c   d   e

Slip-on Garments

f

Open-sewn Garments

g   h

Closed-sewn Garments

i   j   k   l

Limb-encasing Garments

m

SOURCES: (a) *Codex Mendoza*, vol. 3, fol. 60r; (b) *Codex Mendoza*, vol. 3, fol. 68r; (c) *Codex Mendoza*, vol. 3, fol. 64r; (d) *Codex Magliabechiano*, fol. 34r; (e) *Codex Borbonicus*, p. 29; (f) *Codex Magliabechiano*, fol. 58r; (g) *Codex Telleriano-Remensis*, fol. 29r; (h) *Codex Mendoza*, vol. 3, fol. 63r; (i) *Codex Mendoza*, vol. 3, fol. 66r; (j) *Codex Vaticanus A*, fol. 57v; (k) *Códice Matritense de la Real Academia de la Historia*, fol. 73r; (l) *Codex Mendoza*, vol. 3, fol. 68r; (m) *Codex Mendoza*, vol. 3, fol. 65r.

CHART 17
TLAXCALA COSTUME REPERTORY
Examples of Garments Reflecting
the Five Basic Principles of Garment Construction

Draped Garments

a   b   c   d

Slip-on Garments

e

Open-sewn Garments

- - - - - - - - - - - - - -

Closed-sewn Garments

f   g   h

Limb-encasing Garments

i

SOURCES: (a) *Lienzo de Tlaxcala, lámina* 10; (b) *Lienzo de Tlax-cala, lámina* 30; (c) *Lienzo de Tlaxcala, lámina* 4; (d) *Tonalamatl Aubin, lámina* 4; (e) *Tonalamatl Aubin, lámina* 7; (f) *Lienzo de Tlaxcala, lámina* 13; (g) *Lienzo de Tlaxcala, lámina* 21; (h) *Lienzo de Tlaxcala, lámina* 9; (i) *Lienzo de Tlaxcala, lámina* 43.

CHART 18
TARASCAN COSTUME REPERTORY
Examples of Garments Reflecting
the Five Basic Principles of Garment Construction

Draped Garments

  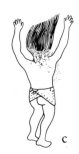  

a   b   c   d   e

Slip-on Garments

f   g

Open-sewn Garments

h   i   j

Closed-sewn Garments

k   l   m

Limb-encasing Garments

- - - - - - - - - - - - - - - - -

SOURCES: (a) *Relación de Michoacán, lámina* 2; (b) *Relación de Michoacán, lámina* 18; (c) *Relación de Michoacán, lámina* 25; (d) *Relación de Michoacán, lámina* 38; (e) *Relación de Michoacán, lámina* 38; (f) *Relación de Michoacán, lámina* 19; (g) *Relación de Michoacán, lámina* 37; (h) *Relación de Michoacán, lámina* 37; (i) *Relación de Michoacán, lámina* 25; (j) *Relación de Michoacán, lámina* 44; (k) *Codex Telleriano-Remensis, fol.* 33v; (l) *Relación de Michoacán, lámina* 41; (m) *Relación de Michoacán, lámina* 30.

197

men wore the enveloping *cicuilli*, a garment the Aztecs scornfully likened to a woman's *huipil*. There are no other Mesoamerican examples of this full, rather short male "tunic," unless the robes of the Mixtec and Borgia Group codices are analogous. That connection is doubtful, however, since those robes appear to be special-purpose garments used in a ritual context.

The Tarascan costume repertory does contain a few parallels with that of the neighboring peoples. The high priest carries the staff and tobacco gourd that are pan-Mesoamerican priestly diagnostics. The *Relaciones geográficas* of the Michoacán area show that the Tarascans too wore the quintessential pan-Mesoamerican military garment—cotton armor. They also had a feathered warrior's costume that vaguely resembles the *ehuatl*, although it is not certain that the Tarascan garment was worn into battle.

The Tarascan women were the only highland group to go about virtually topless. An occasional *quechquemitl*—seemingly out of place in that *sui generis* area of Mesoamerica—is pictured. The presence of the female upper-body garment is puzzling; the *quechquemitl* may have been worn only on special occasions. Of the forty-four illustrations in the *Relación de Michoacán*, only thirteen show living women[4] (there are three sacrifice-execution scenes).[5] Of the thirteen scenes only five show the *quechquemitl*,[6] but the contexts vary enough to suggest that it was not used just for special occasions. Yet in several of the examples the garment is so small that it could not have afforded much warmth. That may indicate that the *quechquemitl* was originally adopted into the Tarascan costume repertory because of religious or historical connotations. The *quechquemitl* is particularly associated with the Gulf Coast.[7] It is also shown being worn by goddesses at the great central Mexican Classic period site Teotihuacán, and it appears later in the costume repertory of the Early Postclassic Toltecs of Tula. Perhaps the Chichimec ancestors of the Tarascans brought it with them as a symbol of prestigious Toltec antecedents.

MIXTEC COSTUME REPERTORY

In comparison with the three preceding groups, the Mixtec costume repertory, summarized in chart 19, includes a number of unique features: (1) the short length of the male capes, (2) instances of some of the male capes being worn over the chest rather than over the back or shoulders, (3) the occurrence of male kilts, (4) the variety of female upper-body garments, (5) the *xicolli* being worn as both a secular and a priestly costume, (6) the occurrence of a male, body-encasing, robelike garment, and (7) the use of limb-encasing jaguar and eagle costumes as ceremonial

rather than martial costumes. Each feature will be considered in turn.

In a comparison of the capes of the Aztecs and Tlaxcalans with those of the Mixtecs the immediately observable difference is the shorter length of the Mixtec garments. The only "long" Mixtec capes come from the highly Hispanicized colonial *Códice de Yanhuitlán*, which dates from around 1545 to 1550. Many of the Mixtec males wear their capes over the chest rather than over the back or shoulder, as did the Aztecs and the Tlaxcalans. The Mixtec chest capes may have been a version of the *quemitl*, a ritual garment that Seler mentioned as having been placed around the necks of idols.[8]

In the two examples of comparable Aztec capes worn in the Mixtec manner, both appear in a religious context. The first occurs in Sahagún's *Primeros memoriales*, worn by Omacatl, the Aztec god of feasting and revelry (fig. 57).[9] The other example is the figure used to illustrate one of the eighteen annual religious ceremonies, Hueytecuilhuitl, in *Codex Telleriano-Remensis* (fig. 58).[10] Neither these two Aztec capes nor the short Mixtec capes agree with the cape descriptions from the 1579–81 *Relaciones geográficas* of the Oaxaca area.

Depictions of a short male kilt appear only occasionally in the Mixtec codices. Aside from one illustration that comes from the Aztec pictorial corpus but depicts a Zapotec ritual (fig. 59),[11] I know of no comparable example. The Borgia Group codices contain a similar garment, however, and there is also a variant of it in the Maya pictorial *Codex Dresden*. The context of all the garments indicates they were special-purpose, ritual clothing.

Mixtec women's clothing presents several interesting contrasts. Among the Aztecs, and probably the Tlaxcalans as well, the *quechquemitl* was strictly a ritual costume, and the only female everyday upper-body apparel was the *huipil*. The Mixtec women, however, had a wider variety of garments for the upper torso. Although the *huipil* apparently was worn in the Mixtec area, it rarely appears in the pictorials. The noble ladies of the Mixtec codices wear short capes and round or triangular *quechquemitl*, all with some degree of decoration. Since the *quechquemitl* is so prevalent in the native pictorials, it is surprising that there is no mention of it in the colonial Spanish texts dealing with the Mixteca.

Among the Aztecs, like the *quechquemitl*, the *xicolli* was also a special-purpose garment worn only for ritual purposes, particularly by the priests. Among the Mixtecs the *xicolli* was utilized to a far greater extent. While they also had a priestly jacket, easily identifiable by black designs on a white ground, most of their *xicolli* were red with a multicolored fringed hem. The garment is the principal costume of the aristocratic lords and rulers of the Mixtec codices.

---

[4] *Relación de Michoacán*, pp. 6, 8, 9, 12, 13, 19, 20, 26, 34, 37–39, 42.

[5] Ibid., pp. 2, 25, 33.

[6] Ibid., pp. 8, 13, 19, 26, 37.

[7] Anawalt, in press.

[8] Seler 1901–1902, pp. 122, 130.

[9] Seler 1960, 2:504, fig. 56.

[10] *Codex Telleriano-Remensis*, fol. IV.

[11] *Codex Vaticanus A*, fol. 55v.

CHART 19

MIXTEC COSTUME REPERTORY
Examples of Garments Reflecting
the Five Basic Principles of Garment Construction

Draped Garments

a   b   c   d   e   f

Slip-on Garments

g

h

Open-sewn Garments

i

j

Closed-sewn Garments

k

l

m

Limb-encasing Garments

n

SOURCES: (*a*) *Codex Zouche-Nuttall*, p. 50; (*b*) *Codex Zouche-Nuttall*, p. 83; (*c*) *Codex Zouche-Nuttall*, p. 82; (*d*) *Codex Vindobonensis* obverse, p. 26; (*e*) *Codex Zouche-Nuttall*, p. 30; (*f*) *Codex Zouche-Nuttall*, p. 12; (*g*) *Codex Zouche-Nuttall*, p. 9; (*b*) *Codex Zouche-Nuttall*, p. 20; (*i*) *Codex Bodley*, p. 14; (*j*) *Codex Selden*, p. 14; (*k*) *Codex Zouche-Nuttall*, p. 66; (*l*) *Codex Zouche-Nuttall*, p. 40; (*m*) *Codex Zouche-Nuttall*, p. 5; (*n*) *Codex Zouche-Nuttall*, p. 32.

FIGURE 57. The deity Omacatl, god of feasting and revelry. *Codex Primeros memoriales*. Seler 1960, 2:504, fig. 46.

Of the six Mesoamerican groups for whom there are pictorial clothing data, only the Tarascans, the Mixtecs, and the Borgia Group include a male body-encasing, tuniclike garment. Because of colonial Spanish descriptions equating the Tarascan *cicuilli* with both the Aztec *xicolli* and a European jacket, I placed the Tarascan garment in the open-sewn category. The Mixtec and Borgia Group robes appear to be narrower tunics that pulled over the head. One of the Mixtec robes (example *d* of chart 10) has the priestly white-with-black-design diagnostic, which reinforces the impression that they were probably ritual garments.

One of the most striking differences between the Aztec-Tlaxcalan costume repertories and that of the Mixtecs is in the use of the limb-encasing jaguar and eagle costumes. Among the former groups those flamboyant garments were utilized predominantly in warfare. They served the important function of achieved-status markers that indi-cated, by their style, color, and degree of elaboration, the prowess of the warriors who wore them. Although the costumes were also sometimes worn for ceremonial occasions, their principal association was decidedly martial. Not so their Mixtec counterparts.

While there is a resemblance between the Aztec and Mixtec limb-encasing garments (both groups had similar jaguar suits and eagle costumes), the Mixtec apparel occurs only in ceremonial contexts. Wherever warfare is indicated in the Mixtec codices—by either physical aggression or a figure accompanied by weapons—cotton or animal-skin armor is shown rather than the limb-encasing costumes. The implications of this difference remain obscure until further research can be done.

Mixtec culture was less complex and controlled than that of the Aztecs, and accordingly the Mixtec costume repertory indicates less standardization in dress. Not only does it contain a wider range of garment types, but there is not a comparable differentiation within a single item of clothing to signal status level, as was needed in the more complex Aztec society. While various styles of Mixtec capes are shown, they appear to be decorative variations on a common theme rather than carefully graded visual status markers. The same situation exists with the *xicolli* and *quechquemitl*, which display variety in color, fringe, and border design. These detailed garments appear to have been well made with much attention to fine decorative finish, a trait reflected in other aspects of Mixtec craftsmanship.

This emphasis on well-made clothing is confirmed by Cortés in his second letter to Charles V. The conquistador, telling about sending some Spaniards out to look at the gold mines, mentioned in reference to the Mixtec area that the people "wore more clothes than any others we have seen, and as it seemed to them, well-designed."[12]

BORGIA GROUP COSTUME REPERTORY

The costume repertory of the Borgia Group codices, summarized in chart 20, resembles that of the Mixtecs in many ways, but there are also decided differences that may offer some interesting clues to provenience. Table 1 presents a comparison of the two repertories. Because the Borgia Group codices are ritual-divinatory manuals, the Mixtec codex that most closely parallels them, the obverse of *Codex Vindobonensis*, is used as the specific Mixtec document for comparison.

Table 1 reveals the degree of correlation between the costume repertories of the Borgia Group and the Mixtec codices. There are several marked differences. The female chest cape does not appear at all in the Mixtec codices, but both *Fejérváry-Mayer* and *Laud* contain several depictions of it. The same contrast occurs with females wearing skirts only. The sole depiction in the Mixtec group is of a

[12] Cortés 1971, p. 92.

FIGURE 58. Figure illustrating the Hueytecuilhuitl ceremony. *Codex Telleriano-Remensis*, fol. 1v.

FIGURE 59. Zapotec ritual scene. *Codex Vaticanus A*, fol. 55v.

child, but the Borgia Group codices contain repeated depictions of topless females.

The Borgia Group also contains a number of figures who wear the male *maxtlatl* in addition to standard women's clothing. The Mixtec codices have no similar androgynous figures.

There is a dramatic difference between the two groups of pictorials in the use of the *xicolli*. The Mixtec codices contain dozens of depictions of the garment, both the aristocratic red secular jacket and its priestly counterpart, the *xicolli* with white-with-black designs. In all the Borgia Group only two *xicolli* appear. Both are worn by priests, yet neither has the white-with-black designs.

Both groups had robes in their costume repertoires. Robes are, however, more prevalent in the Borgia Group, though never in the priestly combination white and black.

The final striking contrast between the two costume repertories is seen in the limb-encasing ceremonial costumes. In the Mixtec codices there are at least 123 jaguar, puma, and eagle garments, 15 of which are found in *Codex Vindobonensis*. In the five core members of the Borgia Grop only 2 limb-encasing costumes can be found, both with the jaguar design.

What can we deduce from these contrasts? How many of the differences can be attributed to the ritual nature of the Borgia Group? The female chest cape, which must represent the *quemitl* — the garment Seler said the Indians tied around the necks of their idols — could be explained in that way. Such an explanation would also apply to the androgynous figures who combine the clothing of both sexes: it is the confusing proclivity of certain earth-fertility-death deities.

The ritual nature of the Borgia Group may also explain why they contain over four times as many robes as the Mixtec pictorials. If the Borgia Group codices are indeed the Mixtecs' religious manuscripts, however, it could be expected that they would reflect the Mixtecs' convention of depicting priestly attire by the use of the white-and-black color scheme; none of the Borgia Group robes does so.

The same argument can be applied to the *xicolli*. Since the Mixtecs made extensive use of both secular and ritual *xicolli*, regularly depicting the latter in a conventional white-and-black color scheme, it could be anticipated that their religious documents would reflect the same pattern. Yet in all the Borgia Group there are only two *xicolli*. In

CHART 20

THE BORGIA GROUP COSTUME REPERTORY
Examples of Garments Reflecting
the Five Basic Principles of Garment Construction

Draped Garments

Slip-on Garments

Open-sewn Garments

Closed-sewn Garments

Limb-encasing Garments

SOURCES: (a) *Codex Laud*, p. 15D; (b) *Codex Fejérváry-Mayer*, p. 32; (c) *Codex Laud*, p. 3D; (d) *Codex Fejérváry-Mayer*, p. 3; (e) *Codex Fejérváry-Mayer*, p. 30; (f) *Codex Laud*, p. 15D; (g) *Codex Fejérváry-Mayer*, p. 25; (h) *Codex Borgia*, p. 59; (i) *Codex Fejérváry-Mayer*, p. 27; (j) *Codex Laud*, p. 15D; (k) *Codex Cospi recto*, p. 1; (l) *Codex Laud*, p. 13D.

Comparison of the Mixtec and Borgia Group Codices Costume Repertories

Garment	Mixtec Codices	Borgia Group Codices
Maxtlatl	*Codex Vindobonensis* obverse: 15% of the *maxtlatl* are decorated	Examples of decorated *maxtlatl*: *Codex Borgia*: 55% *Codex Vaticanus B*: 68% *Codex Cospi*: 11% *Codex Fejérváry-Mayer*: 68% *Codex Laud*: 18%
Hip-cloth	*Codex Vindobonensis* obverse: all hip-cloths are decorated	*Codex Borgia* and *Codex Cospi*: all hip-cloths are decorated *Codex Vaticanus B*: 68% are decorated *Codex Fejérváry-Mayer*: 17% decorated *Codex Laud*: 18% decorated
Male capes	*Codex Vindobonensis* obverse: 2 male capes	*Codex Borgia*: 2 *Codex Vaticanus B*: 0 *Codex Cospi*: 5 *Codex Fejérváry-Mayer*: 12 *Codex Laud*: 9 (2 are the only back capes in the Borgia Group)
Kilt	*Codex Vindobonensis* obverse: 8 *Codex Vindobonensis* reverse: 2 *Codex Zouche-Nuttall*: 1	*Codex Borgia*: none *Codex Vaticanus B*: approximately 19 *Codex Cospi*: 1 (?) *Codex Fejérváry-Mayer*: 5 *Codex Laud*: 7
Female chest capes (*quémitl*)	No female chest capes appear in the Mixtec codices.	*Codex Borgia*: 0 *Codex Vaticanus B*: 1 *Codex Cospi*: 0 *Codex Fejérváry-Mayer*: 3 *Codex Laud*: 6
Female skirt worn topless	The Mixtec codices contain only one topless female, a child.	The Borgia Group codices all contain repeated depictions of topless females.
Rounded and triangular *quechquemitl*	The Mixtec Codices have no really short, rounded *quechquemitl*. The Mixtec codices contain no *quechquemitl* + *maxtlatl* = androgynous figures.	The Borgia Group codices contain a number of very short, rounded *quechquemitl*. The Borgia Group codices contain a number of *quechquemitl* + *maxtlatl* = androgynous figures.
Xicolli	The red *xicolli* is the principal male garment of the Mixtec codices. The white-with-black-design *xicolli* is the priestly garment.	The Borgia Group codices contain only two *xicolli* depictions (*Codex Fejérváry-Mayer* and *Codex Laud*). Both are priests but neither *xicolli* is white-with-black designs.
Armor	The Mixtec codices contain only a few depictions of cotton and animal-skin armor. *Codex Vindobonensis* contains none.	The Borgia Group codices contain no depictions of armor.
Robe	Eleven robes occur in the Mixtec codices. *Codex Vindobonensis* obverse: 3 *Codex Zouche-Nuttall* obverse: 8	The Borgia Group codices contain 48 robes: *Codex Borgia*: 0 *Codex Vaticanus B*: 13 *Codex Cospi*: 9 *Codex Fejérváry-Mayer*: 19 *Codex Laud*: 7
Huipil	The Mixtec codices contain very few *huipil*.	The Borgia Group codices contain very few *huipil*.
Limb-encasing, ceremonial costumes	The Mixtec codice contain at least 123 jaguar, puma, or eagle costumes.	The Borgia Group codices contain only two of these costumes, both jaguar (*Codex Borgia* and *Codex Laud*).

both cases it is priests who wear the garment, but neither has the white-with-black designs. The more stylized of the two (*Codex Laud*, sheet 8) has dots placed over yellow stripes. The closest analogue is found not in the Mixtec codices but on a *xicolli* worn by the Aztec Churubusco Idol, the sculpture now in the National Museum of Anthropology in Mexico City (see fig. 17).

Another pattern in the Mixtec codices is the repeated presentation of individuals in jaguar, puma, or eagle costumes; in all the Borgia Group codices only two limb-encasing costumes—both jaguar suits—are to be found.

Considering the sharp contrast in the occurrence of topless females and androgynous figures, as well as the use of the *xicolli*, robe, and ceremonial costumes, the clothing in the ritual pictorials of the Borgia Group suggests that the books probably did not come from the Mixtec heartland, since they do not reflect Mixtec ritual-clothing patterns. Further, the considerable stylistic variation among the Borgia pictorials—always excepting the twins *Fejérváry-Mayer* and *Laud*—suggests that the manuscripts came not only from different communities but probably also from centers well separated in space.

Considering the impressive evidence associating *Codex Borgia* with the important pre-Hispanic religious and manufacturing center of Cholula, I agree with Nicholson in assigning *Borgia* to the Puebla-Tlaxcala area.[13] And since *Codex Cospi* not only is stylistically similar to *Borgia* but also has an even closer resemblance to the Tizatlán altar paintings found in Tlaxcala, it seems logical to attribute it to the Puebla-Tlaxcala region as well. This may also be the best attribution for *Codex Vaticanus B*. While it resembles *Borgia*, it is much sketchier in both content and style and aesthetically is much inferior. For reasons discussed below, however, the Gulf Coast must also be considered a possibility.

When we are considering the probable homeland of the remaining two Borgia pictorials, the twins *Fejérváry-Mayer* and *Laud*, the emphasis must shift to the Gulf Coast. It is of interest to note[14] that in the late pre-contact period the influence of the polychrome ceramic tradition of Cholula on the local assemblage of Cempoallán, Veracruz, was so great that García Payón dubbed this center *un vástago de Cholula*.[15] This intimate relationship is underscored by specific mention of the Veracruz center as one from which regular ritual pilgrimages to Cholula were undertaken.

It must be remembered that the central-southern section of Veracruz was thriving before the Spanish conquest. The natives of the region were famous for their skill in painting cotton mantles.[16] Further, the inhabitants of the area had the reputation of being particularly wise in ritual and divinatory lore, as descendants of the *tlamatinime*, the wise men of legendary Tamoanchán, who

were supposed to have migrated to this eastern coastal region, taking with them the sacred ritual books.[17] Indeed, among other names, the area was known as Tillan Tlapallan (Place of Writings).

This region of the Gulf Coast, renowned for craftsmen skilled in painting and priests steeped in esoteric religious knowledge, may well have been the homeland for the beautifully drawn, intellectually abstract pictorials *Fejérváry-Mayer* and *Laud*. There is a further factor that argues in favor of such an attribution: bare-breasted women were typical of this tropical zone. While admittedly there is no necessary correlation between semi-nudity and warm climate (recall the nudity practiced in the harsh environment of Tierra del Fuego), the repeated occurrence of topless females in the Borgia Group codices may well be a provenience indicator. With only one exception—a child—toplessness does not occur in the Mixtec codices nor in the Aztec pictorials (bare-breasted Aztec women are almost always stone sculptures, mother goddesses whose exposed breasts emphasizes their maternal aspect). In the central-southern Gulf Coast region, however, bare-breasted women were, and still are today, typical of the area.[18] When considered in conjunction with other Gulf Coast provenience clues, the frequent occurrence of topless women in the Borgia Group codices is definitely significant.

There is still a further argument that can be presented for the central-southern Gulf Coast region as homeland for *Fejérváry-Mayer* and *Laud*. In the July 6, 1519, inventory of gifts Cortés sent back to Spain are listed two native books. As has been mentioned earlier, there are a number of pictorial contenders for this honor, but the Borgia Group twins are prime candidates. Central Veracruz was the first area where the conquistadors landed and where they reconnoitered for five months. Cempoallán was the first large Mesoamerican city they visited. It would be logical to collect two exceptionally well-drawn books to include in the rich gifts chosen to send back to Spain to impress the crown with the exotic appeal of Cortés's newly discovered land.

Archaeological data are needed to strengthen further a central-southern Veracruz Gulf Coast provenience attribution for *Codex Fejérváry-Mayer* and *Laud*. Unfortunately, the area is almost an archaeological blank for the Late Postclassic period; the emphasis in this region principally has been on Preclassic Olmec sites and subsequent Classic Maya connections. Nicholson, who has summarized what knowledge we have of the Postclassic archaeology of the area, has called for Mesoamerican archaeologists to become more deeply involved in the central-southern Gulf Coast Late Postclassic time period, particularly in the areas somewhat north of Cempoallán to at least the Tabasco border on the south, with special

[13] Nicholson 1966*b*, pp. 153–54.
[14] Nicholson MS, p. 58.
[15] García Payón 1949, p. 471.

[16] Alvarado Tezozomoc 1944, pp. 308–309.
[17] Sahagún 1950–69, bk. 10, pp. 187–88, 190–91.
[18] Covarrubias 1947.

emphasis on the Tuxtepec and lower Papaloapán, Playa Vicente, Los Tuxtlas, and Coatzacoalcos zones.[19] Certainly the richly detailed pictorials of the Borgia Group contain a great variety of ritual objects and structures of imperishable materials that are potentially available for archaeological discovery. Indeed, as Nicholson has pointed out, a single archaeological discovery on the order of the Tizatlán altar paintings might prove to be a major turning point in our understanding of the whole Borgia Group provenience question.[20]

LOWLAND MAYA COSTUME REPERTORY

Chart 21, which summarizes the Lowland Maya costume repertory, demonstrates the presence of all four basic Mesoamerican garments of the Late Postclassic period: the loincloth, the hip-cloth, the cape, and the wraparound skirt. The Lowland Maya added a new item of apparel, the female hip-cloth.

Another Lowland Maya garment that has no known Mesoamerican counterpart is the Tulum cape (see examples *l* and *m* of chart 14). The Tulum murals have been described as not truly reflecting the Mayas, being too Mexican or Mixtec in style,[21] yet depictions of the unusual cape are completely lacking in the pictorial data from both the suggested areas. The capes and hip-cloths of examples *l* and *m*, and examples *g* and *k* from Santa Rita, contain the principal Lowland Maya Late Postclassic clothing diagnostic, the notched hem, a feature that appears repeatedly in all three of the Maya codices.

The male kilt (example *d* of chart 21) differs somewhat from the kilt of the Aztecs, the Mixtecs, and the Borgia Group, but the resemblances are close enough to consider it a recognizable variant. That is also true of both the rounded and triangular *quechquemitl* depictions.

Unlike the Mixtec and Borgia Group codices, the Maya pictorials give no indication that the Lowland Mayas wore the robe; but Bernal Díaz del Castillo's reference to the priests of Campeche wearing clothing of long white cotton *manta* that came down to their feet is intriguing.[22] It is particularly so in light of the existence at Chichén Itzá of at least six depictions of Itzá priests clad in robelike garments that reach to their feet.[23]

Two other garments are conspicuously absent in the Lowland Maya costume repertory, the *huipil* and the limb-encasing ceremonial costume. The *Relaciones geográficas* make no reference to Maya women wearing the *huipil* before Spanish contact. There are, however, repeated references to the garment being worn at the time the reports were written (1579 to 1585). The implication is that the *huipil*, an "eastern" garment, came into the Maya Lowlands after the Spanish conquest.

The Lowland Mayas apparently had no limb-encasing animallike garment similar to the jaguar costumes of the neighboring Mixtec and Borgia Group peoples. Evidently such garments were not worn into battle by the Mayas of the Late Postclassic period; there is no mention of them in the Yucatán *Relaciones geográficas*. In describing the Maya warriors of Champotón encountered by the Córdoba expedition of 1517, Díaz del Castillo referred to the Indians as being "dressed in cotton armor and carrying the feathered crests they were accustomed to wear."[24] The implication is that the Lowland Mayas went into battle wearing some form of feathered back ornament strapped on over their *ichcahuipilli*. From a wall mural at the Temple of the jaguars at Chichén Itzá, we know that the Mayas of the Toltec invasion period, A.D. 987, went into battle similarly arrayed (fig. 60).

We must ask ourselves if the Lowland Maya costume repertory reflects what is known of the culture. Because all pictorial data for the group come from ritual-oriented sources, their clothing is seen from a somewhat distorted perspective. But considering the degree to which religion influenced the lives of those people, perhaps such an orientation does not unduly skew the presentation; certainly Late Postclassic Lowland Maya clothing has a quality all its own. Inasmuch as the Mayas were controlled for some two hundred years by the formidable Toltecs, and were subsequently influenced through Lowland Maya trading contacts with the Triple Alliance Empire of the Valley of Mexico, we could expect that there would be noticeable vestiges of the central Mexican highlands in the Maya costume repertory. That is not the case. There are no long capes, no *huipils*, and, particularly, no limb-encasing warrior costumes. Despite strong highland influence, the Lowland Maya dress retained its own distinctive personality. Just as the earlier Mayas held their former Itzá overlords in contempt, so too might they have rejected Mexican clothing styles. Perhaps the native Maya traditions preserved on the east coast of Yucatán through the Toltec period were stronger and more resilient than has been generally acknowledged.

---

[19] Nicholson MS, pp. 55–64, 105.
[20] Nicholson 1966*b*, p. 158.
[21] Mahler 1965, p. 591.

[22] Díaz del Castillo 1967, 1:20.
[23] Tozzer 1957, figs. 100, 196, 669–72.
[24] Díaz del Castillo 1967, 1:22.

CHART 21
LOWLAND MAYA COSTUME REPERTORY
Examples of Garments Reflecting
the Five Basic Principles of Garment Construction

Draped Garments

a b c d e f

Slip-on Garments

g h

Open-sewn Garments

i

Closed-sewn Garments

j

Limb-encasing Garments

- - - - - - - - - - - - - - - -

SOURCES: (*a*) *Codex Madrid*, p. 95; (*b*) *Codex Dresden*, p. 33; (*c*) *Codex Dresden*, p. 23; (*d*) *Codex Dresden*, p. 28; (*e*) *Codex Dresden*, p. 39; (*f*) *Codex Dresden*, p. 22; (*g*) *Codex Madrid*, p. 11; (*h*) *mural*, Structure 5, Temple of the Diving God, Tulum, Quintana Roo, Mexico; (*i*) *Codex Madrid*, p. 84; (*j*) *Codex Madrid*, p. 50.

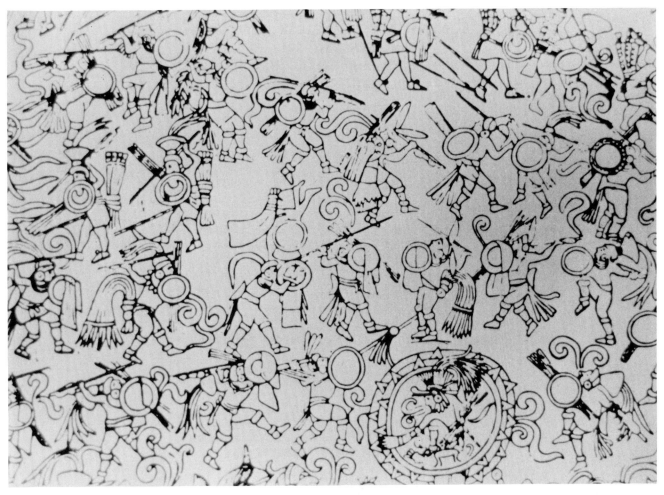

FIGURE 60. Section of a wall mural from the Temple of the Jaguars, Chichén Itzá. Tozzer 1957, fig. 60.

FIGURE 61. Mixtec place glyph including a *xicolli*. *Codex Vindobonensis* obverse, p. 43.

CHAPTER NINE

What the Garments Tell Us

 IN THE PRECEDING discussions the clothing of each of the six costume repertories has been considered only within its own cultural framework. Further information can be gleaned from the same data by examining their pan-Mesoamerican distribution, concentrating on the variations that occur within the costume types themselves.

I have arranged the male and female pan-Mesoamerican costume repertories in two charts (22 and 23) showing garments in columns according to type, thus displaying a summary of the full range of clothing depicted in the extant Mesoamerican codices at the time of Spanish contact. As in the summary charts of the six costume repertories (charts 16 to 21), the examples used are the initial figures from each of the apparel sections. Those garments have already been described and discussed within the context of their own costume repertories. They can also serve to illustrate the type and distribution of clothing worn in pre-Hispanic Mesoamerica.

MALE GARMENTS

The first column on the left in chart 22 contains examples of the *maxtlatl*. The loincloth was utilized by all groups except the Tarascans, and it appears in the full range of social contexts. It was the basic, indispensable male garment. Two styles of the loincloth were worn in Late Post-classic Mesoamerica. From the extant pictorials it appears that the Aztecs and the Tlaxcalans favored the shorter type that encircled the waist, passed between the legs, and tied in front of the crotch, creating a distinctive knot whose two short ends reached no farther than to the knees. The knot appears as a glyph on *mantas* in the

tribute lists, indicating the intended use of the cloth, and it is always found on the front of the limb-encasing warrior costumes. It probably was synonymous with virility; indeed, the word *maxtlatl* was used as a male given name. The second type of loincloth also wrapped around the waist and passed between the legs; it was then knotted in the back, and the two long ends extended, front and back, to the ankles. It was a "southerly" style, and appears in the Mixtec, the Borgia Group, and the Lowland Maya pictorials.

The Aztecs utilized the second type of loincloth, but usually only for deities and their impersonators. (The historical section of *Codex Telleriano-Remensis*, however, shows that style of garment on warriors.) To judge from examples in the only extant Aztec ritual manuscript, *Codex Borbonicus* (as on page 26), the longer-style *maxtlatl* was knotted in front, as was the more common, distinctive-knot type of loincloth that seems to have been the usual secular style.

The second column of chart 22 is devoted to examples of the hip-cloth. If we classify the short, hip-encasing Tarascan costume in that section, the hip-cloth becomes the most widely used garment in the male repertory. Absence of any mention of it in the sixteenth-century sources is considered below.

The cape is the third male draped garment that, with the exception of the Tarascan area, was worn throughout Mesoamerica. Although the capes varied in size, material, and degree of decoration, they were in concept the same simple draped garments and everywhere seem to have served a prominent role as visual status markers.

The male kilt, however, appears to have been as esoteric as the cape was omnipresent. Since male kilts usually appear on deities or their impersonators, it must

CHART 22
PAN-MESOAMERICAN COSTUME REPERTORY
Male Garments

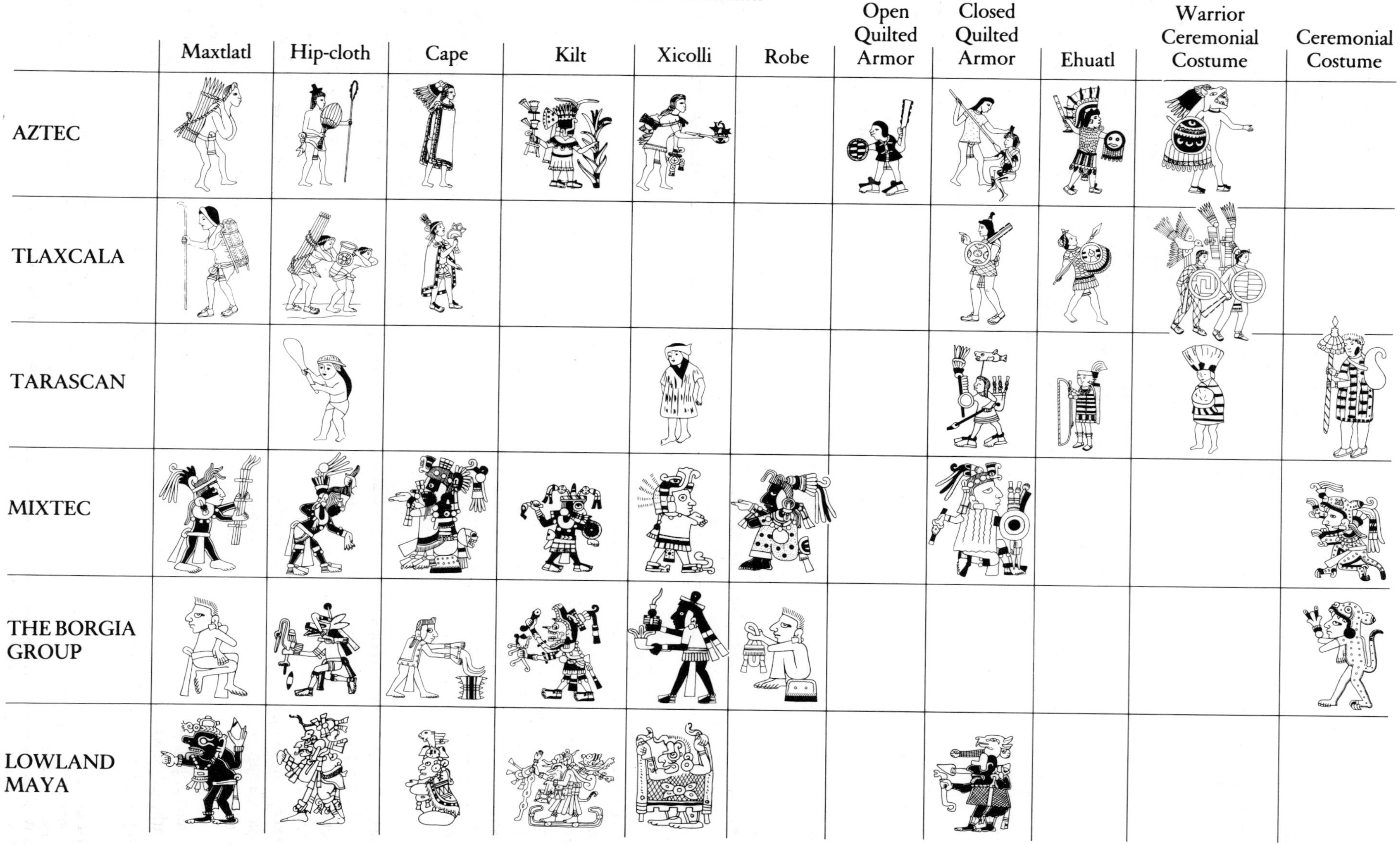

	Maxtlatl	Hip-cloth	Cape	Kilt	Xicolli	Robe	Open Quilted Armor	Closed Quilted Armor	Ehuatl	Warrior Ceremonial Costume	Ceremonial Costume
AZTEC	✎	✎	✎	✎	✎		✎	✎	✎	✎	
TLAXCALA	✎	✎	✎					✎	✎	✎	
TARASCAN		✎			✎			✎	✎	✎	✎
MIXTEC	✎	✎	✎	✎	✎	✎		✎			✎
THE BORGIA GROUP	✎	✎	✎	✎	✎	✎					✎
LOWLAND MAYA	✎	✎	✎	✎	✎			✎			

SOURCES: For sources of Aztec costumes see chart 16. For sources of Tlaxcalan costumes see chart 17. For sources of Tarascan costumes see chart 18. For sources of Mixtec costumes see chart 19. For sources of the Borgia Group costumes see chart 20. For sources of the Lowland Maya costumes see chart 21.

have been a special-purpose garment limited to ceremonial contexts.

Some form of *xicolli* was utilized by all the Mesoamerican groups. Although there is no illustration of the pre-Hispanic Tlaxcalans' *xicolli*, it is known from Fray Motolinía's description that the garment was part of their costume repertory.[1] I have classified the Tarascan *cicuilli* in the *xicolli* column because of Sahagún's reference to it as the "so-called sleeveless jacket,"[2] and because the *Relaciones geográficas* equate it with the Spanish jacket.

The *xicolli* was a ritual garment for the Aztecs, the Tlaxcalans, the Mixtecs, the Borgia Group peoples, and probably the Lowland Mayas. It also served as the principal apparel of the male Mixtec aristocracy. One might suppose, therefore, that the garment would have been quickly eradicated by the missionaries, particularly in the areas where it had strong religious connotations. It is strange, then, that a version of the garment is found today in an area of strongest sixteenth-century missionary concentration, the highland valley of central Mexico.[3]

Figure 62 shows a *xicolli*-like garment being worn in the animal market of Xochimilco in April, 1931. A native of Xochimilco reported seeing the costume worn by the "*chinamperos*" of San Gregorio Atlapulco (a village between Xochimilco and Milpa Alta, in the Federal District), selling their vegetables at the *jamaico* ("charity fair") market. The garment is now called a *cotorina*. The informant reported: "They use *cotorinas* for the cold. The old men still speak a little Nahuatl."[4] He said that the *cotorinas* had been used for years, having seen them from the 1940s through the 1960s. They were taken from Santa Ana Chiautempan, Tlaxcala, and from Chiconcoac, Texcoco, to be sold in the Xochimilco market.

The next column in chart 22 shows that the robe, which was a special-purpose garment, is found only in the pictorials of the Mixtecs and the Borgia Group. It is unfortunate that so little is known about the costume. It was certainly worn by priests in the Late Postclassic period and may have been worn in the preceding period by the Toltecs at Chichén Itzá. It must have been restricted to ritual use.

Examples of open-sewn *ichcahuipilli* ("open-quilted armor" in chart 22) are found only in the Aztec sources, but depictions of closed-sewn cotton armor ("closed quilted armor") appear in the pictorials of all the Indian cultures except the Borgia Group. Since all five codices of the Borgia Group are ritual-divinatory manuals, the nature of their content may explain the exclusion. In pre-Hispanic secular Mesoamerica cotton armor was the essential martial garment.

The feathered *ehuatl*, worn as a warrior costume, is found only in the Aztec and Tlaxcalan pictorials, but a similar feathered costume, also with a short skirt of feathers, appears in one of the forty-four illustrations of the Tarascan colonial document *Relación de Michoacán*.[5] Since the Tarascan garment has the diagnostic skirt, I included it in the *ehuatl* column even though it was unlike the Tarascans to have a costume resembling that of one of their arch foes, the Aztecs.

The variety of uses of the limb-encasing warrior and ceremonial costumes in Late Postclassic Mesoamerica provides one of the most intriguing enigmas of the pan-Mesoamerican costume repertory. That the Aztecs and Tlaxcalans actually wore their elaborate, valuable costumes into battle is confirmed by the eyewitness reports of the conquistadores, as well as by later native accounts supplied to such missionary chroniclers as Sahagún and Durán and the administrators who filled out the 1579–85 *Relaciones geográficas*. Although the splendid limb-encasing garments of the Aztecs and Tlaxcalans were also worn in certain ceremonies, their principal function apparently was for use in battle. It is puzzling, then, that the Mixtecs appear in their jaguar, puma, and eagle versions of the garments only in ceremonial contexts. Can we infer that the Mixtecs were less bellicose than their northern neighbors? Was the Mixtec culture not organized or wealthy enough to attain the necessary quantities of lowland feathers and gems necessary to produce large numbers of those valuable and lavish garments? Which Mesoamerican group had the costume first? These are questions that only further research can answer.

FEMALE GARMENTS

The first column of chart 23 shows skirts representative of those worn by the six Mesoamerican Indian groups for whom pictorial data are available in the codices. The skirt (even more than its male counterpart, the *maxtlatl*, which was not worn by the Tarascans or the Huaxtecs) was obviously the basic, indispensable pan-Mesoamerican female garment. Far less widespread was the hip-cloth (second column), which occurs only in the Lowland Maya repertory. Female capes also appear to have had a limited distribution, occurring only among the Mixtecs and in the Borgia Group codices.

Some form of the *quechquemitl* was in use in all the regions under consideration in this book. Various sizes were worn in the Oaxaca region at some period before European contact; the evidence from the Mixtec codices is irrefutable. The *quechquemitl* also occurs repeatedly in the ritual pictorials of the Borgia Group codices, where certain goddesses are frequently shown wearing it. The garment was often utilized as part of the attire of some of the goddesses of Aztec ritual, but apparently it was never

[1] Motolinía 1971, pp. 78–79.

[2] Sahagún 1950–69, bk. 10, pp. 188–89.

[3] Gibson 1964, pp. 98–100.

[4] Irmgard W. Johnson was most kind in supplying the 1931 *cotorina* photograph and the accompanying information. Her informant was Plácido Villanueva, a native of Xochimilco. The interview was conducted in November, 1974, at Bodega de Etnografía, Museo Nacional de Antropología, Mexico City.

[5] *Relación de Michoacán*, lámina 44.

FIGURE 62. A modern *xicolli* (now called *cotorina*), photographed in the animal market at Xochimilco in April, 1931. Photograph courtesy of I. W. Johnson.

worn by the Mexicas as everyday female apparel. The question then arises, Why was the *quechquemitl* restricted to ritual use among the Aztecs? What made it so special that only goddesses and their impersonators wore it? Where did the *quechquemitl* originate, and what were its symbolic implications?

A recent study indicates that the *quechquemitl* probably originated in the lush, fertile Gulf Coast region, homeland of the Huaxtec and Totonac Indians.[6] The costume was and still is the quintessential female garment of that region and is often found on the early pre-Hispanic Gulf Coast fertility goddesses depicted in stone sculpture and clay figurines.

Although the use of the *quechquemitl* goes far back in time on the central plateau—it is found on clay figurines and carvings of what appear to be goddesses among both the Toltecs and the Teotihuacanos—the Aztecs had their own historical reasons for equating it with ritual fertility and abundance. The garment's presence in their costume repertory no doubt reflects the earlier adoption of religious concepts from the Gulf Coast region.

For the Aztecs, then, the *quechquemitl* was a special-purpose garment that carried explicit connotations of fertility. That apparently was not the case among the Mixtecs, where the history of the garment is both confused and intriguing. Despite repeated depictions of the costume in the Mixtec codices, there is no mention of such a garment in early Spanish documents of the area, nor of Burgoa,[7] Alvarado,[8] Juan de Córdoba,[9] or the Oaxacan *Relaciones geográficas*.[10] A comment on the absence of the *quechquemitl* from the Oaxaca area after the Spanish conquest also comes from a Dominican friar who had been in the region before 1570.

Codex Vaticanus A was compiled between 1569 and 1570; the accompanying gloss is written in Italian, supposedly based on a commentary by Fray Pedro de los Ríos. Folio 61 contains a drawing of two Indian women (fig. 63): the one on the left wears a *quechquemitl*, the other a *huipil*.

[6] Anawalt, 1982.
[7] Burgoa 1934*a*, 1934*b*.
[8] Alvarado 1962.

[9] Fray Córdoba 1942.
[10] Paso y Troncoso 1905, p. iv.

CHART 23
PAN-MESOAMERICAN COSTUME REPERTORY
Female Garments

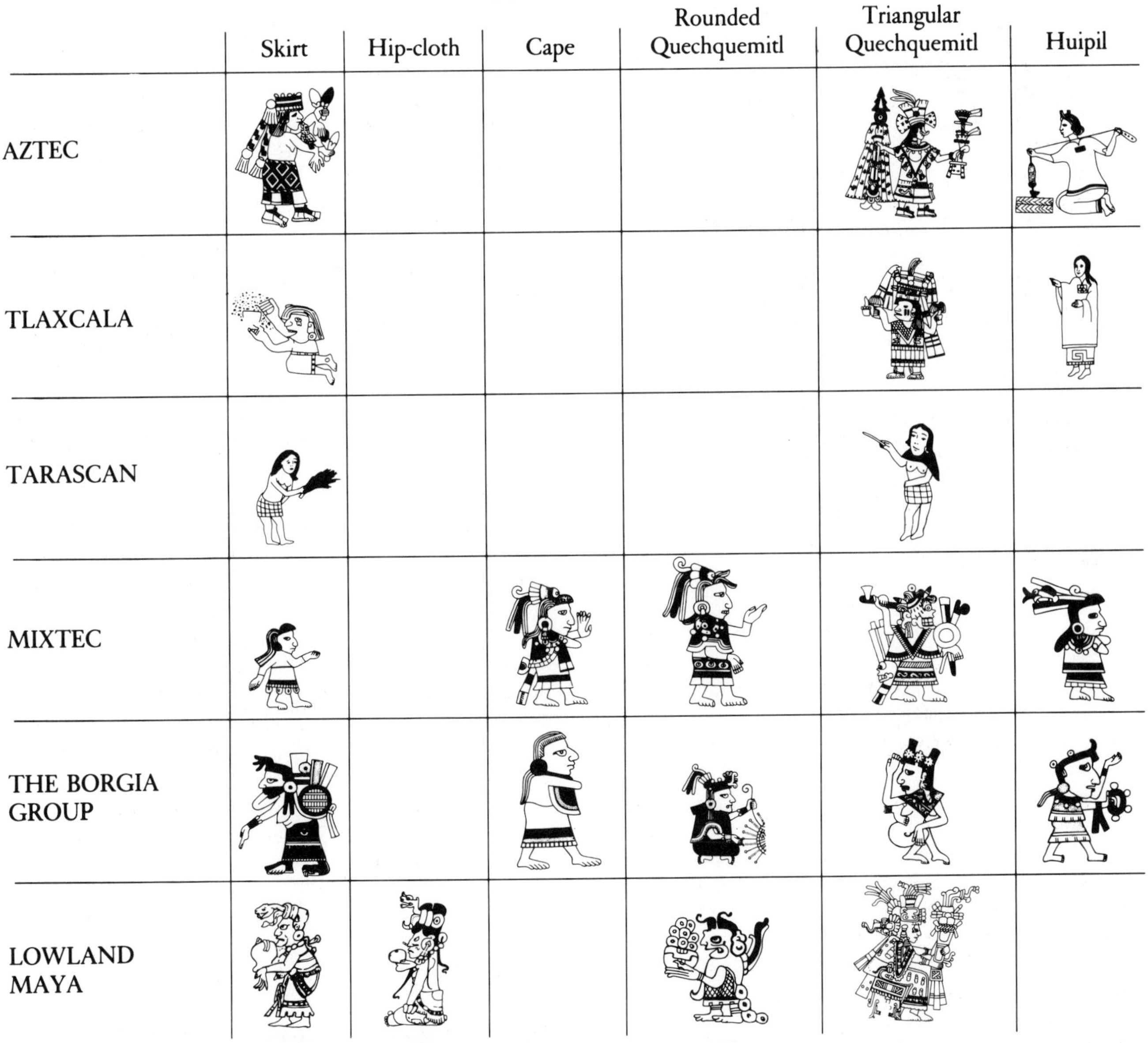

	Skirt	Hip-cloth	Cape	Rounded Quechquemitl	Triangular Quechquemitl	Huipil
AZTEC						
TLAXCALA						
TARASCAN						
MIXTEC						
THE BORGIA GROUP						
LOWLAND MAYA						

SOURCES: For sources of Aztec costumes see chart 16. For sources of Tlaxcalan costumes see chart 17. For sources of Tarascan costumes see chart 18. For sources of Mixtec costumes see chart 19. For sources of the Borgia Group costumes see chart 20. For sources of the Lowland Maya costumes see chart 21.

The commentary states:

The dress of the first [woman] I do not know where it is used, nor have I ever seen it before, but the second is the dress of the Mexicans and of Zapotec, and of the Mixtec, whose [clothing] I have seen. The old men say the manner of dressing of the first woman is that of the Huastec women, which is a nation of this country that is in the northern part of Mexico.[11]

[11] *Codex Vaticanus A*, fol. 61.

Thus it seems that when the friar was in the Oaxaca region, before he wrote the codex commentary, the Mixtec and Zapotec women were wearing a Mexican-style *huipil*, and the *quechquemitl* had disappeared from the area. How is such a dramatic change in feminine apparel over a thirty-year period to be explained? Certainly the *quechquemitl* was being worn in Oaxaca at some time before the compiling of the pre-Conquest Mixtec and Borgia Group codices. In the Mixtec pictorials *Zouche-Nuttall* and *Vindobonensis* it dates back to the fifteenth

FIGURE 63. Indian women wearing *quechquemitl* and *huipil*. *Codex Vaticanus A*, fol. 61r.

century. Perhaps the artists of the later Mixtec codices continued to depict the *quechquemitl* as an example of the aristocratic garb of an earlier age. It is also possible that by the time of Spanish contact there had been a shift away from use of the *quechquemitl* as everyday wear. When the Spaniards arrived, it may have been worn only by idols or human impersonators of goddesses, as was the situation with the Aztecs. In such a case the costume probably would immediately have been forbidden; hence the friar who wrote the commentary in *Codex Vaticanus A* would not have seen it in either central Mexico or Oaxaca.

In many areas the wearing of the *quechquemitl* may have been restricted to highborn ladies. If they were still wearing the garment at the time of the Conquest, it would have represented a pagan status or power symbol and therefore would not have been approved by the Spanish clergy. Even if the *quechquemitl* was not forbidden, the very women qualified to wear it in pre-Contact times would have been the ones in a position to adopt a new status symbol, European dress.[12] That could explain why the *quechquemitl* disappeared from some regions but continued in use in others where it did not have aristocratic connotations. It might have been expected to reenter the Oaxaca area at a later date, but by that time the *huipil*, no doubt encouraged by the early friars, had become established and filled the need for an upper-body garment.

The final column in chart 23 is devoted to the *huipil*, the basic upper-body garment for both the Aztecs and the Tlaxcalans. The *huipil* of the latter is the longest and fullest of the Mesoamerican examples. The costume ap-

12 Heyden 1977.

parently did not exist among the Mayas until after the Conquest, and the few *huipil*-like garments found in the Borgia Group are questionable. There are only a few scattered *huipil* in the Mixtec codices, harbingers of the ubiquitous garment it was to become over that entire area.

SHARED CHARACTERISTICS OF THE PAN-MESOAMERICAN COSTUME REPERTORY

Examples of costumes from the codices have now been analyzed both in the context of their individual cultures and in the pan-Mesoamerica distribution of each garment type. This analysis enables us to define the characteristics of the apparel of the six Indian groups that demonstrate the same fundamental, areawide approach to clothing construction.

1. The costumes in the codices reflect the restraint imposed by Mesoamerican technology. The identical weaving apparatus used throughout the area restricted the width of each piece of woven cloth to the breadth of the backstrap loom that produced it. However, within that restraint no uniform module of textile width resulted. As analogous contemporary ethnographic data indicate, fabric width was determined by intended use.

2. Because the backstrap loom produces textiles finished on all four sides, the material could be worn draped on the body just as it came from the loom without further processing, or several pieces could be joined by simply sewing together the selvages of two or more different webs.

3. Most Mesoamerican clothing was draped.

4. The predominant garments were the male loincloth, hip-cloth, and cape and the female wraparound skirt, blouse, and *quechquemitl*.

5. Mesoamerican garments were nonfitted. Aside from the warrior ceremonial costumes—special-purpose garments worn by only a small percentage of the population—clothing did not encase the limbs or conform to the lines of the body.

6. Aside from the special-purpose warrior ceremonial costumes, Mesoamerican clothing had no sleeves. Despite what appears to be contradictory pictorial evidence, careful comparative analyses indicate that the pre-Hispanic clothing of Middle America was sleeveless.

7. Mesoamerican clothing reflected the sharply stratified societies from which it came. Although the various classes wore the same types of garments, their apparel varied markedly in fabric and degree of ornamentation.

These seven characteristics summarize the fundamental approach to clothing construction of the six Indian societies for which there is pictorial evidence. Although the groups do not collectively represent all the peoples of Mesoamerica, the shared concepts displayed in their clothing repertories indicate that—as in the other areawide cultural traits—the same approach to clothing construction extended throughout Mesoamerica. Given the technological level of pre-Hispanic Middle American weaving, the basic characteristics of the pan-Mesoamerican costume repertory must have been the same throughout the culture area.

Having determined the essential features of Mesoamerican clothing, we still face the problem of reconciling certain garments depicted in the codices with conflicting descriptions in the colonial sources.

INCONSISTENCIES IN COLONIAL COSTUME DESCRIPTIONS

In the preceding chapters some inconsistencies in the documentary reporting have become obvious. Specific clothing types illustrated in the pictorials bear no resemblance to their descriptions in the 1579–85 *Relaciones geográficas*, whereas garments known not to have existed in an area of pre-Hispanic times are reported in the *Relaciones* as having been worn there before Spanish contact. Certain costumes repeatedly found in the codices are never mentioned in the Spanish documents. How are these contradictions to be explained?

The first consideration is the degree of accuracy of the pre-contact information in the *Relaciones geográficas*, written sixty years after the fact. The Spanish administrators who filled out the reports were civil servants of the crown, *alcaldes mayores* and *corregidores* who as salaried local magistrates obtained their pre-Hispanic knowledge from hearsay or from the few remaining aged natives available as informants. Over the years memories dim. If certain garments being worn in the pictorials were never mentioned, the explanation could be that the magistrates did not have that much understanding of indigenous life before the Conquest or simply did not record that information.

Even allowing for faulty memory and possible errors, the fact remains that, in *Relaciones geográficas* from all over Mesoamerica, Nahuatl-derived terms are repeatedly used to describe the same pre-Hispanic garments: the loincloth, *maxtlatl*; the cloak, *tilmatli*; the blouse, *huipil*; and the wraparound skirt, *cueitl*. That was, of course, the clothing the Aztecs of the Valley of Mexico were wearing when Cortés arrived in 1519. How is the common vocabulary to be explained?

The Mixteca-Puebla "international style" that appeared in many parts of Mesoamerica in the late Postclassic period demonstrated the possibility of a pan-Mesoamerican distribution of an iconographic style.[13] It is possible that a unifying clothing fashion could have reached many sections of Middle America in a similar manner. Such an areawide phenomenon occurred in late-fourteenth-century Europe with the spread of the Late Gothic International style;[14] recent decades of the twentieth century

are seeing the rapid demise of regional variation on a global scale as the world adopts Western European–American dress.

The fashion-follows-power explanation would account for the discrepancy between descriptions in the *Relaciones geográficas* and the ignored Mixtec-Lowland Maya male capes and the Mixtec *quechquemitl*, all of which appear in the pictorials. The illustrated garments would then have to be regarded as representatives of a previous era, as archaic clothing carrying important religious-historical significance. An analogous example might be modern Sunday School tracts with their depictions of Christ and the apostles dressed in the archaic flowing robes of the biblical Near East.

The Aztecs' use of one style *maxtlatl* for daily life and another style for their gods and deity impersonators suggests another archaic religious survival. If, as Thompson suggested, *Codex Dresden* is a copy of an earlier thirteenth-century ritual document,[15] such a survival could explain the depictions of the Lowland Maya men's short capes. In the Mixteca the earliest pictorials date from the fifteenth century, but the same type of clothing was still being depicted in post-Conquest *Codex Selden*, compiled in 1556. A Late Postclassic pan-Mesoamerican dress style would also solve the mystery of why the *quechquemitl* had completely vanished from the Oaxaca area by 1550. Perhaps it had not been worn there for some time before Spanish contact but was still illustrated in the codices of the area because it was an important historical-religious symbol of earlier times.

There is an alternate explanation for the disappearance of the *quechquemitl*, as well as for other clothing contradictions. Those changes may have been the result of one of the most powerful influences on early colonial Indian life, the Spanish missionaries. Beginning in the 1530s, the friars were very active in their attempts to Christianize the Indians. For those devoted sixteenth-century clerics commitment to Indian conversion involved far more than simply baptizing the pagan; "heathen" ways had to be eradicated and a uniform, manageable (for the clergy) pattern set up in its place.

Coupled with the friars' dedication to proselytizing was the reduction in native population in the sixty-year period following contact. In 1519 the population of central Mexico was conservatively estimated at 15 million. By 1580, when the *Relaciones geográficas* were compiled, the population in the area had declined to an estimated 1.9 million.[16] The decline was caused primarily by the arrival with the Spaniards of Old World diseases, which wiped out whole Indian communities. To administer and care for the remaining indigenous population, the Spaniards instigated the policy of *congregación*. In many areas of Middle America the Indians were gathered together "within the sound of the bell," in central communities organized

[13] Robertson 1968, p. 88.
[14] Ibid.

[15] Thompson 1972*b*, p. 15.
[16] Cook and Borah 1960.

around the church to make it easier to preach to, teach, supervise, and control them.

That attempt at standardization may also have extended to native dress. Since the friars were troubled by the "immoral" apparel of many Indian groups, what would be more suitable than to put them into a "decent" *huipil* or long *tilmatli*? They were simple garments that all Indian women could make on a backstrap loom, and, even more important to the friars, they were "modest" garments. Judging from the Nahuatl-derived terminology utilized for local dress in all the *Relaciones geográficas*, it appears that, along with the language of central Mexico, Aztec clothing styles may also have been imposed on Indians of non-Nahuatl-speaking regions by the missionaries. That would explain why the costumes described in the 1579–85 *Relaciones geográficas* as being used in an area are often different from the apparel that appears in the extant Late Postclassic pictorials from the same regions. It would also explain the Nahuatl terminology.

The occurrence five decades after the Conquest of Aztec patterns of dress in non-Aztec areas of pre-Hispanic Mesoamerica becomes more understandable when the problems and procedures of the missionaries are understood. That no *cedulario* ("decree") has been found specifically spelling out a standardization-of-dress policy in no way negates its existence; even the compulsive record keeping of the Spaniards was selective and did not stipulate every detail. In some areas certain indigenous pre-Cortesian costume patterns managed to survive, but in other regions specific garment types disappeared completely. The *quechquemitl* is such a case.

If the *quechquemitl* was indeed being worn in Oaxaca when the Spaniards arrived, it was restricted to the ruling class. Since women of that class were in a position to adopt the more prestigious Spanish clothing, the *quechquemitl* may have quickly become *déclassé*. The lower classes probably had little chance to begin using it, because the missionaries were already stipulating the wearing of *huipil*.

In central Mexico, however, the case was different, for there the *quechquemitl* had strong religious connotations. With the surrender of Tenochtitlán the formal aspects of Aztec religion came to an abrupt halt. All public native ritual ceremonies ceased, the native priesthood was suppressed, and all accouterments associated with the indigenous religion were banned. The Aztec *quechquemitl* must thus have disappeared early. How then is the improbable survival of the *xicolli* to be explained? Certainly it too was ritual-oriented; one would think that the association of the jacket with human sacrifice would have immediately spelled its doom. A similarity-of-structure argument is probably the best explanation; of all the pre-Hispanic Mesoamerican costumes, the jacketlike *xicolli* was closest in appearance to a European tailored garment.

Although it lacked the sleeves and fullness of the sixteenth-century overrobe, or surcoat,[17] there was a certain familiarity in its hip-length, coatlike structure. Perhaps its vague resemblance to European dress made possible the survival of the Indian *xicolli*.

The pre-Cortesian costume repertory of the Tarascan area, like so much else about that culture, is puzzling. The presence of the tiny *quechquemitl* may reflect an attempt by the Tarascans' Chichimec founders to associate their lineages with the prestigious Toltec past. Aside from that, there are no other clues in the codices or colonial sources to the antecedents of Tarascan clothing, nor have any of the pre-Hispanic garments survived. Following the Conquest, Tarascan indigenous costumes disappeared almost completely because the area was the center of one of the most thorough of the early colonial social experiments. The first bishop of Michoacán, Vasco de Quiroga (whose tenure lasted from 1537 to 1565), was one of a group of humanists who saw in the New World the opportunity to revive the virtues of early Christianity. Closely following the ideas of Sir Thomas More's *Utopia*, Quiroga imposed new rules of conduct on every aspect of life. The Michoacán experiment resulted in a far-reaching acculturation, and as a result modern Tarascan culture probably shows fewer survivals or adaptations from the pre-Hispanic past than does any other persisting Mexican Indian group.[18]

The antecedents of the Tarascan indigenous garments are not the only unsolved mystery in the Mesoamerican repertory. The dramatic limb-encasing warrior ceremonial costumes are among the most intriguing of all pre-Conquest garments. Where and when did they originate? What were their route and chronology of diffusion? Why did the Mixtecs use the costumes only in a ceremonial context whereas the Aztecs actually wore their valuable feather suits into bloody battle?

Such questions present a stimulating challenge for future pre-Hispanic costume research; such studies will promote a deeper understanding of Mesoamerican civilization. As this book demonstrates, a special aspect of a culture is revealed through a detailed examination of the clothing, an aspect of culture that reflects ideology. Nowhere is this relationship more apparent than with the Aztecs and their military accouterments at the time of the Conquest.

AZTEC MILITARY ATTIRE IN THE CONQUEST

One of the improbable episodes of recorded history is the victory of Hernán Cortés and a few hundred Spanish conquistadors over the fifteen million or more indigenes of central Mexico in 1521.[19] There were several reasons for the Spaniards' success. Cortés's appearance out of the east in an anniversary year prophesied for the return of Quet-

---

[17] Norris 1938, p. 238.
[18] Beals 1969, p. 728.

[19] The following section of chapter 9 appeared in part in Anawalt 1977, pp. 232–33.

zalcoatl was a significant coincidence. The emperor Moctezuma, rendered indecisive by the prophecies, hesitated to oppose the European invaders until they were established within the very confines of his highland capital, Tenochtitlán.

A political factor, the traditional animosity between Moctezuma's empire and the inhabitants of nearby Tlaxcala, motivated the Tlaxcalans to become the invaluable allies and auxiliary troops of the Spanish invaders. Disease also contributed to the Aztecs' defeat; smallpox accompanied the Europeans to Mexico in 1520 and soon grew to epidemic proportions, taking its toll among the Aztecs and their leaders, as well as other Indian groups throughout Mesoamerica.

Despite the importance of those factors, perhaps the most significant element in the Spaniards' success was the contrast in the natives' and the conquistadors' concepts of warfare. Though the Spaniards—with their metal armaments, horses, and trained war dogs—possessed a technological superiority, it was their European tradition of warfare that gave them their greatest advantage. The invaders engaged in total warfare aimed at killing as many of their opponents as possible, wreaking extensive destruction and bringing about the complete overthrow of the enemy. The Aztecs, on the other hand, practiced a limited form of conflict directed toward a different end, and their flamboyant martial attire reflects that.

Although the Indians of Mesoamerica utilized military aggression as a means of expansion, they also viewed war as a sacred duty that complied with the will of the gods. Because of its religious aspects Aztec warfare was highly conventionalized. The time and place of the martial confrontations were carefully negotiated, and battles were almost always of short duration. The warriors' goal was not to kill their enemies but to capture them for sacrifice to the deities, whose continued running of the universe was dependent on their being sustained by the most sacred of foods—human hearts and blood.

Before their exposure to the Spaniards, the natives' concept of defeat was also defined by convention: a city acknowledged itself beaten when the attacking force succeeded in reaching the temple and burning the sanctuary of the local god. From that moment on, the inhabitants believed that divine will had prevailed and that further resistance was useless. Once the fighting stopped, negotiations began, and the bargaining ended in a contract detailing the amount and nature of tribute to be paid to the conquerors.

Given the Mesoamerican concept of limited warfare, the types of weapons used, and the fact that all troop movement was on foot, the Aztecs' pageantlike military attire was actually very practical. Their sturdy cotton armor withstood stones, darts, and lance and war-club thrusts surprisingly well, as shown by the Spaniards' haste to adopt it. Although a warrior wearing feather garments may seem very vulnerable to us, Spanish sources make it clear that the protective *ichcahuipilli* was always worn under the *ehuatl* and *tlahuitztli*, rendering the lightweight, flexible costumes very effective as martial apparel.

In addition to providing bodily protection, the resplendent feather garments and back devices served several other functions. On the battlefield the warrior costumes acted as visual ordering mechanisms, telling a fighting man the location of his unit and commanding officer. The towering back devices served as the standards by which the troops could identify their regiments. They were rallying points in times of adversity, thus sustaining the morale of the warriors.

The theatrical accouterments of Aztec warfare become even more understandable when considered as a system of rewards for a society whose cultural emphasis was aggressive expansion. By granting highly visible and desirable status clothing, the Aztecs effectively motivated young men to perform military feats. The pageantry of Aztec warfare worked very well both as a visual ordering device and as an incentive system—as long as their battles were conducted against like-minded opponents.

It is a measure of the military genius of Hernán Cortés that he perceived the integrative function of Aztec military attire, as he demonstrated at the decisive battle at Otumba on July 7, 1520. The conquistadors had just suffered a devastating defeat at the hands of the Mexicas and had been driven out of Tenochtitlán in the famous rout of Noche Triste. Wounded and exhausted, the Spaniards were attempting to make their way back to their Indian allies in Tlaxcala. When they reached the plains of Otumba, near the great pyramids of Teotihuacán, the massed military forces of the Aztec Empire were awaiting them.

Woefully outnumbered, Cortés realized that the Spaniards' only hope lay in an unexpected move. He scanned the battlefield and identified the Aztecs' commanding officer, who was easily recognizable not only by the rich panoply of his entourage and his own magnificent costume but also by the huge, distinctive feather-and-silver crest strapped on his back. Under Cortés's direction the remaining Spanish troops and cavalry drove through the tightly massed native forces and succeeded in reaching and killing their conspicuous commanding officer. The moment the Indian noble fell and his towering back device passed to the Spaniards, panic spread among the Aztecs, even though they vastly outnumbered the Europeans. The loss of their leader and his symbolic emblem quickly demoralized the warriors, and the tide of the battle turned. Thus, by capturing the Aztec imperial standard, the conquistadors survived the battle at Otumba and were able to reach Tlaxcala, where they mounted the final devastating assault on Tenochtitlán.

That is but one example of the contrasts in native and European concepts of warfare. Between 1519 and 1521, from the first contact with the Spaniards to the final conquest, the Indians were repeatedly caught off balance because the invaders did not follow Aztec martial conventions; the conquistadors did not negotiate before battle, nor did they prefer capturing enemies to killing them.

When the long siege of Tenochtitlán finally ended, there was no bargaining about tribute to be paid to the European conquerors. What followed instead was a cataclysm the Aztecs could never have imagined: the abolition of their political institutions, the destruction of their gods, and the overthrow of their civilization. With their defeat came the destruction of the complex social network that had made possible the pageantry of Aztec warfare. Gone were the sumptuary laws and the ranking of warriors. Gone too was the tribute system that had supported the regular transport of tropical feathers, gems, silver, and gold from the lowlands to the central plateau of Mexico, where skilled artisans had fashioned those valuable materials into the status goods necessary for a sharply stratified society.

At first glance it would appear that all that is left of the complex world the conquistadors discovered are the ruins of temples, the surviving clay and stone artifacts stored in museums, the accounts of the Spanish chroniclers, and the information found in the pictorial documents. Further evidence remains, however. In some of the more conservative Indian villages of present-day Middle America clothing is still being worn that incorporates a blend of Western European and pre-Hispanic traits. Now that the pre-Hispanic Mesoamerican costume repertory has been compiled, a baseline exists that makes possible a study of the changes through which these intriguing modern Indian garments have evolved. Surely it is a fascinating acculturation process, one that began over 450 years ago, when Cortés first set foot on the beach at Veracruz.

FIGURE 64. An Aztec priest carrying a banner bearing the *ilhuitl* ("feast day") symbol. After *Codex Borbonicus*, p. 31.

BIBLIOGRAPHY

Adams, Richard E. W.
  1977 *Prehistoric Mesoamerica*. Boston: Little, Brown.
Aguilar, Fray Francisco de
  1954 *Relación breve de la conquista de la Nueva España*. Mexico City: José Porrúa e Hijos.
Alvarado, Fray Francisco de
  1962 *Vocbulário en lengua Mixteca*. Mexico City: Instituto Nacional Indigenista e Instituto Nacional de Antropología e Historia.
Alvarado Tezozomoc, Hernando
  1944 *Crónica mexicana escrita hacia el año de 1598*. Notas de Manuel Orozco y Berra. Mexico City: Editorial Leyenda.
Anawalt, Patricia
  1976 The *xicolli*: an analysis of a ritual garment. *Actas del 41 Congreso Internacional de Americanistas* 2:223–235. Mexico City.
  1977 What Price Aztec Pageantry? *Archaeology* 30:226–33.
  1980 Costume and control: Aztec sumptuary laws. *Archaeology* 33:33–43.
  1982 Analysis of the Aztec *quechquemitl*: an exercise in inference. In *The Art and Iconography of Late Post-Classic Central Mexico*. Edited by Elizabeth Hill Boone. Pp. 37–72. Washington, D.C.: Dumbarton Oaks.
Anders, F.
  1967 *Summary of the Codex Madrid (Codex Tro-Cortesianus). Museo de América, Madrid*. Graz: Akademische Druck-und Verlangsanstalt.
  1972 *Summary of the Codex Vaticanus 3733 (Codex Vaticanus B). Biblioteca Apostolic Vaticana*. Graz: Akademische Druck-und Velangsanstalt.
Andrews, E. Wyllys, IV
  1965 Archaeology and prehistory in the northern Maya lowlands: an introduction. In *Handbook of Middle American Indians*. Edited by Robert Wauchope. 2:288–330. Austin: University of Texas Press.
Anonymous Conqueror
  1858 El Conquistador Anónimo. In *Colección de documentos para la historia de México*. Publicada por Joaquín García Icazbalceta. Mexico City: Librería de J. M. Andrade. I:568–98.
Antón, Ferdinand
  1965 *Alt-Mexico und seine Kunst*. Leipzig: E. A. Seeman Buch-und Kunstverlag.
Asensio, José Maria, ed.
  1898 *Colección de documentos inéditos relativos al descubrimiento, conquista y organización de las antiguas posesiones españolas de ultramar. Relaciones de Yucatán*. 2 vols. Madrid.

Barlow, R. H.
  1949a *The extent of the empire of the Culhua Mexica*. Ibero-Americana, no. 28. Berkeley: University of California Press.
  1949b *Códice Azcatitlán. Journal de la Société des Américanistes*, new ser., 38:101–35 (Paris, 1949). Commentary in Spanish by Barlow.
Barnett, H. G.
  1942 Invention and cultural change. *American Anthropologist* 44:14–30.
Beals, Ralph
  1969 The Tarascans. In *Handbook of Middle American Indians*. Edited by Robert Wauchope. 8:725–73. Austin: University of Texas Press.
Berdan, Frances Frei
  1975 Trade, tribute, and market in the Aztec Empire. Ph.D. dissertation, University of Texas at Austin.
Boone, Elizabeth Hill
  1975 Two painting styles in the *Codex Magliabechiano*. Paper read at 40th Annual Meeting of Society for American Archaeology, May, 1975, Dallas, Texas.
Borah, W., and Cook, S. F.
  1963 *The aboriginal population of central Mexico on the eve of the Spanish conquest*. Ibero-Americana, no. 45. Berkeley: University of California Press.
Boucher, François
  1966 *20,000 years of fashion: the history of costume and personal adornment*. New York: Abrams.

Bruhn, Wolfgang, and Tilke, Max
1955   *A pictorial history of costume: a survey of costume of all periods and peoples from antiquity to modern times including national costume in Europe and non-European countries.* New York: Praeger.

Burgoa, Fray Francisco de
1934a   *Geográfica descripción.* 2 vols. Mexico City.
1934b   *Palestra historial.* Mexico City.

Burland, Cottie A.
1955   *The Selden Roll: an ancient Mexican picture manuscript in the Bodleian Library at Oxford.* Ibero-Amerikanischen Bibliothek, Monumenta Americana, vol. 2. Berlin: Verlag Gebr. Mann.
1966   *Introduction to Codex Laud (MS Laud Misc. 678, Bodleian Library). True-color facsimile of the old Mexican manuscript.* Graz: Akademische Druck-und Verlangsanstalt.
1971   *Introduction to Codex Fejérváy-Mayer (12014 M). City of Liverpool Museums.* Graz: Akademische Druck-und Verlangsanstalt.

Calnek, E. E.
1971   Settlement pattern and chinampa agriculture at Tenochtitlán. *American Antiquity* 37:104–15.

Carrasco, Pedro
1971   Social organization of ancient Mexico. In *Handbook of Middle American Indians.* Edited by Robert Wauchope. 10:349–75. Austin: University of Texas Press.

Caso, Alfonso
1958   *The Aztecs: people of the sun.* Norman: University of Oklahoma Press.
1960   *Interpretation of the Codex Bodley 2858.* Mexico City: Sociedad Mexicana de Antropología.
1964   *Interpretation of the Codex Selden 3135 (A.2).* Mexico City: Sociedad Mexicana de Antropología.
1965   Mixtec writing and calendar. In *Handbook of the Middle American Indians.* Edited by Robert Wauchope. 3:948–61. Austin: University of Texas Press.
1966   *Interpretation of the Codex Colombino.* Mexico City: Sociedad Mexicana de Antropología.

Chadwick, Robert
1971   Archaeological synthesis of Michoacán and adjacent regions. In *Handbook of Middle American Indians.* Edited by Robert Wauchope. 11:657–93. Austin: University of Texas Press.
– – –, and MacNeish, R. S.
1967   The *Codex Borgia* and the Venta Salada phase. In *Prehistory of the Tehuacán Valley,* vol. 1, *Environment and subsistence.* Edited by D. S. Byers. Pp. 114–31. Austin: University of Texas Press.

Clark, James Cooper, ed.
1938   *Codex Mendoza. The Mexican manuscript known as the Collection of Mendoza and preserved in the Bodleian Library, Oxford.* 3 vols. London: Waterlow & Sons.

Cline, Howard
1972   The *Relaciones geográficas* of the Spanish Indies, 1577–1648. In *Handbook of Middle American Indians.* Edited by Robert Wauchope. 12:183–242. Austin: University of Texas Press.

Closs, Michael P.
1976   New information on the European discovery of Yucatán and the correlation of the Maya and Christian calendars. *American Antiquity* 41:192–95.

Codex Becker I
1961   *Codex Becker 1/II. Museum für Völkerkunde Wien. Inv. Nr. 60306 und 60307.* Graz: Akademische Druck-und Verlagstalt.

Codex Bodley
1960   *Codex Bodley. Facsimile edition of a Mexican painting preserved in the collection of Sir Thomas Bodley, Bodleian Library, Oxford.* Interpreted by A. Caso, translated by R. Morales, revised by J. Paddock. Mexico City: Sociedad Mexicana de Antropología.

Codex Borbonicus
1974   *Codex Borbonicus. Bibliothèque de l'Assemblée Nationale – Paris (Y 120) Vollständige Faksimile-Ausgabe des Codex Im Original-format.* Commentary by Karl Anton Nowotny and Jacqueline de Durand-Forest. Graz: Akademische Druck-und Verlagsanstalt.

Codex Borgia
1963   *Codex Borgia.* In Eduard Seler. *Commentarios al Códice Borgia.* Facsimile ed. 2 vols. Mexico City: Fondo de Cultura Económica.

Codex Colombino
1966   *Codex Colombino.* Facsimile ed. Interpretation by A. Caso, glosses by Mary Elizabeth Smith. Mexico City: Sociedad Mexicana de Antropología.

Codex Cospi
1968   *Codex Cospi (Calendario Messicano 4093). Biblioteca Universitaria Bologna.* Facsimile ed. Introduction and summary by K. A. Nowotny. Graz: Akademische Druck-und Verlagsanstalt.

Codex Dresden
1972   *Codex Dresden.* In J. Eric S. Thompson. *A commentary on the Dresden Codex: a Maya hieroglyphic book.* Pp. 122–47. Philadelphia: American Philosophical Society.

Codex Dresdensis
1975   *Codex Dresden. Sächsische Landesbibliothek Dresden (Mscr. Dresd. R310) Vollständige Faksimile-Ausgabe Des Codex Im Originalformat.* Commentary by Helmut Deckert and Ferdinand Anders. Graz: Akademische Druck-und Verlagsanstalt.

Codex Fejérváry-Mayer
1971   *Codex Fejérváry-Mayer (12014 M). City of Liverpool Museums.* Facsimile ed. Introduction by C. A. Burland. Graz: Akademische Druck-und Verlagsanstalt.

Codex Ixtlilxochitl
1976   *Codex Ixtlilxochitl. Bibliothèque Nationale Paris (MS. Mex. 65–71). Reproduktion des Manuskriptes im Originalformat.* Commentary by Jacqueline de Durand-Forest. Graz: Akademische Druck-und Verlagsanstalt.

Codex Laud
1966   *Codex Laud. (MS Laud Misc. 678, Bodleian Library). True-color facsimile of the old Mexican manuscript.* Introduction by C. A. Burland. Graz: Akademische Druck-und Verlagsanstalt.

Codex Madrid (Codex Tro-Cortesianus)
1967   *Codex Madrid (Codex Tro-Cortesianus). Museo de*

América, Madrid. Facsimile ed. Introduction and summary by F. Anders. Graz: Akademische Druck-und Verlagsanstalt.

Codex Magliabechiano CL.XIII.3
1970 *Codex Magliabechiano, Cl. XIII.3 (B.R. 232). Biblioteca Nazionale Centrale di Firenze.* In *Codices Selecti, phototypice impressi.* Vol. 23. Facsimile ed. Commentary by Ferdinand Anders. Graz: Akademische Druck-und Verlagsanstalt.

Codex Mendoza
1938 *Codex Mendoza.* In *Codex Mendoza. The Mexican manuscript known as the Collection of Mendoza and preserved in the Bodleian Library, Oxford.* Edited and translated by James Cooper Clark. 3 vols. London: Waterlow & Sons.

Codex Paris (Codex Peresianus)
1968 *Codex Paris (Codex Peresianus). Bibliothèque Nationale Paris.* Facsimile ed. Introduction and summary by F. Anders. Graz: Akademische Druck-und Verlagsanstalt.

Codex Primeros memoriales (part)
1972 *Codex Primeros memoriales.* In Thelma D. Sullivan. The arms and insignia of the Mexica. *Estudios de Cultura Nahuatl* 10:155–93.

Codex Selden
1964 *Codex Selden.* Facsimile ed. Interpretation by A. Caso, translated by J. Quirarte, rev. by J. Paddock. Mexico City: Sociedad Mexicana de Antropología.

Codex Telleriano-Remensis
1964 *Codex Telleriano-Remensis.* In *Antigüdades de México, basadas en la recopilación de Lord Kingsborough.* Edited by José Corona Nuñez. 4 vols. 1:151–337. Mexico City: Secretaría de Hacienda y Crédito Público.

Codex Vaticanus A
1964 *Codex Vaticanus A.* In *Antigüdades de Mexico, basadas en la recopilación de Lord Kingsborough,* ed. José Corona Nuñez. 4 vols. 3:7–313. Mexico City: Secretaría de Hacienda y Crédito Público.

Codex Vaticanus B (Codex Vaticanus 3773)
1972 *Codex Vaticanus B (Codex Vaticanus 3773). Biblioteca Apostolica Vaticana.* Facsimile ed. Introduction, summary, and résumé by Ferdinand Anders. Graz: Akademische Druck-und Verlagsanstalt.

Codex Vindobonensis Mexicanus I
1974 *Codex Vindobonensis Mexicanus I. Vollständige Faksimile-Ausgabe Im Originalformat.* History and Description by Otto Adelhofer. Graz: Akademische Druck-und Verlagsanstalt.

Codex Zouche-Nuttall
1902 *Codex Zouche-Nuttall. Facsimile of an ancient Mexican Codex belonging to Lord Zouche of Harynworth, England.* Introduction by Zeila Nuttall. Cambridge, Mass.: Peabody Museum, Harvard University.

Códice Azcatítlan
1949 *Códice Azcatítlan.* In *Journal de la Société des Americanistes,* new ser., 38:101–35. Photographic reproduction.

Códice de Yanbuitlán
1940 *Códice de Yanbuitlán. Edición en facsimile y con estudio preliminar.* Edited by Wigberto Jiménez Moreno and Salvador Mateos Higuera. Mexico City: Museo National de Antroplogía.

Códice Matritense (part)
1972 *Códice Matritense de la Real Academia de la Historia.* In Thelma D. Sullivan. The arms and insignia of the Mexica. *Estudios de Cultura Nahuatl* 10:155–93.

Códice Xolotl
1951 *Códice Xolotl.* In *Códice Xolotl.* Edited by Charles Dibble. Mexico City: Universidad Nacional de México and University of Utah.

Cook, S. F., and Borah, W.
1960 *The Indian population of central Mexico.* Ibero-Americana, no. 44. Berkeley: University of California Press.

Córdoba, Francisco Fernández de
1942 *The discovery of Yucatán: a translation of the original texts.* Edited by Henry R. Wagner. Berkeley, Calif.: Cortés Society.

Córdoba, Fray Juan de
1942 *Vocabulario Castellano-Zapoteco.* Mexico City: Instituto Nacional de Antropología e Historia.

Cordry, Donald, and Cordry, Dorothy
1968 *Mexican Indian costumes.* Austin: University of Texas Press.

Corona Nuñez, José
1958 *Relaciones geográficas de la diocesis de Michoacán 1579–1580. Colección "Siglo XVI."* Guadalajara, Mexico.
1964 *Antigüedades de México, basadas en la recopilación de Lord Kingsborough.* Introduction by Antonio Ortiz Mena, foreword by Agustín Yáñez, interpretation by José Corona Nuñez. 4 vols. Mexico City: Secretaría de Hacienda y Crédito Público.

Cortés, Hernán
1971 *Hernán Cortés: letters from Mexico.* Translated and edited by A. R. Pagden. New York: Grossman.

Covarrubias, Miguel
1947 *Mexico South: The Isthmus of Tehuantepec.* London: Cassell.

Craine, Eugene R., and Reindrop, Reginald C.
1970 *The chronicles of Michoacán.* Norman: University of Oklahoma Press.

Dahlgren de Jordán, Barbro
1954 *La Mixteca: su cultura y historia prebispanica.* Colección Cultura Mexicana. Mexico City: Imprenta Universitaria.

Davies, Nigel
1973 *The Aztecs.* New York: Putnam.

Díaz del Castillo, Bernal
1967 *The true history of the conquest of New Spain.* 2 vols. Translated and edited by Alfred Percival Maudslay. London: Hakluyt Society, 1908. Reprint. Liechtenstein: Kral's Reprint.

Dibble, Charles
1951 *Códice Xolotl.* Publicaciones del Instituto de Historia, 1st ser., no. 22. Mexico City: Universidad Nacional de México and the University of Utah.
1971 Writing in central Mexico. In *Handbook of Middle American Indians.* Edited by Robert Wauchope. 10: 322–31. Austin: University of Texas Press.

Donnan, Christopher B.
  1973   Lummis at Tiahuanaco. *Masterkey* 47:85–93.
Dumond, D. E.
  1976   An outline of the demographic history of Tlaxcala. In *The Tlaxcaltecans: prehistory, demography, morphology, and genetics.* Edited by Michael H. Crawford. Publications in Anthropology, no. 7, pp. 13–28. Lawrence: University of Kansas Press.
Durán, Fray Diego
  1967   *Historia de las Indias de Nueva España e islas de la tierra firme.* Edited by Angel María Garibay K. 2 vols. Mexico City: Editorial Porrúa.

Eworth, Hans
  1938   Portrait of Henry VIII, 1542: After Hans Eworth. Original at Trinity College, Cambridge. In Herbert Norris. *Costume and Fashion.* Vol. 3, plate 13. New York: Dutton.

Fernández, Josefina Barrera
  1965   El arte textil entre los Nahuas. *Estudios de Cultura Nahuatl* 5:143–52.
Florentine Codex
  1950-69   *Florentine Codex.* In Fray Bernardino Sahagún. *Florentine Codex: general history of the things of New Spain.* Edited by Arthur J. O. Anderson and Charles E. Dibble. Monographs of School of American Research, no. 14, pts. 2–13. Santa Fe, N. Mex.: University of Utah and School of American Research.
Frazer, Sir James
  1959   *The new golden bough.* Edited by Theodor H. Gaster. New York: New American Library.
Furst, Jill Leslie
  1978   *Codex Vindobonensis Mexicanus I: A Commentary.* Albany: Institute of Mesoamerican Studies, State University of New York.

Gann, T. W. F.
  1900   *Mounds in northern Honduras.* Smithsonian Institution, Bureau of American Ethnology, 19th Annual Report, pt. 2, pp. 655–92. Washington, D.C.
García Payón, J.
  1949   *Zempoala: compendio de su estudio arqueológico.* Veracruz: Universidad de Veracruz. 1:449–76.
Gelb, I. J.
  1974   *A study of writing.* Rev. ed. Chicago: University of Chicago Press. (Originally published in 1952.)
Gibson, Charles
  1964   *The Aztecs under Spanish rule.* Stanford, Calif.: Stanford University Press.
  1967   *Tlaxcala in the sixteenth century.* Stanford, Calif.: Stanford University Press. (Originally published in 1952 by Yale University Press.)
Glass, John B., with Robertson, Donald
  1975   A census of native Middle American pictorial manuscripts. In *Handbook of Middle American Indians.* Edited by Robert Wauchope. 14:81–252. Austin: University of Texas Press.
Grijalva, Juan de
  1942   *The discovery of New Spain in 1518: a translation of the original texts.* Edited by Henry R. Wagner. Berkeley, Calif.: Cortés Society.

Guzmán, Eulalia
  1951   Huipil y maxtlatl. In *Esplendor del México antiguo.* Edited by Carmen Cook de Leonard. 2:957–82. Mexico City: Centro de Investigaciones Antropológicas de México.

Harvey, H. R.
  1972   The *Relaciones geográficas,* 1579–1586: native languages. In *Handbook of Middle American Indians.* Edited by Robert Wauchope. 12:279–323. Austin: University of Texas Press.
Heyden, Doris
  1977   The *quechquemitl* as a symbol of power in the Mixtec codices. *Vicus Cuadernos, Arqueología Cultural, Etnología* 1:5–24.
– – –, and Horcasitas, Fernando, eds.
  1964   *The Aztecs: The history of the Indies of New Spain, by Fray Diego Durán.* New York: Orion Press.

Jiménez-Moreno, Wigberto
  1941   Tula y los Toltecas segun las fuentes historicas. *Sociedad Mexicana de Antropología Revista* 5:79–83.
  1966   Los imperios prehispánicas de Mesoamérica. *Sociedad Mexicana de Antropología Revista* 20:179–95.
Johnson, Irmgard W.
  1953   El *quechquemitl* y el *huipil.* *Revista Mexicana de Estudios Antropológicos* 13:241–57.
  1958   Un antiguo huipil de frente decorado con pintura. *Revista Mexicana de Estudios Antropológicos* 15–16:115–22.
  1959   Hilado y tejido. In *Esplendor del México antiguo,* ed. Carmen Cook de Leonard. 1:440–78. Mexico City: Centro de Investigaciones Antropológicas de México.
  1960   Un Tzotzapztli antiguo de la región de Tehuacán. Instituto Nacional de Antropología e Historia, *Anales* 11–12:75–85.
  1966   Analisis de un tejido de Tlatelolco. Academia Mexicana de la Historia, *Memorias* 15:127–28.
  1971   Dress and adornment. In *The ephemeral and the eternal of Mexican folk art.* Edited by Rafael Carillo Azpeitia. 1:161–267. Mexico City: Fondo Editorial de la Plástica Mexicana.

Karst, Smiley
  1972   The Mixtec codices as a source in the study of costume variation among women in Pre-Conquest Mexico. Master's thesis, University of California, Los Angeles.
Keesing, Felix M.
  1953   *Culture change.* Stanford, Calif.: Stanford University Press.
Kelley, David
  1973   Costume and name in Mesoamerica. Paper read at 38th Annual Meeting of the Society for American Archaeology, San Francisco, Calif.
  1976   *Deciphering the Maya Script.* Austin: University of Texas Press.
Kirchhoff, Paul
  1952   Mesoamerica: its geographic limits, ethnic composition, and cultural characteristics. In *Heritage of conquest.* Edited by Sol Tax. Pp. 17–30. New York: Macmillan.

Landa, Biship Diego de
1941   *Landa's Relación de las cosas de Yucatán*. Edited by Alfred M. Tozzer. Papers of the Peabody Museum of American Archaeology and Ethnology, vol. 18. Cambridge, Mass.: Harvard University.

Las Casas, Fray Bartolomé de
1951   *Historia de las Indias*. 3 vols. Mexico City: Fondo de Cultura Económica.

1967   *Apologética historia sumaria*. Edited by Edmundo O'Gorman. 2 vols. Mexico City: Universidad Nacional Autónoma de México, Instituto de Investigaciones Históricas.

Lienzo de Tlaxcala
1892   *Lienzo de Tlaxcala*. In *Antigüedades Mexicanas*. Edited by Alfred Chavero. Publicadas por la Junta Colombina de México. Mexico City: Secretaría de Fomento.

Lounsbury, Floyd C.
1974   The inscription of the Sarcophagus Lid at Palenque. In *Proceedings of the Primera Mesa Redonda de Palenque*, 2, pp. 5–19. Pebble Beach, Calif.: Robert Louis Stevenson School, Pre-Columbian Art Research.

1976   A rationale for the initial date of the Temple of the Cross at Palenque. In *Proceedings of the Segunda Mesa Redonda de Palenque*, 3, pp. 211–24. Pebble Beach, Calif.: Robert Louis Stevenson School, Pre-Columbian Art Research.

Lothrop, S. K.
1924   *Tulum: an archaeological study of the east coast of Yucatán*. Carnegie Institution of Washington, Publication no. 335. Washington, D.C.

Mahler, Joy
1965   Garments and textiles of the Maya lowlands. In *Handbook of the Middle American Indians*. Edited by Robert Wauchope. 3:581–93. Austin: University of Texas Press.

Matrícula de tributos
N.d.   *Matrícula de Tributos*. Manuscript in the Museo Nacional de Antropología, Mexico City.

Mendizibal, Miguel Othon de
1943–   *Obras completas*. Vols. 3–6.
47

Miller, Arthur G.
1972   The mural painting in Structure 12 at Tancah and in Structure 5 at Tulum, Quintana Roo, Mexico: implications of their style and iconography. In *Atti del 50 Congresso Internazionale Degli Americanist Roma-Genova, 3–10 September, 1972*. 1:465–77.

Molina, Alonso de
1970   *Vocabulario en lengua castellana y mexicana, y mexicana y castellana*. Mexico City: Editorial Porrúa.

Motolinía, Fray Toribio de Benavente
1950   *History of the Indians of New Spain*. Translated and edited by Elizabeth Andros Foster. Westport, Conn.: Greenwood Press.

1971   *Memoriales o libro de las cosas de la Nueva España y de los naturales de ella*. Edited by Edmundo O'Gorman. Mexico City: Universidad Nacional Autónoma de Mexico, Instituto de Investigaciones Históricas.

Nicholson, H. B.
1957   Review of excavations at Yagul. John Paddock et al.

American Antiquity 23:195–96.
1966a   The Mixteca-Puebla concept in Mesoamerican archaeology: a re-examination. In *Ancient Mesoamerica*. Edited by John A. Graham. Pp. 258–63. Palo Alto, Calif.: Peek Publications.

1966b   The problem of the provenience of the members of the "Codex Borgia Group": a summary. In *Summa Antropológica en Homenaje a Roberto J. Weitlaner*. Pp. 145–58. Mexico City: Instituto Nacional de Antropología e Historia.

1967a   The efflorescence of Mesoamerican civilization: a résumé. In *Indian Mexico Past and Present*. Edited by Betty Bell. Pp. 46–71. Los Angeles: University of California, Latin American Center.

1967b   A "royal headband" of the Tlaxcalteca. *Revista Mexicana de Estudios Antropológicos* 21:71–106.

1967c   A fragment of an Aztec relief carving of the earth monster. *Journal de la Société des Américanistes* 16:81–94.

1971a   Sketch map of Mesoamerica. Manuscript.

1971b   Religion in pre-Hispanic central Mexico. In *Handbook of Middle American Indians*. Edited by Robert Wauchope. 10:395–446. Austin: University of Texas Press.

1971c   Major sculpture in pre-Hispanic central Mexico. In *Handbook of Middle American Indians*. Edited by Robert Wauchope. 10:92–134. Austin: University of Texas Press.

1973a   Phoneticism in the late pre-Hispanic central Mexican writing system. In *Mesoamerican writing systems*. Washington, D.C.: Dumbarton Oaks Research Library and Collection.

1973b   Sahagún's *Primeros memoriales*, Tepepolco, 1559–1561. In *Handbook of Middle American Indians*. Edited by Robert Wauchope. 13:207–18 Austin: University of Texas Press.

1973c   Eduard Georg Seler, 1849–1922. In *Handbook of Middle American Indians*. Edited by Robert Wauchope. 13:348–69. Austin: University of Texas Press.

1974a   Some remarks on the provenience of *Codex Borbonicus. Adeva-Mitteilungen*, December, 1974. No. 40. Graz: Akademische Druck-und Verlagsanstalt.

1979   Ehecatl Quetzalcoatl vs. Topiltzin Quetzalcoatl of Tollan: a problem in Mesoamerican religion and history. Paper read at 42d International Congress of Americanists, Paris. *Actes du 42e Congrès des Américanistes* 6:35–47.

Unpublished manuscript: The problem of the provenience of the members of the "Codex Borgia Group."

Norris, Herbert
1938   Costume and fashion. Vol. 3. New York: Dutton.

Nowotny, Karl A.
1961   *Tlacuilolli: die mexikanischen bilderhandschriften stil und inhalt mit einem katalog der Codex-Borgia-Gruppe*. Monumenta Americana. Vol. 3. Berlin: Verlag Bebr. Mann.

Nutini, Hugo G.
1976   An outline of Tlaxcaltecan culture, history, ethnology, and demography. In *The Tlaxcaltecans: Prehistory, demography, morphology and genetics*. Publications in Anthropology, no. 7, pp. 24–34. Lawrence: University of Kansas Press.

Nuttall, Zelia
1902   *Codex Nuttall: facsimile of an ancient Mexican codex belonging to Lord Zouche of Haryingworth.* Cambridge, Mass.: Peabody Museum of American Archaeology and Ethnology, Harvard University.

Osborne, Lille de Jongh
1935   *Guatemala textiles.* Department of Middle American Research, Tulane University of Louisiana, Publication no. 6. New Orleans.

Pagden, A. R., trans. and ed.
1971   *Hernán Cortés.* New York: Grossman.
Paso y Troncoso, Francisco del
1905– *Papeles de Nueva España.* 2d ser., Geografía y
06   Estadística. 6 vols. Madrid.
Pohl, John M. D.
1978   Political and iconographic considerations in the removal of Male 10-Dog and Male 6-House by Male 8-Deer. Master's thesis, University of California at Los Angeles.
Prescott, W. H.
1922   *The Conquest of Mexico.* 2 vols. New York: Henry Holt and Company.
Proskouriakoff, Tatiana
1964   Portraits of women in Maya art. In *Essays in Pre-Columbian art and archaeology.* Edited by Samuel K. Lothrop et al. Pp. 81–99. Cambridge, Mass.: Harvard University Press.
1965   Sculpture and major arts of the Maya lowlands. In *Handbook of the Middle American Indians.* Edited by Robert Wauchope. 2:469–97. Austin: University of Texas Press.

Quirarte, Jacinto
1975   The wall paintings of Santa Rita, Corozal. *Belize National Studies* 3:5–29.

Redfield, Robert; Linton, R.; and Herskovits, M. J.
1936   Memorandum on the study of acculturation. *American Anthropologist* 38:149–52.
Relación de Michoacán
1956   *Reproducción facsímil del M. s.c. IV. 5 de El Escorial.* Translated and edited by José Tudela, José Nuñez, and Paul Kirchoff. Madrid: Aguilar.
Reyes, Antonio de los
1890   Arte en lengua mixteca. *Actes de la Société Philologique,* vol. 18 (1888; Paris, 1890).
Robertson, Donald
1959   *Mexican manuscript painting of the early colonial period: the metropolitan schools.* New Haven, Conn.: Yale University Press.
1963   The style of the Borgia Group of Mexican pre-Conquest Manuscripts. In *Studies in western art.* Edited by M. Meiss et al. 3:148–64. 20th International Congress on the History of Art, New York, 1961.
1966   The Mixtec religious manuscripts. In *Ancient Oaxaca: Discoveries in Mexican Archaeology and History.* Edited by John Paddock. Pp. 298–312. Stanford, Calif.: Stanford University Press.
1968   The Tulum murals: the international style of the late post-classic. *Verhandlungen des XXXVIII Internationalen Amerikanisten-Kongresses, August 12–18, 1968, Stuttgart-Munich* 2:77–88.
Robertson, Merle Greene, and Jeffers, Donnan Call
1979   *Proceedings of the Tercera Mesa Redonda de Palenque.* Part 4. Monterey, Calif.: Pre-Columbian Art Research, Herald Printers.
Rodas, Flavio N.
1938   *Simbolismos (Maya Quiche) de Guatemala.* Guatemala City: Tipográfia Nacional.
Roys, Ralph L.
1965   Lowland Maya native society at Spanish contact. In *Handbook of Middle American Indians.* Edited by Robert Wauchope. 3:659–78. Austin: University of Texas Press.

Sahagún, Fray Bernardino de
1926   *Historia general de las cosas de Nueva España,* by Bernardino de Sahagún. Edicion completa en facsimile colorido del Codice Florentino que se conserva en la biblioteca Laurenzio-Medicea de Florencia, Italia. Mexico City: Talleres Gráficos del Museo Nacional de Arqueología, Historia, y Etnografía.
1950– *Florentine Codex: General History of the Things of New*
69   *Spain.* Translated and edited by Arthur J. O. Anderson and Charles E. Dibble. Monographs of the School of American Research no. 14, pts. 2–13. Santa Fe, N. Mex.: University of Utah and School of American Research.
Schele, Linda
1974   Observations on the cross motif at Palenque. In *Proceedings of the Primera Mesa Redonda de Palenque,* pt. 1, pp. 41–61. Pebble Beach, Calif.: Robert Louis Stevenson School, Pre-Columbian Art Research.
1976   Accession iconography of Chan-Bahlum in the Group of the Cross at Palenque. In *Proceedings of the Segunda Mesa Redonda de Palenque,* pt. 3, pp. 9–34. Pebble Beach, Calif.: Robert Louis Stevenson School, Pre-Columbian Art Research.
1979   Genealogical Documentation on the Tri-Figure Panels at Palenque. In *Proceedings of the Tercera Mesa Redonda de Palenque,* part 4, pp. 41–70. Monterey, Calif.: Pre-Columbian Art Research, Herald Printers.
Scholes, France V., and Adams, Eleanor B.
1952   *Proceso contra Tzintzicha Tangaxoan el Caltzontzin formado por Nuño de Guzmán, Año de 1530.* Mexico City: Porrúa y Obregon.
Schreider, Helen, and Schreider, Frank
1961   Indonesia: the young and troubled island nation. *National Geographic* 119:579–627.
1962   East from Bali. *National Geographic* 122:236–79.
Sejourné, Laurette
1966   *El Lenguaje de las formas en Teotihuacán.* Mexico City.
Seler, Eduard
1900– *The Tonalámatl of the Aubin Collection.* Berlin and
1901   London: Published at the Expense of His Excellency the Duke of Loubat.
1901– *Codex Fejérváry-Mayer.* Berlin and London: Published at the Expense of His Excellency the Duke of
1902   Loubat.

1902–
1903   *Codex Vaticanus No. 3773 (Codex Vaticanus B)*. Berlin and London: Published at the Expense of His Excellency the Duke of Loubat.

1904   Ancient Mexican feather ornaments. In *Mexican and central American antiquities, calendar systems, and history*. Smithsonian Institution, Bureau of American Ethnology, Bulletin no. 28, pp. 59–74. Washington, D.C.

1960   *Gesammelte Abhandlungen zur Amerikanischen Sprach-und Altertumskunde*. 5 vols. Graz: Akademische Druck-und Verlagsanstalt.

1963   *Commentarios al Códice Borgia*. Facsimile ed. 2 vols. Mexico City: Fondo de Cultura Económica.

1967   *Wort-und Sachregister zu Eduard Seler*. Edited by Ferdinand Andres. Graz: Akademische Druck-und Verlagsanstalt.

Siméon, Rémi
1963   *Dictionnaire de la Langue Nahuatl ou Mexicaine*. Graz: Akademische Druck-und Verlagsanstalt.

Smith, Mary Elizabeth
1973   Picture writing from ancient southern Mexico. Norman: University of Oklahoma Press.

1974   Codex Selden: a manuscript from the valley of Nochixtlan? Paper read at 41st International Congress of Americanists, September, 1974, Mexico City.

Soustelle, Jacques
1961   *Daily life of the Aztecs*. Stanford, Calif.: Stanford University Press.

Spores, Ronald
1967   *The Mixtec kings and their people*. Norman: University of Oklahoma Press.

1974   Marital alliance in the political integration of Mixtec kingdoms. *American Anthropologist* 76:297–311.

Stevens, Captain John
1726   A new dictionary: Spanish and English and English and Spanish. London.

Sullivan, Thelma D.
1972   The arms and insignia of the Mexica. *Estudios de Cultura Nahuatl* 10:155–93.

Swadash, Morris
1967   Lexicostatistic Classification. In *Handbook of Middle American Indians*. Edited by Robert Wauchope. 5:79–115. Austin: University of Texas Press.

Textile Museum
1977   *1976 proceedings of the Irene Emery roundtable on museum textiles: ethnographic textiles of the Western Hemisphere*. Washington, D.C.: Textile Museum.

Thompson, Sir J. Eric S.
1950   *Maya hieroglyphic writing: introduction*. Carnegie Institution of Washington, Publication no. 589. Washington, D.C.

1965   Maya hieroglyphic writing. In *Handbook of Middle American Indians*. Edited by Robert Wauchope. 3:632–58. Austin: University of Texas Press.

1970   *Maya history and religion*. Norman: University of Oklahoma Press.

1972a   *Maya hieroglyphics without tears*. London: Trustees of British Museum.

1972b   *A commentary on the Dresden Codex: a Maya hieroglyphic book*. Philadelphia: American Philosophical Society.

Tonalámatl Aubin
1900–
1901   *Tonalamatl Aubin*. In Eduard Seler. *The Tonalamatl of the Aubin Collection*. Berlin and London: Published at the Expense of His Excellency the Duke of Loubat.

1981   *El Tonalamatl de la Colección de Aubin. Antiguo manuscrito mexicano en la Biblioteca Nacional de Paris (Manuscrit Mexicains No. 18–19)*. Reproduction of the 1900–1901 facsimile edition accompanied by commentary by Eduard Seler. Mexico: Tlaxcala Códices y Manuscritos 1.

Tozzer, Alfred M.
1957   *Chichén Itzá and its cenote of sacrifice: a comparative study of contemporaneous Maya and Toltec*. Memoirs of Peabody Museum of Archaeology and Ethnology, vols. 10–12. Cambridge, Mass.: Harvard University.

Troike, Nancy P.
1974a   Notes on the possible source of the *Codex Zouche-Nuttall* and the *Codex Colombino-Becker*. Paper read at 41st International Congress of Americanists, September, 1974, Mexico City.

1974b   The interpretation of gestures in the *Codex Colombino-Becker*. Paper read at Annual Meeting of American Anthropological Association, November, 1974, Mexico City.

1975   The meanings of postures and gestures in the Mixtec codices. Paper read at 40th Annual Meeting of Society for American Archaeology, May, 1975, Dallas, Texas.

1978   Fundamental changes in the interpretation of the Mixtec codices. *American Antiquity* 43:553–68.

Wagner, Henry R.
1969   *The rise of Fernando Cortés*. Berkeley: Cortés Society, 1944. Reprint. New York: Kraus Reprint.

Warren, J. Benedict
1973   An introductory survey of secular writings in the European tradition on colonial Middle America, 1503–1818. In *Handbook of Middle American Indians*. Edited by Robert Wauchope. 13:42–137. Austin: University of Texas Press.

Weaver, Muriel Porter
1972   *The Aztecs, Maya, and their predecessors: archaeology of Mesoamerica*. New York: Seminar Press.

Zorita, Alonso De
1963   *Breve y sumaria relación de los señores de la Nueva España*. Edited by Joaquín Ramírez Cubañas. Biblioteca del Estudiante Universitario, vol. 32. Mexico City: Universidad Nacional Autónoma de México.

INDEX